Networked Business Models in the Circular Economy

Bogdan Nogalski
WSB University in Gdańsk, Poland

Agnieszka Anna Szpitter
University of Gdańsk, Poland

Adam Jabłoński
WSB University in Poznań, Poland

Marek Jabłoński
WSB University in Poznań, Poland

A volume in the Advances in Finance, Accounting, and Economics (AFAE) Book Series

IGI Global
DISSEMINATOR OF KNOWLEDGE

Published in the United States of America by
IGI Global
Business Science Reference (an imprint of IGI Global)
701 E. Chocolate Avenue
Hershey PA, USA 17033
Tel: 717-533-8845
Fax: 717-533-8661
E-mail: cust@igi-global.com
Web site: http://www.igi-global.com

Library of Congress Cataloging-in-Publication Data

Names: Nogalski, Bogdan, editor.
Title: Networked business models in the circular economy / Bogdan Nogalski [and three others], editors.
Description: Hershey, PA : Business Science Reference, [2019]
Identifiers: LCCN 2018036427| ISBN 9781522578505 (hardcover) | ISBN 9781522578512 (ebook)
Subjects: LCSH: Business networks. | Strategic alliances (Business) | Management.
Classification: LCC HD69.S8 N458 2019 | DDC 658/.046--dc23 LC record available at https://lccn.loc.gov/2018036427

This book is published in the IGI Global book series Advances in Finance, Accounting, and Economics (AFAE) (ISSN: 2327-5677; eISSN: 2327-5685)

British Cataloguing in Publication Data
A Cataloguing in Publication record for this book is available from the British Library.

For electronic access to this publication, please contact: eresources@igi-global.com.

Advances in Finance, Accounting, and Economics (AFAE) Book Series

ISSN:2327-5677
EISSN:2327-5685

Editor-in-Chief: Ahmed Driouchi, Al Akhawayn University, Morocco

MISSION

In our changing economic and business environment, it is important to consider the financial changes occurring internationally as well as within individual organizations and business environments. Understanding these changes as well as the factors that influence them is crucial in preparing for our financial future and ensuring economic sustainability and growth.

The **Advances in Finance, Accounting, and Economics (AFAE)** book series aims to publish comprehensive and informative titles in all areas of economics and economic theory, finance, and accounting to assist in advancing the available knowledge and providing for further research development in these dynamic fields.

COVERAGE

- Taxes
- Microeconomics
- Economics Geography
- Applied Accounting
- Health economics
- Economics of Innovation and Knowledge
- Field Research
- E-finance
- Economic Policy
- Economic Indices and Quantitative Economic Methods

IGI Global is currently accepting manuscripts for publication within this series. To submit a proposal for a volume in this series, please contact our Acquisition Editors at Acquisitions@igi-global.com or visit: http://www.igi-global.com/publish/.

The Advances in Finance, Accounting, and Economics (AFAE) Book Series (ISSN 2327-5677) is published by IGI Global, 701 E. Chocolate Avenue, Hershey, PA 17033-1240, USA, www.igi-global.com. This series is composed of titles available for purchase individually; each title is edited to be contextually exclusive from any other title within the series. For pricing and ordering information please visit http://www.igi-global.com/book-series/advances-finance-accounting-economics/73685. Postmaster: Send all address changes to above address.

Titles in this Series

For a list of additional titles in this series, please visit:
https://www.igi-global.com/book-series/advances-finance-accounting-economics/73685

Metaheuristic Approaches to Portfolio Optimization
Jhuma Ray (RCC Institute of Information Technology, India) Anirban Mukherjee (RCC Institute of Information Technology, India) Sadhan Kumar Dey (RCC Institute of Information Technology, India) and Goran Klepac (Algebra University College, Croatia)
Business Science Reference • ©2019 • 300pp • H/C (ISBN: 9781522581031) • US $205.00

Handbook of Research on Economic and Political Implications of Green Trading and Energy Use
Ramesh Chandra Das (Vidyasagar University, India)
Business Science Reference • ©2019 • 421pp • H/C (ISBN: 9781522585473) • US $225.00

Emerging Research on Monetary Policy, Banking, and Financial Markets
Cristi Spulbar (University of Craiova, Romania) and Ramona Birau (Constantin Brâncuşi University of Targu Jiu, Romania)
Business Science Reference • ©2019 • 322pp • H/C (ISBN: 9781522592693) • US $195.00

Modernization and Accountability in the Social Economy Sector
Augusta Ferreira (University of Aveiro, Portugal) Rui Marques (University of Aveiro, Portugal) Graça Azevedo (University of Aveiro, Portugal) Helena Inácio (University of Aveiro, Portugal) and Carlos Santos (University of Aveiro, Portugal)
Business Science Reference • ©2019 • 351pp • H/C (ISBN: 9781522584827) • US $215.00

Foreign Business in China and Opportunities for Technological Innovation and Sustainable Economics
Anna Visvizi (Deree – The American College of Greece, Greece) Miltiadis Lytras (Deree – The American College of Greece, Greece) Xi Zhang (Tianjin University, China) and Jie Zhao (Anhui University, China)
Business Science Reference • ©2019 • 284pp • H/C (ISBN: 9781522589808) • US $195.00

For an entire list of titles in this series, please visit:
https://www.igi-global.com/book-series/advances-finance-accounting-economics/73685

IGI Global
DISSEMINATOR OF KNOWLEDGE

701 East Chocolate Avenue, Hershey, PA 17033, USA
Tel: 717-533-8845 x100 • Fax: 717-533-8661
E-Mail: cust@igi-global.com • www.igi-global.com

Table of Contents

Detailed Table of Contents

Archetypes of sustainable business models can be used to the elaboration of archetypes of business models that combine the assumptions of sharing economy and circular economy as part of their categorization. The chapter presents the assumptions of conceptualization and operationalization of potential model solutions in the field of using archetypes of sustainable business models in the design of circular business models in digital economy. The chapter has an epistemological character described in ontological, epistemological, and methodological categories, but also with the use of an axiological sense. The aim of the chapter is to develop and indicate the principles of designing business models based on the concepts of sharing economy and circular economy using archetypes of sustainable business models in range of digital environment of business.

The dynamics of ongoing market changes require a new look at business management mechanisms. Often the key element of the organization's operation is to ensure business continuity, which is not easy. This requires strong embeddedness in the decision-making processes resulting from the properly built business model of the organization. A business model becomes a crucial determinant of the organizational success today. The aim of the chapter is to present the place and role of robustness in shaping the business models of organizations embedded in the circular economy. The scope of the chapter includes studies of listed companies that implement the principles of responsible business to ensure their robustness in the short and long term. In the chapter, the author poses a research question: Can the skillful use of the concept of business model robustness in circular economy companies guarantee the organization's ability to ensure business continuity and its high performance?

Circular economy was the subject of interest for many researchers and is currently an inherent part of the sustainable growth concept. Shifting the economy to circular will require transformations in the field of competence, development, innovations, and organizational governance, as well as public awareness. Circular economy creates opportunities for achieving benefits in the economy (the efficiency of production processes, innovations, power safety) as well as in the social and environmental fields (shaping ecological safety). In the chapter, the authors describe such issues as theoretical foundations of the circular economy concept; European guidelines in the field of circular economy; problems and benefits associated with the implementation of circular economy, in light of compliance with sustainable development principles; business solution models together with the prospects for further sustainable development of a company, based on assumptions and models of circular economy.

Sharing economy has emerged as influential economic model in the last decades. A considerable literature has grown up around the sub-themes of sharing economy including business-related, system-related, and other context-related studies. Examining a general phenomenon in a limited scope is a strategy for specific perspective and conclusions. Therefore, examining sharing economy phenomenon in a business and marketing perspective can be useful for business related viewpoint. The study is composed of three parts and begins with a theorotical review of conceptual background. It will then go on to three level structures for this study, including consumer level, business and brand level, and system levels. The remaining part includes context-based studies about level structure. After reviewing topics in contexts, there are presented selected studies about related contexts. The study aims to research sharing economy in a general view and review business- and marketing-related topics and studies.

The increasingly important role of sustainability issues and CSR in business activity has been widely recognized. In order to promote socially responsible decisions, changes in the macro- and micro-environment should be examined. The study offers insight into different aspects of CSR and defines those whose importance is growing, discusses trends, reasons for the state of affairs, and formulates conclusions of possible effects. The focus is on ethical values, in particular trust, and their changing perception which may lead to new business models strengthening and further development.

The use of renewable energy and recycling products is one of the main achievements of organizations. The circular economy (CE) is a new concept which evolves out of a new management assumption in organizations based on recycling, reuse, and repurposing of products. The circular economy provides a framework for facing challenges and a guide for rethinking and redesigning the future. This chapter analyzes the Portuguese market for circular economy organizations based on discussion of the CE conceptual model. The circular economy is expected to contribute positively by introducing new methodologies for the production of raw materials, with new production processes and giving value to eco products. The challenge for Portuguese organizations is to create management "vectors" which promote networking innovation, labor, capital, and eco products. Overall, the conceptual model presented gives importance to Portuguese business decision making for sustainable consumption, which provides advancements in business for the green supply chain.

In the 21st century, the main focus of technological advances is on data. Practice management software (PMS) is having its highest demand in the international market as a tool helping dental services operate in a better way. The main focus of this research is on analyzing the role of the implementation of PMS in dental

Preface

The dynamics of the ongoing market changes determine the strategic behavior of modern enterprises. This is related to the emerging new logic of understanding and conducting a business, caused by the total changes in the economy. This economy, currently operating at the convergence of the digital and real worlds, not only creates the business processes of enterprises but, above all, their business models, because by functioning in network relationships, a specific platform for exchanging value through the generated network effect is created. The context of running a business is conditioned by many factors that shape the image of the market and its attributes. In the era of Industry 4.0, the shape of business is related - among others - to the network economy supported by the digital economy, where new economies emerge including the sharing economy, the Big Data economy and, finally, the circular economy. Thus, the network environment becomes natural, where the conceptualization and operationalization of networked business models is an important factor. By combining these issues in a coherent whole, a significant scientific problem arises and therefore needs to be solved. It is, among others, a way of understanding, constructing and implementing networked business models functioning in the circular economy. How should such business models be built? What are the configuration and interfaces in such business models? How can your organization achieve high performance by owning and operating these business models? These are some of the key selected questions to be answered, especially given that the proposed structure of connections concerning networked business models in the modern economy becomes a multidimensional construct, both in theoretical and application terms. This multidimensional construct is particularly important for the new dimension of today's business. This new dimension changes, inter alia, the value chain where almost everything should be SMART and companies build their competitive advantage on digital DNA among other things. It is also important that we exist in many digital network communities where new business models not only convert payments into profits but also generate social innovations resulting in new forms of monetization through company business models. It is not the revenue model that is important here, but only new payment methods focused on monetization. Therefore, new design thinking is focused on such business models that not only have to provide an economic dimension, but also a social one. This is strongly determined by the network environment. Thus, the specific digital social ecosystem shapes new perspectives for the development of enterprises, which not only affect the sectors of the economy, but also create new behaviors of entire societies in various areas of life. For example, the circular economy has created new ways of thinking about global resources and using them, not only in terms of possessing them but above all in the way they are available and shared. Business models and the approach to configuration caused an avalanche of interpretation in terms of their logic, contributing to the generation of income but also a new value proposition capable of permanent circulation, among other things. Such an understanding - also related to digital transformation - means that such a subversive economy in a holistic approach changes and shapes new business models and, above all, their cause and effect relationships and mutual relationships with strategies, business processes and strategic projects. Such a specific strategic hybrid determines the management mechanisms affecting the key strategic goals of today's enterprises. In this context, by making a constructive comparison of business models functioning in the network economy, we seek mutual social and economic effects. Here circularity then acquires a different dimension and strength of influence. Thus, networked business models in the circular economy can become an important link between key resources, critical success factors and new value drivers for generating new value propositions from many perspectives and in many dimensions, as the world that we are currently observing needs new solutions, new approaches and new interpretations. This can be offered, inter alia, by new networked business models of enterprises operating in the circular economy. The business environment and social space expect such business models.

The contemporary world is changing under the influence of technological development and universal digitalization. Not only are new market opportunities shaped in a geometric way, but threats with huge social impact are also created. The increased number of environmental threats has resulted in a natural need not only to look for ad hoc solutions but, above all, systemic ones. Therefore, the new mechanisms of social impact functioning in the world had to be taken into account at the business level. For example, certain solutions for reducing the adverse impact on the environment were building environmental management systems at company level. However, this turned out to be insufficient. This has indeed affected the reduction of emissions to air, soil and water, and the reduction in resource consumption by companies, but it did not have a cause-and-effect nature in the relationship between ownership and the use of resources. There is a need to change the perspective to project thinking based on prediction at the ideas stage or the idea of running a business. The concept of business models was the best one. Modern ideas have freed up new thinking spaces for architects of modern business. The natural network environment has created a synergistic effect for various network actors. In this approach, the search for effective solutions began, the result of which would be such solutions that would ensure the creation of many values for many recipients, while achieving multiple feedback mainly in the context of the long-term perspective. A specific construct was created, namely network business models in the circular economy, which to some extent can be a kind of panacea for solving many problems of the world, especially in the global dimension. This includes assumptions for the rational use of global natural resources, their ability to renew and be recycled. In this construction we deal with several sources of high efficiency generation. In the context of the network, the network effect is important; in the context of the business model, it is a new income generation logic and a new proposition, mainly of many values; and in the context of the circular economy, it is the ability to manage repeating cycles. This causes a snowball effect which determines the achievement of various results. not only in individual enterprises but also results affecting the economy as a whole, and indeed the world.

The monograph is multidimensional, and its very title referring to networked business models in the circular economy indicates different cognitive perspectives focused on several - both theoretical and practical - problems embedded therein. Therefore, the monograph should reach a wide audience. It should be read by theoreticians and scientists dealing with the issues of constructing and operationalizing innovative business models. It should also be read by students exploring the issues of strategic management and sustainable development. And finally, it should be read by business practitioners, both entrepreneurs and managers, mainly top managers who want to be business virtuosos that can change their organizations and business models. The monograph should be an inspiration for changing the way people think and behave around their organizations. Finally, it should be read by experts looking for inspiration in the development of modern management concepts.

The individual articles presented in the monograph constitute a logically related whole. The structure itself has a systemic character that is supposed to lead the reader in thought disquisition through the meanders of networked business models embedded in the circular economy. In the first chapter by Marek Jabłoński entitled 'The use of sustainable business model archetypes in the design of circular business models in the digital economy', the author points out that the archetypes of sustainable business models can be used for the elaboration of archetypes of business models that combine the assumptions of the Sharing Economy and the Circular Economy as part of their categorization. The article presents the assumptions of the conceptualization and operationalization of potential model solutions in the field of using archetypes of Sustainable Business Models in the design of circular business models in the Digital Economy. The chapter has an epistemological character described in ontological, epistemological and methodological categories, but also with the use of an axiological sense. The aim of the article is to develop and indicate the principles of designing business models based on the concepts of the Sharing Economy and Circular Economy using archetypes of Sustainable Business Models in the framework of the digital environment of business. In the second chapter, entitled 'Robustness in the business models of organizations embedded in the circular economy', Adam Jabłoński claims that the dynamics of ongoing market changes requires a new look at business management mechanisms. Often the key element of the organization's operation is to ensure business continuity. which is not easy. This requires strong embeddedness in the decision-making processes resulting from the properly built business model of the organization. A business model is becoming a crucial determinant of organizational success today. The aim of the chapter is to present the place and role of robustness in shaping the business models of organizations embedded in the circular economy. The scope of the chapter includes studies of listed companies that implement the principles of responsible business to ensure their robustness in the short and long term. In the chapter, the author poses the following research question: Can the skillful use of the concept of business model robustness in circular economy companies guarantee the organization's ability to ensure business continuity and high performance? In the third chapter entitled 'A Sustainable Business Model in the Functioning of Enterprises as the Basis for Creating a Circular Economy - the Present and Development Prospects', Elżbieta Lorek and Agnieszka Lorek claim that the circular economy has been a subject of interest for many researchers and is currently an inherent part of the sustainable growth concept. Shifting the economy to circular will require transformations in the field of competence, development, innovations and organizational governance, as well as public awareness. The circular economy creates opportunities for achieving benefits in the economy (the efficiency of production processes, innovations, power safety), as well as in the social and environmental fields (shaping ecological safety). In the chapter, the authors describe issues such as the theoretical foundations of the circular economy concept; European guidelines in the field of the circular economy; problems and benefits associated with the implementation of the circular economy, in light of compliance with sustainable development principles; and business solution models together with the prospects for further sustainable development of a company, based on assumptions and models of the circular economy. In chapter four, entitled 'The Sharing Economy and Applications - Business and Marketing Perspective', Fatih Pinarbasi argues that the sharing economy has emerged as an influential economic model in recent decades. A considerable amount of literature has grown up around the sub-themes of the sharing economy including business-related, system-related and other context-related studies. Examining a general phenomenon in a limited scope is the strategy for a specific perspective and conclusions. Therefore examining the sharing economy phenomenon from a business and marketing perspective can be useful for a business-related viewpoint. The study is composed of three parts and begins with a theoretical review of the conceptual background. It will then go on to a three-level structure for this study, including consumer level, business and brand level and system levels. The remaining part includes context-based studies about level structure. After reviewing topics in context, selected studies about related contexts are presented. The aim of this study is to research the sharing economy in a general sense and review business and marketing-related topics and studies. In chapter five, entitled 'Competences of startups as entities operating in network structures', Waldemar Jędrzejczyk refers to some important issues. The chapter indicates the most important changes in organizations caused by technological progress. The development of the network business model, according to which both very large and very small organizations are starting to function, has been emphasized. The main focus is on startup entities due to their specific character and increasingly dynamic development. Firstly, the issues which are well recognized in science, enabling the creation of a picture of both startups and their ecosystems, have been presented. Subsequently, the considerations have been narrowed down to the issue of startup competences. The key startup competences in the organizational and individual dimensions, which contribute to success on the startup market, have been defined, based on literature analysis and primary research results. The empirical part concerns Polish startups. The main goal of this chapter is to define the key competences of a startup that will allow it to distinguish itself from other entities in the search for an investor or business partner. Chapter six, entitled 'Redesigning business models with the circular economy: An insight into Italian enterprises' by Francesca Ceruti, Laura Gavinelli, Angelo Di Gregorio and Marco Frey, presents important issues. In recent decades, the circular economy has become a key issue in academic and managerial studies. While there are plenty of contributions to the circular economy such as environmental strategy, a less developed line of studies is that of analyzing the circular economy as a new way of doing business. In this context, Italy initiated the necessary reforms for the transition to the circular economy in 1997, but it was only in 2017 that it adopted a working plan to that end. The chapter presents evidence of a CAWI interview investigating whether Italian firms are adopting the principles of the circular economy, and whether this affects their competitiveness and business performance. The research contributes to the understanding of this new paradigm, by going into detail in terms of the motivations that drive Italian enterprises to adopt the principles of the circular economy, the actions they are taking to be circular economy-oriented, and the possible relationship between the adoption of the circular economy principles and their business performance. Chapter seven, entitled 'An approach to solving the fuzzy knapsack problem in investment and business models is written by Vishnu Pratap Singh. In this chapter, the author studies the knapsack problem with fuzzy weights for single and bi-objective functions. The knapsack problem has been widely used in investment and business models. In real-world decision-making situations, the existence of fuzziness of the weights and profit is a common requirement. To overcome this difficulty, these weights and profit can be considered a triangular fuzzy number. Thus the fuzzy knapsack problem is introduced. The possibility index gives the idea of choosing the solution according to the decision-maker's choice. The dynamic programming approach using multi-stage decision making has been given to different types of decision-makers to find the solution. An investment problem in an imprecise environment has been defined as a fuzzy knapsack problem and the solution procedure is given to demonstrate the methodology. In chapter eight, entitled 'Spiral Management: A New Concept of Social Systems Management' by Justína Mikulášková, Miloš Čambál, Ľuboš Polakovič, and Petra Urbanovičová, the authors claim that Spiral Management and its principles are based on the long-term successful existence of living systems. The principles can be applied to enterprise and organization management. Living systems manage long-term success by acquiring energy from their surroundings (through nutrition), while enterprises acquire customers and employees' energy in order to eliminate entropy (in enterprises manifested as economic losses). Spiral management is based on the synergy of living systems. It describes behavioral patterns in the cyclical development of enterprises as well as the ability of the latter to diagnose their own strategic decisions, including the instructions of how to drive an enterprise towards a long-term success. The current paper describes the theoretical basis of Spiral Management while providing a novel insight into this unique managerial approach and emphasizing its importance for human resource management. Also, the elements of Spiral Management applied in enterprises that want to be competitive and survive turbulent periods are introduced. In chapter nine, entitled 'Legal and Ethical Aspects of CSR. Potential in New Business Model Development', Ewa Barbara Wójcik and Katarzyna Olejko argue that the increasingly important role of sustainability issues and CSR in business activity has been widely recognized. In order to promote socially responsible decisions, changes in the macro- and micro-environment should be examined. The study offers insight into different aspects of CSR and defines those whose importance is growing, discusses trends and reasons for the state of affairs, and formulates conclusions of possible effects. The focus is on ethical values, in particular trust and the changing perception thereof, which may lead to strengthening new business models and further development. Chapter ten, entitled 'Circularity in Portugal. Features of new business challenges', by Ana Cristina Pego, says that the use of renewable energy and recycling products is one of the main achievements of organizations. The circular economy (CE) is a new concept which evolves out of a new management assumption in organizations based on the recycling, reuse and repurposing of products. The circular economy provides a framework for facing challenges and a guide for rethinking and redesigning the future. This article analyses the Portuguese market for circular economy organizations based on a discussion of the CE conceptual model. The circular economy is expected to contribute positively by introducing new methodologies for the production of raw materials, with new production processes and providing value to eco products. The challenge for Portuguese organizations is to create management "vectors" which promote networking innovation, labor, capital and eco products. Overall, the conceptual model presented gives significance to Portuguese business decision-making for sustainable consumption, which provides advancements in business for the green supply chain. Chapter eleven, entitled 'Improving the Way Dental Services Operate: An Albanian Case Study', by Alba Demneri Kruja and Kei Hysi, is the last chapter. It says that, in the 21th century, the main focus of technological advances is on data. Demand for Practice Management Software (PMS) is highest on the international market as a tool for helping dental services operate better. The main focus of this research is on analyzing the role of the implementation of PMS in dental clinics in Tirana, the capital city of Albania. Qualitative and quantitative data was collected through semi-structured interviews and surveys to analyze the case. Low purchasing power, lack of knowledge and informality in Albania are some of the limitations that restrict dentists from implementing new technologies. The results show that PMS implementation adds value to dental clinics through more effective and efficient services and improved customer relationship management.

The monograph affects many key areas of business science and practice. It is embedded mainly in the field of strategic management with a special focus on the concept of business models and sustainable development and it refers and is strongly referenced to the network paradigm. In the context of economic conditions, it is based on the principles of the circular economy. Such a multi-faceted approach makes the monograph holistic. From this perspective, it can be a specific platform for the development of business theory and practice. The editors hope that the monograph will not only make excellent reading but, above all, it will become an inspiration for a wide range of readers interested in seeking explanations for the complex phenomena of the modern world. The editors cordially thank the authors of the individual chapters for sharing their thoughts and experiences, which allowed for a thorough exploration of the complex issue of Networked Business Models in the Circular Economy.

Bogdan Nogalski
WSB University in Poznań, Poland

Agnieszka Szpitter
WSB University in Poznań, Poland

Adam Jabłoński
WSB University in Poznań, Poland

Marek Jabłoński
WSB University in Poznań, Poland

Chapter 1
The Use of Sustainable Business Model Archetypes in the Design of Circular Business Models in the Digital Economy

Marek Jabłoński
WSB University in Poznań, Poland

ABSTRACT

Archetypes of sustainable business models can be used to the elaboration of archetypes of business models that combine the assumptions of sharing economy and circular economy as part of their categorization. The chapter presents the assumptions of conceptualization and operationalization of potential model solutions in the field of using archetypes of sustainable business models in the design of circular business models in digital economy. The chapter has an epistemological character described in ontological, epistemological, and methodological categories, but also with the use of an axiological sense. The aim of the chapter is to develop and indicate the principles of designing business models based on the concepts of sharing economy and circular economy using archetypes of sustainable business models in range of digital environment of business.

DOI: 10.4018/978-1-5225-7850-5.ch001

INTRODUCTION

The conceptualization and operationalization of Sustainable Business Models is based on the assumptions of the joint examination of the Triple Bottom Line concept and the techniques of configuring an effective and efficient resource structure of business model components.

The concept of sustainability, widely explored in science in recent years, can play an important role in shaping and adjusting these innovative business models. As regards the concept of sustainability, the key role is played by a longer perspective of studying business, which, in the context of the dynamic development of new technologies, can lead to a number of problems.

Generally, in theory and practice, several approaches to sustainability can be distinguished:

The classic approach broadly described in the literature and well-recognized as the Triple Bottom Line (Elkington, 1999). This approach is often used by mature companies which create the strategy based on stakeholders analysis and corporate social responsibility (Wang, Sarkis, 2017, p. 1607-1616). Their business model incorporates a balance of ecological, social and economic factors. In their strategy of competitive advantage these companies apply the triple bottom line rules for example by including ecologically friendly products into their offer, undertaking activities for positive impact on environmental protection, and striking a balance between all stakeholders interests. There are different aspects which are described in the range of classical approaches to sustainability, for example: typology (Bergman, Bergman, Berger, 2017), aspect of life cycle of enterprises (Jabłoński, Jabłoński, 2016), rules for corporate social responsibility (Mourougan, 2015), and green supply chain (Fahimnia, Sarkis, Davarzani, 2015, pp.101-114).

The second approach is based on assumptions, for example of S. Schaltegger et al, who say that: 'The value proposition must provide both ecological or social and economic value through offering products and services – business models for sustainability describe, analyze, manage, and communicate (i) a company's sustainable value proposition to its customers, and all other stakeholders, (ii) how it creates and delivers this value, (iii) and how it captures economic value while maintaining or regenerating natural, social, and economic capital beyond its organizational boundaries (Schaltegger, Hansen, Lüdeke-Freund, 2015).' In this holistic approach 'no sustainable value can be created for customers without creating value to a broader range of stakeholders'. This also includes a management approach which aims at achieving success in a fair manner for employees. This topic is widely developed in the literature (Lüdeke-Freund, 2010), (Schaltegger, Lüdeke-Freund, Hansen, 2016), (Boons, Montalvo, Quist, Wagner, 2013).

The third approach addresses the specific aspect of economic sustainability in combination with the emerging shared economy business models that are enabled by the networked economy. It is very important for the sustained continuity of these business models to consider issues such as social, ecological and labor rules, which may be captured in legal requirements but also in social norms and values. The concept of the sharing economy is now widely discussed in literature (Choi, Cho, Lee, Hong, Woo, 2014), (Stephany, 2015), (Cohen, Munoz, 2017), (Belk, 2014).

The fourth approach can be defined as a complex construct that comprises a broader approach that takes into account internal and external factors such as: sustainable business models, network theory, entrepreneurial ecosystems and venture typologies to explore the social constructivist nature of sustainable business models. Entrepreneurial ecosystems are more than just high-growth/high-technology clusters, but complex adaptive systems of interdependent actors that engage in entrepreneurial activities to create economic, social, as well as environmental value (Neumeyer, Santos, 2018, p.4566).

The fifth approach, which has been highlighted in this chapter, is based on the combined use of the assumptions of sustainability and the circular economy, assuming that sustainability is interpreted as the balanced integration of economic performance, social inclusiveness, and environmental resilience, to the benefit of current and future generations. The circular economy is understood as an umbrella concept (a phenomena that creates a relation between pre-existing independent concepts) that aims to develop a regenerative economic system by intentionally slowing, closing, and narrowing material and energy loops (de Pádua Pieronia, Pigossoa, McAloonea, 2018, p. 801).

Sustainability should thus be seen in the context of building competitive advantage with an ethical approach to market play, supporting innovative solutions that have a positive impact on society, creating social value and social profit.

When searching for the optimal configuration of business models operating in the circular economy, the solutions of sustainable business model archetypes developed in the literature can be used. Works on sustainable business model archetypes have been published in recent years by authors such as: N.M.P. Bocken, S.W. Short, P. Rana, S. Evans (Bocken, Short, Rana, Evans, 2014), A.W.H Yip, N. M.P. Bocken (Yip, Bocken, 2018), N. Calvo, O. Villarreal (Calvo, Villarreal, 2018, p. 191). This subject is dynamically developing, and the authors try not only to develop the theoretical framework of this issue but also try to operationalize this concept in various sectors of the economy. The traditional approach to designing circular economy business models is based at least on the stages of the value chain delivery process such as design, production, remanufacturing, distribution, consumption, use, reuse, repair, collection, recycling and recovery. The use of virgin materials and the development of solutions from the sphere of obtaining residual waste should close the circular economy circulation process. The assumptions of the Triple Bottom Line concept, in turn, shape the understanding of a pro-ecological, ethical and economic approach to managing limited resources in a traditional way. The process becomes complicated when the principles of classical economics based on maximizing shareholder value are compared with the sharing economy concept, especially in the context of using this link in circular economy business models. Sustainable business model archetypes can be used after making adjustments to business model archetypes that combine the assumptions of the sharing economy and the circular economy. Sharing economy sustainable development perspectives suggest the use of perspectives to measure sharing economy business models performance in economics, environmental, social and technological areas (Daunoriene, Draksaite, Snieska, Valodkiene, 2015, p. 839). The chapter presents the assumptions of the conceptualization and operationalization of potential model solutions in the field of using sustainable business model archetypes in designing circular business models in the Digital Economy. The chapter has a theoretical character and describes recommendations for the development of the proposed solution in ontological, epistemological and methodological categories, but also with the use of the axiological sense. The aim of the chapter is to develop and indicate the principles of designing business models based on sharing economy and circular economy concepts, using sustainable business model archetypes.

THE ASSUMPTIONS OF DIGITAL ECONOMY BUSINESS MODELS

The digital economy is largely based on the principles of the network of links between market players, where communication platforms shape the potential to effectively deliver the proposed value not only to customers, who are usually the users of these platforms, but they are fully designed to build a community of supporters who after some time should foster the monetization of business models.

Figure 1 shows the attributes of the resource sharing process in the context of the assumptions of the concept of business models.

The Sharing Business Model Compass presented in Figure 6 shows six key areas, which include shared resources, a governance model, a platform type, technology, transaction type, and a business approach. These areas shape the structure of the designed business model in terms of its configuration and functionality. The compass confirms that there is a multitude of scenarios and alternative constructs designed in this concept of business models. Examples of business models of companies referring to the assumptions of the sharing economy concept include companies such as Uber, BlaBlaCar, ZipCar, finansowo.pl, Polak potrafi, iParkomat, Ulala Chef, Skiltrade and others.

Figure 1. Sharing Business model compass
Source: (Cohen, Munoz, 2017).

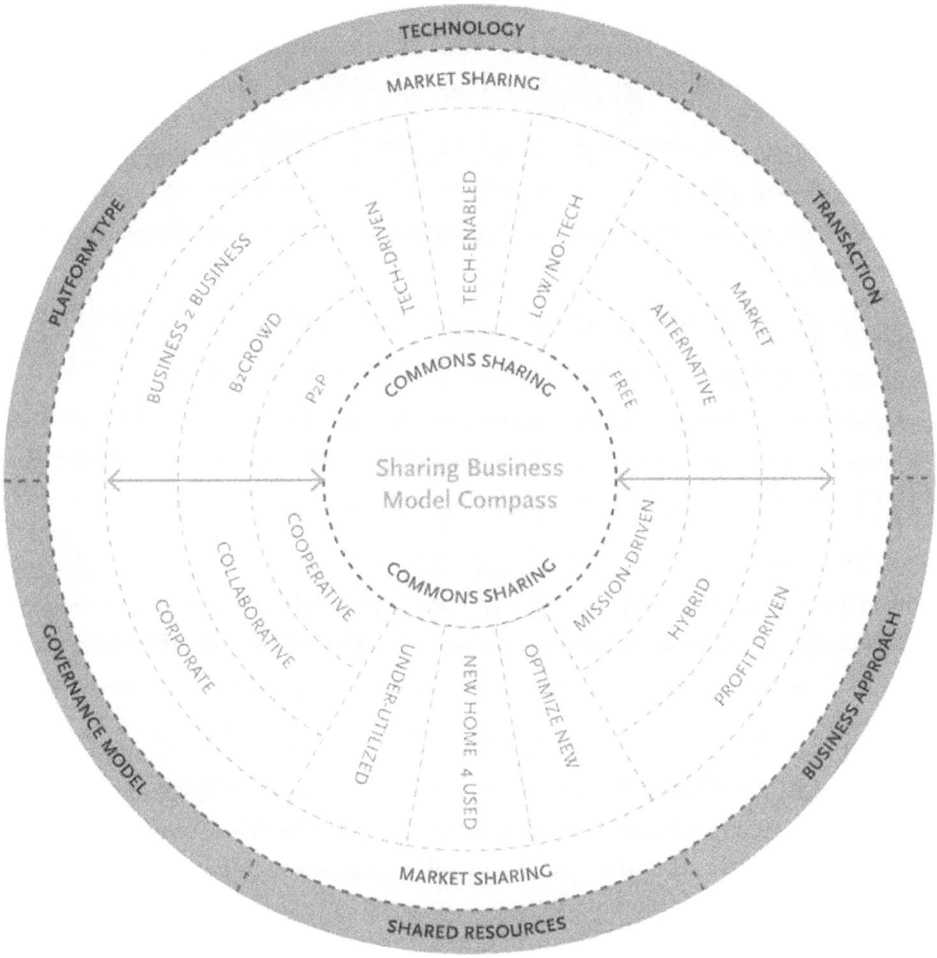

Designing, reconfiguring and adjusting business models are processes that are implemented properly throughout the life cycle of the business model by the creators of innovative business ventures.From a broader perspective, the conceptual and technological sphere of the design process at least should be distinguished. Both are important in the business environment in terms of the sharing economy and Open Data.

THE THEORETICAL AND PRACTICAL FRAMEWORK OF DIGITAL ECONOMY SUSTAINABLE BUSINESS MODELS

The issue of sustainability expands the scope of its impact also into the area of the digital economy. In addition to classical three pillars underlying the assumptions of this approach, namely Economy, Environment and Society, the fourth component of technology is also used. This is particularly important in the use of sharing economy digital platforms. Table 1.

Each of the variables that characterize the assumptions of Sustainable Business Models for the Digital Economy reveal a new perspective on building a fair process of delivering value to stakeholders. In the case of the digital economy in particular, a phenomenon of the co-creation of value for and with communities occurs. It is significantly reflected in the Sharing Economy.

The sharing economy is widely discussed in the relevant literature. Many authors interpret this concept differently. Table 2 shows a few narrow and broad definitions of sharing economy assumptions.

The sharing economy is the result of several overlapping concepts, technologies and solutions of a social nature. A. Acquier, T. Daudigeosb and J. Pinksec graphically showed the central place of the sharing economy compared to the following concepts: the Access Economy; the Community-Based Economy; the Platform economy, the Access Platform, Community Based Access, and the Community Based Platform. The Access Economy includes a set of initiatives sharing underutilized assets (material resources or skills) to optimize their use. The Platform Economy is the second core of the sharing economy. It is defined as a set of indirect initiatives of decentralized exchanges among peers via digital platforms. The community-based economy is the third core of the economy. It refers to coordinating initiatives through non-contractual, non-hierarchical or non-monetized forms of interactions in order to perform work, participate in the project or create exchange relationships (Acquiera, Daudigeosb, Pinksec, 2017, pp. 3-7). Figure 2.

In the sharing economy, roles are assigned to three entities that create a triadic B2B platform relationship. These include service enablers such as Uber, Airbnb, Luxe, etc., service providers such as drivers, hosts in homes and customers, such as passengers, guests, and users. A customer may be a firm (B2B) or an individual (B2C) (Kumar, Lahiri, Bahadir Dogan, 2018, p. 147) Figure 3 shows the relationship between the actors constituting the structure of the sharing economy business model.

This approach emphasizes the role of partnership in the creation of value, which should be sustainable to maintain the cohesion of the business model as well as synergy between the expectations and needs of its participants. If this partnership is not preserved and some participants of the business model achieve more favorable conditions for themselves, then these models may wobble and lose their effectiveness

Table 1. Sharing economy sustainable development perspectives

Sustainability area	Definition	Perspectives	References
Economy	The economic perspective is defined as an organizational domain that emphasizes the practices, discourses, and material expressions associated with the production, use, and management of resources (adapted from Circles of Sustainability, 2011:9).	Production and Resourcing; Exchange and Transfer; Accounting ; Consumption and Use; Labour and Welfare; Infrastructure; Wealth and Distribution	Circles of Sustainability (2011)
Environment	The ecological perspective is defined as an organizational domain that emphasizes the practices, discourses, and material expressions that occur across the intersection between the organizational and the natural realms (adapted from Circles of Sustainability, 2011: 10).	Materials and Energy; Water and Air ; Built-Form and Transport; Emission and Waste	Circles of Sustainability (2011)
Society	The social perspective is defined as an organizational domain that emphasizes the practices discourses, and material expressions associated with the formal and informal processes; systems; structures; and relationships actively support the capacity of current and future generations to create healthy and liveable communities (adapted from McKenzie, 2004:12,13)	Social equity; Health equity; Community development; Social support; Human rights; Labor rights; Social responsibility; Social justice; Social integration; Cultural competence; Human adaptation	Omann & Spangenberg (2002); James et all (2015).
Technology	The technological perspective is define as an organizational domain that support and enhance a "good life" for all of its employees, customers and society as well without compromising the Earth's ecosystem or the prospects of later generations (adapted from Vergragt, 2006:7).	Intermediate; Progressive; Alternative ; Light-capital; Laborintensive; Indigenous; Low-cost; Soft; Liberatory	Akubue (2000)

Source: (Daunoriene, Draksaite, Snieska, Valodkiene, 2015, p. 839).

Table 2. Narrow and broad definitions of the sharing economy

Narrow definitions	
Author	**Definition**
Benkler (2004)	The sharing economy refers to a class of resources or goods that are amenable to being shared within social sparing systems rather than allocated through markets Social sharing also constitutes "alternative modality of production " based on gifting and the free participation among "weakly connected participants"
Belk (2014)	"True sharing" and "pseudo-sharing" are distinguished. "Sharing is an alternative to private ownership that is emphasized in both marketplace exchange and gift-giving." Pseudo-sharing is a phenomenon whereby commodity exchange and potential exploitation of consumer co-creators present themselves in the guise of sharing or business relationship masquerading as communal sharing
Cockayne (2016)	The "on demand" or "sharing" economy is a term that describes digital platforms that connect consumers to a service or commodity through the use of a mobile application or website.
Eckhardt and Bardhi (2016)	The access economy, (...) also known as sharing or peer-to-peer economy, (...) provides temporary access to consumption resources for a fee or for free without a transfer of ownership.
Frenken and Schor (2017)	The sharing economy can be defined as "consumers granting each other temporary access to under-utilized physical assets ("idle capacity"), possibly for money.
Stephany (2015)	The value-sharing economy is using under-utilized assets and making them accessible online to a community, leading to a reduced need for ownership of those assets.
Broad definitions	
Habibi et al. (2017)	We suggest a sharing-exchange continuum that helps distinguish the degree to which actual sharing is being offered.
Lessig (2008)	The sharing economy can be described as the hybrid economy, which is either a commercial entity that aims to leverage value from the sharing economy, or it is a sharing economy that builds upon a commercial entity to better support its sharing aims.
Muñoz and Cohen (in this issue)	A socio-economic system enabling an intermediated set of exchanges of goods and services between individuals and organizations, which aim to increase efficiency and optimization of under-utilized resources in society.
Schor (2014)	Sharing activities fall into four broad categories: recirculation of goods, increased utilization of durable assets, exchange of services and sharing of productive assets.
Botsman (2013)	An economic model based on sharing underutilized assets from spacer to skills to stuff for monetary or non-monetary benefits.

Source: (Acquiera, Daudigeosb, Pinksec, 2017, p. 3)

Figure 2. The sharing economy as a result of several overlapping concepts
Source: (Acquiera, Daudigeosb, Pinksec, 2017, pp. 3-7).

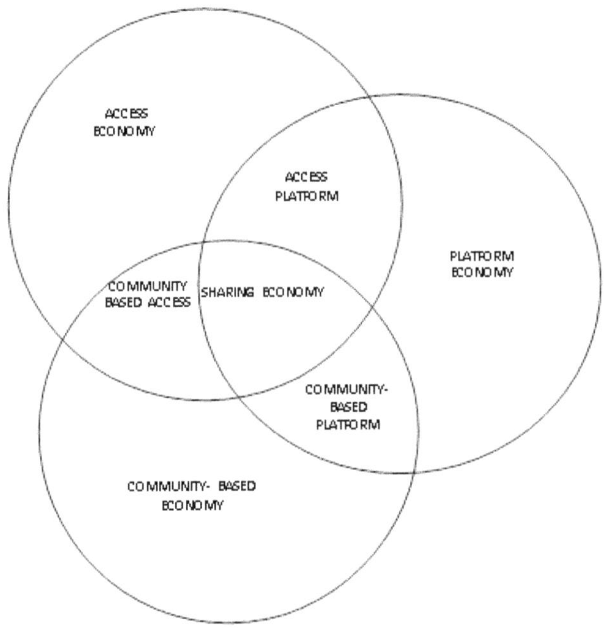

Figure 3. Conceptual framework of the sharing economy business model
Source: (Kumar, Lahiri, Bahadir Dogan, 2018, p. 148).

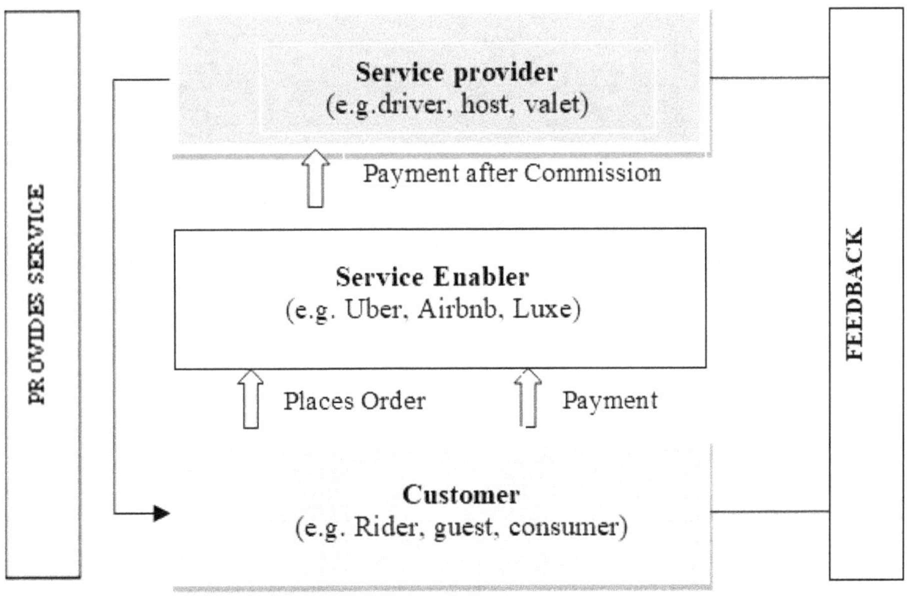

and efficiency. Therefore, the application of sustainable business model archetypes can successfully improve the balance between organizing, human and technological aspects.

SUSTAINABLE BUSINESS MODEL ARCHETYPES RULES

Sustainable business model archetypes are introduced to describe groupings of mechanisms and solutions that may contribute to building up the business model for sustainability. The aim of these archetypes is to develop a common language that can be used to accelerate the development of sustainable business models in research and practice. The archetypes are: Maximise material and energy efficiency; Create value from 'waste'; Substitute with renewables and natural processes; Deliver functionality rather than ownership; Adopt a stewardship role; Encourage sufficiency; Re-purpose the business for society/ environment; and Develop scale-up solutions (Bocken, Short, Rana, Evans, 2014, p. 42).

A wide range of sustainable business model archetypes is shown in Figure 4.

Figure 4. The sustainable business model archetypes
Source: (Bocken, Short, Rana, Evans, 2014, p. 48).

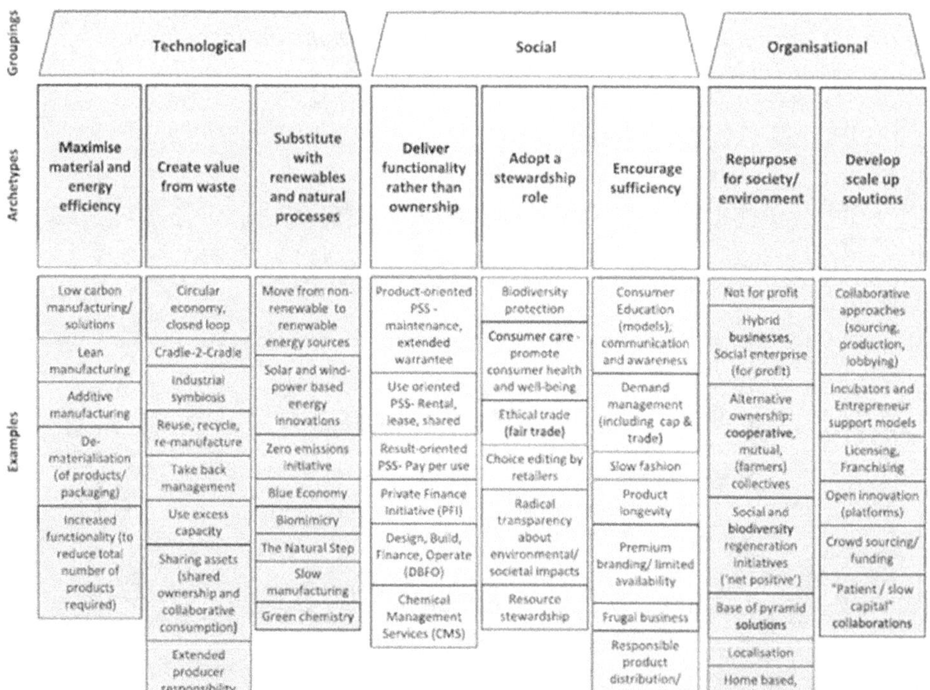

Figure 5. Sustainable business model archetype 'deliver functionality, rather than ownership'
Source: (Bocken, Short, Rana, Evans, 2014, p. 51).

Value proposition	Value creation & delivery	Value capture
• Provide services that satisfy user needs without users having to own psyhical products. • Business focus shifts from manufacturing 'stuff' to maximizing consumer use of products, so reducing production throughput of materials and better aligning manufacturers' and consumers' interests	• Delivery through product/service offerings require significant changes within the firm to deliver this and may incentivize redesign for durability, reparability and upgradability. • Potentially, more direct consumer contact and consumer education to shift away from ownership. Supply chains become more integrated	• Consumers pay for the use of the service, not for ownership of products. • Cost of ownership of psyhical products are bome by the company and/or partners.

In the context of the axiological approach to defining sustainable business model archetypes, as well as to show the advantage of functionality over ownership, three types of values were identified: Value Proposition, Value Creation & Delivery, and Value Capture.

Sustainable business model archetypes suitable for the Digital Economy create new resource optimization opportunities for sustainable development. This archetype is about shifting substantially towards the pure service models that is, delivering functionality on a pay-per-use basis, rather than selling ownership of a product. In doing so, this may fundamentally change the material throughput requirements of the industrial system. The literature suggests the following potential benefits of such an approach, which result from better alignment of the customer's (and societies) needs with that of the manufacturer:

- Breaks the link between profit and production volume (but probably not usage volume)
- Can reduce resource consumption,
- Motivation and opportunity to deal with through-life and endof-life issues as the manufacturer retains ownership of assets,
- Enhanced efficiency in use,
- Enhanced product longevity/durability,
- Reuse of materials. (…) This archetype has the potential to change consumption patterns, in particular by reducing the need for product ownership. In addition, it may incentivize manufacturers to develop products that last longer and design for upgradability and reparability, potentially

reducing resource use.(…) The archetypes aim to: Categorise and explain business model innovations for sustainability; Provide mechanisms to assist the innovation process for embedding sustainability in business models (e.g. through case studies and workshops); Define a clearer research agenda for business models for sustainability; and Provide exemplars for businesses to de-risk the SBM innovation process. The eight archetypes developed are:

1. Maximise material and energy efficiency
2. Create value from 'waste'
3. Substitute with renewables and natural processes
4. Deliver functionality, rather than ownership
5. Adopt a stewardship role
6. Encourage sufficiency
7. Re-purpose the business for society/environment
8. Develop scale-up solutions ((Bocken, Short, Rana, Evans, 2014, p. 55).

It is important to indicate such sustainable business model archetypes that are suitable for the digital economy based on the use of technology platforms that gather communities. Change in the priority from ownership to availability and designing scalable business solutions is becoming a stimulus for designing business models that take into account social factors, making them more environmentally friendly. They also contribute, to a very large extent, to the development of intelligent business models, where the value of a higher order (ideological value) is built into its logic.

CIRCULAR ECONOMY BUSINESS MODELS

The dynamics of the transformation of business models from the neoclassical approach, based on the assumptions of the classical economy, towards solutions that include social elements and the assumptions of the Sharing Economy can be observed. Evolutionary change in designing business models also occurs, from classical business models through sustainable business models to circular business models. Figure 6.

The issue of circular business models has been developing very dynamically in recent years, and the definitions of this concept have been evolving in many directions. Many different approaches have been proposed for designing either circular or sustainable business models, however there is no consensus of an integrated vision of both concepts (de Pádua Pieronia, Pigossoa, McAloonea, 2018, p. 799).

The assumptions of the circular economy are based on the application of the following principles, which, in whole or in part, constitute a configuration of business models focused on their implementation. ReSOLVE is a checklist of CE

Figure 6. Comparison of traditional, sustainable, and circular business models
Source: (Geissdoerfer, Naomi Morioka, Monteiro de Carvalho, Evans, 2018, p. 714).

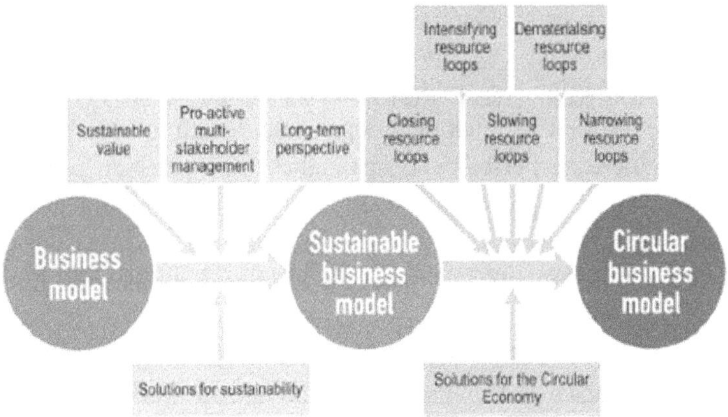

Table 3. Deployment of sustainability dimensions into circular business models.

Sustainability dimensions	Circular business models		
	Value proposition	**Value creation and delivery system**	**Value capture**
Economic	Offerings (products and services) with economic margin to ensure profit	Incentives for actors in the supply chain to extend product use and return disposal to the value system	Profit (or at least not negative result) to each stakeholder
Environmental	Products and services designed to minimise natural resources depletion	Eco-efficient production and logistic operations	Reduced environmental burden by extracting more value from less natural resource consumption
Social	Maximize product and service value for society well-being	Pro-active approach towards stakeholders in the closed loops	Further environmental consciousness on the value of products
Protection of future generations	Long-term capacity to address economic, environmental and social concerns	Incremental and radical changes in the system level to ensure long-term partnerships	Preparation of current production systems to be make "perfect" circular economy viable in the future

Source: (Geissdoerfer, Naomi Morioka, Monteiro de Carvalho, Evans, 2018, p. 714).

(circular economy) requirements proposed by the Ellen MacArthur Foundation that consists of six actions: regenerate, share, optimise, loop, virtualise, and exchange, each presenting an opportunity for CE implementation (EMF, 2015a). The scope and interpretation of these six activities covers the following areas:

1. **Regenerate:** Shift to renewable energy and materials, reclaim, retain and regenerate health of ecosystems, return recovered biological resources to the biosphere.
2. **Share:** Keep product loop speed low, maximise utilisation of products by sharing them among users, reuse products throughout their technical lifetime, prolong life through maintenance, repair and design for durability.
3. **Optimise:** Increase performance/efficiency of a product, remove waste in production and the supply chain, leverage big data, automation, remote sensing and steering.
4. **Loop:** Keep components and materials in closed, loops and prioritise inner loops.
5. **Virtualise:** Deliver utility virtually.
6. **Exchange:** Replace old materials with advanced non-renewable materials, apply new technologies (Manninen, Koskela, Antikainen, Bocken, Dahlbo, Aminoff, 2018, p. 418).

The literature recognizes digital business models and digital technologies as factors facilitating the transition to the circular economy. They can be used to overcome the challenges of the circular economy (Bressanelli, Adrodegari, Perona, Saccani, 2018, p. 218). Digitalisation can boost the transformation towards a more sustainable circular economy. It can help closing the material loops by providing accurate information on the availability, location and condition of products. Digitalisation also enables more efficient processes in companies, helps minimise waste, promotes longer life for products and minimises the transaction costs. Thus, digitalisation boosts the circular Economy business models by helping to close the loop, slow the material loop and narrow the loop with increased resource efficiency (Anticainen, Uusitalo, Kivikyto – Reponen, 2018, p. 45). Therefore, it seems reasonable to say that digital technologies support the emergence of sustainable and circular business models to a greater extent than traditional solutions.

THE DESIGN OF CIRCULAR BUSINESS MODELS WITH THE USE OF SUSTAINABLE BUSINESS MODEL ARCHETYPES – CONCEPTUALIZATION AND OPERATIONALIZATION

Sustainable business model archetypes can be used in the process of designing circular business models that use digital technologies. Sustainability archetypes can be used for their conceptualization and operationalization. Table 4 presents a range of possibilities of applying sustainable business model archetypes defined in the relevant literature in the design of digital business models.

Table 4. Sustainable business model archetypes for the design of digital business models

NO,	Sustainable Business Model Archetypes	Possibilities of applying Sustainable Business Model Archetypes in the design of digital business models.
1.	Maximise material and energy efficiency.	Application in IT platforms that use Big Data technologies for collecting data on the efficiency of technological devices, technological processes, and tools optimizing the selection of engineering materials for specific applications. Internet of Things and Tools Analytics.
2.	Create value from 'waste'	IT platforms used to collect data on waste in the field of environmental protection processes. Waste purchase, sale and storage platforms.
3.	Substitute with renewables and natural processes.	Business models of companies that trade in certificates in the field of renewable energy sources. Platforms that use Big Data technology in the field of renewable energy sources.
4.	Deliver functionality, rather than ownership	Business models that use the concept of the sharing economy.
5.	Adopt a stewardship role	Service Enablers business models for services focused on social and pro-environmental activities.
6.	Encourage sufficiency	IT platforms to optimize the use of resources, technologies, properties and services.
7.	Re-purpose the business for society/ environment	IT platforms aimed at building attitudes and pro-social activities using community building, such as Crowdsourcing, Croudfounding and others.
8.	Develop scale-up solutions	IT tools used to manage the scalability of business, technology, tools and human resources.

Source: Own study

The proposals presented for the areas of the application of activities defined as those that create circular business models are innovative and cover a wide range of possibilities. Particularly, they may have a significant application as substantive content for the use of tools in the field of the Access Economy, the Community-Based Economy, the Platform Economy, the Access Platform, Community- Based Access, and the Community Based Platform. All these platforms make it possible to optimize resources as well as manage their availability and use, which has a positive impact on the implementation of sustainable management and development principles.

CONCLUSION

In the context of the analysis of the contemporary approach to business models, the broader and more transparent generation of solutions focused on environmental and social aspects appeared. Current and future digital solutions support and will continue to support the concept of the circular economy to a large extent. Business models, through their structure and place in the economy, are used to operationalize this concept. Large data sources and resources in the form of IT platforms gathering communities through designed functionalities can identify the various innovative formulas of activities consistent with the idea of the circular economy such as regenerating, sharing, optimizing, looping, virtualising, and exchanging. Within these thematic areas, the use of sustainable business model archetypes is an important element in building mature solutions of the circular economy concept in the formula of business models. The principles of designing circular economy business models should be based on the use of the achievements in the field of knowledge and experience in the application of sustainable business model archetypes to shape their expected configuration and functionality. Circular economy solutions currently represent a higher generation of solutions that arise from the sustainable management approach, therefore they should use the existing theoretical and practical achievements in this field.

REFERENCES

Acquiera, A., Daudigeosb, T., & Pinksec, J. (2017). Promises and paradoxes of the sharing economy: An organizing framework. *Technological Forecasting & Social Change*, 125.

Anticainen, M., Uusitalo, T., & Kivikyto-Reponen, P. (2018). Digitalisation as an Enabler of Circular Economy. *Procedia CIRP*, 73.

Belk, R. (2014). You are what you can access: Sharing and collaborative consumption online. *Journal of Business Research*, *67*(8), 1595–1600. doi:10.1016/j.jbusres.2013.10.001

Bergman, M. M., Bergman, Z., & Berger, L. (2017). An Empirical Exploration, Typology, and Definition of Corporate Sustainability. *Sustainability*, 9.

Bocken, N. M. P., Short, S. W., Rana, P., & Evans, S. (2014). A literature and practice review to develop sustainable business model archetypes. *Journal of Cleaner Production*, 65.

Boons, F., Montalvo, C., Quist, J., & Wagner, M. (2013). Sustainable innovation, business models and economic performance: An overview. *Journal of Cleaner Production*, 45.

Bressanelli, G., Adrodegari, F., Perona, M., & Saccani, N. (2018). The role of digital technologies to overcome Circular Economy challenges in PSS Business Models – and exploratory case study. *Proccedia CIRP*, 73.

Calvo, N., & Villarreal, O. (2018). Analysis of the growth of the e-learning industry through sustainable business model archetypes: A case study. *Journal of Cleaner Production, 191*, 26–39. doi:10.1016/j.jclepro.2018.04.211

Choi, H. R., Cho, M. J., Lee, K. B., Hong, S. G., & Woo, C. R. (2014). *The Business Model for the Sharing Economy between SMEs* (Vol. 11). WSEAS Transactions on Business and Economics.

Cohen, B., & Munoz, P. (2017). *Sharing Business Model Compass*. Retrieved from https://ladiaria.com.uy/articulo/2017/4/un-modelo-para-entender-la-economia colaborativa/#

Daunoriene, A., Draksaite, A., Snieska, V., & Valodkiene, G. (2015). Evaluating Sustainability of Sharing Economy Business Models. *Procedia: Social and Behavioral Sciences*, 213.

de Pádua Pieronia, M., Pigossoa, D. C. A., & McAloonea, T. C.,(2018). Sustainable qualifying criteria for designing circular business models. *Procedia CIRP*, 69.

Elkington, J. (1999). *Cannibals with forks: the triple bottom line of 21. century business*. Oxford, UK: Capstone.

EMF. (2015a). *Towards a Circular Economy - Business Rationale for an Accelerated Transition*. EMF.

Fahimnia, B., Sarkis, J., & Davarzani, H., (2015). Green supply chain management: A review and bibliometric analysis. *International Journal Profuction Economics*, 162.

Geissdoerfer, M., Morioka, S., Monteiro de Carvalho, M., & Evans, S. (2018). Business models and supply chains for the circular Economy. *Journal of Cleaner Production*, 190.

Jabłoński, A., & Jabłoński, M. (2016). Research on Business Models in their Life Cycle. *Sustainability*, 8.

Kumar, V., Lahiri, A., & Bahadir Dogan, O. (2018). A strategic framework for a profitable business model in the sharing Economy. *Industrial Marketing Management*, 69.

Lüdeke-Freund, F. (2010). *Towards a Conceptual Framework of 'Business Models for Sustainability*. Paper presented at Knowledge Collaboration & Learning for Sustainable Innovation, Delft, The Netherlands.

Manninen, K., Koskela, S., Antikainen, R., Bocken, N., Dahlbo, H., & Aminoff, A. (2018). Do circular economy business models capture intended environmental value propositions? *Journal of Cleaner Production*, 171.

Mourougan, S. (2015). Corporate Social Responsibility for sustainable business. *IOSR Journal of Business and Management, 17*(5).

Neumeyer, X., & Santos, S. C. (2018). Sustainable business models, venture typologies, and entrepreneurial ecosystems: A social network perspective. *Journal of Cleaner Production*, 172.

Schaltegger, S., Hansen, E. & Lüdeke-Freund, F., (2015). Business Models for Sustainability: Origins, Present Research, and Future Avenues. *Organization & Environment*. . doi:10.1177/1086026615599806

Schaltegger, S., Lüdeke-Freund, F., & Hansen, E.G. (2016). Business Models for Sustainability - A Co-Evolutionary Analysis of Sustainable Entrepreneurship, Innovation, and Transformation. *Organization & Environment, 29*.

Stephany, A. (2015). *The Business of Sharing: Making it in the New Sharing Economy*. Palgrave Macmillan. doi:10.1057/9781137376183

Wang, Z., & Sarkis, J. (2017). Corporate social responsibility governance, outcomes, and financial performance. *Journal of Cleaner Production*, 162.

Yip, A. W. H., & Bocken, N. M. P. (2018). Sustainable business model archetypes for the banking industry. *Journal of Cleaner Production*, 174.

Chapter 2
Robustness in the Business Models of the Organizations Embedded in the Circular Economy

Adam Jabłoński
WSB University in Poznań, Poland

ABSTRACT

The dynamics of ongoing market changes require a new look at business management mechanisms. Often the key element of the organization's operation is to ensure business continuity, which is not easy. This requires strong embeddedness in the decision-making processes resulting from the properly built business model of the organization. A business model becomes a crucial determinant of the organizational success today. The aim of the chapter is to present the place and role of robustness in shaping the business models of organizations embedded in the circular economy. The scope of the chapter includes studies of listed companies that implement the principles of responsible business to ensure their robustness in the short and long term. In the chapter, the author poses a research question: Can the skillful use of the concept of business model robustness in circular economy companies guarantee the organization's ability to ensure business continuity and its high performance?

DOI: 10.4018/978-1-5225-7850-5.ch002

INTRODUCTION

The dynamics of the ongoing market changes requires a new look at business management mechanisms. Often the key element of the organization's operation is to ensure business continuity, which is not easy. This requires strong embeddedness in the decision-making processes resulting from the properly built business model of the organization. A business model becomes a crucial determinant of the organizational success today. As it can be understood in multiple ways, its conceptualization and operationalization under conditions of pressure, expectations and market uncertainty is interesting. A business model that is the mapping of tangible and intangible assets that create value in a short and long term ensures return from the degree of the potential used for all actors gathered around the organization.

In this interpretation, it is important to build a business model that will resist market changes while adjusting to market expectations. This resistance often manifests itself in the robustness of the business model itself. It can be understood as maintaining the high effectiveness of the business model when aggregating and incorporating the aspects of strategic and operational changes. As the changes apply, inter alia, to the principles of running a business in the circular economy, it is therefore important to implement strategic activities taking into account the circular economy.

It is significant to link the concept of business models towards their robustness in the circular economy. A constructive comparison of business model assumptions with its robustness shapes a new dimension of the effectiveness of companies, especially in the network environment. In such an environment, the way also opens to the principles of using the circular economy to achieve high company performance through the skillful use of the business model. The aim of the paper is to present the place and role of robustness in shaping the business models of organizations embedded in the circular economy. The scope of the paper includes the studies of listed companies that implement the principles of responsible business to ensure their robustness in the short and long term. The author poses a research question: Can the skillful use of the concept of business model robustness in circular economy companies guarantee the organization's ability to ensure business continuity and its high effectiveness?

The scientific management issue presented is related to the definition of mechanisms that ensure the robustness of business models of companies that use the circular economy to ensure their ability to survive while achieving high effectiveness. The analysis of both the national and international achievements of management sciences in the context of the evolution of the management problem allows for the statement of several facts that are theses, namely:

- Management problems are empirical (they have their sources and occur inside and outside the organization),
- Management problems in a pragmatic sense evolve (change) under the influence of changes taking place in the environment (and inside the organization), which results in the loss of the assumed effectiveness of the methods of solving them (they require improvement),
- Management problems emerge faster than the progress of science,
- Science notices problems with a certain delay and develops methods for solving them (Szarucki, 2016, p.47).

BUSINESS MODELS: STRATEGIC ASSUMPTIONS

The concept of business models in management sciences results in much controversy and different looks. There are a lot of definitions of business models that are characterized by different parameters and interpretations. Currently, the essence of understanding a business model is widely discussed, both in terms of reference to a given paradigm, and its place in the criterion of the environment and cause and effect relationships and correlations between other ontological entities. In such a community, a business model leads the way, determining new decision-making centres and creating new impulses in shaping, appropriating and capturing value. A business model, being a benchmark and a reference point that ensures the materialization of strategic ideas through the constructive comparison of various factors, becomes a platform of strategic accessories that often have a resource dimension. Potentially, new technology may not be an obvious business model, so in such situations, technology teams need to expand their perspective to find a suitable business model to be able to capture the full value of this technology (Chesbrough, 2010). A business model and business model innovation are not directly observable. We observe the specific arrays of activities devoted to the creation, delivery and appropriation of value, and we have decided to call these arrays "business models" and respectively, model innovations. "Thus, the business model and business model innovation are, of course, conceptual abstractions, theoretical constructs" (Foss, Saebi, 2018). There are many interpretations of the concept of a business model. A business model can be used, among others, to generate revenues and / or to create the value of an organization. According to R. Amit, C.Zott, a business model is a specific way, a method by which an organization can generate revenues (Amit, Zott, 2000). D. Teece defines a business model as a system of how a firm delivers value to customers and converts payment into profits (Teece, 2010). Timmers regards a business model as an architecture for the flows of products, services and information including the description of various activities and different roles of individual network participants (Timmers, 1998). J.Magretta points out that a business model is stories that explain how companies operate (Magretta, 2003, p.470). An interesting interpretation of the business model is presented by A.Osterwalder and Y.Pigneur, who point out that a business model describes how the organization creates value and ensures and derives profits from the value created (Osterwalder, Pigneur, 2012). Baden-Fuller, MacMillan, Demil, and Lecocq define business model as "the logic of the firm, the way it operates and how it creates value for its stakeholders" (Baden-Fuller et al, 2010). Ch.Nielsen, N.Bukh define a general business model as a meta model or ontology for the business model, paying attention to the operating system and the ability to generate value (Nielsen, Bukh, 2008). Generally speaking, the concept refers to the description of the articulation between different BM (Business Model) components or 'building blocks' to produce a proposition that can generate value for - consumers and thus for the organization (Demil, Lecocq, 2010). The business model says "how the company communicates, creates, delivers, and captures value out of a value proposition" (Abdelkafi, 2012).. There are many definitions of business models, but it is crucial to use such a definition that will ensure high organization's effectiveness by the monetization of the business model, taking into account the relevant sales structure.

Robustness in business models. THE CONCEPT OF STAKEHOLDERS AND THE BUSINESS MODELS OF PUBLIC ORGANIZATIONS

The robustness of the business model is now becoming one of the key elements of business continuity management towards a long-term value and high effectiveness management system. Four factors that influence business model robustness are identified: (1) component dynamics, (2) tolerance to variation, (3) feedback about effectiveness, and (4) adaptability (Täuscher, Abdelkafi, 2015). The robustness of a designed BMs is seldom tested vis-à-vis the fast and unpredictable changes in digital technologies, regulation and markets (Haaker et al, 2017). Yuliya Snihur and Christoph Zott argue that firms implementing BMI (business Model Innovation) can design their new business models so as to acquire legitimacy and simultaneously discourage imitation using three elements of the new business model—content, governance, and structure—in conjunction or independently (Snihur, Zott, 2013). In this perspective, it is important to skillfully manage change through its implementation, taking into account factors that trigger it in the environment and inside the organization. The robustness of the business model stems from the organizational DNA. It is the organizational DNA that is the source of managers' decisions related to the conceptualization and operationalization of the business model. It becomes the foundation and platform for its first monetization. This approach generates the first value proposition and the income generation logic that converts payments into profits. It is also worth noting that the robustness of the business model does not exclude its permanent evolution as part of its market exploitation. The robustness of the business model should be considered taking into account the life cycle of the organization. At each stage of the organization's development there are other features of business model robustness. It is also related to the immune system built into the business model. In the opinion of the author, the robustness of the business model is the ability to recognize, neutralize and destroy negative factors and structures affecting the business model. In a more general sense, it means the ability to actively and passively protect the business model from organizational pathogens. Then, the attributes (features) of business model robustness, which may be primary and secondary, gain particular importance.

Table 1 shows the features of the primary and secondary immune systems depending on the life cycle of the organization along with the evolution of its business model. This analysis includes the following features:

- Sales revenues (thousands PLN) - revenue that is a product of the number of products, works, services, goods and materials sold and a relevant unit sale price,
- Net profit (thousands PLN) - actual profitability measure, i.e. the sales margin and discounts after deducing operating costs and taxes.
- Tax efficiency (%) – a ratio of the amount of final tax due to the value of the tax base (it informs about actual taxation of income, i.e. tax base, taxpayer),
- Fixed assets (thousands PLN) - part of the assets of an economic entity with an anticipated period of use longer than one financial year,
- Current assets (thousands PLN) - assets that will be used (e.g. raw materials), sold (e.g. products) or otherwise used in the near future (up to one year from the balance sheet date),
- The cost of capital (%) – a financial indicator that informs about the average relative cost of capital employed in financing the investment by the enterprise,
- Product, process, organizational and technological innovations - product innovations concern goods or services, consisting of the launch of a new product or significant improvement of an already existing product; process (technological) innovations involve implementing new or introducing significant improvements in the methods used by the organization for manufacturing, distribution and supporting activities in the field of products or services, while organizational innovations allow for the implementation of a new organizational method in the operating principles adopted by the

company, which has not been applied in a given company so far, and which aims to improve its operation.
- The competencies of managers and other employees (change in the Management Board compared to the previous year).

These factors allow for introducing the most important aspects of the company's operation.

The features adopted are adequate to the organization's life cycle along with the evolution of its business model. The assessment of a BMfS (Business Model for Sustainability)' scalability and robustness is even more challenging since firms need to connect their value proposition (to customers) and their societal value proposition in a scalable and reinforcing manner (Tauscher, Abdelkafi, 2018).

The robustness of the business model is associated with its protection. Business model protection is required, especially in business continuity management. The better protection of the business model, the longer it can be exploited. To protect the business model, one should define its key attributes, which are also its know-how.

CIRCULAR BUSINESS MODELS

The circular economy is currently one of the crucial development areas at both the macroeconomic and organizational levels. The circular economy should be considered in a systemic approach, which is used to achieve goals focused on the efficient use of resources and it should take into account the assessment of the organization's life cycle and its business model. Life Cycle Assessment is "a tool for the analysis of the environmental burden of products at all stages in their life cycle — from the extraction of resources, through the production of materials, product parts and the product itself, and the use of the product to the management after it is discarded, either by reuse, recycling or final disposal (in effect, therefore, 'from the cradle to the grave') (Guinée, 2002). The systemic approach enables the circular economy to integrate social, economic and natural aspects at every level of management:

- **A Micro Level:** Through the creation of eco-designs, eco-products, waste minimization, the introduction of environment management system, etc.
- **A Meso Level:** Through the creation of industrial eco-parks,
- **A Macro Level:** The creation of eco-cities, eco-communities, and eco-regions (Geng, Doberstein, 2008).

The circular economy aims to decouple prosperity from resource consumption, i.e., how can we consume goods and services and yet not depend on extraction of

Table 1. Features of the primary and secondary immune systems depending on the life cycle of the organization along with the evolution of its business model

	Features	The organization's life cycle along with the evolution of its business model.	**Features**
No	**Primary immune system built into the business model**		**Secondary immune system built into the business model**
	Initial capital First value proposition for customers Dynamic innovations Primary competencies of the first Board	**Incubation**	-
	-	**Growth**	Growth rate of revenue Growth rate of profit Growth rate of fixed and current assets Tax efficiency Cost of capital Increased product, process, organizational and technological innovations Increased quality of products and processes Increased competencies of managers and other employees
	-	**Maturity**	Stability of revenues Stability of profit Stability of fixed and current assets Stabilized competencies of managers and other employees
	-	**Decline**	Sustainable decline in revenues Sustainable decline in profit Sustainable decline in fixed and current assets High quality products Low product, process, organizational and technological innovations High competencies of experienced managers and other employees

Source: own study

virgin resources and thus ensure closed loops that will prevent the eventual disposal of consumed goods in landfill sites. Production and consumption also have associated "contamination transfers" to the environment at each step. In that sense, the circular economy is a movement towards the weak sustainability described earlier. It proposes a system where reuse and recycling provide substitutes to the use of raw virgin materials. By reducing our dependency on such resources, it improves our ability, and the ability of future generations to meet their needs. The circular economy makes sustainability more likely (Sauvé et al, 2016).

In a circular economy, growth is decoupled from the use of scarce resources through disruptive technology and business models based on longevity, renewability, reuse, repair, upgrade, refurbishment, capacity sharing, and dematerialization (Accenture Strategy, 2014).

Linder and Williander define a circular business model as "a business model in which the conceptual logic for value creation is based on utilizing the economic value retained in products after use in the production of new offerings" (Linder, Williander, 2015, p.2). According to Den Hollander and Bakker, a circular business model describes how an organization creates, delivers, and captures value in a circular economic system, whereby the business rationale needs to be designed in such a way that it prevents, postpones or reverses obsolescence, minimizes leakage and favours the use of 'presources' over the use of resources in the process of creating, delivering and capturing value." (Hollander, Bakker, 2016) According to Roos, "A circular value chain business model (or green business model) is one in which all intermediary outputs that have no further use in the value creating activities of the firms are monetised in the form of either cost reductions or revenue streams" (Roos, 2014, p.257). A circular business model is how a company creates, captures, and delivers value with the value creation logic designed to improve resource efficiency through contributing to extending useful life of products and parts (e.g., through long-life design, repair and remanufacturing) and closing material loops (Nußholz, 2017, p. 12). Circular business models proved they could potentially be coherent with a firm economic performance. Indeed, they can participate to its competitiveness through production costs cutting. More ambitiously, they can generate additional turnover by penetrating new markets and gaining new customers, and protect corporations against the volatility of raw material prices in traditional markets. Some of these strategies seem to enable improvements of operating profit and profitability (Beulque, Aggeri, 2016).

Laubscher and Marinelli identified six key areas for integration of the circular economy principles with the business model:

1. **Sales Mode:** A shift from selling volumes of products towards selling services and retrieving products after first life from customers,

2. Product design/material composition—the change concerns the way products are designed and engineered to maximize high quality reuse of product, its components and materials,
3. **IT/Data Management:** In order to enable resource optimization a key competence is required, which is the ability to keep track of products, components and material data,
4. **Supply Loops:** Turning towards the maximization of the recovery of own assets where profitable and to maximization of the use of recycled materials/ used components in order to gain additional value from product, component and material flows,
5. **Strategic Sourcing for Own Operation:** Building trusted partnerships and long-term relationships with suppliers and customers, including co-creation
6. **HR/Incentives:** A shift needs adequate culture adaptation and development of capabilities, enhanced by training programs and rewards (Laubscher, Marinelli, 2014).

RESEARCH METHODS ADOPTED

The appropriate research methods have been defined for the implementation and achievement of the intended purpose of the paper. As part of defining the multidimensional construct of the business model and its robustness, it is important to conduct a proper literature review suitable to the assumptions adopted. A literature review is not a prelude to proper research, but a separate research method. After all, the methodological discipline of this research affects the quality of applications, and further the correctness of hypotheses posed or interpretations of empirical research (Czakon, 2011). In this case, a critical literature review was conducted. The critical review is characterized by a characteristic approach to the synthesis of multidisciplinary research, conducted by means of various methods when criticism of the available literature and the questioning of existing findings of researchers are required (Barnett-Page, Thomas, 2009). The characteristic feature of critical reviews is that they focus on the creation of new theories (Dixon-Woods, 2006, p. 35). The various stages of the review are subordinated to this goal. For this reason, less emphasis is put on the systematicity and repeatability of search, selection, critical evaluation and synthesis methods. Instead of a standard assessment of the critical methodical quality of sophisticated research, a more specific assessment of resources is made here in terms of their theoretical utility (Orłowska et al., 2017, p. 355).

At the same time, when conducting a critical literature review, key words were defined, which were a basis for the selection of scientific papers that are the source of the theory and its review. The selection of literature focused on scientific papers that have been published in well-known world scientific journals in the last five years.

Using the existing research tools to build robustness-focused business models, the use of longitudinal research was proposed. According to J.R. Kimberly, longitudinal scientific research consists of such techniques, methodologies and activities that enable the observation, description and/or classification of organizational phenomena in such a way that processes can be identified and empirically documented (Kimberly, 1976).

Paradoxically, longitudinal research is conducted primarily in order to discover dynamics, and the dynamics of phenomena is a factor hindering research. For this reason, conducting research, especially static analyses, is not able to manage this task (Stańczyk-Hugiet, 2014, p.52).

The set of the following principles may be applied to the assessment of business model by means of longitudinal research:

1. The long observation of the business model allows the evaluation of its revolution or evolution;
2. The frequency of research may enable the adjustment of the business model at the individual stages of the company's operation;
3. The researcher's observation may determine the emergence of the business model's ability to be scalable;
4. The observation has a positive effect on the selection of business model attributes that are adequate to the needs;
5. Scientific research is proactive, informing not only about the past, but also about the future development of the business model (Jabłoński, 2016, p.95).

Simultaneously, qualitative research was used to examine the robustness of the business model.

The characteristic features of qualitative research include the use, implementation and presentation of results (Kaczmarek et al., 2016, p.17). There are five main reasons for using qualitative research:

1. To build new theory when prior theory is absent, underdeveloped, or flawed
2. To capture individuals' lived experiences and interpretations
3. To understand complex process issues
4. To illustrate an abstract idea
5. To examine narratives, discourse, or other linguistic phenomena (Graebner, 2012).

It is worth noting that qualitative research is explanatory rather than conclusive (Silverman, Marvasti, 2008).

For the purposes of the paper, the following assumptions of R.Dubin's eight-element model of scientific theory development were used:

1. Defining theory units, that is the basic elements that will form relationships in the process studied.
2. Describing relationships and principles underlying relationships between theory units.
3. Indicating theory boundaries that allow the process of explaining reality to focus on the most important forces and relationships and demarcation with other theories.
4. Inferring system states, that is how the system behaves, when certain forces operate and relationships between theory units occur.
5. Proposing a theoretical model that logically and consistently describes cause and effect relationships.
6. Operationalizing the model, i.e. finding empirical indicators that can be tested and measured.
7. Formulating hypotheses or research questions that allow for determining the state of empirical indicators in the testing process.
8. Testing, i.e. verifying hypotheses or making an attempt to answer research questions. (Dubin, 1983).

RESEARCH FINDINGS

Two well-known stock exchange indices, the Circular Index and the Respect Index were compared in the research process that included longitudinal research and qualitative research. They were analyzed in terms of differences and common features as part of initial information, dimensions (criteria) considered, the stages of research creating a list of companies composing each index, as well as final outcomes obtained thanks to individual stages of the company analysis. Attempts were made to find the advantages of each index. As regards the Circular Index, the focus was more on economic, social, environmental and circular dimensions, and then the individual steps of selecting companies for the Circular Index were described in detail. Subsequently, the criteria and stages for the Respect Index were presented in order to select the appropriate list of companies. Also, the quotations of Respect Index companies were compared with the quotations of WIG (Warsaw Stock Exchange Index) companies listed on the Warsaw Stock Exchange. A list of Respect Index companies at the time this index was established was made as well as a list of companies that changed over the past few years to eventually reach 28 participants in 2017. It was these companies that were analyzed below in terms of value propositions for customers, share capital (PLN x1000, Q3 2017), sales revenues (PLN x1000), net profit (PLN x1000), tax efficiency (%), fixed assets and current assets, the cost of capital (%), as well as in terms of the existence of innovative products, processes and organizational and technological innovations and the competencies of managers and other employees (whether there was a change in the Management Board compared to the previous year). The table below presents comparative analysis of the Circular Index and Respect Index in relation to the selected criteria adopted.

Both indices focus on economic, social and environmental dimensions. In addition, as regards the Circular Index, the company's circulatory aspect is considered. Research consists of several stages to be able to make a list of companies that meet the criteria of each of these indices, The Respect Index consists of three stages, and the Circular Index of five. However, both indices are aimed at selecting a list of companies that operate in a responsible, sustainable manner, as well as are focused on pro-environmental activities

CIRCULAR INDEX

Each of the Circular Index dimensions focuses on the following goals:

1. In the economic dimension, economic value is generated and distributed; research and development expenditure and employment must be maximized;
2. In the social dimension, accidents at work, job insecurity, absence from work, staff turnover and loss of productivity should be minimized;
3. In the environmental dimension, hazardous waste, used water and used energy should be minimized;
4. Taking into account the circular dimension, outlays from primary material and materials from recycling and re-use, the life span (life cycle) and intensity of products used and the efficiency of the recycling process must be maximized.

At the first stage, the indicators defined in Table 3 may be the examples of sustainable development indicators and circular indicators:

At the second stage, the Delphi technique is recommended to determine weights for sustainable development indicators as well as circularity indicators. This technique aims to isolate the maximum amount of unbiased information and quantify uncertainty. Crucial steps in the Delphi method include:

Table 2. Comparative analysis of the Circular Index and Respect Index in relation to the selected criteria adopted

Comparative criterion	Circular Index	Respect Index
Preliminary information	– the index refers to a single company, not a supply chain, – a set of new indicators related to the circularity dimension was proposed, – the suggested method may also be different. Instead of the AHP (Analytic Hierarchy Process), a Delphi method can be used.	The study of companies is conducted periodically (annually) and includes Polish companies listed on the WSE
Dimensions considered	– The Circular Index construction consists of four dimensions: – economic, – – social – – environmental – – circular.	The criteria used are grouped by the following areas: - environmental – environmental factors – social – social factors – governance – economic factors
Stages of a study that creates a list of companies	There are five stages to achieve the proposed sustainable development index: a) Stage 1 - Selection of circular and sustainable development indices, b) Stage 2 - Determining the weighs of indices, c) Stage 3 - Normalization, d) Step 4 - Aggregation method for building the index, e) Step 5 - Construction of the index.	The study creating the final list of Respect Index companies consists of three stages. The first and second stages are carried out independently, without the participation of the companies themselves and only on the basis of public information. The third stage, on the other hand, includes direct visits to the premises of the companies studied, after prior approval for participation in the project.
Final outcome	The Sustainable Circular Index for a company is created by a set of indicators related to social, economic and environmental sustainability, circularity and appropriate weights. The Circular Index is very versatile and simple because it allows the assessment of the sustainable development and circularity of manufacturing companies by conducting the comparative analysis of companies from the same or different industries.	The study enables updating the Respect Index. The current composition of the Respect Index is published on the http://odpowiedzialni.gpw.pl/ website. After verification that takes into account the criteria adopted in accordance with the best management standards in the area of corporate governance, information governance, investor relations, environmental, social and employee factors, only those companies that meet these criteria are included.

Source: Own study.

Table 3. Examples of sustainable development indicators and circular indicators for the Circular Index.

Social	– Number of accidents per year in the organization, – The loss of performance by the organization, – Percentage of women employed by the organization, – Composition of management bodies and division of employees by sex, age and other criteria – Percentage of temporary employees in the organization, – Absence rate in the organization, – Injury type and rate, illnesses, lost days, absences and work-related deaths, – Staff turnover in the organization – Total number and rate of new employees.
Economic	– Direct economic value generated and distributed (operating costs, remuneration and employee benefits, payments to capital providers) – Expenditure on research and development, – Number of employees
Environmental	– The rate of hazardous waste, – The rate of non-hazardous waste, – The amount of water used annually in industrial processes, – The amount of energy consumed annually.
Circular	– Input data in the production process, – A tool during the use stage, – Recycling effectiveness

Source: Own study.

1. Defining and selecting experts;
2. The number of internal stages,
3. The structure of the questionnaire in each round of research

The number of internal stages can range from two to seven, and the number of participants from three to fifteen. Information requires knowledge and reliable experience in the field of sustainable development and cyclicality, therefore a targeted approach is recommended in the selection of experts. Interviews should be carried out with academic staff / experts on research topics to verify the validity of sustainable development and cyclical indicators examined and rank them according to their importance for the sustainability and cyclicality of enterprises. Each indicator rating should be measured with a score from 1 to 5, where 1 means "insignificant" and 5 means "very important" so that companies can be considered sustainable or circular, depending on indicators. In order to obtain a measure of the consistency of panel responses, a Kendall's concordance coefficient (W) should be used for each round. This coefficient is used to examine the degree of the relationship between the rankings of several objects by several experts. This coefficient varies between "0", which indicates no agreement between experts, and "+1", which indicates the total consensus between experts in the ranking of various factors.

The third stage includes normalization. It is necessary to integrate selected indicators into a complex sustainable circulation indicator because they were expressed in different units. Sometimes, however, there is no need to normalize indicators, as in the case of indicators already expressed in the same unit.

At the fourth stage, which talks about an aggregation method for building the index, there are different linear aggregation methods. The most common methods are additive, multiplicative or additive weights. Their use depends on a set of assumptions. For example, to adopt a linear method, it is necessary to observe independence between variables, and all indicators should have the same unit of measurement. Multiplicative aggregation is appropriate when strictly positive indicators are expressed in different coefficient scales and it involves partial sustainability. The proper selection of the components of complex indicators and their weights is of key importance for the aggregation process. A simple method of weighing factors is widely used in practice as it is transparent and easy to understand by non-experts.

At the fifth stage, the final set of indicators is selected to assess the sustainability and cyclicality of companies.

The Sustainable Circularity Index suggested can be used by managers who consider the following issues:

1. The set of sustainable development and cyclicality indicators should be adapted to the type of a manufacturing enterprise,
2. Weights of the dimensions of sustainable development and cyclicality and relevant indicators should be available by a panel of experts via the Delphi technique,
3. The suggested aggregation method is a simple method of weighing factors (SAW - Simple Additive Weighting).

RESPECT INDEX

On 19 November 2009, the Warsaw Stock Exchange introduced Central and Eastern Europe's first index of responsible companies as a response to investing in accordance with the requirements of corporate social responsibility, including environmental protection. The Respect Index is an index of corporate social responsibility, and its name is an acronym for words that best define the pillars of CSR:

- Responsibility
- Ecology
- Sustainable development
- Participation

- Environment
- Community
- Transparency

The Respect Index is a revenue index because its calculation takes into account changes in the prices of shares of companies included in the index, as well as revenue related to possessing them: revenue from dividends and pre-emptive rights. The blocks of shares of companies in the index (rounded off to the nearest thousands) constitute the number of shares in free trading reduced by the number of shares introduced to the public trading. Since the first publication in 2009, the Respect Index increased its value by 85%.

The index is calculated continuously at minute intervals. After the opening of the session, the opening value of the index is published, however, only when the company's share price allows for the valuation of at least 65% of the index portfolio in this session. However, the index closing value is given after the session has ended. The shares of the largest companies in the Respect Index are limited to 25% in the case of an index with less than 20 participants. When the number of index participants exceeds 20 companies, these shares amount to a maximum of 10%.

Stage One: At the beginning the fulfillment of the liquidity criterion is examined, i.e. those that are included in the WIG20, mWIG40 and sWIG80 indices.

Stage Two: The practices of companies are analyzed in terms of corporate governance, information governance and investor relations. They are evaluated by the Warsaw Stock Exchange together with the Association of Stock Exchange Issuers, taking into account publicly available data published by companies (reports, websites).

Figure 1. Respect Index and WIG values in 2009-2017
Source: http://odpowiedzialni.gpw.pl/.

Stage Three: It covers the area of environmental, social and employee factors. The level of company maturity in these areas is assessed by means of surveys completed by the companies. These surveys are thoroughly verified by Deloitte. The results of the third stage are used to publish the final list of companies in the Respect Index.

The criteria used are grouped by the following areas:

- Environmental – environmental factors::
    - Environment management,
    - Limiting the environmental impact,
    - Biodiversity,
    - Environmental aspects of products / services.
- Social – social factors:
    - OHS,
    - Human resources management,
    - Supplier relationships,
    - Dialogue with stakeholders,
    - Social reporting.
- Governance – economic factors:
    - Strategic management,
    - A code of conduct,
    - Risk management,
    - Fraud risk management,
    - Internal audit and a control system,
    - Customer relationships.

THE SUMMARY OF COMPARISON

The comparison of the Circular Index with the Respect Index shows that they analyze similar aspects of companies, although the selection of a list of companies that meet the criteria generated by those indexes is different. However, both of them focus on studying economic, environmental and social aspects. The Circular Index is very versatile and simple as it allows the assessment of the sustainable development and cyclicality of manufacturing companies in the form of the comparative analysis of companies from the same or different industries. The Respect Index, on the other hand, takes into account the criteria adopted in accordance with the best management standards in terms of corporate governance, information governance, investor relations, covering the area of environmental, social and employee factors.

Table 4. Comparative analysis of the first, historical index of socially responsible companies (Respect Index) with the 2017 edition of the respect index

The first, historical index of socially responsible companies (Respect Index) was as follows.	The 2017 edition of the RESPECT INDEX included 28 companies (in alphabetical order)
▪ APATOR SA ▪ BANK PBH ▪ Barlinek SA ▪ Ciech SA ▪ Citi Handlowy ▪ ELEKTROBUDOWA SA ▪ Grupa LOTOS SA ▪ GRUPA ŻYWIEC SA ▪ ING Bank Śląski SA ▪ KGHM Polska Miedź ▪ Mondi Świecie SA ▪ PGNiG SA ▪ PKN ORLEN SA ▪ Telekomunikacja Polska SA ▪ Zakłady Azotowe w Tarnowie – Mościcach SA ▪ Zakłady Magnezytowe „ROPCZYCE" SA	▪ Agora S.A. ▪ Apator S.A. ▪ Bank Handlowy w Warszawie S.A. ▪ Bank Millennium S.A. ▪ Bank Ochrony Środowiska S.A. ▪ Bank Pekao S.A. ▪ Bank Zachodni WBK S.A. ▪ Budimex S.A. ▪ Elektrobudowa S.A. ▪ Energa S.A. ▪ Fabryki Mebli „FORTE" S.A. ▪ Giełda Papierów Wartościowych w Warszawie S.A. ▪ Grupa Azoty S.A. ▪ Grupa LOTOS S.A. ▪ ING Bank Śląski S.A. ▪ Inter Cars S.A. ▪ Jastrzębska Spółka Węglowa S.A. ▪ KGHM Polska Miedź S.A. ▪ Lubelski Węgiel Bogdanka S.A. ▪ mBank S.A. ▪ Orange Polska S.A. ▪ PCC Rokita S.A. ▪ PGE S.A. ▪ PGNIG S.A. ▪ PZU S.A ▪ Tauron PE S.A. ▪ Trakcja PRKiI S.A. ▪ Zespół Elektrociepłowni Wrocławskich Kogeneracja S.A.

Source: Own study.

AN ANALYSIS OF SOCIALLY RESPONSIBLE COMPANIES IN THE RESPECT INDEX

Among the 28 companies analyzed there are companies from various areas of activity. They include power, banking, automotive, railway or telecommunications branches. Despite such diversity, companies have met the Respect Index requirements. The period of activity in the market is not a barrier here, as it is possible to find recently established companies in this index (e.g. PGE S.A. in 2007 or Grupa LOTOS S.A. in 2003), as well as companies with long histories (e.g. Bank Handlowy w Warszawie S.A. in 1870 or Grupa Azoty S.A. in 1927). There is also diversity in the amount of the share capital, which ranges from several million zlotys (e.g. Apator S.A. Orange Polska S.A.) to several billion zlotys (e.g. PGE S.A.).

Table 5. Value proposition for customers of individual companies

Company	Year of establishment	Value proposition for customers	Share capital (in PLN x 1000, Q3 of 2017)
Agora S.A.	1989	15 subsidiaries conducting mainly internet, printing, cinema and radio activity as well as activity in the outdoor advertising segment	47 665
Apator S.A.	1993	production and sale of measuring instruments, control and measurement, distribution and control equipment, SCADA-class information systems and telemechanics devices cooperating with them, security devices and other network devices for distributed systems	3 311
Bank Handlowy w Warszawie S.A.	1870	banking services	522 638
Bank Millennium S.A.	1989	banking services	1 213 117
Bank Ochrony Środowiska S.A.	1990	banking services	628 732
Bank Pekao S.A.	1929	banking services	262 470
Bank Zachodni WBK S.A.	2001	banking services	993 335
Budimex S.A.	1968	the largest construction group in Poland offering services in the road, rail, airport infrastructure, construction, energy, industrial and ecological sectors, and developing in the facility management sector (real estate and infrastructure facilities) and waste management	No data
Elektrobudowa S.A.	1953	the largest company in Poland operating in the electrical installation industry, dealing with the production of electric power devices, comprehensive electrical installation services and the construction of complete facilities for the needs of energy and industry	10 003
Energa S.A.	2006	one of the four largest domestic electricity suppliers and one of the three largest power suppliers in Poland; the core business includes electricity and heat production, and distribution, and and gas trading	4 521 612
Fabryki Mebli „FORTE" S.A.	1992	one of the largest European self-assembly furniture manufacturers	23 931
Giełda Papierów Wartościowych w Warszawie S.A.	1991	provides the possibility of stock exchange trading in securities (shares, bonds, pre-emptive rights, etc.) and financial instruments that are not securities (options, futures) admitted to trading on the stock market	41 972
Grupa Azoty S.A.	1927	one of the key capital groups in the fertilizer and chemical industry in Europe	495 977
Grupa LOTOS S.A.	2003	a capital group comprising a dozen or so production, commercial and service companies, mainly from the industry of exploration, production and processing of crude oil and distribution of petroleum products (fuels, asphalt, oils, greases, paraffins, etc.)	184 873

Company	Year of establishment	Value proposition for customers	Share capital (in PLN x 1000, Q3 of 2017)
ING Bank Śląski S.A.	1988	banking services	130 100
Inter Cars S.A.	1998	the largest distributor of spare parts for passaenger cars, delivery vans and lorries in Central and Eastern Europe	28 336
Jastrzębska Spółka Węglowa S.A.	1993	the largest producer of high quality hard coking coal; a significant coke producer in the European Union in terms of production volume; the core activity is the production and sale of coking coal for energy purposes and the production and sale of coke and coal derivatives.	587 058
KGHM Polska Miedź S.A.	1961	mining and processing of copper ore located in the largest deposit in Europe in south-western Poland	2 000 000
Lubelski Węgiel Bogdanka S.A.	1970s	one of the market leaders among hard coal producers in Poland	170 068
mBank S.A.	1986	banking services	169 248
Orange Polska S.A.	1991	telecommunications operator, the dominant fixed telephony services provider in Poland	3 937
PCC Rokita S.A.	2003	the producer and distributor of products for the plastics, cosmetics, construction, textile, and domestic detergent and industrial chemistry industries	19 853
PGE S.A.	2007	an electric power sector company	19 165 048
PGNIG S.A.	1982	a natural gas and petroleum exploration and extraction company	5 778 315
PZU S.A	1998	A company operating in the property and personal insurance sector; the oldest, most experienced and largest insurance company in Poland	86 352
Tauron PE S.A.	2006	an enterprise comprising companies from the energy sector, the second largest in Poland (after PGE SA)	8 762 747
Trakcja PRKiI S.A.	2004	A company specializing in railway construction and in the energy sector (performance of works related to the broadly defined railway and road infrastructure with the use of modern machinery park and construction of power systems and remote control systems)	41 120
Zespół Elektrociepłowni Wrocławskich Kogeneracja S.A.	1900	three production plants which are network heat and electricity producers	252 503

Source: Financial statements and data from the websites of companies in the Respect Index

Table 6. Summary of financial data of individual companies

Company	Sales revenues (PLNx1000)			↑/ ↓/ ~	Net profit (PLNx1000)			↑/ ↓/ ~	Tax efficiency (%)			↑/ ↓/ ~
	2014	2015	2016		2014	2015	2016		2014	2015	2016	
Agora S.A.	628 891	659 520	576 059	~	(25 984)	4 759	(56 491)	~	(22,57)	188,34	(6,62)	~
Apator S.A.	186 205	195 978	265 839	↑	48 998	58 351	77 709	↑	4,54	3,03	2,19	↓
Bank Handlowy w Warszawie S.A.	2 874 362	2 415 140	2 414 782	↓	947 312	626 419	601 580	↓	18,87	20,78	21,29	↑
Bank Millennium S.A.	2 175 787	2 411 823	2 456 372	↑	619 511	814 157	652 651	~	21,66	13,31	25,68	~
Bank Ochrony Środowiska S.A.	No data	No data	No data	~	60 828	(39 317)	(67 973)	↓	16,78	(15,66)	(19,31)	↓
Bank Pekao S.A.	No data	No data	No data	~	2 725 100	2 293 478	2 279 800	↑	18,89	18,99	21,29	↑
Bank Zachodni WBK S.A.	No data	No data	No data	~	1 994 632	1 756 210	2 081 720	~	19,52	19,31	21,42	~
Budimex S.A.	4 552 765	4 768 675	5 207 194	↑	156 069	208 008	381 916	↑	20,34	19,66	18,23	↓
Elektrobudowa S.A.	1 064 485	1 204 228	928 509	~	29 101	47 162	53 121	↑	21,10	20,09	17,07	↓
Energa S.A.	45 176	60 000	68 000	↑	650 537	841 000	784 000	~	0,65	4,08	2,48	~
Fabryki Mebli „FORTE" S.A.	821 146	954 706	1 104 556	↑	74 612	77 936	97 195	↑	18,93	12,04	18,07	~
Giełda Papierów Wartościowych w Warszawie S.A.	189 996	191 781	175 454	~	52 907	96 905	116 085	↑	15,06	11,72	10,71	↓
Grupa Azoty S.A.	1 847 250	1 776 651	1 552 332	↓	214 633	209 055	224 775	~	5,24	0,06	2,21	~
Grupa LOTOS S.A.	26 243 106	20 482 298	18 110 016	↓	(1 285 910)	(37.102)	1 160 834	↑	(16,81)	(79,12)	18,72	~
ING Bank Śląski S.A.	No data	No data	No data	~	961 500	1 127 100	2 826 800	↑	19,40	18,93	23,38	~
Inter Cars S.A.	3 398 051	3 974 204	4 779 523	↑	95 669	93 913	109 391	~	11,74	5,15	9,38	~
Jastrzębska Spółka Węglowa S.A.	6 814 900	6 934 900	6 731 300	~	(657 100)	(3 285 200)	4 400	~	(34,26)	(18,79)	77,55	↑
KGHM Polska Miedź S.A.	20 492 000	20 008 000	19 156 000	↓	2 451 000	(5 009 000)	(4 449 000)	~	20,88	(2,21)	(17,05)	↓
Lubelski Węgiel Bogdanka S.A.	2 010 499	1 883 118	1 781 776	↓	272 942	(278 029)	175 896	~	20,92	(18,77)	18,26	~
mBank S.A.	No data	No data	No data	~	1 174 096	1 301 233	1 219 339	~	20,59	16,21	22,34	~

continued on following page

Table 6. Continued

Company	Sales revenues (PLNx1000)			↑/ ↓/ ~	Net profit (PLNx1000)			↑/ ↓/ ~	Tax efficiency (%)			↑/ ↓/ ~
	2014	2015	2016		2014	2015	2016		2014	2015	2016	
Orange Polska S.A.	11 885 000	11 435 000	11 248 000	↓	567 000	257 000	(1 762 000)	↓	3,08	1,91	(0,17)	↓
PCC Rokita S.A.	1 035 492	970 493	1 021 903	~	69 412	89 116	205 235	↑	7,16	5,76	8,41	~
PGE S.A.	9 671 000	10 929 000	10 847 000	~	5 453 000	1 768 000	1 598 000	↓	0,44	1,23	4,54	↑
PGNIG S.A.	34 304 000	36 464 000	33 196 000	~	2 822 000	2 136 000	2 349 000	~	22,17	29,13	26,82	~
PZU S.A	No data	No data	No data	~	2 967 627	2 342 196	2 417 000	~	19,61	20,45	20,26	~
Tauron PE S.A.	8 689 799	9 173 030	7 995 328	~	1 146 443	(3 453 908)	(166 253)	~	2,22	0,09	11,48	~
Trakcja PRKiI S.A.	966 084	763 399	826 198	~	49 797	35 161	28 699	↓	15,97	15,56	3,47	↓
Zespół Elektrociepłowni Wrocławskich Kogeneracja S.A.	508 431	551 212	598 709	↑	168 490	141 735	149 156	~	1,17	8,24	9,58	↑
Przedsiębiorstwo	Fixed assets			↑/ ↓/ ~	Current assets			↑/ ↓/ ~	Cost of capital (%)			↑/ ↓/ ~
	2014	2015	2016		2014	2015	2016		2014	2015	2016	
Agora S.A.	956 622	928 844	880 860	↓	239 171	290 462	234 371	~	No data	No data	No data	~
Apator S.A.	334 887	339 873	342 697	↑	60 913	70 550	97 537	↑	6,9	7,9	9,0	↑
Bank Handlowy w Warszawie S.A.	2014 - 49 843 665		2015 - 49 506 792			2016 – 45 209 916		↓	No data	No data	No data	~
Bank Millennium S.A.	2014 - 60 484 050		2015 - 66 065 250			2016 - 68 394 601		↑	No data	No data	No data	~
Bank Ochrony Środowiska S.A.	2014 - 19 479 980		2015 - 20 785 831			2016 - 20 602 566		~	No data	6,6	7,04	↑
Bank Pekao S.A.	2014 - 167 625 000		2015 - 168 785 600			2016 - 174 214 900		↑	No data	No data	No data	~
Bank Zachodni WBK S.A.	2014 - 121 607 365		2015 - 125 477 589			2016 - 131 417 988		↑	No data	No data	No data	~
Budimex S.A.	1 199 133	1 316 650	1 387 569	↑	2 115 395	2 625 013	3 232 437	↑	No data	No data	No data	~
Elektrobudowa S.A.	201 893	215 554	214 875	~	710 891	682 952	687 150	~	No data	20,66	No data	~
Energa S.A.	10 857 563	10 865 000	11 073 000	↑	1 259 442	1 678 000	3 307 000	↑	No data	No data	No data	~

continued on following page

Table 6. Continued

Company	Sales revenues (PLNx1000)			↑/ ↓/~	Net profit (PLNx1000)			↑/ ↓/~	Tax efficiency (%)			↑/ ↓/~
	2014	2015	2016		2014	2015	2016		2014	2015	2016	
Fabryki Mebli „FORTE" S.A.	272 857	293 050	466 362	↑	349 767	388 344	374 778	~	No data	No data	No data	~
Giełda Papierów Wartościowych w Warszawie S.A.	480 087	472 253	472 942	~	251 636	261 770	291 788	↑	No data	9	No data	~
Grupa Azoty S.A.	4 881 906	5 240 330	5 632 399	↑	518 656	615 617	810 857	↑	No data	No data	No data	~
Grupa LOTOS S.A.	8 045 780	8 357 331	8 327 458	~	6 244 967	5 552 584	6 203 096	~	No data	No data	No data	~
ING Bank Śląski S.A.	2014 - 96 742 400		2015 - 106 105 900			2016 - 113 529 400		↑	11,5	8,07	8,04	↓
Inter Cars S.A.	524 442	659 157	726 165	↑	1 348 103	1 641 374	1 933 154	↑	No data	8,5	8,5	~
Jastrzębska Spółka Węglowa S.A.	13 085 900	10 324 700	9 097 300	↓	2 283 400	1 487 500	2 422 300	~	No data	No data	No data	~
KGHM Polska Miedź S.A.	33 569 000	30 448 000	27 202 000	↓	6 805 000	6 316 000	6 240 000	↓	No data	No data	No data	~
Lubelski Węgiel Bogdanka S.A.	3 717 831	2 978 573	2 908 459	↓	605 152	616 156	839 970	↑	No data	No data	No data	~
mBank S.A.	2014 – 113 603 463		2015 - 119 115 370			2016 - 128 215 265		↑	No data	No data	No data	~
Orange Polska S.A.	21 688 000	20 521 000	20 163 000	↓	2 298 000	2 643 000	2 227 000	~	No data	No data	No data	~
PCC Rokita S.A.	883 991	951 136	1 026 611	↑	287 047	240 807	340 572	~	No data	No data	No data	~
PGE S.A.	33 097 000	35 788 000	39 079 000	↑	4 252 000	3 752 000	5 572 000	~	7,85	7,26	7,56	~
PGNIG S.A.	37 692 000	36 959 000	36 236 000	↓	11 234 000	12 866 000	13 436 000	↑	No data	No data	No data	~
PZU S.A	2014 - 67 572 761		2015 - 105 429 009			2016 - 125 345 000		↑	No data	No data	No data	~
Tauron PE S.A.	26 617 011	24 866 370	25 855 329	~	3 723 519	1 607 786	1 817 047	~	7,94 – 10,03	7,43 – 9,05	6,39 – 7,79	↓
Trakcja PRKiI S.A.	603 625	632 789	657 078	↑	468 928	299 500	356 980	~	No data	No data	No data	~
Zespół Elektrociepłowni Wrocławskich Kogeneracja S.A.	1 339 287	1 451 459	1 462 339	↑	288 397	329 207	297 508	~	7,1	6,5	7,1	~

continued on following page

Table 6. Continued

Company	Sales revenues (PLNx1000)			↑/ ↓/ ~	Net profit (PLNx1000)			↑/ ↓/ ~	Tax efficiency (%)			↑/ ↓/ ~
	2014	2015	2016		2014	2015	2016		2014	2015	2016	

Company	Product, process, organizational and technological innovations			Competencies of managers and other employees (change in the Management Board compared to the previous year)			Y/ N
	2014	2015	2016	2014	2015	2016	
Agora S.A.	Stopklatka TV channel launch	the Helios cinema chain expanded by four more cinemas; a new Radio Pogoda music station was launched	launching a TV channel under the METRO brand; the Helios cinema chain expanded by four more cinemas (41 in total)	Yes	No	No	Y
Apator S.A.	Acquisition of 30% shares of Apator Rector Sp. z o.o.	No data	No data	Yes	Yes	Yes	Y
Bank Handlowy w Warszawie S.A.	the development of the Smart Banking Ecosystem; the first place in Poland in the ranking evaluating Euromoney transaction banking Cash Management Survey 2014; the first place in the prestigious Ministry of Finance Treasury Securities Dealer ranking	launching a sales app; the development of the Smart Banking Ecosystem; the introduction of a mobile banking application - Citi Mobile; a new private banking offer - Citigold Private Client; the first place in Poland in the ranking evaluating transaction banking, the Euromoney Cash Management Survey 2015	a new format of the physical distribution of banking products - Smart Mini; the introduction of the CitiPlanner tool for iPad that enables investment consulting; work on Citibank Online- Redesign +, a new transaction service; the first place in the Ministry of Finance ranking for the position of the Treasury Securities Dealer (for the fifth time in a row); the combination of the SEPA Direct Debit product with currency exchange platform Citi FX Pulse	Yes	Yes	Yes	Y
Bank Millennium S.A.	No data	No data	No data	No	No	Yes	Y
Bank Ochrony Środowiska S.A.	No data	No data	No data	Yes	Yes	Yes	Y
Bank Pekao S.A.	the second place in the BANK monthly magazine's "50 largest banks in Poland" ranking; they received a special prize "Innovator of the banking market in 2013"; the second place in the category of the best account for small and medium-sized companies in the Forbes monthly magazine's "Best Banks for Business" ranking; and others	the "Innovators 2015 - Transactions Services" title in the international Global Finance magazine's ranking and others; the integration of the Pekao Biznes24 system with the largest EDI platform in the country; the acquisition of 100% of the share capital of UniCredit CAIB Poland S.A.	Innovator of the Year 2016 in the area of transaction banking; the highest 5-star rating for Private Banking; distinction in the 4th edition of the e-Commerce Polska awards 2016 competition; and others	No	Yes	No	Y
Bank Zachodni WBK S.A.	No data	No data	No data	No	Yes	Yes	Y

continued on following page

Table 6. Continued

Company	Sales revenues (PLNx1000)			↑/ ↓/~	Net profit (PLNx1000)			↑/ ↓/~	Tax efficiency (%)			↑/ ↓/~
	2014	2015	2016		2014	2015	2016		2014	2015	2016	
Budimex S.A.	the title of the best construction company listed on the Warsaw Stock Exchange; Honorary Diploma of the Bridge Work of the Year; and others				the completion of the first major project in the industrial segment "Construction of the Municipal Waste Treatment Plant in Białystok" in the "design and build" format; maintaining the market leader position in the infrastructure market; and others	the completion of the construction of 87 km of dual carriageways and motorways; signing a conditional agreement for the construction of a waste incineration plant in Vilnius (Lithuania); and others			Yes	Yes	Yes	Y
Elektrobudowa S.A.	No data				No data	No data			No	Yes	Yes	Y
Energa S.A.	No data				No data	No data			No	Yes	Yes	Y
Fabryki Mebli „FORTE" S.A.	No data				the opening of a company kindergarten with a "YELLOW ELEPHANT" nursery branch for employees' children in Ostrowa Mazowiecka; in the FORTE Branch in Ostrowa Mazowiecka a modern logistics center with a high-bay warehouse was established	Initiating the establishment of a new warehouse centre, a clipboard production plant and a furniture factory with logistics infrastructure in the Suwałki Special Economic Zone			Yes	Yes	No	Y
Giełda Papierów Wartościowych w Warszawie S.A.	No data				No data	No data			Yes	Yes	Yes	Y
Grupa Azoty S.A.	No data				No data	No data			No	No	Yes	Y

Company	Product, process, organizational and technological innovations			Competencies of managers and other employees (change in the Management Board compared to the previous year)			Y / N
	2014	2015	2016	2014	2015	2016	
Grupa LOTOS S.A.	No data	No data	No data	No data	No data	No data	No data

continued on following page

Table 6. Continued

Company	Sales revenues (PLNx1000)			↑/↓/~	Net profit (PLNx1000)			↑/↓/~	Tax efficiency (%)			↑/↓/~
	2014	2015	2016		2014	2015	2016		2014	2015	2016	
ING Bank Śląski S.A.	recycling ATMs; the Golden Bell award in the "Mobile Bank - Best Offer of the Year 2013" category; the winner of TotalMoney.pl rankings; the provision of an Individual Pension Security Account; a winner in the Ranking of Responsible Companies in the "Banking, financial and insurance sector" category; it was the first bank in Poland to make V.me by Visa wallet available to the public; Konto z Lwem Direct account for companies, recognized as "The Best Company Account 2014" by Money.pl; the Economic Award of the President of Poland nomination in the category of "Economic Governance and Corporate Social Responsibility"; the eighth time in the RESPECT Index				No data			No data	No	No	No	N
Inter Cars S.A.	Motointegrator – a telephone and internet service targeted at individual drivers and fleet owners				25th anniversary of the company's existence; 374 branches in 14 geographic markets from the Baltic Sea to the Balkans; a plan to launch 80 new branches;			No data	No	No	Yes	Y
Jastrzębska Spółka Węglowa S.A.	No data				No data			No data	No data	No data	No data	No data

continued on following page

Table 6. Continued

<table>
<tr><th rowspan="2">Company</th><th colspan="3">Sales revenues (PLNx1000)</th><th rowspan="2">↑/ ↓/ ~</th><th colspan="3">Net profit (PLNx1000)</th><th rowspan="2">↑/ ↓/ ~</th><th colspan="3">Tax efficiency (%)</th><th rowspan="2">↑/ ↓/ ~</th></tr>
<tr><th>2014</th><th>2015</th><th>2016</th><th>2014</th><th>2015</th><th>2016</th><th>2014</th><th>2015</th><th>2016</th></tr>
<tr><td>KGHM Polska Miedź S.A.</td><td colspan="3">launching operation in the area of Głogów Głęboki-Przemysłowy at the level less than 1 200 m; obtaining a license to search for and recognize deposits of potassium magnesium salts in the vicinity of Puck; sending the first transport of copper concentrate to a steel plant in Japan; and others</td><td colspan="3">entering into a contract with Tele-Fonika Kable for the sale of copper wire rod in 2016-2018 with an option to extend it for a further two years; the commencement of commercial production by the Sierra Gorda mine in Chile; the first place in the "Philanthropy Leaders" competition in Poland, a merger of two Canadian companies - as a result, the company implementing the Ajax project in Canada becomes part of KGHM International Ltd.</td><td colspan="2">the 55th anniversary of KGHM Polska Miedź S.A.; an agreement between KGHM Polska Miedź S.A and China Minmetals Corporation for the sale of copper cathodes in 2017-2021; receiving the prestigious Gold Card of a Safe Work Leader; the 50th anniversary of KGHM Zanam operations; the 20th anniversary of the merger of the Polkowice mine and the Sieroszowice mine; resuming raw copper production at Głogów I Copper Smelter in modern technology</td><td>No</td><td>Yes</td><td>Yes</td><td>Y</td></tr>
<tr><td>Lubelski Węgiel Bogdanka S.A.</td><td colspan="3">No data</td><td colspan="3">No data</td><td colspan="2">No data</td><td>No</td><td>No</td><td>Yes</td><td>Y</td></tr>
<tr><td>mBank S.A.</td><td colspan="3">No data</td><td colspan="3">No data</td><td colspan="2">No data</td><td>No</td><td>No</td><td>Yes</td><td>Y</td></tr>
<tr><td>Orange Polska S.A.</td><td colspan="3">No data</td><td colspan="3">No data</td><td colspan="2">No data</td><td>Yes</td><td>Yes</td><td>Yes</td><td>Y</td></tr>
<tr><td>PCC Rokita S.A.</td><td colspan="3">No data</td><td colspan="3">No data</td><td colspan="2">No data</td><td>Yes</td><td>No</td><td>No</td><td>Y</td></tr>
<tr><td rowspan="2">Company</td><td colspan="8">Product, process, organizational and technological innovations</td><td colspan="3">Competencies of managers and other employees (change in the Management Board compared to the previous year)</td><td rowspan="2">Y / N</td></tr>
<tr><td colspan="3">2014</td><td colspan="3">2015</td><td colspan="2">2016</td><td>2014</td><td>2015</td><td>2016</td></tr>
</table>

continued on following page

Table 6. Continued

Company	Sales revenues (PLNx1000) 2014 / 2015 / 2016	↑/↓/~ ; Net profit (PLNx1000) 2014	Net profit (PLNx1000) 2015 / 2016 ; ↑/↓/~ ; Tax efficiency (%) 2014	Tax efficiency (%) 2015	Tax efficiency (%) 2015 / 2016	Tax efficiency (%) 2016	↑/↓/~
PGE S.A.	A Partnership Agreement between PGE S.A., TAURON Polska Energia S.A., ENEA S.A. and KGHM Polska Miedź S.A., according to which TAURON Polska Energia S.A., ENEA S.A. and KGHM Polska Miedź S.A., as Business Partners, will acquire from PGE SA, on the basis of a separate agreement, a total of 30% of shares (each Business Partners will acquire 10% of shares) in a special purpose vehicle - PGE EJ 1 sp. z o. o., which is responsible for the preparation and implementation of the investment consisting of the construction and operation of the first Polish nuclear power plant	Acting as a leader in the construction and operation of the first Polish nuclear power plant with a capacity of approximately 3,000 MW ("Project"), in the future PGE EJ 1 sp. z o. o. is to act as a power plant operator	on 30 November 2016, PGE Polska Grupa Energetyczna S.A., Energa S.A., Enea S.A. and PGNiG Termika S.A. submitted a conditional binding offer for the purchase of conventional and combined electrical power and heat EDF assets	No	No	Yes	Y
PGNIG S.A.	PGNiG Upstream International AS acquired shares in a package of four deposits located on the Norwegian Continental Shelf from Total E&P Norge AS; PGNiG and Qatar Liquefied Gas Company Limited (3) entered into an additional agreement to the liquefied natural gas sales contract (LNG)	PGNiG Obrót Detaliczny Sp. z o.o. introduced a "Flexible price" discount programme; launching a "Price deregulation" discount programme for strategic clients; the commencement of the Wysin-2H shale gas exploration well in Pomerania; the opening of the first non-Polish natural gas mine in Pakistan	The purchase of Przedsiębiorstwo Energetyki Cieplnej S.A. in Jastrzębie-Zdrój; a contract with Grupa Azoty S.A.; a contract with Grupa PGE and Grupa PKN Orlen for gas fuel supplies; the commencement of gas extraction from the Rizq deposit in Pakistan; the commencement of natural gas supplies to the Ukrainian market.	Yes	Yes	Yes	Y
PZU S.A	The introduction of a revolutionary service -Direct Claim Settlement; the issuance of five-year Eurobonds for an amount of EUR 500 million; the creation of the first fleet of replacement vehicles in Poland at PZU partner car rental companies with 300 hybrid Toyota Auris cars; and others	signing a preliminary agreement for the purchase of 25.19% of Alior Bank; the pilot implementation of the Everest Platform in external channels; completing the PZU Lithuania sale transaction	the acquisition of a separated part of Bank BPH by Alior Bank (a PZU subsidiary); launching, in cooperation with business partners, the Witelo fund, whose aim will be to invest in the world's leading venture capital funds; the acquisition of Polmedic from Radom and Artimed from Kielce	Yes	Yes	Yes	Y

continued on following page

Table 6. Continued

Company	Sales revenues (PLNx1000)			↑/ ↓/~	Net profit (PLNx1000)			↑/ ↓/~	Tax efficiency (%)			↑/ ↓/~
	2014	2015	2016		2014	2015	2016		2014	2015	2016	
Tauron PE S.A.	a consortium agreement between TAURON and 22 institutions, including: 18 universities, 2 institutes and 2 enterprises that establishes the Institute of Technology and Innovation Highway; a consortium agreement for the Integrated Cooperation Platform for the Life Cycle of Product Service Technologies Management (ICP4Life) project	an agreement between TAURON, PGE, ENEA and KGHM for the purchase of shares in a PGE EJ 1 special purpose vehicle responsible for the preparation and implementation of the investment consisting of the construction and operation of the first Polish nuclear power plant with a capacity of approx. 3, 000 MWe; a preliminary conditional agreement between the RSG subsidiary and SRK for the sale of a marked part of KWK Brzeszcze; the adoption of the Sustainable Development Strategy for 2016-2018 with a perspective up to 2020	Declaration of TAURON regarding the application of Best Practices for WSE Listed Companies 2016; launching a programme involving the reorganization of the area of maintenance services in Grupa Kapitałowa TAURON; an agreements between TAURON, PGE, ENEA, ENERGA, PSE and the Association of Private Energy Sector Employers regarding the rules for participation in the Tripartite Energy Industry Team; Launching the TAURON PRO Programme; the commencement of TAURON's operations in the scope of natural gas trading on the ICE exchange; the establishment of Magenta Grupa TAURON; the conclusion of an agreement regarding the conditions for the further implementation of the "Construction of a gas and steam unit in Stalowa Wola" project	Yes	Yes	Yes!	Y					

Company	Product, process, organizational and technological innovations			Competencies of managers and other employees (change in the Management Board compared to the previous year)			Y / N
	2014	2015	2016	2014	2015	2016	
Trakcja PRKiI S.A.	a contract with PKP Polskie Linie Kolejowe S.A. for the execution of the supplementary order involving the performance of design and construction works at the Łódź Widzew railway station from km 4,100 to km 7,200 of a railway line no. 17; a conclusion of two annexes to the contract for designing and performance of construction works on the Kraków-Medyka state border railway line - on the Podłęże - Bochnia section from km 16,000 to 39,000 as part of the "Modernization of the E 30/CE 30 railway line, Kraków - Rzeszów section, stage III " project; and others;	A contract between Trakcja PRKiI S.A. and PKP PLK S.A. for the preparation of detailed designs and performance of works for LCS Warszawa Okęcie as part of the POIiS 7.1-19.1.a project titled "Modernization of the railway line No. 8, Warsaw Okęcie – Radom section (LOT A, B, F)"; a contract between the subsidiary company from the Issuer, AB Kauno Tiltai and the City of Vilnius for the construction of the Trans-European network node - stage III of the western bypass of the city of Vilnius - from Ozo Str. to Ukmergės Str; and others	A consortium agreement between Trakcja PRKiI S.A. as a consortium leader with PKP PLK S.A. for the performance of construction works under the Tender No. 1 - Modernization of the Jaworzno Szczakowa - Trzebinia section; and others	Yes	Yes	Yes	Y
Zespół Elektrociepłowni Wrocławskich Kogeneracja S.A.	No data	No data	No data	No data	No data	No data	No data

Source: Financial statements and data from the websites of companies in the Respect Index.

Taking into account sales revenues of companies in the Respect Index in the years 2014-2016, it should be noted that only in seven companies did value increase year to year.

In six cases, there is a decrease in the value of sales revenues. These values fluctuate in 15 companies examined.

Statistics for net profit look similar. Nine companies recorded a continuous increase in net profit from year to year, five of them recorded decline, while net profit fluctuated in fourteen companies.

When analyzing tax efficiency, an increase can be observed for five companies. A decrease in its value was recorded for eight companies, and fluctuations occurred in fifteen cases.

The value of fixed assets rose in ten companies in the years 2014-2016. However, the value of fixed assets fell in six of them and only in four of them, fluctuations in the value of fixed assets were observed.

As regards the value of current assets, it increased in eight companies and fell in only one company, while it fluctuated in eleven companies. It should be noted that

Figure 2. Change in the value of sales revenues. net profit and tax efficiency in 2014-2016 for companies in the respect index
Source: Own study.

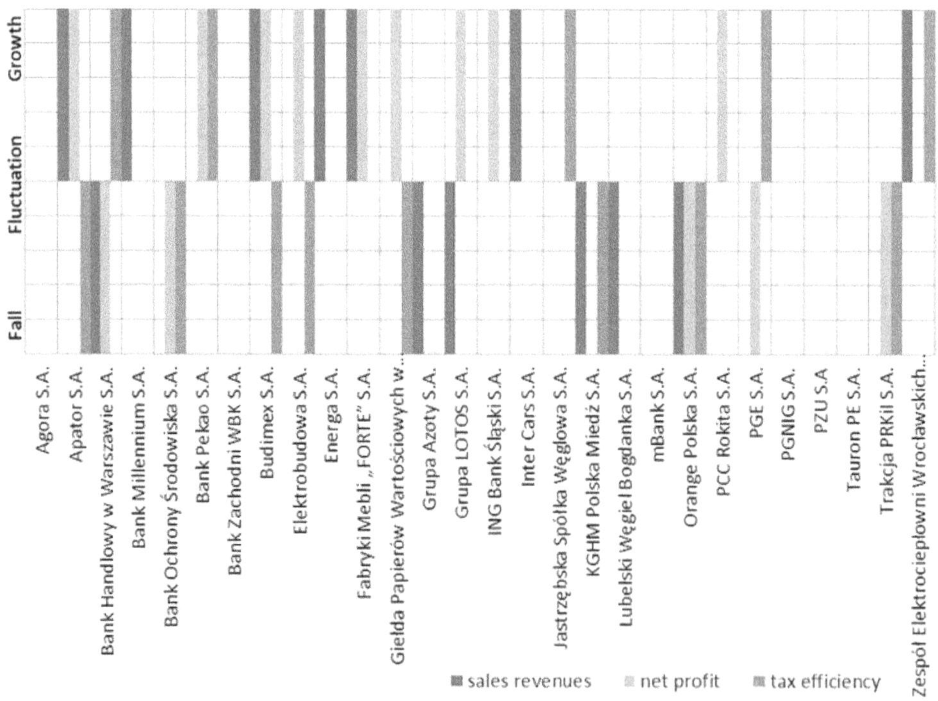

for eight companies, the total value was characterized for all assets without dividing them into fixed assets and current assets. These are mainly banks. As many as six of banks recorded an increased value of assets in the years 2014-2016 and in one company there was a decrease, and in one company total value fluctuated.

While studying changes in the management boards of 28 companies in the Respect Index in 2014-2016, changes in positions occurred in as many as 24 cases. In one of them there were no changes, while for one of them no relevant data was obtained.

CONCLUSION

To sum up the discussion, an important factor is to find appropriate rules that ensure the robustness of business models in the circular economy. The robustness of business models can ensure the organization's ability to make permanent changes. These changes that can be approved, implemented and subdued, together with the acceptance of new trends in management and the degree of their use, generate an environment favourable to robust business models. Then a business model is also the source of the creation of value in every sphere of its and organization's life cycle. Then this responsible management becomes a fact and the rate of return from its operationalization is visible in the organization's performance. The management of the organization's life cycle with the use of the circular economy determines the creation of special value for both the actors of the network where a company is embedded as well as the company itself towards the robustness of its business model. Answering the research question posed: Does the skillful use of the concept of business model robustness among circular economy companies guarantee the

Figure 3. Change in the value of fixed assets, current assets and total assets (mainly banks) in the years 2014-2016 for companies in the respect index
Source: Own study.

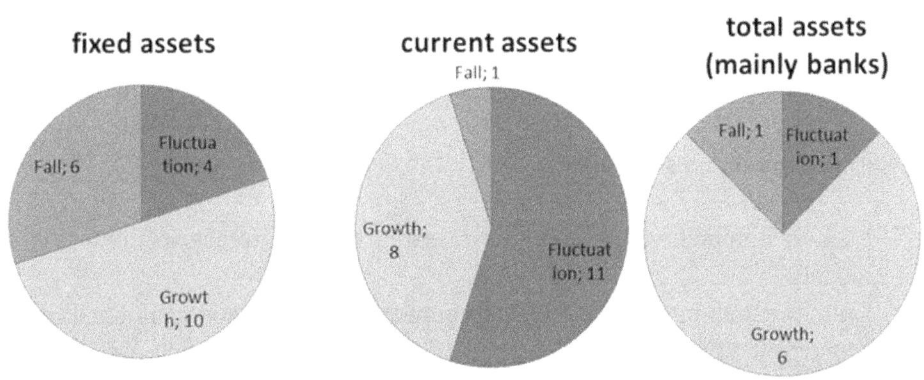

Figure 4. Changes in the management boards of companies in the respect index in the years 2014-2016
Source: Own study.

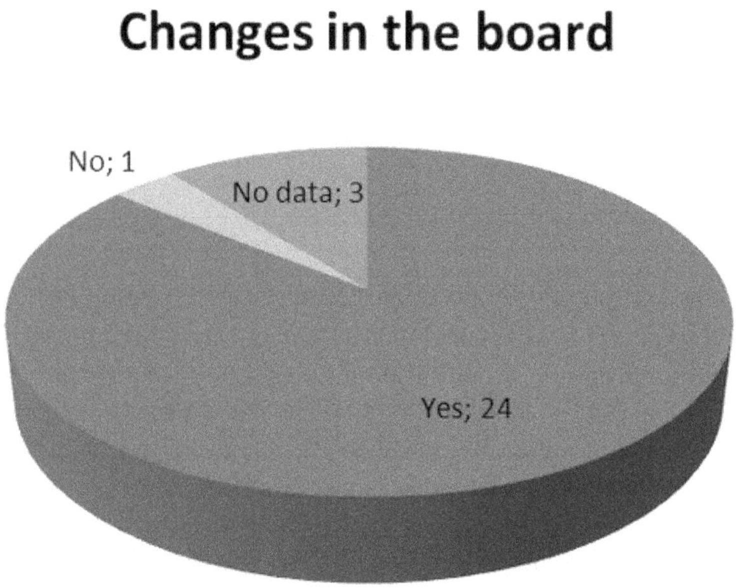

organization's ability to ensure business continuity and its high effectiveness?, it can be concluded, by verifying and synthesizing the results obtained from qualitative research, that the skillful use of the concept of business model robustness among circular economy companies guarantees the organization's ability to ensure business continuity and its high effectiveness.

Further research related to the robustness of business models among circular economy companies may focus on:

- The relationship between the robustness of the business model and the high effectiveness of organizations embedded in the circular economy
- Analyzing business continuity based on a robust business model,
- The circular economy in the context of the concept of business models.

Research limitations include:

- Lack of comprehensive scientific research into the robustness of business models
- Little research into the relationship between business models in the circular economy

- Little research into the relationship between the robustness of business models and organization's effectiveness and ensuring its continuity in the circular economy sector.

REFERENCES

Abdelkafi. N. (2012). Open Business Models for the Greater Good – A Case Study from the Higher Education Context. *Die Unternehmung, 60*(3).

Accenture Strategy. (n.d.). *Circular Advantage Innovative Business Models and Technologies to Create Value in a World without Limits to Growth.* Retrieved from https://www.accenture.com/t20150523T053139Z__w__/usen/_acnmedia/Accenture/ConversionAssets/DotCom/Documents/Global/PDF/Strategy_6/Accenture-Circular-Advantage-Innovative-Business-Models-Technologies-Value-Growth.pdf

Amit, R., & Zott, C. (2010). *Value Drivers of E-commerce Business Models.* Working Paper No. 2000-2006. INSEAD.

Baden-Fuller, C., MacMillan, I., Demil, B., & Lecocq, X. (2010). Long Range Planning call for papers for the Special Issue on "Business Models" by Volume 43. Issues 2–3. Pages 143-462 (April–June 2010). Academic Press.

Barnett-Page, E., & Thomas, J. (2009). Methods for the Synthesis of Qualitative Research: A Critical Review. *BMC Medical Research Methodology, 9*(1), 59. doi:10.1186/1471-2288-9-59 PMID:19671152

Beulque, R., & Aggeri, F. (2016). Circular Business Model Innovation: Key Patterns and Challenges to unleash recycling value creation potential. EGOS.

Chesbrough, H. (2010). Business Model Innovation: Opportunities and Barriers. *Long Range Planning*, 43.

Czakon. W. (2011). Metodyka systematycznego przeglądu literatury. *Przegląd Organizacji*, 3.

Demil, B., & Lecocq, X. (2010). Business Model Evolution: In Search of Dynamic Consistency. *Long Range Planning, 43*(2-3), 227–246. doi:10.1016/j.lrp.2010.02.004

Den Hollander, M., & Bakker, C. (2016). Mind the Gap Exploiter: Circular Business Models for Product Lifetime Extension. *Proceedings of the Electronics Goes Green.*

Dixon-Woods, M., Debbie Cavers, S., Agarwal, A. E., Arthur, A., Harvey, J., Hsu, R., … Sutton, A.J. (2006). Conducting a Critical Interpretive Synthesis of the Literature on Access to Healthcare by Vulnerable Groups. *MC Medical Research Methodology*, 6. doi:10.1186/1471-2288-6-35

Dubin, R. (1983). Theory Building in Applied Areas. In Handbook of Industrial and Organizational Psychology. Wiley.

Foss, N.J., & Saebi, T. (2017). Business Models and Business Model Innovation: Between Wicked and Paradigmatic Problems. *Long Range Planning*. doi:10.1016/j.lrp.2017.07.006

Geng, Y., & Doberstein, B. (2008). Developing the Circular Economy in China: Challenges and Opportunities for Achieving 'Leapfrog Development'. *International Journal of Sustainable Development & World Ecology*, 15.

Graebner, M. E., Martin, J. A., & Roundy, P. T. (2012). Qualitative data: Cooking without a recipe. *Strategic Organization*, *10*(3), 276–284. doi:10.1177/1476127012452821

Guinée, J. B. (2002). Handbook on Life Cycle Assessment: Operational Guide to the ISO Standards. Springer Science+Business Media B.V. doi:10.1007/BF02978897

Haaker, T., Bouwman, H., Janssen, W., & De Reuver, M. (2017). Business model stress testing: A practical approach to test the robustness of a business model. *Futures*, *89*, 14–25. doi:10.1016/j.futures.2017.04.003

http://odpowiedzialni.gpw.pl/

Jabłoński, A. (2016). Longitudinalne badania modeli biznesu przedsiębiorstw. *Zeszyty Naukowe Uniwersytetu Ekonomicznego w Krakowie*, *6*(954), 95–110. Doi:10.15678/ZNUEK.2016.0954.0606

Kaczmarek, M., Olejnik, I., & Springer, A. (2016). Badania jakościowe. metody i zastosowania. CeDeWu.

Kimberly, J. R. (1976). Issues in the Design of Longitudinal Organizational Research. *Sociological Methods & Research*, *4*(3), 321–348. doi:10.1177/004912417600400303

Laubscher, M., & Marinelli, T. (2014). Integration of Circular Economy in Business. *Proceedings of the Conference: Going Green—CARE INNOVATION*.

Linder, M., & Williander, M. (2015). Circular Business Model Innovation: Inherent Uncertainties. *Bus. Strateg. Environ.*

Magretta, J. (2003). *What Management Is. How it Works and Why It Is Everyone's Business*. London: Profile Books.

Nielsen, C., & Bukh, N. (2008). *What Constitutes a Business Model.: The Perception of Financial Analysts. Working Paper.* Series Department of Business Studies No.4. Aalborg University.

Orlowska. A.. Mazur. Z.. Raguna. M. (2017). Systematyczny przegląd literatury: Na czym polega i czym różni się od innych przeglądów. *Ogrody Nauk i Sztuk*, 7. doi:10.15503/onis2017.350.363

Osterwalder, A., & Pigneur, Y. (2012). *Tworzenie modeli biznesowych. Podręcznik wizjonera*. Gliwice: Helion.

Roos, G. (2014). Business model innovation to create and capture resource value in future circular material chains. *Resources*, 3.

Sauvé, S., Bernard, S., & Sloan, P. (2016). Environmental sciences. sustainable development and circular economy: Alternative concepts for trans-disciplinary research. *Environmental Development*, 17.

Silverman, D., & Marvasti, A. B. (2008). Doing Qualitative Research: A Comprehensive Guide. *Sage (Atlanta, Ga.)*.

Snihur, Y., & Zott, C. (2013). *Legitimacy without Imitation: How to Achieve Robust Business Model Innovation.* Paper to be presented at the 35th DRUID Celebration Conference, Barcelona, Spain.

Stańczyk-Hugiet, E. (2014). Badania longitudinalne w zarządzaniu. czyli jak dostrzec prawidłowości w dynamice. *Organizacja i Kierowanie*, 2.

Szarucki, M. (2016). *Koncepcja doboru metod w rozwiązywaniu problemów zarządzania*. Kraków: Wydawnictwo Uniwersytetu Ekonomicznego w Krakowie.

Täuscher, K., & Abdelkafi, N. (2015). Business Model Robustness: A System Dynamics Approach. *Proceedings of the 15th EURAM Conference*.

Tauscher, K., & Abdelkafi, N. (2018). Scalability and robustness of business models for sustainability: A simulation experiment. *Journal of Cleaner Production*, 170.

Teece, D.J. (2010). Business Models. business strategy and innovation. *Long Range Planning*, *43*(2).

Timmers, P. (1998). Business Models for electronic markets. *Electronic Markets*, *8*(2), 3–8. doi:10.1080/10196789800000016

Chapter 3
A Sustainable Business Model in the Functioning of Enterprises as the Base for Creating Circular Economy:
The Present and Development Prospects

Elżbieta Lorek
University of Economics in Katowice, Poland

Agnieszka Lorek
University of Economics in Katowice, Poland

ABSTRACT

Circular economy was the subject of interest for many researchers and is currently an inherent part of the sustainable growth concept. Shifting the economy to circular will require transformations in the field of competence, development, innovations, and organizational governance, as well as public awareness. Circular economy creates opportunities for achieving benefits in the economy (the efficiency of production processes, innovations, power safety) as well as in the social and environmental fields (shaping ecological safety). In the chapter, the authors describe such issues as theoretical foundations of the circular economy concept; European guidelines in the field of circular economy; problems and benefits associated with the implementation of circular economy, in light of compliance with sustainable development principles; business solution models together with the prospects for further sustainable development of a company, based on assumptions and models of circular economy.

DOI: 10.4018/978-1-5225-7850-5.ch003

INTRODUCTION

The economic and social crisis, which affected many world economies, drew attention to the need to implement major structural reforms in the economy. Many countries see opportunities in taking counter-crisis actions, which should create chances for the development of circular economy. Shifting the economy to circular will require transformations in the field of competence, development, innovations and organizational governance, as well as public awareness. It applies to companies from different sectors of the economy. Active environmental protection policy creates the need for new products, services and technologies. Launching innovative mechanisms in eco and low-emission policy will create a new type of services and products. It will shape a market, with companies from around the world intensively working on preparing for it. Companies, which will be the first to claim the opening market segment, will ensure a leading position for themselves. By implementing the principles of sustainable development, enterprises define strategic assumptions differently, creating market opportunities through using these customer groups, who are environmentally-aware and prefer high quality goods. Circular economy creates great opportunities for economic growth and social development. The benefits which can be achieved by business after the transition into the circular economy model include: increased growth, innovativeness and competitiveness, cost reduction, decreased power consumption and CO_2 emissions, balancing the supply chain and increased resource safety.

Based on the analysis of the subject literature, the political assumptions of the EU in this field, and using many years of experience of the Authors resulting from the participation in expert and science-research works, the chapter attempts to identify and evaluate the barriers in creating a sustainable enterprise within a circular economy. The following subchapters will describe such issues as:

- Theoretical foundations of the circular economy concept,
- European guidelines in the field of circular economy,
- Problems and benefits associated with the implementation of circular economy, in light of compliance with sustainable development principles,
- Business solution models together with the prospects for further sustainable development of a company, based on assumptions and models of circular economy.

THE CONCEPT OF CIRCULAR ECONOMY

Circular economy was the subject of interest for many researchers and is currently an inherent part of the sustainable growth concept. Many assumptions and theoretical bases regarding the concept of circular economy were presented in the papers of W.R. Stahel (1976). In the 1970s and 80s, W. Stahel and G. Reday (Stahel, Reday 1976, 1981) presented a vision of circular economy and its impact on creating job vacancies, economic competitiveness, raw material savings and preventing waste generation. A comprehensive circular economy model was introduced in world literature by D. Pearce, R. Turner (1990 p.35-42), which were inspired by the view of Kenneth Boulding (1966).

Generally speaking, two trends may be distinguished in the discussion on circular economy, which translate into its various definition and/or interpretation:

1. **The First Trend:** Oriented mainly at minimizing the consumption of resources and the need to create closed material flow circuits, hence, decreasing environmental pressure. Bastein, Roelofs, Hoogendoorn (2013 p. 4) states that "a circular economy is an economic and industrial system based on the reuse of products and raw materials, and the restorative capacity of natural resources". Sauvé et al. (2016, p. 49) suggest that circular economy applies to production and consumption of goods through closed material flows, which internalize external environment effects associated with acquiring natural resources and generating waste in broad terms. They believe that the main objective of circular economy is limiting the consumption of resources, contamination and waste at each stage of a product lifespan. According to Preston (2012, p. 1) "circular economy is an approach, which will change the function of resources in the economy. Factory waste would become a valuable contribution to another process – and products could be repaired, reused or modernized instead of being disposed of". Mitchell (2015, p.2) goes even further and emphasizes the importance that maintaining usability of resources for as long as possible, as well as draining the maximum value of the product and materials through using them as long as possible, then reclaiming and reusing them have in circular economy.

In the same vein the concept of a closed circulation economy is presented in many documents and studies of international institutions. European Commission in the document "Closing the loop - An EU action plan for the Circular Economy" (COM(2015) 614 final) states that in circular economy: "the value of products, materials and resources is maintained in the economy for as long as possible, and the generation of waste minimised". EEA (2014, p. 11) argues that circular economy "applies mainly to the physical and material aspects of resource management – it concentrates on recycling, limiting and reusing physical expenditure on the economy and using waste as resource, leading to a decreased consumption of primary materials." The approach focused on minimizing resource consumption is also present in the Club of Rome analyses (2015,2016), which underline the need to switch to: „circular economy, where products are designed for ease of recycling, reuse, disassembly and remanufacturing should replace the traditional, linear 'take, make & dispose' model that has dominated the economy so far".

2. **The Second Trend:** Approaches including additional dimensions and extending beyond the issue of natural resource management. This trend is, e.g., strongly visible in the literature on the Chinese model of circular economy, which is associated with the political changes undergoing in China in this respect[1] (see Su B., Heshmati A., Geng Y. and X. Yu 2013; Geng Y. and Doberstein B. 2008). The authors point out that a closed-circuit economy sector extends beyond issues associated with managing materials and covers other aspects, such as power efficiency, land management, soil and water protection as well as social and ethical aspects. As we can read in the work of F. Qiao, N. Qiao (2013, p. 253)„circular economy implies the holistic value principle and sustainable value principle, which can remedy the ethical flaws of the traditional linear model. As an ethical and sustainable development approach, circular economy contributes to the Copernican change in the field of economic ethics". An extensive analysis of the understanding of the concept of circular economy in relation to the Chinese and European economy is included in the article by McDowall W. et all (2017). In this article, the authors state that "circular economy concept lies at the heart of Chinese environmental political rhetoric" and the Chinese authorities underlines „the need to build a resource saving and environment friendly society and ecological civilization" (McDowall W. et all 2017).

On the ground of European economy, a broader discussion on circular economy can be found in the following analyses:

- Analyses of French Environmental and Energy Management Agency ADEME (ADEME, 2014 p. 4), which states that the goal of circular economy is to limit the impact of resource consumption on the environment and improving social welfare;
- Reports prepared by Ellen MacArthur Foundation (2012, 2013, 2015). The reports include a definition of circular economy describing it as: an industrial system, with its concept and design based on regeneration and recovery.

> In this system, the "product service life end" concept is replaced upon its processing, changes towards the use of renewable energy, elimination of the use of toxic chemicals, which hinder reusing the product, and aiming for the elimination of waste thanks to excellent engineering of materials, products or systems, including business models, and he main objective is to enable an effective flow of materials, energy, work and information, in order for the natural and social capital to be rebuilt (Ellen MacArthur Foundation, 2013, p. 26).

A wider approach is also found in the European scientific discourse on the circular economy. For example, Heck (2006) argues that in the debate on circular economy, using sustainable energy had not yet gained an equal status, compared to recycling and waste management. To this end, it is suggested that a transition to a circular economy would require rising to a challenge, which is creating sustainable power supplies, as well as taking determined actions in several other areas, such as agriculture, water, soil and biodiversity. . He states that: "only few countries so far are working on holistic, systemic, and interdisciplinary approaches for Circular Economy" (Heck 2006, p. 6). Acc. to Ghisellini et al. (2016), a radical transformation of all processes along the entire lifespan of products manufactured by innovative entities has the potential of not only material or power recovery, but also improving the entire life and economy model. In this approach, the main goal of the implementation of circular economy solutions is „to achieve a better balance and harmony between economy, environment and society".

The widest way of defining the circular economy refers to the concept of sustainable development, but this is a relatively rare approach. According to a study by Kirchherr J, Reike D. and Hekkert M. (2017), who analysed 114 definitions of circular economy, only 13% of them referred to all three dimensions of sustainable development. These authors formulated their own broad definition of the circular economy, which reads (Kirchherr J, Reike D. and Hekkert M. 2017, pp. 224-225): „A circular economy describes an economic system that is based on business models which replace the 'end-of-life' concept with reducing, alternatively reusing, recycling and recovering materials in production/distribution and consumption processes, thus operating at the micro level (products, companies, consumers), meso level (eco-industrial parks) and macro level (city, region, nation and beyond), with the aim to accomplish sustainable development, which implies creating environmental quality, economic prosperity and social equity, to the benefit of current and future generations."

Coming back to the point, the sole concept of circular economy is an attempt at creating a comprehensive model including the production and consumption spheres, taking into account their relationship with the natural environment (description taken from: Lorek E., Lorek A. 2011). Including such relationships in economic theories became a necessity in light of humanity gaining the technological possibilities enabling the achievement of global growth barriers. It should be noted that the Earth's natural environment is an evolving homeostat, in a dynamic quasi-balance, which mainly depends on the balance of power acquired from the Sun and radiated into space. This energy causes a transition of high entropy resources (mainly through photosynthesis) into low entropy resources. Such a transition under the impact of external energy applies to both renewable, as well as non-renewable resources, provided that, however, the time horizon of such a transition for non-renewable resources is equal to geological epochs, hence, is totally incongruent in terms of human time scale. Since the law of entropy growth is a natural law, there is a spontaneous trend of low entropy resources passing into high entropy resources. The natural cycle of matter in nature and ecobalance are hence created. Human activity is a part of that cycle for obvious reasons, both through acquiring renewable and non-renewable low entropy resources from the environment, as well as depositing waste-type, hence, high entropy substances in the environment. The term "low entropy" or "high entropy" resources is a relative term from every point of view, depending on the available technologies and the profitability of acquiring these resources for the purposes of production and/or consumption. According to this criterion, the term "high entropy resources" means resources, which are unavailable or unprofitable for current technologies. Waste is a particularly important issue in the circular economy concept. Substances located in the environment are waste from the point of view of the economy, however, from the environmental perspective it does not have to be so. Three cases are possible:

- A deposited substance may be included into the environmental flow of the matter – there are no objective criteria (an environmental criterion has to be taken into account in this case) to recognize it as waste, mainly because the natural environment, as an evolving homeostat, does not have own objective function (success or defeat of its individuals or species is totally indifferent to it - it only leads to a balance of another kind),
- A deposited substance may be available for future technologies (a technological criterion has to be taken into account in this case) – an anthropogenic deposit is created,
- The substance will be unavailable in the natural flow cycle of the matter, as well as for future technologies - it is a total waste.

A diagram of circular economy is shown in Figure 1.

The circular economy model, although based on the natural flow of a substance in the environment, differs from the functioning of nature because it has its own

Figure 1. Scheme of circular economy
Source: own elaboration.

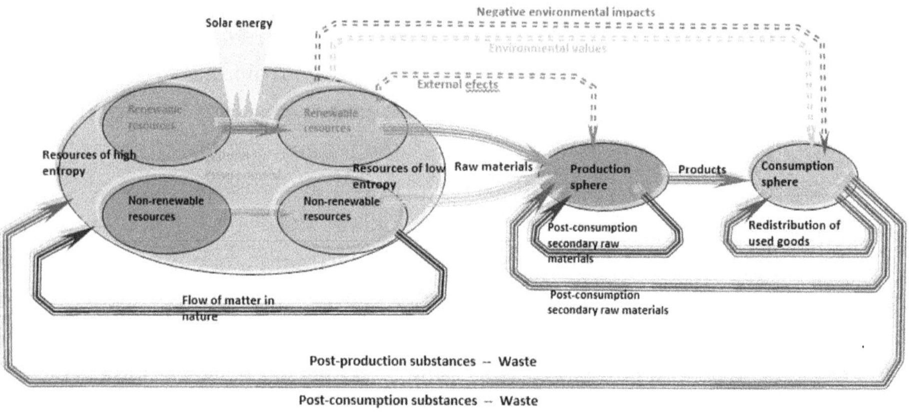

(anthropocentric) objective function, being the welfare of human societies. Substances deposited in the environment and the exploitation of natural resources induce dynamic changes of the environment, causing the setting of a new ecological balance, which through direct impacts (amenity uses - e.g. climate change derivatives, recreational or just aesthetic advantages of the environment) and indirect, i.e., changing resource availability for production fields, creates uses in the consumption sphere, which are the direct cause of people benefiting from welfare. The derivatives of climate changes (droughts, floods) due to the global nature, and issues with communal waste, due to concentration around big agglomerations and management difficulties are especially important[2].

Two subsystems may be distinguished in a circular economy model (Fiedor ed. 2002, p. 235):

- Economy subsystem, including consumer goods production (P), consumption sphere (C), usefulness, being the measure of welfare (U) and recycling (r);
- Environmental subsystem, including natural resources (R) - divided into renewable (RR) and exhaustible (ER) – and waste (W). Moreover, the assimilation ability of the environment (A), resource renewal (regeneration) rate (y) and their exploitation rate (h) were taken into account.
- Given the above relations and structural elements, it is possible to determine several essential functions of the environmental subsystem (Pearce et all 1990, Pearce, Turner 1990):
    1. Natural resources used in the production form - through the consumption process - usefulness (welfare expressed quantitatively).

2. In case of waste, the environment becomes their reservoir, and their impact depends on such factors as: extent of recycling, and the relationships between the amount of waste and the assimilation ability of the environment ($W>A$ or $W<A$).
3. The ecological impacts of management in the sphere of resources depend mainly on the relationship between the rate of renewal and the rate of exploitation.
4. Relation between the economy and the environment mainly involve also direct (positive or negative) impact of management on the level of prosperity. The issue is associated with extra-economic functions of the natural environment, such as: aesthetic, recreational or psychological[3].

The need to maintain ecological function within the development process stems from the fact that ecosystems are not a fully replaceable factor in the production of consumer goods. Their impact on the prosperity of a generation and future generation is also associated with "extra-economy uses" of the environment, in the scheme of circular economy. Replacing these uses with other production factor or even with other elements co-creating the natural capital is generally not possible and usually not socially acceptable. The basic condition of international environmental justice is the stability of natural capital. It conditions the upkeep of the ecological functions of the natural environment. Two basic management principles can be derived from the principle of natural capital resource constancy:

1. The renewable resources exploitation rate cannot exceed the rate of their regeneration (renewal); $h<y$;
2. The amount of waste (contaminants) discharged into the environment cannot exceed its assimilation ability; $W<A$.

The above management principles may be recognized as potentially operationalizationable economic policy objectives, however, they do not include the management of non-renewable (exhaustible) resources). In the case of maintaining the stability of non-renewable resources considered in the category of inter-generation justice, taking into account the above principles, may lead to a decline in the material prosperity of current generations. However, it is hard to fit in with the principle of inter-generation justice. The current exploitation of non-renewable resources cannot affect the prosperity of future generations if:

- The eco-functions of the natural environment will not be essential for future generations,
- These functions will be replaced by other factors,

- Losses for future generations arising as a result of current exploitation of non-renewable resources (from the point of view of prosperity), shall be adequately compensated by earlier generations.

EUROPEAN GUIDELINES ON DEVELOPING CIRCULAR ECONOMY

Already in 2015, the European Commission deemed circular economy to be a key element of creating a competitive economy based on sustainable development (see Closing the loop – An EU action plan for the Circular Economy, COM/2015/0614 final). The reduction of greenhouse gas emissions, protection of natural resources and improved waste management efficiency are, in fact, necessary. Of course, this is a global challenge providing many parties with great development opportunities and chances. The entities driving the ongoing changes are, surely: a business sector with the capital and an innovative approach towards challenges, but also the consumers, who have become more active market participants over the previous years.

The guidelines of the European Union on the transition into circular economy are aimed at protecting an enterprise against the shortage of resources and price instability, providing new business and innovation opportunities, more efficient production and consumption ways. Circular economy should contribute to the creation of local jobs for people with different qualifications, and the development of opportunities for social integration and cohesion. At the same time, it should contribute to energy savings and allow to avoid irreversible damage caused by the use of resources at a level exceeding the Earth's regeneration ability in terms of climate and biological diversity, and air, soil and water pollution. In circular economy, the value of products, materials and resources is maintained as long as possible, and waste generation should be kept at a minimum, which would constitute a significant contribution to EU's efforts aimed at developing a sustainable, low-emission, resource-efficient and competitive economy. Actions in favour of circular economy are, therefore, strictly related to the main priorities of the EU, such as employment and economic growth, investment schedule, climate and power policies, social agenda and supporting industrial innovations, together with global efforts for sustainable development. Business entities, such as enterprises and consumers, are of crucial meaning in the implementation of this process. Local, regional and national authorities enable the transformation of the economy, but also the EU plays a key role in supporting this process (COM/2015/0614 final). The implementation of circular economy will require long-term involvement at every level, starting with the Member States, through regions and cities, to enterprises and consumers. The objectives designated by EU to be achieved within the implementation of circular economy, primarily apply to effective resource management and reaching sustainable production and consumption patterns.

Based on the guidelines in the regulation, a correct circular economy model is presented in Figure 2.

Circular economy begins at the very start of a product's lifespan. Both the engineering, as well as production stages impact the processes of raw material acquisition, raw material utilization and waste generation throughout the entire lifespan of a product. Better engineering is supposed to facilitate recycling and contribute to better design of the products, while simultaneously maintaining a single market and competition, and enabling innovations. The EU regulation on the implementation of circular economy manifests a EU environmental protection philosophy that the environment should be protected mainly through manufacturing products with minimized impact. First of all, and within the directives and regulations on the Eco-Project (for ex. Erp *Energy Related Products* Directive 2009/125/EC, which stipulates the principles of setting Eco-Project requirements for energy related products, and the EU regulation 2017/1369 on FEL stipulating the Framework for Energy Labelling, which replaces the LErP directive – Labelling of Energy Related Products, 2010/30/EU on indications through labelling and standard product information), the Commission developed mandatory requirements regarding

Figure 2. The circular model according to the European Union guidelines
Source: own elaboration

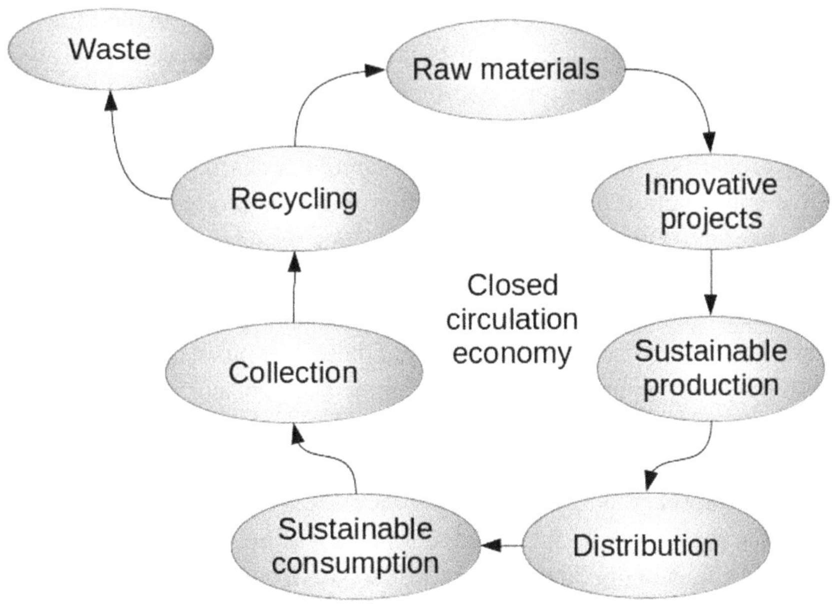

engineering and labelling products, in the field of electrical equipment. This should create a direct economic stimulus for the manufacturing of products, which can be more easily recycled or reused.

In the field of production processes, the European Commission emphasizes the important role of renewable materials in these processes, especially the sustainable acquisition of resources on a global scale. According to the guidelines, production processes should be evaluated in terms of environmental and social impacts, with BAT standards presented for individual industry branches in BREF (the basis for implementing these solutions is Directive 2010/75/EU of the European Parliament and of the Council of 24 November 2010 on industrial emissions) reference documents used for that purpose. The EU promotes a number of tools helpful in issuing integrated permits for industrial systems, such as, e.g. eco-project (for ex. Directive 2009/125/EC), energy labelling (for ex. Regulation (EU) 2017/1369), ecological designation (for ex. Regulation (EC) No 66/2010), green public procurements and other regulations regarding products. It also applies to the promotion and utilization of the EU eco-management and auditing system EMAS (Regulation (EC) No 1221/2009).to a greater extent.

The actions taken by the European Commission are aimed at studying, whether voluntary EU energy labelling might increase its effectiveness and the contribution to circular economy. The frequently used practices of artificial shortening of the product lifespan might limit their service life. This is why the EU commenced works aimed at identifying such practices and determining the ways to dissolve them. The ongoing works aimed at making green product become more trustworthy and ensure better enforcement of binding regulations, including the updating of the guidelines on unfair trade practices. The Commission is currently studying product environmental footprint, a method of measuring environmental effectiveness of products, and also the possibilities of applying that method for measuring or transmitting information regarding greenness. The development of circular economy might also favour innovative consumption forms, such as using the same products or infrastructure (sharing economy), consuming services and not products, and utilizing IT or digital platform technologies. These new consumption styles are often developed by entrepreneurs or citizens and disseminated at a national, regional or local level. The Commission supports the introduction of these new business and consumption models through the “Horizon 2020” programme and cohesion policy funds.

Dissemination of EU methods for measuring and labelling environmental effectiveness should increase the consumers’ level of acceptance for ecological marking of products. It is eco-labelling, which is classified as so-called product-oriented tools, and this causes increased eco-awareness among the consumers. It is an eco-aware consumer or organization that are decisive in terms of eco-product market development. Developing product and organization environmental footprint methods by the Joint Research Centre of the European Commission will enable the execution of an action plan in favour of resource-efficient Europe, including the introduction of sustainable consumption and production. A joint EU approach towards reliable environmental information is based on the evaluation of the entire lifespan, enabling the Member States and the private sector to assess the environmental effectiveness of products, services and enterprises, related information and comparison, as well as providing full information on the product environmental footprint.

Waste management and development of the recycling sector play an important role in circular economy. EU's cohesion policy is to play a crucial part in closing the investment gap for the purposes of better waste management and supporting the application of waste hierarchy. Within the last twenty years, these funds had been commonly used throughout the entire EU, in order to develop waste management infrastructure. As part of the current financing programme (2014-2020), the *ex ante* requirements must be met in order to guarantee new investments in the waste management sector, which must be in line with waste management plans developed by Member States in order to achieve the objectives in the field of recycling. It means that financing new landfills will be granted only in exceptional situations (e.g. mainly for hazardous waste). In circular economy, materials that can be recycled are reintroduced into the economy as a new raw material, which allows an increase of supply safety. These "recycled resources" can be sold or shipped, similar to primary resources from traditional natural resource deposits. A key factor in the creation of a dynamic market for recycled raw materials is a sufficient demand, driven by the use of recycled resources in products and infrastructure.

Transition into a circular economy is a change of the entire system. Apart from targeted actions at each stage of the value chain and in crucial sectors, it is necessary to create conditions, in which a circular economy can succeed, and in which it is possible to mobilize funds. Innovations will play the main role in this systemic change in order to fully change the production and consumption manners and transform waste into high quality products.

Sustainable Production and Consumption the Foundation of Building a Sustainable and Durable Enterprise: Possibilities and Barriers

A circular economy in the modern approach is a system of interconnected vessels. This concept takes into account environmental processes and their functioning balance, as well as the relationships with the society and economy. Due to the complexity of the processes, which should be taken into account, implementing the aforementioned assumption is very complicated and encounters numerous obstacles. Hence, it was concluded that the main issues with implementing circular economy are related to:

1. **Shortcomings in the Theory of the Subject:** The literature of the subject and in the documentation, circular economy is defined in different ways. Its determined priorities and scope are also different. The shortcomings also apply to detailed issues, and, for example, there is no scientifically supported definition of "an ecological product" and "an ecological organization".
2. **Concentrating on Issues Associated With Waste Management and Recycling:** It is necessary to implement a broader approach towards the issue of introducing circular economy and a wider consideration (if feasible) of environmental and social arguments. A major part of the legislative records of the EU in the field of creating circular economy concentrates on the issue of waste (disposing of used materials and managing them). Comparing the characteristics of circular economy with available literature, it can be argued that it lacks certain elements, or they are not explicitly marked. It applies to, i.a., the concept of inhibiting the life cycle shortening, and maintaining products and material at their highest value and usability for as long as possible. Moreover, although it was mentioned in the action plan that circular economy might create local jobs at all skill levels and under all social integration and cohesion opportunities, it can be argued that a bigger stress could be placed on its role in improving social welfare. Similarly, despite using the term "resources", which might also apply to energy resources, we can say that these issues are not sufficiently appreciated and deployed in real life.
3. **Policy Incoherence:** European policy, despite many efforts made in this matter, still remains too fragmented. Examples might include the power policy priorities in the scope of developing the use of renewable resources. Including the combustion of timber (which is a significant part of power resources classified as "solid biofuels") as a resource meeting ecological criteria and being compliant with the circular flow concept seems controversial. Although, admittedly, it is a renewable resource (and from this point of view, using it is coherent with the concept of circular economy), the regeneration takes too much time. In addition, using timber in the power sector on a large scale poses a threat of predatory exploitation of resources and disturbing the ecosystem functioning, which is not coherent with the idea of circular economy, assuming maintained balance in the entire environment – society – economy ecosystem.
4. **Shortcomings in Methods of Measuring Environmental Effectiveness of Products and Organizations:** Measurements are made based either on the direct impact of a product or organization on the environment or according to a direct and indirect impact along the entire product life cycle (LCA – Life Cycle Analysis) (E. Lore, 2007, p. 107). It is often impossible to reliably assess the environmental effectiveness due to the lack of complete information on direct and indirect environmental impacts of a product or organization. Enterprises

state that requirements associated with environmental information regarding the products they intend to market, are different in various countries.

5. **Shaping the Demand Side:** Insofar as it is possible to impact the behaviour of several thousand enterprises in the EU through instruments, then in the case of millions of consumers it is very difficult. Choices made by millions of consumers may support or hinder the development of circular economy. Consumer decisions largely depend on achieving reliable information about the product, their range, prices and existing legislation. A significant barrier is also fixed human behaviours and habits. According to a report by Ellen MacArthur Foundation and McKinsey Center for Business and Environment (2015), business managers and consumers maturing in linear production systems and consumption patterns rarely look for opportunities associated with circular economy development. This is one of the most serious, yet underrated, barriers against an efficient implementation of circular economy solutions. Consumer studies show the vast gap between the intentions and actions. According to a survey from 2014 (European Commission 2014), almost all Europeans (96%) believe that Europe should more effectively utilize the resources, only 21% leased or rented a product instead of purchasing it, and only 27% benefited from sharing schemes.
6. Another practical barrier is the practices of international companies aimed at shortening a product life cycle. Planned limitation of product life-spans is a problematic issue in many respects – decreasing the durability of consumer goods means expanding the consumption of resources and the amount of waste to be processed. For example, according to a survey Flash Eurobarometer 367: Attitudes of Europeans towards building the single market for green products (European Commission 2013), almost a half (47%) of the respondents decided not to return a faulty product for repair within the last year, because its costs turned out too high. As indicated by the data cited by the European Economic and Social Committee, the average service life of household appliances is currently 6-8 years, while 20 years ago it was 10-12 years. European Economic and Social Committee states also that according to the report of the ADEME (Agence de l'Environnement et de la Maîtrise de l'Energie) of 2007, only 44% defective equipment is repaired. According to the retailers, in the event of equipment with expired warranty, the attempt to repair a defect is made in the case of only 20% items. Moreover, further ADEME analysis of 2010 indicates that in France in 2006-2009, the number of attempted repairs, especially in the field of household appliances, declined significantly (European Economic and Social Committee 2014).

Many companies around the world develop their long-term action plan according to the principles of sustainable development and based on the assumptions of circular economy. Already in 2010, the World Business Council for Sustainable Development (WBCSD) published a document titled "Vision 2050. The new agenda for business" "(WBCSD 2010), which defines the challenges facing the business in a 40-year perspective and indicates market opportunities enabling sustainable development for companies in the long run. This document calls business to select a path of development, where sustainable growth would ensure social welfare. The report points to nine crucial areas, and in all of them, to actions that have to be taken, for 9 bn people in 2050 to live worthily, effectively using limited resources on Earth. This message to the business falls within the the main objective of sustainable development (cross-generational justice), which is retaining natural resources for future generations. In order to rise to these challenges, business has a number of implementation tools at its disposal, such as, e.g., implementing environmental management systems (ISO, EMAS), the BAT standard (*Best Available Technology*) – modern technologies, eco-friendly materials and resources for production, and finally, correct recycling. We could add a number of issues such as: the development of clean technologies, renewable energy sources, improving power and material efficiency, changing the consumption and production model to a more sustainable one, integrated product policy, green public procurements, green jobs or, finally, eco tax reform. It is estimated that economic benefits for EU enterprises, which may result from preventing waste generation, eco-engineering and reuse, might amount to as much as EUR 600 bn (net) or 8% of the annual turnover. Eco-benefits are estimated at a 2-4% decrease of the total annual greenhouse gas emissions[4].

Implementing circular economy models based on the circular model will bring multidimensional benefits in light of the sustainable model, i.e. (Rizos et all, 2017):

- Economic benefits (GDP growth, employment, investments, etc.),
- Social benefits (equalling social chances and mitigating inequalities, etc.),
- Environmental benefits (resource utilization, emissions reduction, reduced waste generation, etc.)

The aforementioned circular economy potential, translates to specific business management methods and opportunities. One of the examples of the classification, developed by H. Stageman (2015) was used to distinguish the following circular economy business models:

1. **Circular Input Models**: Intended for the creation of products and expenditure, which are adequate for circular economy, to be used for the production of renewable fuels, and biodegradable and recycling materials. It constitutes a base for sustainable production and consumption.

Table 1. Potential benefits associated with implementing circular economy in EU countries

Aspect	Description	Source
Economic	In this study the target date for the changes to be obtained in terms of decoupling is set for 2030, and were considered case study of: Finland, France, the Netherlands, Spain and Sweden. Analysis concern three scenarios: 1.The renewable-scenario: There was no significant net effect on employment unless the respective countries would give priority to using of domestic biomass then significant number of jobs will be created- Up to 15,000 new jobs could be created in Finland and Sweden, respectively, up to 50,000 jobs in the Netherlands, and up to 100,000 jobs in France and Spain. There would be a surplus in the balance of trade with a third to two-thirds of a percentage point of GDP in all analysed countries. 2.The energy efficiency scenario: the effect on employment would be positive and add new jobs in the range of 15,000 people in Finland, 20,000 people in Sweden, 100,000 people in the Netherlands and 200,000 people in France and Spain, respectively. The trade balance would be improved in most countries, but less so than in the renewable scenario. France and Spain are likely to experience the largest trade surplus gains at 0.4% of GDP. 3.The material efficiency scenario: the effect on employment would be more significant – representing more than 50,000 people in Finland and Sweden, respectively, more than 100,000 in the Netherlands, more than 200,000 in Spain and more than 300,000 people in France. The same goes for the trade balance – the estimated trade surplus improvement would be in the magnitude of 1-2% of GDP. In case of implementation of all the different decoupling strategies: the number of additional jobs would exceed 75,000 in Finland, 100,000 in Sweden, 200,000 in the Netherlands, 400,000 in Spain and half a million in France and The improvement in the trade balance would be around - or even above – 1,5% of GDP in all of the countries studied – representing a few billion euros a year in Finland, more than five billion euros a year in Sweden, around 15 billion euros a year in the Netherlands, 20 billion euros in Spain and 50 billion euros in France.	Club of Rome (2015
	In this study the target date for the changes to be obtained in terms of decoupling is set for 2030, and were considered case study of: Poland and Czech Republic. Analysis concern three scenarios: 1.The renewable-scenario: There could be a small positive net effect on employment if the Czech Republic and Poland would give priority to using domestic biomass in substituting coal and other fossil fuels. In Poland there would be a small gain in the balance of trade, with up to a third of a percentage point of GDP, while the trade balance in the Czech Republic would not be significantly affected. 2.The energy efficiency scenario: the effect on employment would be positive and add in the range of 50,000 new jobs in the Czech Republic and 100,000 new jobs in Poland. The trade balance would not be affected in Poland, while there might be a small loss in the Czech Republic. 3.The material efficiency scenario: around 100,000 jobs in the Czech Republic, while in Poland the employment outcome depend on the development of the agricultural (and forestry) sector. The trade balance surplus would considerable in both the Czech Republic and Poland, in excess of 2% of GDP in both countries. In case of implementation of all the different decoupling strategies: the number of additional jobs would exceed 150,000 in the Czech Republic while the number would depend on the development of the agricultural sector in Poland, and the improvement in the trade balance could amount to more than 2% of GDP in both the Czech Republic and Poland.	Club of Rome (2016)
	Based on the developed macro-econometric model it was estimated that improving resource productivity in the EU by 2% could help in the creation of two million additional jobs by 2030.	Cambridge Econometrics and BIO Intelligence Service (2014)
	Depending on the execution level of the objectives associated with implementing circular economy, EEB estimated that it is possible to create approximately 635 000-750 000 additional jobs by 2025 and circa 710 000-870 000 by 2030.	EEB (2014)
	In a study conducted by this organization, it was estimated that the target recycling level of 70% in the EU might lead to creating more than 563 000 new jobs net. The number includes newly formed “direct” jobs, as well as “indirect” and “linked” vacancies.	Friends of the Earth (2010)

Table 1. Continued

Aspect	Description	Source
	In the sectors of mobility, food and constructions, technological development in combination with organizational innovations would allow a 3% growth of raw material utilization effectiveness in Europe by 2030, which translates to joint annual benefits in the amount of EUR 1.8 tn. This, in turn, would lead to a GDP increase of 7%. This primarily includes benefits associated with saving resources in the amount of EUR 0.6 tn, as well as benefits not linked with resources and external benefits (for example, non-monetary health benefits linked with decreasing pollution, noise, etc.) estimated at EUR 1.2 tn.	Ellen MacArthur Foundation and McKinsey Centre for Business and Environment (2015)
	The newest report estimates that although some developing business models regarding, e.g., the production of electric and autonomous vehicles or sharing economy are growing rapidly, the investments in circular economy still represent only 10% of the traditional investments. Further section of the report estimates that in the three aforementioned sectors (mobility, food, construction) there is a possibility of additional investments of up to EUR 320 bn, which could be used until 2025, provided actions are taken in this scope by political or business policy makers; it could help achieving an additional GDP growth of 7%.	Ellen MacArthur Foundation and SYSTEMIQ (2017)
	Within the assessment of the effects of the waste management legislation review, the European Commission estimated the impact of regulations regarding waste on the creation of new jobs. The scenarios are based on political options regarding assumed objectives for recycling, limiting waste disposal and the possibilities of implementing bans regarding the disposal of plastic / paper / glass metal waste until 2025. The study estimates that various scenarios may create from 136 000 to 178, 000 full-time jobs until 2025 and most of them in the recycling sector. The study also notes that the biggest benefits resulting from creating jobs would be manifested in EU States, which are most in the need of improvements in their waste management systems.	European Commission, 2015
Environmental	Case study of Finland, France, the Netherlands, Spain and Sweden 1.**The renewable-scenario**: for all five countries led to an estimated 50% reduction in carbon emissions. 2.**The energy efficiency scenario**: cut carbon emissions in all five countries by roughly 30%. 3.**The material efficiency scenario**: cut carbon emissions in all the countries by between 3 and 10%. In case of implementation of all the different decoupling strategies: Carbon emissions are likely to be cut by two thirds or more, almost 70% in Spain.	Club of Rome (2015)
	Case study of Poland and the Czech Republic 1.The renewable-scenario: in both the Czech Republic case study and the one for Poland led to an estimated 50% reduction in carbon emissions. 2.The energy efficiency scenario: is likely to cut carbon emissions in the Czech Republic by 33% and in Poland by 35%. 3.The material efficiency scenario: is likely to cut carbon emissions in Czech by 8% and in Poland by 7%. In case of implementation of all the different decoupling strategies: carbon emissions are likely to be cut by more than two-thirds (69% in Czech and 69,5% in Poland)	Club of Rome (2016)
	Improving the productivity of EU resources by 3% would lead to decreasing greenhouse gas emissions by 25% until 2030.	Cambridge Econometrics and BIO Intelligence Service (2014)

continued on following page

Table 1. Continued

Aspect	Description	Source
	Depending on how ambitious objectives are adopted, EEB estimates that it is going to be possible to avoid from 56.5 Mt to 96.5 Mt of greenhouse gas emissions by 2025, which is associated with limiting the practices of wasting food and dissemination of reusing materials in the textile and furniture industries. EEB estimates that the greenhouse gas emission reduction potential in 2030 in these sectors might be from 74.652 Mt to 115.0 Mt. The report also indicated opportunities for saving water consumption from 26.1 Ml to 52.2 Ml and from 34.8 Ml to 60.9 Ml by 2025 and 2030, respectively. The calculations of these values are based on the assumptions regarding decreased water consumption resulting from reuse of textiles. It is estimated that reuse of textiles leads to decreased use of fertilizers and pesticides in cotton production. In light of the above, EEB also estimates a decrease in the use of fertilizers and pesticides, as well as positive environmental impacts resulting from avoiding land development for agricultural purposes.	EEB (2014)
	The study states that circular economy in the three researched sectors (mobility, food and construction) might decrease greenhouse gas emissions by up to 48% until 2030 and 83% until 2050. The paper also shows the impact on the consumption of primary resources in these sectors. The study estimates that it is possible to achieve a decreased consumption of primary materials by up to 32% and 53% until 2030 and 2050, respectively, in terms of materials used in the automotive and construction sectors, land usufruct, and water and fertilizer consumption for agricultural needs.	Ellen MacArthur Foundation and McKinsey Centre for Business and Environment (2015)
	The impact assessment included a review of the legislation regarding waste management and the estimation of the impact of greenhouse gas emissions in the case of the suggested EU legislation on waste was fully implemented. The impact assessment included a presentation of the implementation effects of various objectives regarding recycling and target levels of redirecting biodegradable communal waste to landfills, and it was stated that they can lead to a reduction of between 42 455 to 65 556 Mt CO_2eq by 2015 and 2035, respectively.	European Commission, 2015
	The study estimated environmental benefits resulting from saving materials in the food and industrial manufacturing sectors, as well as hotel and gastronomic services. The study estimates that improved efficiency of raw material utilization in the evaluated sectors might cause a 2-4% reduction of the total annual emission of greenhouses gases in the EU.	Lawton et al. (2013)
Social	The impact on the creation of new jobs was presented in the section including economic benefits	See the economic part
	The study takes into account the aspects associated with employment. The authors of the elaboration estimate that circular economy in Great Britain might help compensate certain job losses, which are expected among qualified mid-level positions due to industrial changes. Some of the presented scenarios also provide for high demand for qualified mid-level employment, which might lead to the transfer of qualified mid-level employees to sectors created thanks to the growth of circular economy. The study expects that circular economy has higher regional unemployment reduction potential in areas with the highest unemployment rates, and also contributes to decreasing regional differences in unemployment.	Morgan & Mitchell (2015)

Source: development on the basis of given sources and Rizos V., Tuokko K. and Behrens A. (2017) "The Circular Economy. A review of definitions, processes and impacts", CEPS Research Reports No 2017/8, April 2017

2. **Waste Value Models:** Where recycling and upcycling play a key role. Waste generate in one production process become useful, as material in another production process. This is beneficial in enterprises where there are significant waste streams or where other product waste can be processed into new materials.
3. **Lifespan Models:** Expanded product lifespan may be achieved in different ways: overhaul, modernization, regeneration or remarketing (also known as recommerce) of the same product. In markets, where new products are better

Table 2. Business models in circular economy

The resolve framework according Ellen MacArthur Foundation		Business models according WBCSD	
Name	**Examples of action**	**Five business models**	**Three disruptive technologies**
REGENERATE	-Shift to renewable energy and materials -Reclaim, retain, and restore health of ecosystems -Return recovered biological resources to the biosphere	CIRCULAR SUPPLIES: Use renewable energy and bio-based or fully recyclable inputs	DIGITAL TECHNOLOGIES such as Internet of Things (IoT), big data, blockchain, and RFID help companies track resources and monitor utilization and waste capacity
SHARE	-Share assets (e.g. cars, rooms, appliances) -Reuse/ secondhand -Prolong life through maintenance, design or durability, upgradeability, etc.	RESOURCE RECOVERY: Recover useful resources out of materials, by-products or waste	PHYSICAL TECHNOLOGIES such as 3D printing, robotics, energy storage and harvesting, modular design technology and nanotechnology help companies reduce production and material costs and reduce environmental impact
OPTIMISE	-Increase performance/ efficiency of product -Remove waste in production and supply chain -Leverage big data, automation, remote sensing and steering	PRODUCT LIFE-EXTENSION: Extend product lifecycles by repairing, upgrading and reselling, as well as through innovation and product design	BIOLOGICAL TECHNOLOGIES such as bio-energy, bio-based materials, biocatalysis, hydroponics and aeroponics help companies move away from fossilbased energy sources
LOOP	-Remaufacture products or components -Recycle materials -Digest anaerobically -Extract biochemicals from organic waste	SHARING PLATFORM: Connect product users to one another and encourage shared use, access or ownership to increase product use	
Virtualise	-Books, music, travel, online shopping -Autonomous vehicles etc.	PRODUCTS AS A SERVICE: Move away from product ownership and offer customers paid access to products, allowing companies to retain the benefits of circular resource productivity or ownership to increase product use	
EXCHANGE	-Replace old with advanced non-renewable materials -Apply new technologies (e.g. 3D printing) -Choose new product/ service (e.g. multimodal transport)		

Source: Ellen MacArthur Foundation. Growth Within: A Circular Economy Vision for a Competitive Europe; Ellen MacArthur Foundation: Cowes, UK, 2015 and WBCSD, 2017, CEO Guide to the Circular Economy, www.wbcsd.org/Clusters/Circular-Economy/Resources/CEO-Guide-to-the-Circular-Economy (16.03.2018).

than their predecessors, it is highly likely that used products in that market will be of a new value (economic). One of the alternatives may be offering such products in another and a less developed market (country).

4. **Platform Modeless:** An important method for a more effective utilization of products is making them available to a wider range of users. Sharing can be paid or free of charge (sharing models), through leasing services, while existing goods may be used on demand or through amending ownership rights regarding things, which were not or already are not used (secondary market).
5. **Product in A Service Model**: Instead of selling the goods, a company remains the owner of a product. A product is made available to one or more users, although under a lease or rental agreement. Such a solution is currently functioning – namely, leasing companies. More and more enterprises are interested in the application of this model type, since the rental or leasing cost is lower than purchasing a product. There is also another benefit. Disassembly or reusing products is well organized. That is why this model includes also the product lifespan expansion model.

Another division of business solutions in circular economy was presented in the reports of the Ellen MacArthur Foundation & McKinsey Center for Business and Environment (2015) and WBCSD (2017). . Circular economy types are shown in Table 2.

An important element of the above concept is effective product engineering. The engineering process assumes that the end product must have the slightest possible environmental impact over the entire lifespan and a smaller negative impact after the period of use (engineering in the categories of increasing efficiency and productivity of products – maintenance, reuse/numerous use, regeneration/refurbishing, recycling). It is estimated that 80% of the environmental costs associated with the impact of products, services and processes on the natural environment are determined at the engineering stage. The application of the product lifespan evaluation and eco-engineering might provide tangible benefits in achieving objectives in the field of developing circular economy - in particular, through enabling effective raw material utilization, reducing environmental impact of products and waste. It contributes to saving energy, water and improving environmental and economic parameters (Polski Ruch Czystej Produkcji 2015).

Another indispensable element for the possibility to implement the aforementioned solutions is the application of modern IT technologies. For example, Porter and Heppelman (2014, 2015) describe how a service-based model, supported by the "Internet of Things" and the development of digital technologies will increase customer involvement. Using the "Internet of Things" means that most suppliers will be able to monitor and maintain constant contact with their digital equipment, foresee problems before they appear and remedy them without a failure. Porter and Heppelman believe that: the possibility to stay in contact with a product and trace its use changes customer relations – shifts the centre of gravity from sales – being mainly a one-time transaction – to constant relations with the customers in order to maximize customer product satisfaction for as long as possible.

Another thing, which could facilitate the use of modern digital technologies is enabling the upkeep of control over the products and planning their return and another life cycle. Hence, the producers would be encouraged to manufacture things that are durable and work well, can be regenerated, renewed or recycled at the end of their lifespan. Therefore, the process may be profitable, competitive, as well as eco-responsible. Peter Lacy and Jakob Rutqvist, the authors of a book titled "Waste to Wealth" (2015), also consider such solutions as one of the possible paths leading to circular economy and describe how the manufacturers should "take into account the entire product lifespan when deciding on a strategy". In this scenario, the products "must be designed in terms of optimum use, maintenance, reuse, regeneration and recycling, in order to avoid such problems as quick value decline, short lifespan, low utilization index and low recycling / return level". However, it should be noted that an essential element for the effective implementation of the aforementioned solution is the presence of relevant legislation on the part of the public authorities.

CONCLUSION

The holistic approach towards the environment represented by sustainable development is increasingly taken into account by business circles. The „sustainable development" concept is the basis for the creation of an enterprise of the future – a *„sustainable enterprise*" [Grudzewski W.M., Hejduk I. K. et al. 2010, p. 275]. The development of such an enterprise favours the implementation of sustainable production in the economy, which is such a model of conducting business activity in the scope of the manufacturing industry, which minimizes environmental impact. Production processes use very large amounts of natural resources and generate excessive waste. They also manufacture products of low quality and durability, which fill landfills after a short period of use. Using a sustainable production model provides numerous benefits for organizations, such as:

- Financial gains,
- Changes in the operation of organizations based on the application of good environmental protection practices,
- Improving the image of enterprises among consumers and the environment.

The circular economy concept has been gaining importance since the mid 1970s. The significance of circular economy stems from its ability to shape effectiveness and savings in terms of production processes due to a greater extent of waste utilization, and at the same time, due to extended product lifespan. The implementation of a new management method is supported by the European Commission via a number of regulatory proposals, programmes and projects, as well as financial instruments. Circular economy creates opportunities for achieving benefits in the economy (the efficiency of production processes, innovations, power safety), as well as in the social and environmental fields (shaping ecological safety). Circular economy aims for reducing the effects of the negative impact of production and consumption processes on the natural environment. Its determinant is the resource and power efficiency, associated with the utilization of waste generated as a result of production and consumption. The prerequisite for success is creating interconnections and relations in the system between enterprises, enterprises and consumers, as well as the State, enterprises and the consumers. They are indispensable, especially due to the exchange of information regarding the demand for raw materials/waste, the possibilities of their use for generating power and heat

Circular economy, as a new model, requires an innovative approach towards business. In the process of straying away from the *take-make-consume-dispose* pattern, innovators appear who offer completely new solutions addressing the needs and expectations of new consumers, generating greater value, without the need of consuming so many resources. All of the new proposals of business models regarding the economy of co-sharing, eco-design, reusing or recycling, drive the new, responsible consumption manner. Together with the development of circular economy, we can expect the creation of new job vacancies. Changing consumption and production patterns to more sustainable is the basis for manufacturing and consuming a sustainable product. In order to get there, it is, most of all, necessary to introduce and apply in economy of a number of so-called product-oriented instruments credible for a consumer, namely, such that the consumer is able to select products in the same product group, distinguished by a minimized environmental impact. It is associated with the need to introduce proper education and information. Works on the implementation of sustainable production and consumption have been undergoing in the EU for several years. The European Commission is working on the creation of a single market for eco-products, at the same time developing efficient tools for this purpose, such as, e.g. environmental footprint determinations for products and organizations, with these actions undoubtedly going to revolutionize the organizational approach towards environmental issues, including the mitigation of environmental impact.

The EU creating a single market for green-products will force the enterprises to respect the methods of evaluating the environmental impact of products. This will be supported by the development of uniform methods of determining the environmental footprint of a product and organization on the market. This will create a reliable tool to differentiate them, without exposing the company to high study execution costs. The European Commission is gradually introducing the developed methods into EMAS, green public procurements and CE marking. The introduction of harmonised environmental footprint determination methods should ensure comparable and reliable ecological information for the producers, consumers and investors. The growth of the contemporary market indicates clear trends towards the ecologization of production, products and services, and consumption. Therefore, the enterprises taking market opportunities and rapid adjustment of investment development activities against these requirements, guarantees competitive leverage over longer periods.

REFERENCES

ADEME. (2014). *Economie Circulaire: Notions*. Author.

Bastien, T., Roelofs, E., Rietveld, E., & Hoogendoorn, A. (2013). *Opportunities for a Circular Economy in the Netherlands*. TNO, Report commissioned by the Netherlands Ministry of Infrastructure and Environment.

Boulding, K. (1966). The Economics of the Coming Spaceship Earth. In H. Jarrett (Ed.), *Environmental Quality in a Growing Economy*. Baltimore, MD: Johns Hopkins University.

Cambridge Econometrics and BIO Intelligence Service. (2014). *Study on modelling of the economic and environmental impacts of raw material consumption*. Final Report prepared for the European Commission.

Club of Rome. (2015). *The Circular Economy and Benefits for Society Jobs and Climate Clear Winners in an Economy Based on Renewable Energy and Resource Efficiency*. Retrieved from www.clubofrome.org

Club of Rome. (2016). *The Circular Economy and Benefits for Society Jobs and Climate Clear Winners in an Economy Based on Renewable Energy and Resource Efficiency*. Retrieved from www.clubofrome.org

Communication from the Commission to the European Parliament, the Council, the European Economic and Social Committee, & the Committee of the Regions. (2005). *Closing the loop - An EU action plan for the Circular Economy*. COM/2015/0614 final.

Directive 2009/125/EC of the European Parliament and of the Council of 21 October 2009 establishing a framework for the setting of ecodesign requirements for energy-related products (Text with EEA relevance), Official Journal of the European Union L 285/10

Directive 2010/30/EU of the European Parliament and of the Council of 19 May 2010 on the indication by labelling and standard product information of the consumption of energy and other resources by energy-related products (Text with EEA relevance), Official Journal of the European Union L 153/1

Directive 2010/75/EU of the European Parliament and of the Council of 24 November 2010 on industrial emissions (integrated pollution prevention and control) Text with EEA relevance, Official Journal of the European Union L 334/17

EEA (European Environment Agency). (2014). *Resource-efficient Green Economy and EU policies*. Luxembourg: Publications Office of the European Union.

EEB (European Environmental Bureau). (2014). Advancing Resource Efficiency in Europe: Indicators and waste policy scenarios to deliver a resource efficient and sustainable. *Europe*.

Elen MacArthur Foundation. (2012). *Towards the Circular Economy: Vol. 1. An economic and business rationale for an accelerated transition*. Retrieved from https://www.ellenmacarthurfoundation.org/publications

Ellen MacArthur Foundation. (2013). *Towards the Circular Economy: Vol. 2. Opportunities for the consumer goods sector*. Retrieved from https://www.ellenmacarthurfoundation.org/publications

Ellen MacArthur Foundation. (2015). *Towards a Circular Economy: Business rationale for an accelerated transition*. Retrieved from https://www.ellenmacarthurfoundation.org/publications

Ellen MacArthur Foundation and McKinsey Center for Business and Environment. (2015). *Growth Within: A Circular Economy Vision for a Competitive Europe*. Retrieved from https://www.ellenmacarthurfoundation.org/publications

Ellen MacArthur Foundation and SYSTEMIQ. (2017). *Achieving 'Growth Within': A €320-Billion Circular Economy Investment Opportunity Available to Europe up to 2025*. Retrieved from https://www.ellenmacarthurfoundation.org/publications

European Commission. (2013). *Flash Eurobarometer 367: Attitudes of Europeans towards building the single market for green products*. Author.

European Commission. (2014). *Flash Eurobarometer 388: Attitudes of Europeans towards waste management and resource efficiency*. Author.

European Commission. (2015). *Commission Staff Working Document: Additional analysis to complement the impact assessment SWD (2014) 208 supporting the review of EU waste management targets*. Author.

European Commission. (n.d.). *Press releases database*. Retrieved from http://europa.eu/rapid/press-release_MEMO-15-6204_pl.htm

European Economic and Social Committee 2014/C 67/05: Opinion of the European Economic and Social Committee on 'Towards more sustainable consumption: industrial product lifetimes and restoring trust through consumer information' (own-initiative opinion). *Official Journal of the European Union, C, 67*(23).

Fiedor, B. (Ed.). (2002). Podstawy ekonomii środowiska i zasobów naturalnych. Wydawnictwo C.H.Beck.

Friends of the Earth. (2010). *More Jobs Less Waste - Potential for Job Creation through higher rates of recycling in the UK and the EU*. Author.

Geng, Y., & Doberstein, B. (2008). Developing the circular economy in China: Challenges and opportunities for achieving 'leapfrog development'. *International Journal of Sustainable Development and World Ecology, 15*(3), 231–239. doi:10.3843/SusDev.15.3:6

Ghisellini, P., Cialani, C., & Ulgiati, S. (2016). A review on circular economy: The expected transition to a balanced interplay of environmental and economic systems. *Journal of Cleaner Production, 114*, 11–32. doi:10.1016/j.jclepro.2015.09.007

Grudzewski, W. M., Hejduk, I. K., Sankowska, A., & Wańtuchowicz, M. (2010). *Sustainably w biznesie czyli przedsiębiorstwo przyszłości. Zmiany paradygmatów i koncepcji zarzadzania*. Warszawa: Wyd. Poltext.

Heck, P. (2006). *Circular Economy related international practices and policy trends: Current situation and practices on sustainable production and consumption and international Circular Economy development policy summary and analysis. Institut für angewandtes Stoffstrommanagement*. IfaS.

Kirchherr, J., Reike, D., & Hekkert, M. (2017). Conceptualizing the circular economy: An analysis of 114 definitions. *Resources, Conservation and Recycling, 127*, 221–232. doi:10.1016/j.resconrec.2017.09.005

Lacy, P., & Rutqvist, J. (2015). *Waste to Wealth. The Circular Economy Advantage*. Palgrave Macmillan.

Lawton, Carter, Lee, Tan, de Prado Trigo, Luscombe, & Briscoe. (2013). *The opportunities to business of improving resource efficiency*. Study prepared by AMEC Environment & Infrastructure and Bio Intelligence Service.

Lorek, E. (2007). *Polska polityka energetyczna w warunkach integracji z Unią Europejską*. Wyd. AE Katowice.

Lorek, E., & Lorek, A. (2011). *Efektywne zarządzanie dobrami środowiskowymi w ujęciu modelowym*. Uniwersytet Ekonomiczny w Krakowie.

McDowall, W., Geng, Y., Huang, B., Bartekov'a, E., Bleischwitz, R., Türkeli, S., . . . Doménech, T. (2017). Circular Economy Policies in China and Europe. *Journal of Industrial Ecology*. Retrieved from https://www.researchgate.net/publication/316722262

Mitchell, P. (2015). Employment and the circular economy - Job Creation through resource efficiency in London. Report produced by WRAP for the London Sustainable Development Commission, the London Waste and Recycling Board and the Greater London Authority.

Morgan, J., & Mitchell, P. (2015). Employment and the circular economy Job creation in a more resource efficient Britain. *Green Alliance*. Retrieved from https://tinyurl.com/gmrnosb

Pearce, D., Barbier, E., & Markandya, A. (1990). *Sustainable Development, Economics and the Enviroment in the Third World*. Edward Elgar Pub.

Pearce, D. W., & Turner, R. K. (1990). *Economics of Natural Resources and the Environment*. Baltimore, MD: Johns Hopkins University Press.

Polski Ruch Czystszej Produkcji. (2015). *Gospodarka o obiegu zamkniętym – nowe wytyczne Komisji Europejskie*. Retrieved from www.cp.org.pl/2015/12/forum-cp-j-baran-circular-economy.htm

Porter, M. E., & Heppelmann, J. E. (2014). How Smart, Connected Products Are Transforming Competition. *Harvard Business Review*.

Porter, M. E., & Heppelmann, J. E. (2015). How Smart, Connected Products Are Transforming Companies. *Harvard Business Review*.

Preston, F. (2012). A Global Redesign? Shaping the Circular Economy. *Briefing Paper*. London: Chatham House.

Qiao, F., & Qiao, N. (2013). Circular Economy: An Ethical and Sustainable Economic Development Model. *Prakseologia, 154*, 253-272.

Regulation (EC) No 1221/2009 of the European Parliament and of the Council of 25 November 2009 on the voluntary participation by organisations in a Community eco-management and audit scheme (EMAS), repealing Regulation (EC) No 761/2001 and Commission Decisions 2001/681/EC and 2006/193/EC, Official Journal of the European Union L 342/1

Regulation (EC) No 66/2010 of the European Parliament and of the Council of 25 November 2009 on the EU Ecolabel (Text with EEA relevance), Official Journal of the European Union L 27/1

Regulation (EU) 2017/1369 of the European Parliament and of the Council of 4 July 2017 setting a framework for energy labelling and repealing Directive 2010/30/EU (Text with EEA relevance.)

Regulation (EU) 2017/1369 of the European Parliament and of the Council of 4 July 2017 setting a framework for energy labelling and repealing Directive 2010/30/EU (Text with EEA relevance.), Official Journal of the European Union L 198/1

Rizos, V., Tuokko, K., & Behrens, A. (2017). *The Circular Economy. A review of definitions, processes and impacts.* CEPS Research Reports No 2017/8.

Sauvé, S., Bernard, S., & Sloan, P. (2016). Environmental sciences, sustainable development and circular economy: Alternative concepts for trans-disciplinary research. *Environmental Development, 17*, 48–56. doi:10.1016/j.envdev.2015.09.002

Stahel, W., & Reday, G. (1976). *Report The Potential for Substituting Manpower for Energy*. New York: Vantage Press.

Stahel, W., & Reday, G. (1981). *Jobs for Tomorrow, the Potential for Substituting Manpower for Energy*. New York: Vantage Press.

Stegeman, H. (2015). *The potential of the circular economy.* Retrieved from https:/economics.rabobank.com/publications/2015/july/the-potential-of-the-circular-economy

Su, B., Heshmati, A., Geng, Y., & Yu, X. (2013). A review of the circular economy in China: Moving from rhetoric to implementation. *Journal of Cleaner Production, 42*, 215–227. doi:10.1016/j.jclepro.2012.11.020

Vision 2050: The New agenda for business. (n.d.). World Business Council for Sustainable Development (WBCS). Retrieved from http://www.wbcsd.org/vision2050.aspx

WBCSD. (2017). *CEO Guide to the Circular Economy.* Retrieved from www.wbcsd.org/Clusters/Circular-Economy/Resources/CEO-Guide-to-the-Circular-Economy

ENDNOTES

1 The transition of Chinese economy into a circular economy model took place in 2002, during the 16th National Congress of the Communist Party of China and was associated with the high level of environmental degradation in the country.

2 Generally speaking, environmental issues come in two forms: extensive (determined by the scale of the phenomenon) or intensive (determined by the concentration of the phenomenon).

3 D.Pearce, E. Barbier, A. Markandya. Sustainable Development, Economics and the Enviroment in the Third World, Aldershot 1990. cf. also: D. Pearce, K. Turner, Economics of Natural Resources and the Environment, New York 1990.

4 The European Commission. Press releases database: http://eu-ropa.eu/rapid/press-release_MEMO-15-6204_pl.htm [Access: 2/4/2016].

Chapter 4
Sharing Economy and Applications:
Business and Marketing Perspective

Fatih Pinarbasi
https://orcid.org/0000-0001-9005-0324
Istanbul Medipol University, Turkey

ABSTRACT

Sharing economy has emerged as influential economic model in the last decades. A considerable literature has grown up around the sub-themes of sharing economy including business-related, system-related, and other context-related studies. Examining a general phenomenon in a limited scope is a strategy for specific perspective and conclusions. Therefore, examining sharing economy phenomenon in a business and marketing perspective can be useful for business related viewpoint. The study is composed of three parts and begins with a theorotical review of conceptual background. It will then go on to three level structures for this study, including consumer level, business and brand level, and system levels. The remaining part includes context-based studies about level structure. After reviewing topics in contexts, there are presented selected studies about related contexts. The study aims to research sharing economy in a general view and review business- and marketing-related topics and studies.

DOI: 10.4018/978-1-5225-7850-5.ch004

INTRODUCTION

Freedom in a commons brings ruin to all. (Hardin, 1968)

Hardin (1968) (as also cited in (Feeny et al., 1990) mentioned a metaphor about a pasture and capacity of commons. If one of herdsman would add an additional animal to his herd, then another herdsman, then another. What would be the result of this? For years it would be not a problem because of tribal wars, poaching and diseases. Because they could keep the capacity balanced. But what would happen if conditions are better for these problems? Every herdsman would like to add additional animals to their herds. Finally, tragedy starts, each man is locked into a system which force him to a limited capacity world. This is the economic starting point for sharing economy or more basicly "sharing."

As sharing is an old phenomenon as humankind (Belk, 2014), the extended or augmented form of sharing has been seen in consumption patterns for years. Sharing economy one of reflections in consumption pattern in economy, is popular concept in recent years for both scholars and practitioners. For consuming side, many years ago Belk (1988) stated that possessions of people both contribute and reflect identities. After years, Belk (2014) updated the statement with "you are what you share" conclusion. According to author it was indicating that people may be entering a new economy which includes a post-ownership characteristic.

The production and consumption patterns of people on earth have been an important factor throughout history. When the historical stages are examined, the change of people's production methods, for example the industrial revolution, is an important development which also affects other factors. How we consume products and services following this is an important research topic. How to get products and services, how to consume them and how to keep consuming them are important questions. The sharing economy is a concept that leads to changes that involve consumption patterns at this stage.

In addition to the conceptual conception of the share economy, it will be useful to examine statistics for economic significance. In 2015 sharing economy revenues were $15 billion and five key sharing sectors – car sharing, travel, staffing, finance and music and video streaming- were estimated to reach $335 billion by 2025 (PwC, 2015).

As importance of sharing economy and its applications is clear, this is originating the first part of title "sharinge economy and applications". Sharing economy has a wide range of research areas including law to sustainability, tourism to accommodation and etc. Concluding a specific study relies on limiting scope well. In this study, the limit of scope including business and marketing applications in sharing economy which leads to "business and marketing perspective" part.

Study consists of two parts. While first part relates to sharing economy concept and its details, latter part focuses on applications of sharing economy. Second part has three parts which implicating three contexts of research studies. First context refers to consumer context and it is mostly micro-perspective which implies studying consumers in micro level. Second context refers to business/brand side of sharing economy. Finally, last context takes sharing economy as system.

SHARING ECONOMY AND HISTORICAL BACKGROUND

In this section, the conceptual background of sharing economy will be given. Definitions, scope, similiarities and differences from other concepts and historical developments are the topics for this section.

What is Sharing Economy and What is the Scope of it?

One of formal definition of sharing economy, according to (Botsman, 2013);

An economic model based on sharing underutilized assets from spaces to skills to stuff for monetary or non-monetary benefits.

Mair and Reischauer (2017) defines sharing economy as web markets individuals use which are mediated by digital platform operated by an organization. Individuals use these web markets to access and redistribute resources by using various forms of compensation.

While sharing economy concepts are able to reduce transaction costs, increase convenience and reduce search costs (Nadler, 2014), "Sharing economy" term covers wide range of digital platforms and offline activites (Schor, 2016). According to Acquier et al. (2017) sharing economy had a nature of contested and umbrella concept and it had three foundational cores; access economy, platform economy, community-based economy.

In another study Hamari et al. (2016) discussed about four aspects of sharing economy. These aspects of sharing economy are;

- Online collaboration,
- The notion of sharing online,
- Consumer ideology,
- Social commerce

According to Schor (2016) activities of sharing economy have four categories; recirculation of goods, exchange of services, sharing of productive assets, increased utilization of durable assets.

In addition to definitions and categorization, the connection with sharing economy and social/economic life would be useful for understanding sharing economy well. Mair and Reischauer (2017) discussed three implications/recasts of sharing economy to social/economic activities. First recast was related to boundaries between production and consumption, as the boundaries were blurring. In sharing economy, the platform was produced by an organization, there was not a general "producing" company in system, people could be producer. For example, Airbnb platform was an infrastructure, hosts and guests trade accommodation service. Second recast was related to distinction between casual labor and full employment. Finally, last recast was related do boundary between public and private. Overlapping of private and public concepts was important in sharing economy.

What is Common With Other Concepts?

Sharing economy has common characteristics with other concepts like colloborative economy, collaborative consumption and peer economy. Botsman (2013) discussed the commonalities of these concepts with sharing economy. Distributed power, one of common characteristics, refers to distributing of power from centralized institutions to networks consisting of individiuals and communities. Disruptive drivers which have four components, is another characteristic. These drivers are technological innovation, economic realities, values shift and environmental pressures. Last common characteristic refers to innovative and efficient asset utilization.

At this stage, what is the difference between concepts is important. It must be noted that, there is blur space between topics by definitions. Collaborative economy refers to an economy which transforming how people can produce, finance, consumer and learn. This economy is built on distributed networks and has four components; production, finance, education and consumption (Botsman, 2013).

According to Botsman (2013) collaborative consumption is an economic model. It includes swapping, sharing, renting and trading activites for products and services, it also enables access over ownership. Collaborative consumption is a similar concept to sharing economy and it was studied in many studies in a similar context to sharing economy. For example, Möhlmann (2015) studied collaborative consumption by two quantitative studies, one for B2C car sharing service (car2go) and other for C2C online community accommodation marketplace (Airbnb). The aims of study were two parts. First part was about satisfaction and other was about rechoose. According to results; utility, cost savings, trust and familiarity were significant factors for both study. Peer economy refers to marketplaces which enable direct trade and share of assets based on peer trust (Botsman, 2013).

In difference between sharing economy and collaborative consumption; CC includes share, swap, rent and trade functions, while SE includes sharing function. In sharing economy, “underutilized” part is also important issue.

What is the Historical Development of Sharing Economy?

According to Cheng (2016) sharing economy concept had been popular in media, after (R Botsman a Rogers (2010)’s book on collaborative consumption had been published. The emergence and adoption of sharing economy relies on four fources; new technological advancements, increased public awareness about deterioration of environment, increasing need for community engagement and national and global economic conditions (Nadler, 2014).

One of important factors for emergence of sharing economy is technology. Hamari et al. (2016) mentioned that sharing economy phenomenon emerged from technological developments which simplified sharing through information systems on the internet. Web 2.0 technologies also important for historical development of sharing economy. As Web 1.0 technology relys on one-to-one relationship, Web 2.0 is consistent with sharing economy (Belk, 2014). Uber case is an appropriate example for technological ease for taxi service. With integration of mobile apps between consumers and drivers, with advancements in payment systems for easier payment methods, taxi service or ride-sharing services has been easily adapted to traditional consumers’ behaviours.

After widespreadity of sharing economy, Zervas et al. (2017) studied the impact of sharing economy to hotel industry by Airbnb context. According to results, hotel room pricing become less agressive which could benefit to all consumers. This benefit was not limited to participants of sharing economy, so there was an aggreate benefit.

LEVELS OF SHARING ECONOMY

According to Ferrell et al. (2017), sharing economy had a structure, including agents facilitate in exchanging, independent providers and consumers. The facilitate action took place offen through web-based platforms.

In line with this conclusion, in this section a three-level structure will be used for structural understanding of Sharing Economy. This refers to the lowest level of individual consumers in the structure, and is related to why individuals engage in consumption and sharing activities. The medium level in this structure refers to the platforms in which the opportunities of joint activity in sharing economy are provided. The highest level in this structure is the macro dimension as a system of sharing economy.

Factors for evolving of sharing system are lower costs, acquiring equivalent product benefits and transactional and flexibility utility (Ferrell et al., 2017). In terms of consumer part of sharing economy, reasons of participating to sharing economy are important issues. We are living in a limited space, time, money world. So people would like to lower costs for services like accommodation, transportation etc.

Let's think of two customers who have a short-term idea of lodging in a region. One of them is planning to stay in the hotel in the context of traditional hospitality management. He must use generic pricing structures of hotels which changes by seasons, he has to adapt to standart periods of accommodation. The other one is using an accommodation based sharing economy service, which enables him to examine and choose appropriate prices, decide periods of accommodation. The second one also has social networking opportunities by choosing hosts in sharing economy. The difference with these two example customers refers main difference and in same time some of motivations for sharing economy.

Second level refers to platforms in sharing economy. These platforms are like meeting point for sharing activity. For example, Airbnb defines itself as, according to their website (Airbnb, 2016); *"Founded in 2008, Airbnb is a global travel community that offers magical end-to-end trips, including where you stay, what you do and the people you meet."* If the example from first level continues, one group of people could start an entrepreneur to gather people for a specific service. This service could be an accommodation service which the second person in example could use to reach other people.

Third level refers to macro dimension which implying interacting with other environments. For example, using of sharing economy could affect hotel industry in accommodation context. When using of alternative accommodation increases, unemployment could happen in traditional hotel industry. In another example car sharing service could affect traditional taxi sector. As with positive results, negative consequences may also arise.

In next section examples of studies will be presented consistent with this section.

SHARING ECONOMY IN A BUSINESS AND MARKETING PERSPECTIVE

There are three basic contexts at the point of evaluating the share economy from the operational and marketing perspectives. These; consumer, brand / business and system contexts. Along with the many different contexts such as ethics (Gonzalez-

Figure 1. Contexts in sharing economy

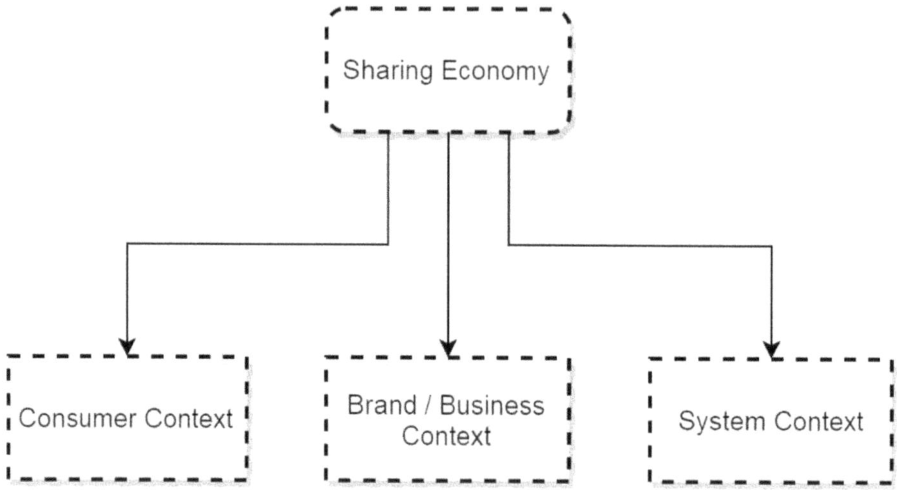

Padron, 2017), law, economics, urban (Jin et al., 2018) and transport (Standing et al., 2018) related to the sharing economy, these three contexts are constrained in accordance with the purpose of working in this work.

Consumer context in this study refers to consumers who use the sharing economy. In this context, there are various sub-themes such as perception, awareness, use and suggestion of sharing economy. The other context, the brand / business context, refers to companies that are another actor of the shared economy, and therefore to the business part. Given these two contexts of work, one can talk about the mass of businesses that individually or collectively use a service, and the mass of businesses that bring that service to consumers. In the final context of the study, the sharing economy is treated as a system, far from consumers or brands. In the context of the system, there will also be a business-centric perspective.

Consumer Context in Sharing Economy

As in most operations in the business world, there is a consumer in the center of sharing economy. The consumer plays a more intensive role in sharing economy than other concepts. From this point of view, the first context of the sharing economy is the consumption.

Consumer behaviour is a compexy structure which is affected by many factors including personal, social, behavioral etc. Therefore, several theories/models are used in consumer context of sharing economy. For example, norm activation model and theory of planned behaviour used in Kim et al. (2018)'s study. According to results, norm activation model and theory of planned behaviour were found effective in explaining consumer behaviour related to sharing service.

Decision Making and Motivations

The issue of how consumers are influenced in the decision-making process in the sharing economy is another research topic. Mauri et al. (2018) studied sharing economy with personal reputation subject. By studying with personal reputational attributes and product descriptions, they concluded that 40% of popularity variation was explained by personal reputation. This study was related to specific nature of Airbnb which included profile information and product descriptions content.

Beyond being influenced one of important topics in sharing economy is motivations of consumers to participate in sharing economy and related consumption activities. Hamari et al. (2016) studied motivations of participating behaviour of consumers to collaborative consumption. With 168 participant study, they concluded that participation in collobarative consumption was related to factors including enjoyment of activity, economic gains and sustainability.

Role of Trust and Related Factors

After motivations part, trust and reputation is another issue in decision making process. Phua (2018) studied reviews and implemented content analysis to complaints. According to results, trust is a major factor, besides customer service and technology channels. In another study, Ert et al. (2016) studied trust and reputation topic in accommodation context by examining photos of host and conducting experiment. According to study, trusthworthiness of host (perceived from photo) lead to higher price and higher purchase chance. Also, it was found that reputation of host which communicated with review score did not affect listing price or booking probability.

Importance of trust issues in sharing economy manifest itselfs in some applications in sharing economy. For example, usage of trust artefacts by Airbnb was studied in Teubner et al. (2016)'s study. They studied economic value variable and concluded that indicators about trust, like "superhost" status, rating scores of hosts and duration of membership, provided economic value.

Risk issue is a complex issue which must be studied in different contexts, like age, social characteristics etc. For example, in Amaro et al. (2018)'s study, in millenials context, perceived risk did not have significant effect on booking on Airbnb.

Traditional Marketing/Consumer Relations Concepts

One of the topic in consumer context is segmentation. Lutz and Newlands (2018) studied sharing economy by Airbnb brand in accodomation context. Their aim was segmenting customers and they used a mixed method approach for that. The comparing parts of the study was shared rooms and entire homes. According to results of the study, accodomation choice of consumers were could estimated by education, gender, travel modality and income variables. For brand side of conclusion, authors concluded that Airbnb was using marketing logic to implement their listings regarding to consumer segments. Lastly, non-alignment of host targeting and guest choice was leading to potential inefficiency. In another study Guttentag et al. (2018) studied motivations of tourists about using Airbnb while using segmentation approach. According to results, participants were splitted into five groups; money savers, collaborative consumers, interactive novelty seekers, home seekers and pragmatic novelty seekers.

Sharing economy is also studied in common/classic relations from literature in service context. For example, service quality and loyalty relationship is a common relationship in service context. Cheng et al. (2018) studied car-hailing services by online and offline context. Relationship between service quality and loyalty was mediated by attitudes towards the sharing economy. Thus relationship in academic literature was approved in sharing economy context.

Beyond the general and traditional research areas in sharing economy, there are also context-specific researches in sharing economy and related concepts. Example researches include the topics; the refusal of host in peer to peer accommodation (Karlsson et al., 2017), gamification and badge system for hosts (Liang et al., 2017), effect of seller's facial image and expression to consumer (Fagerstrøm et al., 2017)

In addition to themes in this context, selected studies are presented in Table 1.

Brand / Business Context in Sharing Economy

Another important concept after the consumer in Sharing economy is brands / businesses. Studies on brands / businesses that express the platform in which the transactions are made is also important for the sharing economy.

Management Perspective in Business Activities

Firstly, in management perspective, the way of managing organizations and competitiveness is important for companies in sharing economies. Parente (2018) studied sharing economy in a global perspective for companies context. In the study which ecosystem of sharing economy was discussed, authors concluded main

Table 1. Selected studies for consumer context in sharing economy

Author	Date	Topic	Summary
Chang and Wang	2018	Degree of Risk and Generations of Customers	Sentiment analysis to online reviews was applied in study to compare degrees of risk by customers' generations. In accommodation context, Generation X cared cleanliness, reviews and overall star rating. Generation Y and Z paid more attention to review, cost and cleanliness.
Tussyadiah and Park	2018	Host Descriptions and Trust	In Airbnb context, multi-stage approach study conducted to examine host self-presentations patterns and responses of consumers. Results concluded that hosts presented themselves in two way; a well-traveled individual and an individual of certain passion. Responses of consumers were different according to two types.
Böcker and Meelen	2017	Motivations for Intented Sharing Economy Participation	Motivations for participating to sharing economy were examined through different sectors. With a study among 1330 participants, it was found that motivations differed by between socio-economic groups, the role of people (user / provider), and sectors.
Priporas et al.	2017	Service Quality and Customer Perceptions	Customer perceptions of service quality in sharing economy by Airbnb accommodation were examined. It was found that convenience and assurance were the important factors for measuring service quality.
Zhu et al.	2017	Consumer Motivations for Adoption of Mobile Applications	Motivations for adoption of mobile applications were examined, while social cognitive theory was used as framework. Overall perceived value of ridesharing applications was affected by functional, social and economical values.

features of sharing economy companies, and differences between sharing economy firm internationalizations and international business theories. In another study, Key (2017) examined domains for digital marketing channels in sharing economy. In the study three areas in digital marketing was discussed for sharing economy; e-mail marketing, search engine marketing and social media marketing. Author also discussed about branded mobile application which was related to sharing economy context.

Roh (2016) studied sharing economy in social entrepreneurship context in their study. Authors concluded that sharing economy could provide opportunities for social enterprises and presented that information and communication technologies based (ICTs) sharing economy could be a new business model for social entrepreneurship.

Common Context with Consumer

Brand context has common side with consumer context in studies, as there is a brand side in brand-consumer relationships. Yang et al.(2018) studied Airbnb brand and its relations with consumer in a different context. They used Aristotle's rhetorical theory to examine relations. In the study, three key cues were determined; credibility, accommodation characteristics and emotinal bonding. These cues were related to trust in Airbnb hosts, after that trust to hosts was related to brand trust to Airbnb.

Concepts in which the human-brand relationship is intense may also be important in the shared economy, where human interaction is intense. In a brand-related context, Yannopoulou et al. (2013) studied Airbnb and Coachsurfing brands in user-generated brand context and social media. According to results, brand identity of Coachsurfing relied on notion of human relationships and cultural diversity, while brand narrative of Airbnb relied on people's stories.

In addition to these studies in themes, selected studies are presented in Table 2.

System Context in Sharing Economy

Sharing economy has a system dimension other than consumer and business dimensions. First situation is the competition in which sharing economy lives. Another situation is related to developments in the Sharing economy affect other systems that result in interactions with other systems.

Competition of Sharing Economy Platforms

Varma et al.(2016) studied Airbnb in a competitive perspective. They used both Airbnb users and traditional hotel executives for research and evaluated Airbnb's

Table 2. Selected studies for brand / business context in sharing economy

Author	Date	Topic	Summary
Lee and Kim	2018	Brand personality	Brand personality of Airbnb was examined with involvement level and gender variable.
Liu and Mattila	2017	Online targeted adversiment	Online advertising strategies for Airbnb brand were examined with click-through intention and purchase intention. The characteristics about Airbnb used as variables with consumers' senses of power.
Richard and Cleveland	2016	Hotel Chains and Branded Marketplaces	The future of hotel chain was evaluated and a scenario related to branded marketplaces was presented.
Habibi et al.	2017	Managerial Perspective on Sharing Economy	Sharing economy concept was examined in a managerial perspective. Exchange and sharing concepts were compared, recommendations were presented.
Lombardi and Schwabe	2017	Business model for Energy Storage Systems	A business model in sharing economy was developed for energy storage systems. It was concluded that the simulated business model could increase the profitability of battery storage system, comparing to single use type business model.

presence in hospitality sector. According to results; while major players of sector do not evaluate Airbnb as distruptive or competitor, small and mid-range ones evaluating adjustments for increased competition.

When the effects of the sharing economy are considered as the system, one of the important issues in the study concerns the destructive structure. For accommodation side, Guttentag and Smith (2017) examined Airbnb as disruptive innovation as regards to hotel industry. In study which 800 online survey was collected, it was found that two thirds of participants had used Airbnb as substitute to hotel. In traditional hotel attributes situation, Airbnb was outperforming budget hotels/motels, while underperforming in upscale hotels. Regarding the situation of mixed outcomes between Airbnb and mid-range hotels, it was concluded that Airbnb had signalling characteristics to disruptive innovation but it was not exactly consistent with concept of disruptive innovation. Apart from consistency with disruptive innovation, the nature of sharing economy is consonant with social media and new technologies. The disruptive impact of sharing economy in media context was studied in Laurell and Sandström (2018) 's study. It was found that while traditional media focused on impact of entrants in sharing economy to society, social media was playing an accelerating role for entrants.

Effects of Sharing Economy

Beyond the disruptiveness side of sharing economy, implication of sharing economy on transportation system is an interesting topic for transportation researches. What will be changes after Uber enters a market? How will consumer and taxi drivers behave to this change? Will the traditional taxi revenue decrease or not? These are questions rising with Uber spreading. Kim et al.(2018) studied this topic for New York and concluded compelling finding. After Uber settled into center of Manhattan, taxis started to serve outside areas of center. Increasing service coverage did help to taxi drivers about market share.

Impact of sharing economy to accomodation is another topic for research. Akbar and Tracogna (2018) researched sharing economy in hotel industry by transaction cost theory. Strategic and tactical suggestions were presented for hotel industry in this study. Lastly, three features from transaction cost theory; frequency, asset specifity and uncertainty were mentioned by authors. By revising their business models hotel industry could leverage their capacities to deal with these three features.

One of the other topics in system context is stages of consumption in sharing economy. The question is whether consumers attitudes or willingnesses are changing in different stages of consumption, according to external/internal variables. Zhang et al. (2018) studied sharing economy in co-creation context with customer context together. Although their study measured willingness to pay premium price, the main focus of study was stages of consumption related to sharing economy. These stages are pre-consumption, mid-consumption and post-consumption. The values which activity involved used in this study were emotional, functional and social values. Pre-consumption stage had functional and social values significant, mid-consumption stage had all three values significant and finally post-consumption stage had only social value based activities significant.

Selected studies in system context are presented in Table 3.

FUTURE RESEARCH DIRECTIONS

One of the suggestions for future studies is examining advancements in digital technologies in consumer context. As technology develops and new tools becoming developed, people will try and also be affected. Effects on consumer behaviour is always popular topic in consumer research and it will be in future, too.

One of the other suggestion for future studies is testing consumer behaviours in different cultures. Differences between cultures may lead to different conclusions in the understanding and interpretation of the sharing economy. Cultures with high level

Table 3. Selected studies for system context in sharing economy

Author	Date	Topic	Summary
Wang and Nicolau	2017	Price determinants	Price determinants of sharing economy was studied in accommodation context. 180.553 accommodation rental offers from 33 cities were examined and 25 variables were explored for relationship between prices and its determinants.
Bin et al.	2016	Employment in Tourism Industry	The effect of sharing economy to employment in tourism industry was examined. Results concluded that there would be positive outcome by generated new job positions, because of lower accommodation cost and increasing amount of tourists. On the other hand there would be negative outcome by loss of jobs in low-end hotels.
Gibbs et al.	2018	Pricing	A hedonic pricing model was used for sharing economy. Factors influencing pricing significantly in sharing economy were found as; physical characteristics, host characteristics and location.
Tussyadiah and Pesonen	2016	Travel Patterns	The effects of peer-to-peer accommodations on travel industry were examined. Increase in travel frequency, increase of participated range of activites,increase in length of stay and expansion in destination selection were affected.
Guttentag	2015	Airbnb as Disruptive Innovation	Airbnb brand was evaluated through disruptive innovation theory.

of individualism differs from cultures with high level of collectivism. For example, car-sharing service in a sharing economy would result different in different cultures according to individualism level.

Platforms on sharing economy is also an important topic for research. According to collaborative nature of platforms, consumer behaviour and effects of it always be alive. Therefore, the changing dynamics would form new research questions.

Lastly, sharing economy in a macro system is ongoing issue for research. Employment, environment, sustainability, transportation etc. are the other topics which are affected by sharing economy.

Motivations of participation to sharing economy differ regarding to diversity of activites and platforms (Schor, 2016). This refers to diversity nature of sharing economy activities. Consumers' attitudes and behaviours are being shaped according to industries, companies and their own networks. Therefore every new research question could start with, "what if.." and could result in "how would consumers in X industry behave according to situation Y in Z context?"

For new researches in sharing economy, it would be useful to examine review based (or including previous studies part) studies in literature. Cheng (2016), Prayag and Ozanne (2018), Yang et al. (2018) included this type of content in their studies.

CONCLUSION

The concept of sharing economy, which is one of popular topics in recent years in this study, has been discussed with the perspective of business and marketing. It is useful to focus on the concept of sharing economy, which has a very broad scope, with a limited scope.

In sharing economy, invidiuals even strangers can connect, share information, exchange and cooperate easily, so this has a transformative characteristic (Schor, 2016). This transformativeness could be used for changing lots of things including competiteveness, economical structure, regulations, marketing activities etc. In this study, the effects of different fields are examined from the perspective of business and marketing and some examples are given. But the implication of sharing economy is not limited to these perspectives, it is affecting many areas of economy and it will continue, either.

As there was a three-degree structure in this study, conclusion will match it. First degree in sharing economy referred to consumer related context. The context included three themes; decision making and motivations, role of trust, traditional marketing and consumer relations. The main questions in this contexts are;

- Why people participate to sharing economy?
- How people experience sharing economy?
- What is/are the main motivation(s) for attending sharing economy activities?
- How important is trust in sharing economy context?

Second degree in sharing economy was related to business/brand side of sharing economy. The main parts of this context were management perspective and common context with consumer. The questions rising with this context are;

- How is management perspective affected by sharing economy?
- How is the relationship between companies and consumers shaped by sharing economy?
- How will brand related concepcts affected by sharing economy?

Last degree in sharing economy was related to system side of sharing economy. Competitiveness in sharing economy and the effects of sharing economy to other systems were the topics for this context. As sharing economy develops, it interacts with other systems and other businesses. Therefore, the implications of sharing economy to other systems is important issue. The questions rising with this context are;

- How will the competitiveness in sharing economy take place?
- How will sharing economy influence other systems?
- How will other systems respond to sharing economy?

All these questions in these contexts are current questions for recent years and some of these questions will be discussed in next years. Therefore, after a comprehensive review of business and marketing related concepts, it is important to examine sub topics compatible with the new contexts. These new contexts would include new research questions.

If we discuss the concept of Sharing economy in general, products or services of people's production and consumption methods have a structure that affects other rings, like the first ring of a chain. The change in the mode of production experienced in the industrial revolution influenced many other concepts and systems as a chain. The change in the consumption pattern in the Sharing economy may have a similar spirit. Differences such as having a product on its own, sharing it while not using it, and using a service more than one person will affect consumption behavior. In this respect, it will be the case that businesses and brands are affected by these differentiated consumer behaviors.

In addition to these present changes, there is a concept of technology that is very effective and constantly evolving today. With the increase and development of technology, new platforms and new forms of consumption can emerge. In this regard, careful examination of these changes and the effects of these changes will be important for new investigations.

REFERENCES

Acquier, A., Daudigeos, T., & Pinkse, J. (2017). Promises and paradoxes of the sharing economy: An organizing framework. *Technological Forecasting and Social Change*, *125*, 1–10. doi:10.1016/j.techfore.2017.07.006

Airbnb. (2016). *About Us*. Retrieved 12 July 2018, from https://press.atairbnb.com/about-us/

Akbar, Y. H., & Tracogna, A. (2018). The sharing economy and the future of the hotel industry: Transaction cost theory and platform economics. *International Journal of Hospitality Management*, *71*, 91–101. doi:10.1016/j.ijhm.2017.12.004

Amaro, S., Andreu, L., & Huang, S. (2018). Millenials' intentions to book on Airbnb. *Current Issues in Tourism*, *0*(0), 1–15. doi:10.1080/13683500.2018.1448368

Belk, R. (2014). You are what you can access: Sharing and collaborative consumption online. *Journal of Business Research*, *67*(8), 1595–1600. doi:10.1016/j.jbusres.2013.10.001

Belk, R. W. (1988). Possessions and the Extended Self. *The Journal of Consumer Research*, *15*(2), 139–168. doi:10.1086/209154

Bin, F., Qiang, Y., & Law, R. (2016). Effect of sharing economy on tourism industry employment. *Annals of Tourism Research*, *57*, 264–267. doi:10.1016/j.annals.2015.11.018

Böcker, L., & Meelen, T. (2017). Sharing for people, planet or profit? Analysing motivations for intended sharing economy participation. *Environmental Innovation and Societal Transitions*, *23*, 28–39. doi:10.1016/j.eist.2016.09.004

Botsman, R. (2013). *The Sharing Economy Lacks A Shared Definition*. Retrieved 12 July 2018, from https://www.fastcompany.com/3022028/the-sharing-economy-lacks-a-shared-definition

Botsman, R., & Rogers, R. (2010). *What's Mine Is Yours: The Rise of Collaborative Consumption*. New York: Harper Business.

Chang, W.-L., & Wang, J.-Y. (2018). Mine is yours? Using sentiment analysis to explore the degree of risk in the sharing economy. *Electronic Commerce Research and Applications*, *28*, 141–158. doi:10.1016/j.elerap.2018.01.014

Cheng, M. (2016). Sharing economy: A review and agenda for future research. *International Journal of Hospitality Management*, *57*, 60–70. doi:10.1016/j.ijhm.2016.06.003

Cheng, X., Fu, S., & de Vreede, G.-J. (2018). A mixed method investigation of sharing economy driven car-hailing services: Online and offline perspectives. *International Journal of Information Management*, *41*, 57–64. doi:10.1016/j.ijinfomgt.2018.03.005

Ert, E., Fleischer, A., & Magen, N. (2016). Trust and reputation in the sharing economy: The role of personal photos in Airbnb. *Tourism Management*, *55*, 62–73. doi:10.1016/j.tourman.2016.01.013

Fagerstrøm, A., Pawar, S., Sigurdsson, V., Foxall, G. R., & Yani-de-Soriano, M. (2017). That personal profile image might jeopardize your rental opportunity! On the relative impact of the seller's facial expressions upon buying behavior on Airbnb™. *Computers in Human Behavior*, *72*, 123–131. doi:10.1016/j.chb.2017.02.029

Feeny, D., Berkes, F., McCay, B. J., & Acheson, J. M. (1990). The Tragedy of the Commons: Twenty-two years later. *Human Ecology*, *18*(1), 1–19. doi:10.1007/BF00889070 PMID:12316894

Ferrell, O. C., Ferrell, L., & Huggins, K. (2017). Seismic Shifts in the Sharing Economy: Shaking Up Marketing Channels and Supply Chains. *Journal of Marketing Channels*, *24*(1-2), 3–12. doi:10.1080/1046669X.2017.1346973

Gibbs, C., Guttentag, D., Gretzel, U., Morton, J., & Goodwill, A. (2018). Pricing in the sharing economy: A hedonic pricing model applied to Airbnb listings. *Journal of Travel & Tourism Marketing*, *35*(1), 46–56. doi:10.1080/10548408.2017.1308292

Gonzalez-Padron, T. L. (2017). Ethics in the Sharing Economy: Creating a Legitimate Marketing Channel. *Journal of Marketing Channels*, *24*(1-2), 84–96. doi:10.1080/1046669X.2017.1347005

Guttentag, D. (2015). Airbnb: Disruptive innovation and the rise of an informal tourism accommodation sector. *Current Issues in Tourism*, *18*(12), 1192–1217. doi:10.1080/13683500.2013.827159

Guttentag, D., Smith, S., Potwarka, L., & Havitz, M. (2018). Why Tourists Choose Airbnb: A Motivation-Based Segmentation Study, Why Tourists Choose Airbnb: A Motivation-Based Segmentation Study. *Journal of Travel Research*, *57*(3), 342–359. doi:10.1177/0047287517696980

Guttentag, D. A., & Smith, S. L. J. (2017). Assessing Airbnb as a disruptive innovation relative to hotels: Substitution and comparative performance expectations. *International Journal of Hospitality Management*, *64*, 1–10. doi:10.1016/j.ijhm.2017.02.003

Habibi, M. R., Davidson, A., & Laroche, M. (2017). What managers should know about the sharing economy. *Business Horizons*, *60*(1), 113–121. doi:10.1016/j.bushor.2016.09.007

Hamari, J., Sjöklint, M., & Ukkonen, A. (2016). The sharing economy: Why people participate in collaborative consumption. *Journal of the Association for Information Science and Technology*, *67*(9), 2047–2059. doi:10.1002/asi.23552

Hardin, G. (1968). The tragedy of the commons. *Science*, (162): 1243–1248. doi:10.1126cience.162.3859.1243 PMID:5699198

Jin, S. T., Kong, H., Wu, R., & Sui, D. Z. (2018). Ridesourcing, the sharing economy, and the future of cities. *Cities (London, England)*, *76*, 96–104. doi:10.1016/j.cities.2018.01.012

Karlsson, L., Kemperman, A., & Dolnicar, S. (2017). May I sleep in your bed? Getting permission to book. *Annals of Tourism Research*, *62*, 1–12. doi:10.1016/j.annals.2016.10.002

Key, T. M. (2017). Domains of Digital Marketing Channels in the Sharing Economy. *Journal of Marketing Channels*, *24*(1-2), 27–38. doi:10.1080/1046669X.2017.1346977

Kim, K., Baek, C., & Lee, J.-D. (2018). Creative destruction of the sharing economy in action: The case of Uber. *Transportation Research Part A, Policy and Practice*, *110*, 118–127. doi:10.1016/j.tra.2018.01.014

Kim, Y. G., Woo, E., & Nam, J. (2018). Sharing economy perspective on an integrative framework of the NAM and TPB. *International Journal of Hospitality Management*, *72*, 109–117. doi:10.1016/j.ijhm.2018.01.008

Laurell, C., & Sandström, C. (2018). Comparing coverage of disruptive change in social and traditional media: Evidence from the sharing economy. *Technological Forecasting and Social Change*, *129*, 339–344. doi:10.1016/j.techfore.2017.09.038

Lee, S., & Kim, D.-Y. (2018). Brand personality of Airbnb: Application of user involvement and gender differences. *Journal of Travel & Tourism Marketing*, *35*(1), 32–45. doi:10.1080/10548408.2017.1284030

Liang, S., Schuckert, M., Law, R., & Chen, C.-C. (2017). Be a “Superhost”: The importance of badge systems for peer-to-peer rental accommodations. *Tourism Management*, *60*, 454–465. doi:10.1016/j.tourman.2017.01.007

Liu, S. Q., & Mattila, A. S. (2017). Airbnb: Online targeted advertising, sense of power, and consumer decisions. *International Journal of Hospitality Management*, *60*, 33–41. doi:10.1016/j.ijhm.2016.09.012

Lombardi, P., & Schwabe, F. (2017). Sharing economy as a new business model for energy storage systems. *Applied Energy*, *188*, 485–496. doi:10.1016/j.apenergy.2016.12.016

Lutz, C., & Newlands, G. (2018). Consumer segmentation within the sharing economy: The case of Airbnb. *Journal of Business Research*, *88*, 187–196. doi:10.1016/j.jbusres.2018.03.019

Mair, J., & Reischauer, G. (2017). Capturing the dynamics of the sharing economy: Institutional research on the plural forms and practices of sharing economy organizations. *Technological Forecasting and Social Change*, *125*, 11–20. doi:10.1016/j.techfore.2017.05.023

Mauri, A. G., Minazzi, R., Nieto-García, M., & Viglia, G. (2018). Humanize your business. The role of personal reputation in the sharing economy. *International Journal of Hospitality Management*, *73*, 36–43. doi:10.1016/j.ijhm.2018.01.017

Möhlmann, M. (2015). Collaborative consumption: Determinants of satisfaction and the likelihood of using a sharing economy option again. *Journal of Consumer Behaviour*, *14*(3), 193–207. doi:10.1002/cb.1512

Nadler, S. (2014). *The sharing economy: what is it and where is it going?* (Thesis). Massachusetts Institute of Technology. Retrieved from http://dspace.mit.edu/handle/1721.1/90223

Parente, R. C., Geleilate, J.-M. G., & Rong, K. (2018). The Sharing Economy Globalization Phenomenon: A Research Agenda. *Journal of International Management*, *24*(1), 52–64. doi:10.1016/j.intman.2017.10.001

Phua, V. C. (2018). Perceiving Airbnb as sharing economy: The issue of trust in using Airbnb. *Current Issues in Tourism*, *0*(0), 1–5. doi:10.1080/13683500.2018.1440539

Prayag, G., & Ozanne, L. K. (2018). A systematic review of peer-to-peer (P2P) accommodation sharing research from 2010 to 2016: Progress and prospects from the multi-level perspective. *Journal of Hospitality Marketing & Management, 27*(6), 649–678. doi:10.1080/19368623.2018.1429977

Priporas, C.-V., Stylos, N., Rahimi, R., & Vedanthachari, L. N. (2017). Unraveling the diverse nature of service quality in a sharing economy: A social exchange theory perspective of Airbnb accommodation. *International Journal of Contemporary Hospitality Management, 29*(9), 2279–2301. doi:10.1108/IJCHM-08-2016-0420

PwC. (2015). *The Sharing Economy - Consumer Intelligence Series*. Retrieved from https://www.pwc.com/us/en/industry/entertainment-media/publications/consumer-intelligence-series/assets/pwc-cis-sharing-economy.pdf

Richard, B., & Cleveland, S. (2016). The future of hotel chains, The future of hotel chains: Branded marketplaces driven by the sharing economy, Branded marketplaces driven by the sharing economy. *Journal of Vacation Marketing, 22*(3), 239–248. doi:10.1177/1356766715623827

Roh, T. H. (2016). The Sharing Economy: Business Cases of Social Enterprises Using Collaborative Networks. *Procedia Computer Science, 91*, 502–511. doi:10.1016/j.procs.2016.07.129

Schor, J. (2016). Debating the sharing economy. *Journal of Self-Governance and Management Economics, 4*(3), 7–22. doi:10.22381/JSME4320161

Standing, C., Standing, S., & Biermann, S. (2018). The implications of the sharing economy for transport. *Transport Reviews, 0*(0), 1–17. doi:10.1080/01441647.2018.1450307

Teubner, T., Saade, N., Kawlitschek, F., & Weinhardt, C. (2016). It's only pixels, badges, and stars: On the economic value of reputation on Airbnb. *27th Australasian Conference on Information Systems*. Retrieved from http://ro.uow.edu.au/acis2016/papers/1/56

Tussyadiah, I. P., & Park, S. (2018). When guests trust hosts for their words: Host description and trust in sharing economy. *Tourism Management, 67*, 261–272. doi:10.1016/j.tourman.2018.02.002

Tussyadiah, I. P., & Pesonen, J. (2016). Impacts of Peer-to-Peer Accommodation Use on Travel Patterns, Impacts of Peer-to-Peer Accommodation Use on Travel Patterns. *Journal of Travel Research, 55*(8), 1022–1040. doi:10.1177/0047287515608505

Varma, A., Jukic, N., Pestek, A., Shultz, C. J., & Nestorov, S. (2016). Airbnb: Exciting innovation or passing fad? *Tourism Management Perspectives*, *20*, 228–237. doi:10.1016/j.tmp.2016.09.002

Wang, D., & Nicolau, J. L. (2017). Price determinants of sharing economy based accommodation rental: A study of listings from 33 cities on Airbnb.com. *International Journal of Hospitality Management*, *62*, 120–131. doi:10.1016/j.ijhm.2016.12.007

Yang, S.-B., Lee, H., Lee, K., & Koo, C. (2018). The application of Aristotle's rhetorical theory to the sharing economy: An empirical study of Airbnb. *Journal of Travel & Tourism Marketing*, *0*(0), 1–20. doi:10.1080/10548408.2018.1455622

Yannopoulou, N., Moufahim, M., & Bian, X. (2013). User-Generated Brands and Social Media: Couchsurfing and AirBnb. *Contemporary Management Research*, *9*(1), 85–90. doi:10.7903/cmr.11116

Zervas, G., Proserpio, D., & Byers, J. W. (2017). The Rise of the Sharing Economy: Estimating the Impact of Airbnb on the Hotel Industry. *JMR, Journal of Marketing Research*, *54*(5), 687–705. doi:10.1509/jmr.15.0204

Zhang, T. C., Jahromi, M. F., & Kizildag, M. (2018). Value co-creation in a sharing economy: The end of price wars? *International Journal of Hospitality Management*, *71*, 51–58. doi:10.1016/j.ijhm.2017.11.010

Zhu, G., So, K. K. F., & Hudson, S. (2017). Inside the sharing economy: Understanding consumer motivations behind the adoption of mobile applications. *International Journal of Contemporary Hospitality Management*, *29*(9), 2218–2239. doi:10.1108/IJCHM-09-2016-0496

KEY TERMS AND DEFINITIONS

Collaborative Consumption: It refers to consumption activity in collaborative way for goods and services.

Collaborative Economy: It refers to an economic system based on collaborative structure.

Consumer Behaviour: Actions of consumers related to consuming activities.

Disruptive Innovation: It refers to the situation of destructing old market/structures while implementing new actions.

Sharing Economy: It refers to sharing action of things people own as a good, service, etc.

Sharing Economy Platform: It refers to online place which trades take place at.

Chapter 5
Competences of Startups as Entities Operating in Network Structures

Waldemar Jędrzejczyk
Czestochowa University of Technology, Poland

ABSTRACT

The chapter indicates the most important changes in the organizations caused by technological progress. The development of the network business model, according to which both very large and very small organizations are starting to function, have been emphasized. The main attention has been focused on startup entities due to their specific character and more and more dynamic development. Firstly, the issues well recognized in science, enabling the creation of a picture of both startups and their ecosystems, have been presented. Then the considerations have been narrowed down to the issue of the startup competences. The basic/key startup competences in organizational and individual dimension, which are the contribution to the startup market success, have been defined. It was based on literature analysis and primary research results. The empirical part concerns Polish startups. The main goal of this chapter is to define the key competences of a startup that will allow to distinguish it from other entities in the searching for an investor or business partner process.

DOI: 10.4018/978-1-5225-7850-5.ch005

INTRODUCTION

Nowadays, organizations are increasingly departing from the traditional organizational structure - characteristic for industrial enterprises - towards a network structure. This trend, in its most radical form, is reflected in the concept of Industry 4.0, which projects a complete paradigm shift from "centralized production" to "decentralized production". In the paradigm of "centralized production", complete production tasks are carried out in a single company. Such systems are based on centralized management and control. Decentralization paradigm indicates a departure from centralized management and control. "Networks of autonomous production resources capable of responding to different situations, self-configuring, knowledge-based, sensor-based, spatially dispersed and including appropriate planning and management systems will be set up" (Kagermann, Helbig, Hellinger, & Wahlster, 2013). Functioning in the network requires a change in a way of working and managing and makes the organizations focus on their own key competences and shift other activities to co-operators.

There are both very large and very small enterprises in network structures. Each individual one brings to the network the strengths of different entity types. The synergy effect occurs - the network structure limits the weaknesses of individuals. It is more flexible and innovative. Large organizations command significant resources - unique infrastructure, capital, industry and business knowledge, specialized competences as well as market and customer access. These resources enable testing of new solutions on a large scale and in real conditions. Small businesses, on the other hand, are characterized by high decision-making autonomy, more efficient management, high speed, high flexibility and higher product quality - they usually focus on only one product or service. If the cooperation model is properly designed, it can be beneficial for all parties (World Economic Forum, 2018). Network structures are typically used on the B2B market.

Many of the small entities, which see their chances for business success in the network model, are the so-called start-ups. Startups are newly created companies or temporary organizations looking for a business model that ensures their profitable growth. They pose an important element of creating innovative products and services, but their actions are not based on a stable business model - its business model determines the way in which a new entity intends to create and deliver value to its target customers: how it will function, win customers and earn money. The startup organization characteristics are as follows (Łopusiewicz, 2013, pp. 8-9):

- Low start-up costs,
- Increased risk in comparison to standard projects,
- Increased return on investment compared to standard projects.

The most significant aspect is the increased risk of the project. "Most startups collapse. Most new products do not succeed on the market. Most new business ventures never reach their full potential" (Ries, 2011). The startup success is determined by two groups of factors: external and internal. External factors create a startup environment, called the ecosystem - startups have no possibility of influencing the ecosystem. Internal factors pose the main startup potential (Grow Advisors, 2017) - they can be modified, they depend on a startup. The evolution of the ecosystem is a relatively slow process. All startups operate in the same environment - on a regional/country scale[1]. It shows that their success is primarily determined by the idea, knowledge and other unique resources and the ability to interact with the environment. These elements can be referred to as startup competences.

In this chapter, the main focus will concern internal factors. The main goal is to define the key competences of a startup, which will distinguish it from other entities in the process of searching for an investor or business partner.

WHAT IS ALREADY KNOWN ABOUT STARTUP ENTITIES?

Start-ups are becoming more and more popular in the field of science - both research units and consulting and advisory companies, mainly because they constitute a relatively new type of organization. The startup concept as an innovative undertaking in the management theory and practice has been widely used only for a decade. This term would refer exclusively to projects closely related to the IT or technology sector until recently. Nowadays, any project characterized by the features defined in the introduction is determined as a startup, regardless of the sector type. It is also a result of the high development dynamics of these entities and their impact on the economy (Boyoung, Hyojin, & Youngok, 2018) and lack of well-established comprehensive knowledge in this area.

The analysis of the previous research shows that the knowledge about the startups is becoming wider and wider. The following issues have been well identified (Deloitte, 2016; Startup Genome, 2017; Beauchamp, Krysztofiak-Szopa, & Skala, 2017; Beauchamp, Krysztofiak-Szopa, & Skala, 2018):

- Age of people who create startups,
- Places where startups founders gained their previous experience,
- Education of people who set up startups,
- Business model (activities) of startups,
- Areas of activity, broken down into those where startups generate regular revenues and those where revenues are highly irregular,
- Sources of financing (financing model),

- Nationality of the startup founder,
- Market,
- Institutions with which startups cooperate create partnership relations,
- Start-ups lifespan,
- Stages (levels) of start-ups development/life cycle.

This knowledge allows one to create an image, both of startups themselves and of their ecosystems (Piscione, 2013, pp. 15-51). It helps to understand the idea of startups, their strengths and weaknesses as well as the rules of their functioning. However, many questions remain unanswered, including the most important ones: what attributes/competences should a startup have in order to make the project successful on the market, so that the idea or a small business could be transformed into a large, global enterprise.

Research and analyses in the start-up area are difficult due to the lack of a clear definition of this type of entities. The studies usually give the definitions proposed by S. Blank and E. Ries as a baseline. According to S. Blank, a startup is "a temporary organization dealing with the search for a scalable, repeatable and profitable business model" (Blank, Dorf, 2012, p. 19). E. Ries (2011, p. 8), on the other hand, understands the term as "a human institution created to build new products or services in extremely uncertain conditions". Thus, it can be concluded that a basic feature of each start-up is its innovative character and short life cycle:

- People are the basic resource (with almost zero remaining resources at the beginning of the startup operation),
- Startups are to create new, innovative products or services,
- The business model is dynamic,
- The activities are carried out under the uncertainty conditions (experimentation concerns both The market, the product/service and the customer),
- These are newly created entities (startups have no history or experience), which operate as startups for a few years at most (they collapse or if they achieve success and an established position on the market, they cease to be considered startups – they are considered "normal" companies).

Due to lack of an unambiguous start-up definition (different eligibility criteria and various values adopted in individual parameters, e.g. years of run activity) and lack of a separate legal form for these entities – in most countries, including Poland, it is not possible to unambiguously determine the total number of start-ups, and as a result, of the research population.

The startup world market is developing very dynamically today – this regularity also applies to Poland. It is highly probable that this trend will continue to grow in the upcoming years. The main expansion determinants of the startup market are as follows (Compass, 2015):

1. Low Building Cost of a Startup Company: The cost of building a startup counts in thousands, not millions of dollars. This has resulted in a decrease in expenditures on new product development in the last decade, which has fallen tenfold;
2. Development of new IT technologies, which enable the provision of services at significantly lower prices;
3. An access to finance through venture capital funds (VCs) has become easier. It has reduced the amount of capital needed to set up a start-up, an investment risk of VC funds and the capital cost, with the fund being able to invest less capital in a larger number of companies. Therefore, there is no need to look for external co-investors;
4. A change of management methods and philosophy. High dynamics of changes in the environment and its uncertainty translate into increased difficulties in managing organizations. As a result, management concepts evolve – the management philosophy changes and new management methods emerge. Startups require both a new approach to management and new management methods. The fundamental principles of management, from hierarchical organizational structures to long-term planning, do not "work" for startups. One of the predestined management methods for startups is Lean Startup[2];
5. The rate at which customers assimilate new technologies through Internet access is increasing. Therefore, the entrepreneurs have access to cheap distribution of products and services and a startup can become a micro international enterprise at once.

Dynamic environment, civilizational progress, quickly progressing world virtualization, increased societies welfare, growing consumerism and diametrically shortened product life cycle make it necessary for organizations to constantly seek new opportunities to build a competitive advantage. Classical competing forms lose their value in favor of new ones, such as: inter-organizational cooperation, sustainable development, ecology, trust and organization's agility – flexibility and speed. Low-budget forms of distinguishing oneself from the competition, based on knowledge, intuition, creativity, innovation and new technologies, are becoming increasingly important. These are the main sources of a competitive advantage, characteristic for highly innovative organizations (Jeon, 2018). And startups are undoubtedly such organizations.

BASIC STARTUP COMPETENCES

Basic startup competences, both at the organizational and individual level, result directly from the startup definition. These include the following competences:

- Understanding the Idea of Startup: The awareness that the idea itself and launching the project is a very important, but small contribution to the final success. Creating a business plan, visual creation and an efficient website is a matter of a few weeks. However, further stages, such as product creation and development, search for financing sources, promotion, reaching out to investors and customers, convincing them to the offer, are a matter of a few or even several months of intensive work on the project;
- Understanding the Startup Business Philosophy: When making a decision to start a startup, one should essentially focus on implementing innovation and continuous development, not on making a quick profit – profit is supposed to be a derivative of innovation and development;
- An Interdisciplinary Team Acquisition and Integration: Startup requires three types of competences: business, technical and graphic. It is rare for one person to have all competences. Therefore, startups should be created by specialists from various fields, so that there is someone to deal with the project in specific areas, such as market and competition research, product/service design, negotiations and product development, marketing and distribution.

On the basis of the singularized competences, it can be stated that a startup is not only an entity or a project, but also a certain attitude and culture, whose fundamental values are: openness, ambition, sacrifice, development, risk and cooperation.

Basic startup competences at the organizational level also include (on the basis of a literature analysis indicated by various authors) (Zacharakis, & Meyer, 2000; Teece, 2010; Lee, & Noh, 2014):

- Product/service innovativeness (added value generated by the product, uniqueness degree)
- Business plan/business model (How will the startup earn money? What is its main source of funding? Does the business model already exist somewhere else? Is the project focused on generating revenues? Is the project scalable? How does the startup intend to reach its customers? What channels will it use to do this? Who forms the target audience? How does the competition look like, both at home and abroad? How does the product/service stand out from the competition?),

- Financial projections (revenue statement, costs and their forecasts, financial result, investment outlays, project valuation, product valuation),
- Team/ team's competences (both hard and soft, including motivation, successes and experiences of individual startup members, with the greatest attention focused on the team leader),
- Product/service development stage (Is there already a prototype? Has the product/service already been tested on the market? Does it already have customers/users?).

Basic startup competences, according to the investors or large organizations which are interested in supporting or cooperating with startups, should "match" the business strategy of these organizations.

Possessing an interdisciplinary team was distinguished among the competences at the organizational level, which determine the startup strength. Team competences consist of the competences of the team individual members. In a startup team, the founder's/startup leader's (CEO's) competences are given the highest priority. The competences that should characterize the startup CEO (most frequently indicated by different authors) include (Baron, & Markman, 2003; Kim, & Cho, 2014; Cho, & Gumeta, 2015; Boyoung, Hyojin, & Youngok, 2018):

- Having a vision (one must know what and how to achieve),
- Flexibility of action,
- Decision-making rapidity,
- How to function in chaos,
- Inspiring co-workers/subordinates,
- Focus,
- The ability to work independently and effectively,
- Communicativeness,
- Opportunity recognition,
- Coping with stress,
- Self-control,
- Understanding oneself,
- Knowing one's own boundaries,
- Comfort with ambiguity,
- Peace,
- Work management and measurement,
- Self-knowledge,
- Perseverance,
- Quick and effective learning,

- Work-life balance
- Integrity and trust,
- Customer orientation.

Most of the singularized competences are interdisciplinary and non-technical. These competences are usually considered so-called soft competences, which are usually difficult to develop and preferably innate. The distinguished competences correlate with the startup specificity – agility, innovativeness and concentration/orientation.

KEY COMPETENCES OF POLISH STARTUPS: RESEARCH RESULTS

Research Method

The main aim of the research is to develop a reference competency model of startups. This model will define the competences that should be characteristic of a startup in order to achieve a relatively high probability of market success[3].

The main goal of the research presented in this study is to determine the key competences of a startup, which will distinguish it from other entities in the searching for an investor or business partner process. Two basic research stages were distinguished in a research process:

Stage 1: Identification of start-ups key competences, which constitute their strength in the founder's opinion – start-up's competences, especially in the first phases of the development cycle, can be identified with the founder's competences;

Stage 2: Identification of start-ups key competences in the consulting and investment groups assessment – a set of competences definition that a start-up should have in order to be recognized as innovative by a potential investor and receive support from him/her.

In order to emerge on the market, a startup needs to obtain financing for the project. In the first phases of the development cycle, at the stages of ideation, vision and molding, a startup can only be based on the founder's contribution[4]. However, operating costs will appear over time, for which external financing will have to be found. Without investment capital, startups do not stand a chance for development. In order for a startup to obtain financing from external sources, it must convince potential investors of its idea.

Key Competences of Polish Startups: Founders' Opinions

The research was conducted in March 2018. It was of a qualitative nature. The individual interview technique was applied, using a standardized interview questionnaire. The research sample included 24 startups registered in the Wielkopolska region. The sample selection was intentional – the request to take part in the research was addressed to startups registered in institutions such as incubators or operating within investment funds. In the surveyed startups the founders were the respondents. Characteristics of the studied startup population included: 1) the sector in which start-ups operate, 2) the start-up functioning period (registration date), 3) the stage of development the tested start-up is currently at, and 4) the start-up financing source.

The study involved 19 startups dealing with the latest technologies and 5 startups operating in other areas. There were 3 start-ups on the market that had been functioning for less than a year. 17 startups were at an early stage of activity. 14 startups financed the project from their own resources, 6 used a bank loan and 4 used other external financing sources. The studied startup population structure was similar to the population structure on which the organizations such as Startup Poland and Deloitte Polska conducted research in Poland.

In the research part, which aimed to identify the key competences of the startup, the respondents were asked two basic questions:

1. What attributes/competences should a startup have?
2. What competences should be characteristic of people who create a startup?

The research results are presented graphically in Figure 1 and Figure 2 – only those competences indicated by 25% of the respondents, both in the organizational and individual dimension, were considered to be the key competences.

There are 10 key competences (organizational competences), which in the founders' opinion constitute the strength of each startup (Figure 1). The most important ones are knowledge of the market/the competition as well as technical knowledge in a given field (know-how) – 71% of respondents' answers each. Knowledge of the market allows us to find a market niche. Technical knowledge is essential to create a product. These competences can be considered complementary. Other important competences (response rate of at least 50%) are: readiness for change, financial capital and expert knowledge. Readiness for change is a highly desirable competence due to the high risk of project's failure – before the proper entity's functioning model is found, many smaller or larger corrections or even a radical change of performing direction may occur. Financial capital is necessary to cover operating costs. With the startup development, not only the financial needs increase, but also the needs

Figure 1. Respondents' answers to the question: What attributes/competences should a startup have?
Source: own elaboration

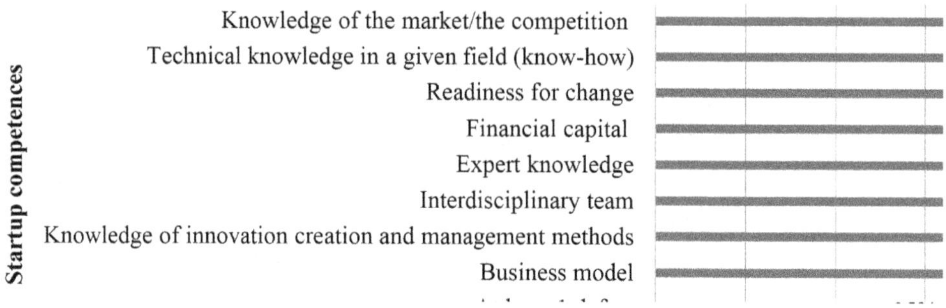

Figure 2. Respondents' answers to the question: What competences should be characteristic of people who create a startup?
Source: own elaboration

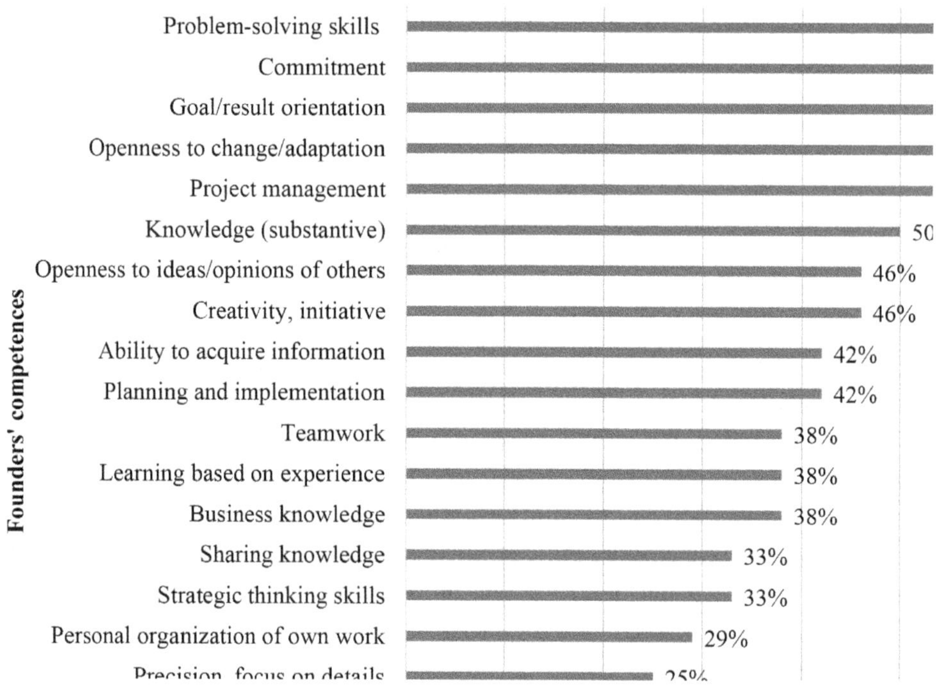

regarding expert knowledge, such as management and business practice. A common phenomenon is the investor becoming the startup mentor. In the key competences set, the following features have been also singularized:

- Interdisciplinary team,
- Business model,
- Knowledge of innovation creation and management methods,
- Prototype,
- At least 1 defeat.

These competences can be considered as important as those with high response rates. An interdisciplinary team is necessary to ensure tasks are carried out at a high level in all startup operation areas, especially in the successive development cycle phases, as well as in molding, validation, scaling and maturity phases. A specific business model enables the startup idea to be understood by all startup members. Knowledge of innovation creation and management methods is indispensable due to the start-up specificity – start-ups are considered innovative by definition. Creating a prototype enables the project's empirical verification. At the same time, it is an announcement of the first revenues. The startup creation process, regardless of the final result, increases the level of business, technological and managerial competences. Therefore, even an earlier idea's failure is treated as a method of developing the competences of startupcreators.

Organizational competences are derivatives of individual competences. The study distinguished 20 key competences that should characterize startup members – startup founders in particular (Figure 2). The most important ones are problem-solving skills and commitment – 71% and 67% of respondents' responses respectively. "Constant problems", in view of the startup organization distinguishing features, can be considered as a domain of startups, in each phase of development. Thusly, the ability to solve problems is incredibly important. Involvement is no less crucial. The founder should concentrate only on the startup project – in fact, it is impossible to create a startup "after hours". The competences indicated by no less than a half of the respondents also include: goal/results orientation, project management skills, openness to change, adaptability and knowledge of the subject matter.

The singularized individual competences are in line with the managerial competences scope – interdisciplinary competences dominate in the distinguished set. They are referred to as cross-cutting ones. This means that startups should be created by people with highly developed competences, both hard and soft ones. People who are:

- Strongly motivated to act,
- Creative and open,
- Determined to achieve the set targets,
- Open to continuous development,
- Experienced in project management,
- Positively oriented towards people.

Distinguished individual competences translate into specific startup competences, e.g. knowledge of the market correlates with the ability to obtain information and focus on the customer. Readiness for change correlates with openness to change or changes adaptation and openness to ideas/opinions of others. At least 1 failure correlates with learning from experience.

Polish Start-Ups Key Competences: In Consulting and Investment Groups Assessment

The research was carried out in March 2018 in the Wielkopolska region. It was of a qualitative nature. The individual interview technique was applied, using a standardized interview questionnaire. The research subjects were experts representing two consulting and investment groups supporting startups – a deliberate selection. The groups requested to participate in the study appointed one representative each. They were considered experts in the survey. Both respondents are decision-makers in the entity they represent: expert 1 – operational director, expert 2 – Investment. Both entities' residence is registered in the Wielkopolska region

In the research part, which aimed to identify the startup key competences from the consulting and investment groups perspective, experts were asked three basic questions:

1. What factors have a significant impact on the decision to grant financial support to a startup?
2. What knowledge and skills should characterize a startup in order for an investment fund to be willing to invest in the project – to decide to start cooperation with a startup?
3. What features should startupcreators have?

The assessments of experts were concurrent. The survey has shown that consulting and investment groups primarily invest in start-ups which want to develop and gain knowledge and expect commitment and support from the investor in addition to financial resources. Evaluating the startup, they take into account following factors:

1. Innovations diagnostics,
2. Access to a given technology and owned resources (in case of technological start-ups),
3. The existence of substitute and complementary goods on the market,
4. A minimum payback period of the investment,
5. Minimum profit,
6. A possibility to modify the idea/design/product,
7. A final minimum ratio between profits and costs,
8. An idea,
9. Market potential, business risk, attractiveness of the idea, strategy and competition,
10. A real possibility of selling innovations,
11. The real existence of a market need that will be met by innovation,
12. The idea/project scalability on the basis of the initial business model,
13. The value of the product offered by startup,
14. Knowledge of methods and tools for creating and managing innovations, such as lean startup, design thinking, agile or general project management,
15. Constructed prototype.

In addition, the important factors are also: the percentage of involvement in the project – in the first expert's opinion, who stressed that his fund invests only in startups which can devote 100% of their work to the product/service; and the startup motivation level – in the second expert's opinion, who pointed out that a sufficiently high level of startup motivation to the project and showing initiative in case of failure is also important for his organization.

Both experts stressed the fact that their funds do not invest in projects operating in areas they do not have the knowledge and experience about.

The factors that determine the decision on granting financial support to a startup entity by a consulting and investment group are the factors that depend on startups. The most important ones are: the idea, market intelligence and risk assessment. Only one of the indicated factors does not depend on the evaluated startups - the projects area in which the funds invest.

The factors which have a significant impact on the decision on granting financial support to a startup and cooperating with it are derivatives of both the knowledge and startup skills at the organizational level, as well as the individual characteristics of the startup-creators.

The evaluations of experts in this area were also concurrent. The survey showed that startups should have knowledge and skills such as (the answers have been sorted into broader categories):

- General business understanding, processes occurring in a startup, competitors' activities, awareness of the startup operational and financial goals – business knowledge,
- The ability to make objective assessments and decisions, also in complex situations and under pressure – problem-solving and decision making,
- The ability to plan and implement the plan effectively; effectively achieve set goals – planning and implementation,
- The ability to learn from one's own and others' experience – learning from experience,
- The ability to use creative thinking to solve problems and take new initiatives to improve results – initiative and creativity,
- The ability to assertively express one's own opinions and reflections in a clear, concrete and professional way; the ability to listen to others – interpersonal skills;
- The ability to work effectively in a team, create appropriate emphatic relations and support the group development in achieving team goals – cooperation in a team;
- Effective team work organization, delegating tasks, motivating, monitoring progress, effective implementation of changes – team management.

According to the experts, the most important features, which should absolutely characterize startup-creators, are as follows:

- Willingness to learn,
- Flexibility,
- Understanding of their product and the purpose of its production and launch,
- Perseverance,
- self-discipline.

Based on the research results analysis, it can be concluded that both consulting and investment groups have a clearly defined startup picture. In their opinion, such entities must be characterized not only by a good idea or project, but also (and above all) by substantial preparations for market entry.

DISCUSSION

As stated in the introduction to this chapter, the startup success is determined by factors that can be divided into external and internal. The factors dependent on the startup are internal factors. They determine the startup potential. They can be depicted be competences.

The issue of the startup competence has been frequently raised in the domain-specific literature. However, the problem is often presented unilaterally – papers usually address recommendations and good practices to organizations/institutions that are interested in cooperation with startups, so that the decision on financing or wider cooperation is burdened with the lowest possible risk. Thereby, the interests of investors or business partners are more important than those concerning start-ups. The competences distinguished in the theoretical part of this chapter were used to construct interview questionnaires, which were used in the empirical research.

Firstly, an attempt was made to determine the key startup competences, both in organizational and individual dimensions, which state the startup potential and constitute its identity. The survey shows that startups pay more attention to individual than organizational competences. This is because startup competences can be identified with the founder's competences, especially in the first phases of the development cycle. Individual competences generate organizational competences over time.

The external entity's decision to finance or cooperate with a startup is made not only on the basis of the startup identity, but also on the basis of its image. Therefore, an attempt to determine the key startup competences, which create their image (desired competences in the consulting and investment groups' assessment), was made. The research shows that external entities pay more attention to organizational competences than to individual ones. The one-to-one relation (the external entity evaluation in relation to the founders' assessment) in the organizational dimension concerns such competences as: the knowledge of the market, competition and methods of creating and managing innovation, prototype and ability to learn from experience. Several of the competences singularized by experts can be reduced to one indicated by the founders – to a business model. Many startup competences at the organizational level indicated by experts can be identified with individual competences indicated by the founders.

By comparing the key startup competences indicated by startup creators with the key competences expected by external entities, it is possible to identify the competence gap. Its size generates the probability of possible cooperation between entities.

CONCLUSION

A characteristic feature of startup projects is innovation. It distinguishes start-ups from other newly-emerging enterprises. Startups introduce new services or products on the market under their own business model. They are also characterized by high flexibility and operation rapidity, as well as lower operating costs – both in terms of company construction as well as product development and distribution. The competition paradigm's change (change of competition forms and main competitive advantage sources) caused an emergence of a demand for a new type of entities on a niche market – highly innovative organizations. Therefore, despite a small percentage of successful startups, their development is becoming more and more dynamic. Startups usually operate in network structures on the B2B market.

One of the key determinants of the startup success on the market is obtaining financing. In the process of searching for an investor or business partner it is necessary to distinguish oneself from other competing entities – startups are evaluated on the basis of factors that can be identified with competences. Both organizational and individual competences are taken into account. The important issue is to make the competence gap – the difference between the start-up competences which determine the start-up potential and the competences desired by external entities – as small as possible.

Many centers and institutions are involved in the presented research stream, e.g. the research team from the SWPS University is currently conducting the first edition of the study entitled "Determinants of success. Global research on personality traits of startup CEOs"[5], which aims primarily at finding the answers to two fundamental questions: 1) Are there any common features which characterize the startup CEOs? and 2) Are there universal competences that drive the development of a young company?

The analyses and research results presented in this chapter have not completely exploited the issues. There is a need for further research in the field of startup competences, which the author and his team intend to continue.

REFERENCES

Baron, R. A., & Markman, G. D. (2003). Beyond social capital: The role of entrepreneurs' social competence in their financial success. *Journal of Business Venturing*, *18*(1), 41–60. doi:10.1016/S0883-9026(00)00069-0

Beauchamp, M., Krysztofiak-Szopa, J., & Skala, A. (2017). *Polskie startupy. Raport 2017*. Warszawa, Poland: Fundacja Startup Poland.

Beauchamp, M., Krysztofiak-Szopa, J., & Skala, A. (2018). *Polskie startupy. Raport 2018*. Warszawa, Poland: Fundacja Startup Poland.

Blank, S., & Dorf, B. (2012). *The Startup Owner's Manual. The Step-By-Step Guide for Building a Great Company*. Pescadero, CA: K&S Ranch Press.

Boyoung, K., Hyojin, K., & Youngok, J. (2018). Critical Success Factors of a Design Startup Business. *Sustainability*, *10*(9), 1–15. doi:10.3390u10092981 PMID:30607262

Cho, S., & Gumeta, H. (2015). Factors affecting university students' start-up intention: Comparative study on Korean and Chinese universities. *Journal of Korean Entrepreneurship*, *10*(3), 150–152.

Compass. (2015). *The Global Startup Ecosystem Ranking 2015*. Retrieved https://ec.europa.eu/futurium/en/system/files/ged/the_global_startup_ecosystem_report_2015_v1.2.pdf

Deloitte. (2016). *Diagnoza ekosystemu startupów w Polsce*. Retrieved https://www2.deloitte.com/content/dam/Deloitte/pl/Documents/Reports/pl_Deloitte_raport_startupy.pdf

Grow Advisors. (2017). *The Startup Ecosystem. White Paper*. Retrieved http://www.startupcommons.org

Jeon, Y. (2018). Analysis of the impact of start-up mentoring on strengthening business capabilities of one-man design entrepreneur-focusing on 'Creative Maestro Job Creation Project'. *Journal of Digital Convergence*, *16*, 343–349.

Kagermann, H., Helbig, J., Hellinger, A., & Wahlster, W. (2013). *Recommendations for Implementing the Strategic Initiative INDUSTRIE 4.0: Securing the Future of German Manufacturing Industry. Final Report of the Industrie 4.0 Working Group*. Forschungsunion.

Kim, B., & Cho, S. (2014). Factors affecting university students' start-up intentions: Focus on knowledge and technology based start-up. *Journal of Korean Entrepreneurship*, *9*(4), 86–106.

Lee, S. H., & Noh, S. H. (2014). A study on the success factors of ICT Convergence type-specific start-up enterprise - Mainly the case study. *Journal of Digital Convergence*, *12*(12), 203–215. doi:10.14400/JDC.2014.12.12.203

Łopusiewicz, A. (2013). *Start-up Od Pomysłu Do Sukcesu*. Warszawa, Poland: Edgard.

Piscione, D. P. (2013). *Secrets of Silicon Valley: What Everyone Else Can Learn from the Innovation Capital of the World*. New York, NY: Palgrave Macmillan.

Ries, E. (2011). *The Lean Startup. How Constant Innovation Creates Radically Successful Businesses*. London, England: VIKING.

Ries, E. (2011). *The Lean Startup: How Today's Entrepreneurs Use Continuous Innovation to Create Radically Successful Businesses.* New York, NY: Crown Publishing Group.

Startup Genome. (2017). *The Global Startup Ecosystem Report 2017.* Retrieved https://startupgenome.com

Teece, D. J. (2010). Business models, business strategy and innovation. *Long Range Planning, 43*(2), 172–194. doi:10.1016/j.lrp.2009.07.003

World Economic Forum. (2018) *Collaboration between Start-ups and Corporates. A Practical Guide for Mutual Understanding*. White Paper. Author.

Zacharakis, A., & Meyer, D. (2000). The potential of actuarial decision models: Can they improve the venture capital investment decision? *Journal of Business Venturing, 15*(4), 323–346. doi:10.1016/S0883-9026(98)00016-0

ENDNOTES

1 There are specific economic ecosystems which favor the development of young, innovative companies.

2 The Lean Startup method was created by E. Ries.

3 The study is conducted in a research team leaded by the author of this paper. The main research stream concerns the competence issue, both currently desirable and prospective, in relation to sectors, varieties and organization types, professional groups and key positions in organizations. In the startup area, the main contractor is Agnieszka Kulej.

4 There are various needs necessary for proper functioning at the particular startups' life stages and the importance of several key areas elements (such as financing, legal regulations, human capital, social capital and institutional environment) changes.

5 https://infoshare.pl/global_ceo_research.

Chapter 6
Redesigning Business Models With Circular Economy:
An Insight on Italian Enterprises

Francesca Ceruti
Laboratory Resources Valorization, Italy

Laura Gavinelli
University of Milano-Bicocca, Italy

Angelo Di Gregorio
University of Milano-Bicocca, Italy

Marco Frey
Sant'Anna School of Advanced Studies, Italy

ABSTRACT

In the last decades, circular economy has become a key in the academic and managerial studies. While there are plenty of contributions on circular economy like environmental strategy, a less developed line of studies is that analyzing circular economy as a new way of doing business. In this context, Italy has initiated the necessary reforms for the transition to the circular economy in 1997, but it is only in 2017 that it has adopted a work plan on that. The chapter presents the evidence of a CAWI interview investigating if the Italian firms are adopting the principles of circular economy and if this affects their competitiveness and business performance. The research contributes to the understanding of this new paradigm by getting into detail with the motivations that drive Italian enterprise to adopt the principles of circular economy, the actions they are taking to be circular economy-oriented, and the possible relationship between the adoption of the circular economy principles and their business performance.

DOI: 10.4018/978-1-5225-7850-5.ch006

INTRODUCTION

In recent decades, there has been a growing attention of the academic and managerial world to issues related to circular economy (Pearce and Turner 1989; Andersen (2007; Ellen MacArthur Foundation, 2013; Su et al. 2013; Ghisellini et al. 2016; Lieder and Rashid, 2016; Geissdoerfer et al. 2017). Circular economy refers to those business models that go beyond the traditional linear approach of production, consumption and disposal of the product, to move towards circular models, where the disposal phase is in particular replaced by the recycling/reuse of products and materials with the goal of transforming waste in a resource for a new production cycle (EMAF, 2013). In Ghisellini et al. (2016: 766) circular economy is "a regenerative system in which resource input and waste, emission, and energy leakage are minimised by slowing, closing, and narrowing material and energy loops. This can be achieved through long-lasting design, maintenance, repair, reuse, remanufacturing, refurbishing, and recycling".

The minimization of wastes and their impact on the environment are key issues in this type of economy. As a matter of fact, the circularization can be activated along the entire value chain to create closed loop value (Wells and Seitz, 2005; Guide and Van Wassenhove, 2009; Stindt and Sahamie, 2014; Govindan et al., 2015), influencing the choice of resources and materials that are used in production, the eco-design concept (Bakker et al., 2014), as well as the procurement of raw materials, the production and re-manufacturing processes, distribution, consumption models, disposal techniques, recycling and re-use of products, and as a new frontier, the development of secondary raw materials (Italian Ministry of the Environment, 2017).

Due to the importance of circular economy, a growing number of countries are launching specific laws on it. For instance, Germany was the first in Europe with a law on circular economy, passed in 1996. In 2000, Japan adopted a law to promote circular economy, while China introduced the circular economy model in 2008-10, moving from waste recycling to more efficient production, distribution and consumption models. The US Environmental Protection Agency (EPA) adopted the "SMM Sustainable Materials Management" approach to the sustainable management of materials, trying to prolong their life cycle. The United Kingdom has a specific programme called the "Waste and Resource Action Programme", which started in 2010. In addition, the UK model of industrial symbiosis - "NISP, National Industrial Symbiosis Programme" – has involved more than 15,000 British enterprises from 2003 to 2013, and more than 25 countries have adopted it (Italian Ministry of the Environment, 2017). France has passed a law on energy transition for green growth in 2015, stating that they will adopt a national strategy for circular economy every 5 years. The Netherlands set an ambitious national target in 2016 with the goal of becoming a 100% circular economy by 2050.

In this context, although Italy has initiated the necessary reforms for the development of a circular economy with the Ronchi Decree in 1997, it is only in 2017 that it has adopted a work plan for the 2017-2022 period with the aim of promoting the efficiency of resources and circular economy (Italian Ministry of the Environment, 2017). Italy is poor in raw materials and for that reason it is particularly sensitive to the theme of circular economy. More in detail, its per capita domestic consumption of raw materials is equal to about 10 tons per year, confirming that Italy is one of the most virtuous countries of the G7 and the EU28, whose average per capita consumption is about 13.3 tons per year (EUROSTAT, 2016). The progressive reduction in the import of resources, which passed from 225 million tonnes in 2005 to 155 million tonnes in 2015 (OECD, Green Growth Indicators, 2016) confirms this trend. Moreover, in the 2017 OECD Report (OECD, Green Growth Indicators 2017), Italy is, together with Estonia, United Kingdom, Denmark and Slovakia, the country with the greatest overall improvement achieved towards green growth, compared to 2000.

The chapter presents a research investigating if the Italian firms are adopting the circular economy paradigm and if this affects their competitiveness and business performance. Through the evidence of the research the chapter contributes to the understanding of this new paradigm, by getting into detail with: 1) the motivations that drive Italian enterprises to adopt the principles of circular economy; 2) the actions they are taking to be circular economy-oriented; 3) the possible relationship between the adoption of the circular economy principles and their business performance.

BACKGROUND

Circular Economy: Definition and Features

The notion of circular economy is based on a variety of ideas derived from different scientific disciplines and concepts (Yap, 2005; Andersen, 2007; Charonis, 2012, Preston, 2012; Lett, 2014; Naustdalslid, 2014; Prendeville et al., 2014; Ghisellini et al., 2016; Korhonen et al., 2018).

Some scholars see circular economy like a way to optimize the use of raw materials by increasing efficiency, moving from open cycles to closed cycles of materials and energy, by adopting less expensive industrial processes (Frosch, 1992; Erkman, 1997; Ehrenfeld and Gertler, 1997; Chiu and Yong, 2004; Andersen, 2007). Furthermore, it prevents the loss of materials (Mirabella et al., 2014) and considers waste as a potential resource (Zaman and Lehmann, 2013; Park and Chertow, 2014). Consequently, in the principles of circular economy, nothing that contains available energy or useful material is lost (Frosch, 1992).

Other authors focus instead on circular economy as a competitive environmental strategy that aims, primarily with cleaner production and eco-design (Van Berkel et al., 1997; Ramani et al., 2010; Winkler, 2011) to achieve waste minimization, environmental conservation, energy efficiency and economic development (EMAF, 2013). In circular economy, industrial wastes become valuable inputs that the enterprise can repair, reuse and recycle using cost-effective waste management techniques, as well as obtaining eco-efficient and value-added products and processes (EC, 1997; Van Berkel et al., 1997; Gwehenberger et al., 2003; Frondel et al., 2004; Van Berkel, 2007).

Circular economy is also described as a new productive model, which is opposed to the traditional one. While the typical re-use and regeneration activities of circular economy are labour intensive, the linear model of production and consumption is resource intensive (Stahel, 2013).

In the present work for circular economy we mean an economic system designed to regenerate itself, in which the waste of a production largely becomes raw material for a different production, or which can be started to reuse or recycle in order to minimize waste, when not cancel them. The aim is to put always the raw or semi-finished material back into circulation (Circular Economy Network, 2018). This definition is added to those identified by Korhonen et al. (2018) as that based on the Ellen MacArthur Foundation definition (EMAF, 2013). With the aim of maximizing the use of products and materials already placed on the market, and minimizing the consumption of raw materials and related waste, the circular model requires enterprises to adopt technologies and business models that are based on renewability, reuse, repair, updating, knowledge sharing and dematerialization (EMAF, 2014).

Circular Economy and Performance

A particularly interesting and less developed line of studies is the one studying circular economy as a new way of doing business (Andersen, 2007; Bocken et al., 2016). In this perspective, the advantages that are achievable with this new approach seem to be multiple and widespread at various levels: the macroeconomic level, the social level and the enterprise one. At a macroeconomic level, circular economy favours the recycling and reuse of materials (Sherwin and Evans, 2000; Prendeville et al., 2014), reducing the dependence on natural resources from the exporting countries. Circular economy can also help to reduce the effects of the price fluctuation of raw materials, as well as the aggressive pricing policies adopted by other countries (Preston, 2012; EMAF, 2013; Lett, 2014). Circular economy benefits the enterprise and society as a whole with a better supply chain, low volatility of resource prices, and better customer relations (Singh et al., 2017). Moreover, when adopting a cleaner production approach the enterprise takes into account the environmental impact of the entire life cycle of its products. In doing that, it pursues a more rational procurement and use of material and resources and use of materials and at the same time pursues a higher quality standards and product's performances (Van Berkel et al., 1997; Graedel and Allenby, 2003; Ramani et al., 2010; Ghisellini et al., 2016).

At social level, circular economy can lead to a reduction of negative externalities for society, to new job opportunities and collective well-being (EMAF, 2013).

Finally, at the enterprise level, management theories suggest that integrating circular economy principles into business operations can lead to sustainable competitive advantage (Park et al. 2010) and to a more integrated corporate and environmental value creation (Singh et al., 2017).

So, circular economy is also related in the literature to performance and competitiveness. In this light, the adoption of the circular economy principles seems to help enterprises increase their competitiveness and enhance their environmental and economic performance. To transform all this into a real competitive advantage, firms are encouraged to take action on several levels, like procurement and supply chain (Hall, 2001; Sarkis, 2006; Darnall et al., 2008; Seuring e Muller, 2008; Zhu et al., 2010), environmental and technological innovation (Murphy e Gouldson, 2000; Sherwin ed Evans, 2000; Zhu et al., 2010), organizational matters (Judge and Elenkov, 2005; Murphy and Gouldson, 2000; Seuring and Muller, 2008) and external collaborations (Darnall et al., 2008), which might lead to industrial symbiosis (Su et al., 2013; Wen and Meng, 2015; Yu et al., 2015).

From a managerial point of view, the adoption of circular economy models can also help enterprises to reduce costs (Geng et al., 2010; Mirabella et al., 2014). Furthermore, profits increase when environmental performance increases, especially among those enterprises that are able to put on the market products that can be perceived as distinctive also thanks to the environmental strategies carried out by their producers, like for instance, pollution prevention (Schroeder et al., 2002). In light of what has been so far illustrated, it seems that those enterprises that are willing to incorporate the issue of circularity in their strategies, have to care more about the long-term implications of environmental challenges, and avoid concentrating only on "green" products (Park et al., 2010). The challenge consists in "going beyond," maintaining the competitiveness of their business models (Kleindorfer et al., 2005) and the consequent value creation, while adopting the principles of circular economy.

CIRCULAR ECONOMY AMONG ITALIAN ENTERPRISES

An Insight on Italian Context

The research presented in the chapter concerns Italy, which is one of the most important industrial and manufacturing contexts in the world. From the point of view of circular economy, Italy is characterized by a limited raw materials endowment, but is also technologically advanced and with high expertise on environmental protection. For this reason, it can compete at international stage by seizing the opportunities that the transition to circular economy is generating.

To date, the literature has not provided an exhaustive picture on how and how much the paradigm of circular economy is changing the business models of Italian enterprises. In particular there is still much to investigate on the attitude of enterprises towards the principles of circular economy (Xue et al., 2010; Singh et al., 2017), their motivations to adopt these principles (Clarkson, 1995; Yayan, 2007; Agan et al., 2013), the actions undertaken (Agan et al., 2013), as well as the effects of circular economy on business performance (Rao, 2002; Zhu et al., 2007; Zailani et al., 2012; Agan et al., 2013) .

To achieve the aforementioned objectives, a quantitative survey was carried out on a national scale, through a CAWI - Computer Assisted Web Interview - questionnaire. The survey is divided into 5 different sections: attitude towards circular economy, motivations, actions, performance, description of respondents. The average time for the compilation of the questionnaire was 20 minutes. The list of potential participants was extrapolated from the LeFac.com database - TBS Group and contains the direct contacts of owners and managers of the main enterprises operating in Italy. For reasons of accessibility and timeliness, the sample was set according to a non-probabilistic sampling criterion (Molteni and Troilo 2007). The potential recipients of the questionnaire are chairmen/CEOs or general managers, division directors, directors of market research, communication managers, brand managers, marketing directors, communication directors, brand directors, sales managers; CFOs, marketing managers, directors of PR and press office; international marketing managers, events and promotion managers. The enterprises contacted were 4,349.

The enterprises that took part in the survey are 116, with a response rate of 2.6% (13.96% if the partially completed questionnaires are also considered). The collected statistical data were treated in an aggregate way to guarantee the privacy of respondents. Observing the list of respondents (Table 1) we note that the service sector is more represented (60.34%) than the production sector (39.66%). Among the services, the first by number are communication & media (12.07%), followed by trade (9.48%) and finance (8.62%). Owing to firm size, large firms represent the sample for 50.86%, while the medium-sized firms are 28.45% of the sample, the small ones represent 14.66% and the micro enterprises total 6.03% of respondents. The organizational functions contacted during the survey were of two types: top managers - including owners, general directors, CEO, CFO - and officials - including marketing, sales, communication, and IT. The top managers account for 38.79% of the sample, while the officials are 61.21%. Over half of the sample operates in Business to Business context (57.17%), while 36.78% of respondents operate mainly

Table 1. Sample description

Variable	Category	%
Dimension	Big	50.86%
	Medium	28.45%
	Small	14.66%
	Micro	6.03%
Industry	Manufacture	39.66%
	Service	26.72%
	Media & Communication	12.07%
	Commerce	9.48%
	Finance	8.62%
	No-profit	3.45%
Business function	Top Management	11.21%
	Director	27.59%
	Manager	61.21%
Customer	B2C	36.78%
	B2B	57.17%
	B2G	6.04%

Source: Authors' Elaboration

in Business to Consumer. The Business to Governance is residual accounting for 6.04%.

All questions were asked using a 5-point Likert scale and were organized according to the following constructs (Table 2):

- Attitude to circular economy ($\alpha = 0.676$)
- Internal and external motivations to adopt the principles of circular economy ($\alpha = 0.856$)
- Actions (eco-design, product implementation, end of life of the product) ($\alpha = 0.946$)
- Performance (environmental performance, economic performance, relation with the customer) ($\alpha = 0.953$)

To evaluate the correlation between the descriptive variables of the sample and the construct variables, three dummy variables were created indicating respectively firm dimension (SME - Small and Medium Enterprises), industry (Manufacture) and organizational function (Board). It should be noted that in the creation of the dummy "Manufacture" variable 4 non-profit firms were excluded. In addition, the dummy "Board" variable includes both top managers and directors.

Results

As shown in Table 3, the results are presented distinguishing by firm size (large, medium, small, micro), industry (manufacturing vs. services) and organizational

Table 2. Theoretical constructs used in the research

Construct	Subtheme	Code	Item	Literature
Attitude α = 0.676	**n.a.**	ATT 1	CE is more resource and energy efficient	Xue et al., 2010; Singh et al., 2017
		ATT 2	CE is waste management	
		ATT 3	CE is a radical approach to the way we make and use waste material	
		ATT 4	CE is a cost effective practice	
Motivation α = 0.856	**Internal**	MOT 1	The firm owners/managers see environmental responsibility within social responsibility context	Clarkson, 1995; Yayan, 2007; Agan et al., 2013; Helmig et al., 2016
		MOT 2	Our employees voluntarily engage in actions devoted to circular economy	
	External	MOT 3	Market insists to manufacture affordable products by minimizing the environmental impacts	
		MOT 4	Community demands the adoption of circular economy	
		MOT 5	Regulatory institutions insist to follow stringent rules and regulations in development of eco-efficient waste management methodology in production process	
		MOT 6	Financial institutions claim the considerations of environmental parameters of the firms	
		MOT 7	Customer demands motive us in our environmental efforts	

continued on following page

Table 2. Continued

Construct	Subtheme	Code	Item	Literature
Actions $\alpha = 0.946$	**Ecodesign**	ACT 1	To conduct R&D on environmental issues	Agan et al., 2013
		ACT 2	To design environmentally friendly products	
		ACT 3	To design environmentally friendly production process	
		ACT 4	To use more environmentally friendly materials	
		ACT 5	To design environmentally friendly business processes	
		ACT 6	To develop environmentally friendly packaging	
	Product implementation & end of life	ACT 7	Water filtering systems	
		ACT 8	To use air filters	
		ACT 9	To give/sell solid waste to recycling companies	
		ACT 10	To burn solid waste for energy production	
		ACT 11	To reduce energy consumption	
		ACT 12	To reduce raw materials	
		ACT 13	To reduce waste/emissions/water	
		ACT 14	To develop reuse process	
		ACT 15	To buy/use recycled materials	
		ACT 16	Recycling within the firm	
		ACT 17	To develop recycling process	
		ACT 18	To give priority to the use recyclable materials	

continued on following page

Table 2. Continued

<table>
<tr><th>Construct</th><th>Subtheme</th><th>Code</th><th>Item</th><th>Literature</th></tr>
<tr><td rowspan="17">Performance α = 0.953</td><td rowspan="6">Environmental</td><td>PER 1</td><td>Significant improvement in its overall environmental situation</td><td rowspan="17">Rao, 2002; Zhu et al.; 2007; Zailani et al., 2012; Agan et al., 2013; Schramm-Klein, 2015</td></tr>
<tr><td>PER 2</td><td>Significant improvement in its compliance to environmental standards</td></tr>
<tr><td>PER 3</td><td>Significant reduction in emission of air pollutants</td></tr>
<tr><td>PER 4</td><td>Significant reduction in energy consumption</td></tr>
<tr><td>PER 5</td><td>Significant reduction in material usage</td></tr>
<tr><td>PER 6</td><td>Significant reduction in consumption of hazardous materials</td></tr>
<tr><td rowspan="5">Economic</td><td>PER 7</td><td>Cost reduction</td></tr>
<tr><td>PER 8</td><td>Profits improvements</td></tr>
<tr><td>PER 9</td><td>Increased productivity</td></tr>
<tr><td>PER 10</td><td>Increased market share</td></tr>
<tr><td>PER 11</td><td>Higher ROI Return on investment</td></tr>
<tr><td rowspan="6">Customer Relationships</td><td>PER 12</td><td>To improve firm brand image</td></tr>
<tr><td>PER 13</td><td>To strength brand reputation</td></tr>
<tr><td>PER 14</td><td>Competitive advantage over competitors</td></tr>
<tr><td>PER 15</td><td>Customer satisfaction</td></tr>
<tr><td>PER 16</td><td>Customer loyalty</td></tr>
<tr><td>PER 17</td><td>Attracting new customer</td></tr>
</table>

Source: Authors' Elaboration

function of the respondent (top management, director, manager). For each of these constructs and variables - dimension, sector and function - the significance of the Pearson correlation is below calculated (Table 4).

An introductory question to the survey concerned the level of awareness of respondents on circular economy. On average, the level of awareness of respondents corresponds to 3.24 on a Likert scale 1-5, where 1 corresponds to no awareness and 5 to maximum awareness. The average value shows that the perception on this topic is not yet completely clear or assimilated among the respondents.

Construct 1 - Attitude: The most common association with circular economy is that related to the way firms make and use waste material (average evaluation of 4.24 on a 1 to 5 scale) (Table 3). The second answer option chosen by respondents is related to energy efficiency (average evaluation of 4.09), followed by profitable practice (3.64) and waste management (3.47).

The results change if we focus on those who declared a maximum awareness on circular economy (13.79% of the responding sample gave a rating equal to 5 on a 1-5 scale). For these firms, in fact, the first association is on more resource and energy efficiency (their average assessment equal to 4.63, quite higher than the average of the entire sample which is equal to 4.09).

Respondents with minimal awareness (rating of 1 and 2 on a 1-5 scale) exceed the average of the entire sample on the first option - approach to the way we make and use waste material - with a high rating of 4.71 (the average rating is 4.24).

Crossing the answers with the description of respondents, no high deviations emerge from the sample average except for the small firms that have a strong association of circular economy with the way they make and use waste materials (4.53) and manufacturing companies (4.37).

No items correlate to the variables of firm size, industry and organizational function (Table 4).

Construct 2 - Motivation: The motivations that drive respondents to adopt the principles of circular economy are both internal and external. A first result that emerges is that the internal motivations are a more incisive driver than the external ones. In fact, they collect an average rating of 3.51, against the external motivations that are equal to 2.85 (average rating).

Among the internal motivations, what fosters the most toward circular economy is the management's orientation towards environmental responsibility within social responsibility context (average assessment equal to 3.81). It follows the lever of the employees, who voluntarily engage in actions devoted to circular economy (3.21).

Among the external motivations, the one that records the highest average rating is the market demand that insists on having affordable and environmentally friendly

Table 3. Results

Code	Average	Big	Medium	Small	Micro	Manifacture	Service	Top management	Director	Manager
ATT 1	4.09	4.10	3.82	4.29	4.71	4.15	4.03	3.77	3.94	4.21
ATT 2	3.47	3.37	3.61	3.59	3.29	3.67	3.35	3.85	3.28	3.48
ATT 3	4.24	4.25	4.09	4.53	4.14	4.37	4.15	4.31	4.34	4.18
ATT 4	3.64	3.54	3.85	3.41	4.00	3.63	3.61	3.46	3.72	3.63
MOT 1	3.81	3.95	3.67	3.76	3.43	3.87	3.83	4.23	3.88	3.70
MOT 2	3.21	3.32	3.03	3.29	2.86	3.13	3.29	3.46	3.09	3.21
MOT 3	3.16	3.39	2.88	2.88	3.14	3.26	3.09	3.00	3.22	3.15
MOT 4	2.83	3.03	2.52	2.88	2.43	2.70	2.95	2.54	2.72	2.93
MOT 5	2.97	3.07	2.82	3.12	2.43	3.09	2.92	2.92	3.16	2.89
MOT 6	2.67	2.90	2.55	2.53	1.71	2.67	2.73	2.54	2.44	2.80
MOT 7	2.60	2.73	2.52	2.65	1.86	2.78	2.50	2.62	2.41	2.69
ACT 1	2.62	2.88	2.55	2.29	1.57	3.07	2.39	3.23	2.66	2.49
ACT 2	2.53	2.80	2.45	2.29	1.29	3.02	2.27	3.00	2.34	2.54
ACT 3	2.61	2.98	2.52	2.00	1.43	3.11	2.29	2.77	2.50	2.63
ACT 4	3.03	3.15	3.12	2.53	2.86	3.35	2.86	4.00	2.75	2.99
ACT 5	3.21	3.44	3.00	3.00	2.71	3.43	3.09	4.00	3.09	3.11
ACT 6	2.55	2.61	2.58	2.47	2.14	3.15	2.18	3.69	2.44	2.39
ACT 7	2.78	2.90	3.06	2.41	1.29	3.33	2.50	3.62	2.47	2.76
ACT 8	3.28	3.58	3.39	2.53	2.00	3.65	3.12	4.08	2.69	3.39
ACT 9	3.18	3.10	3.64	3.06	2.00	3.39	3.08	4.15	3.00	3.08
ACT 10	1.83	2.03	1.91	1.24	1.14	2.00	1.70	1.62	1.53	2.00
ACT 11	3.55	3.73	3.48	3.29	3.00	3.65	3.53	3.92	3.34	3.58
ACT 12	2.88	3.07	2.76	2.71	2.29	2.98	2.82	3.15	2.75	2.89
ACT 13	3.08	3.25	3.03	2.59	3.00	3.30	2.95	3.92	2.91	3.00
ACT 14	2.78	2.86	2.85	2.59	2.14	2.93	2.70	3.00	2.59	2.82

continued on following page

Table 3. Continued

Code	Average	Big	Medium	Small	Micro	Manifacture	Service	Top management	Director	Manager
ACT 15	2.92	2.97	2.82	2.94	3.00	3.04	2.85	3.08	2.94	2.89
ACT 16	2.91	2.81	3.03	2.88	3.14	3.13	2.74	3.77	2.75	2.82
ACT 17	2.60	2.68	2.76	2.53	1.43	2.87	2.50	2.62	2.75	2.54
ACT 18	2.80	2.80	2.91	2.71	2.57	2.80	2.85	3.23	2.84	2.70
PER 1	3.37	3.51	3.30	3.41	2.43	3.54	3.30	3.38	3.13	3.48
PER 2	3.41	3.56	3.45	3.12	2.57	3.78	3.20	3.46	3.41	3.39
PER 3	3.23	3.42	3.00	3.12	3.00	3.50	3.12	3.31	3.09	3.28
PER 4	3.36	3.56	3.27	3.29	2.29	3.59	3.29	3.38	3.13	3.46
PER 5	3.32	3.49	3.21	3.00	3.14	3.50	3.26	3.85	3.09	3.32
PER 6	2.95	3.14	3.06	2.71	1.43	3.33	2.73	3.46	2.56	3.03
PER 7	2.69	2.73	2.79	2.41	2.57	2.76	2.70	3.00	2.63	2.66
PER 8	2.47	2.53	2.64	2.29	1.57	2.59	2.44	2.54	2.31	2.52
PER 9	2.32	2.42	2.39	2.12	1.57	2.43	2.27	2.38	2.16	2.38
PER 10	2.45	2.47	2.52	2.59	1.57	2.65	2.36	2.92	2.28	2.44
PER 11	2.39	2.37	2.67	2.29	1.43	2.59	2.30	2.85	2.13	2.42
PER 12	3.70	3.76	3.88	3.65	2.43	3.85	3.65	3.69	3.59	3.75
PER 13	3.70	3.76	3.88	3.53	2.71	3.80	3.68	3.92	3.66	3.68
PER 14	3.08	3.15	3.18	3.18	1.71	3.35	2.94	3.23	2.72	3.21
PER 15	3.07	3.19	3.18	3.00	1.71	3.33	2.92	3.23	2.88	3.13
PER 16	2.94	2.95	3.15	3.06	1.57	3.00	2.92	3.00	2.81	2.99
PER 17	2.98	3.05	3.15	3.06	1.43	3.26	2.86	3.38	2.78	3.00

Source: Authors' Elaboration

Table 4. Correlations between constructs and descriptive variable of the sample

Construct	Code	SME	Manifacture	Board
Attitude α = 0.676	ATT 1	-.018	.069	-.181
	ATT 2	.086	.146	-.015
	ATT 3	-.014	.114	.078
	ATT 4	.099	.012	.005
Motivation α = 0.856	MOT 1	-.126	.017	.119
	MOT 2	-.100	-.068	-.005
	MOT 3	-.197**	.071	.000
	MOT 4	-.188**	-.115	-.115
	MOT 5	-.093	.072	.088
	MOT 6	-.202**	-.023	-.144
	MOT 7	-.111	.122	-.095
Actions α = 0.946	ACT 1	-.179	.223**	.109
	ACT 2	-.181	.250***	-.001
	ACT 3	-.252***	.271***	-.018
	ACT 4	-.091	.181	.046
	ACT 5	-.172	.123	.085
	ACT 6	-.042	.335***	.138
	ACT 7	-.084	.275***	.013
	ACT 8	-.213**	.185	-.104
	ACT 9	.055	.106	.082
	ACT 10	-.180	.130	-.185**
	ACT 11	-.134	.045	-.024
	ACT 12	-.142	.058	-.007
	ACT 13	-.132	.127	.071
	ACT 14	-.065	.085	-.037
	ACT 15	-.036	.079	.036
	ACT 16	.070	.146	.083
	ACT 17	-.057	.136	.064
	ACT 18	.004	-.018	.100

continued on following page

Table 4. Continued

Construct	Code	SME	Manifacture	Board
Performance α = .953	PER 1	-.120	.104	-.117
	PER 2	-.130	.244***	.011
	PER 3	-.153	.152	-.048
	PER 4	-.170	.128	-.110
	PER 5	-.155	.107	-.006
	PER 6	-.142	.223**	-.075
	PER 7	-.038	.030	.033
	PER 8	-.058	.070	-.067
	PER 9	-.104	.078	-.075
	PER 10	-.025	.132	.014
	PER 11	.014	.129	-.040
	PER 12	-.060	.090	-.055
	PER 13	-.059	.055	.025
	PER 14	-.064	.170	-.141
	PER 15	-.109	.181	-.066
	PER 16	-.009	.034	-.052
	PER 17	-.055	.156	-.017

*** p= 0.001; ** p= 0.05
Source: Authors' Elaboration

products (3.16). The regulatory institutions also guide the change towards eco-efficient waste management in the production process (2.97).

Crossing the answers with the descriptive data of the respondents there are discrepancies with respect to the average evaluation of the sample, taking into account the firm size variable: the larger the company, the higher the motivations to adopt the principles of circular economy. In fact, the average evaluation of large firms is higher than the one of the entire sample (respectively 3.20 against 3.03). This is true both with internal motivations (evaluated by large firm with 3.64 and with 3.51 by the entire sample) and external motivations (average evaluation equal to 3.02 for large firms and equal to 2.85 for the entire sample). The small firm size correlates negatively with the following external motivations: the market insists to manufacture affordable products by minimizing the environmental impacts (-.197 **); community demands the adoption of circular economy (-.188 **); financial institutions claiming the assessment of environmental parameters of the firms (-2.22 **).

Construct 3 - Actions: The actions undertaken by firms have been investigated with respect to two sub-themes: eco-design, and product implementation till its end-of-life. About the product design actions according to the principles of circular economy (eco-design) the average level of practice compared to the actions related to the implementation and management of the product is slightly lower, gaining respectively an evaluation equal to 2.76 versus 2.88.

More in detail, among the eco-design actions, the most adopted is the design of environmentally friendly business processes (3.21), while the least considered is the development of environmentally friendly packaging (2.55).

Considering the management of the product (implementation and end-of-life), the most implemented action is the reduction of energy consumption (3.55), followed by the use of air filters (3.28). As a third option, respondents give or sell solid waste to recycling companies (3.18). Finally, they rarely burn solid waste for energy production (1.83).

In general, respondents take actions toward circular economy at a medium and medium level. This indicates that the level of implementation of its principles is not yet consolidated among respondents.

Crossing the actions with the descriptive variables of respondents differences occur with respect to firm size and industry. Considering firm size, the larger the firms, the higher their evaluation on eco-design actions. The averages for eco-design are in fact 2.98 for large companies with a statistically significant correlation for the item "to design environmentally friendly production process" (-.252 ***).

As for industry, firms operating in manufacturing the average evaluation on eco-design is higher than the one of the entire sample (3.19 for manufacturing firms, against 2.76 for the entire sample). The industry shows positive and significant correlations to the items "to conduct R & D on environmental issues" (.223 **), "to design environmentally friendly products"(.250 ***), "to design environmentally friendly production process" (.271 ***) and "to develop environmentally friendly packaging" (.335 ***).

The organisational function of respondents impacts the average evaluation on eco-design actions. The top management declares on average an overall level of adoption corresponding to 3.45 against 2.69 declared by managers. Nonetheless, the variable "organisational function" is not significantly related to any eco-design item.

Thinking about product implementation and end-of-life, the average evaluation of manufacturing firms and top managers is higher than the one of the entire sample (2.88), being respectively equal to 3.09 and 3.35. Statistically significant correlations were found, referring to all three descriptive variable - firm size, industry and organisational role. Referring to firm size, there is a negative correlation between SMEs and the adoption of air filters (-.213 **). As for the industry variable, there is a positive correlation between respondents operating in manufacturing sector and the use of water filtering systems (.275 ***). Finally, the correlation between the organisational role and the item "burn solid waste for energy production" is negative (-.185 **).

Construct 4 - Performance: The impact of circular economy on firm performance is recorded at three levels: environmental performance, economic performance and the company's relationship with customers.

Regarding the environmental performance, the average rating is 3.27 on a 1 to 5 scale, where 1 means no incidence and 5 maximum incidence of circular economy on the response option. The most significant result is that of a significant improvement in the firm compliance with environmental standards (3.41), followed by a significant improvement in the overall environmental situation (3.37) and a significant reduction in energy consumption (3.36). The lowest average rating is instead about the significant reduction in emission of air pollutants (3.23).

The economic performance is the one that obtains the lowest average rating compared to the three types (2.46). Among the response options, the one obtaining the highest average rating is cost reduction (2.69), followed by profits improvement (2.47) and increased market share (2.45). The lower evaluation option, on the other hand, is about an increase in productivity (2.32). Cost cutting is present on average in the minds of respondents, while the relationship between circular economy and production capacity is still struggling to consolidate.

Finally, adopting the principles of circular economy improves the relationship of the firm with its customers. The respondent sample expresses an average rating on all the response options of 3.25. The results that circular economy mostly brings in this area are referred to a strengthened brand image and a strengthened brand reputation (both valued at 3.70), followed by a competitive edge over competitors (3.08). Instead, adopting the principles of circular economy affects less customer loyalty (average rating of 2.94).

In short, the relationship between circular economy and business performance gets an average rating of 3.03 on a 1-5 scale. Among the three areas of performance, it is the relationship with the customer that mostly benefits from the fact that the enterprise adopts the principles of circular economy. On the other hand, the economic performance is not yet fully recognized within the sample, being the one that obtains the lowest average rating (2.46 on a 1-5 scale).

Crossing the evaluation of the impact of circular economy on business performance with the descriptive variables of respondents, some discrepancies emerge with respect to firm size. As for environmental performance, the larger the firms the higher the average evaluation (3.45 by large firms, against 3.27 by the entire sample).

A different situation occurs with respect to the other two types of performances – economic performance and relationship with customers, where medium-size firms give a higher average evaluation on the benefits obtained in customer relations (3.40 against 3.25 of the entire sample), and on economic performance (2.60 against 2.46 of the sample).

In short, while for large firms the most important impacts of being circular are found in environmental performance – followed by relations with customers and economic performance – for SMEs the order is relations with customers as the highest performance, followed by environmental performance and economic one.

Taking into account the business sector, the respondents operating in manufacturing sector perceive higher benefits than those who operate in service industry for all three types of performances. The average evaluation on the benefits gained on environmental performance is 3.54 for manufacturing industry and 3.15 for service industry, the one on relations with customers is about 3.43 for manufacturing firms and 3.16 for respondents operating in service industry, while the evaluation on economic performance is equal to 2.60 in manufacturing industry and to 2.42 in services.

Lastly, as for the "organisational function" variable, the higher the role played by the respondent within his/her organization, the higher more positive the perception of the impact of circular economy on all three performances. In fact, top management values the environmental performance with an average rate of 3.47, the relations with customers with 3.41 and the economic performance with 2.74, while the average evaluations of managers are respectively equal to 3.33, 3.29 and 2.48.

No correlations between descriptive variables – firm size and organisational role – and performance - environmental, economic and relations with customers – were found, except a positive correlation between manufacturing firms and environmental performance, more specifically referring to the items "significant improvement in the overall environmental standards" (.244 ***) and "significant reduction in consumption of hazardous materials" (.223 **).

The Role of Communication

Within the performance theme, a sub-theme emerged during the data processing. It is that of the use of communication tools by respondents in the management of their relationship with their stakeholders. Details on the single items used to investigate this theme are provided in Table 5.

As shown in Table 6, communication is an area in which the connection with circular economy is particularly weak. The average rating is in fact equal to 2.25 on a 1 to 5 scale. Among the most used tools to spread messages and results related to being circular certifications are the first answer option with an average rating of

Table 5. Items used for the communication theme

Construct	Code	Item	Literature
Communication **α = 0.944**	COM 1	Company homepage	Adapted from Schramm-Klein et al. 2015
	COM 2	Dedicated section in company website	
	COM 3	Social media	
	COM 4	Newsletter	
	COM 5	Separate social report/environmental report	
	COM 6	Environmental report integrated in annual report	
	COM 7	Public relations	
	COM 8	Advertising	
	COM 9	Flyers/brochures	
	COM 10	In-store advertising	
	COM 11	Info points. multimedia terminals	
	COM 12	Certifications	

Source: Authors' Elaboration

Table 6. Tools used by respondents to communicate circular economy

Code	Average	Big	Medium	Small	Micro	Manifacture	Service	Top management	Director	Manager
COM 1	2.28	2.46	2.27	2.00	1.57	2.35	2.21	2.38	2.50	2.17
COM 2	2.59	2.92	2.45	2.12	1.71	2.67	2.53	2.31	2.66	2.62
COM 3	2.45	2.61	2.45	2.29	1.43	2.50	2.42	2.38	2.56	2.41
COM 4	2.18	2.34	2.21	1.94	1.29	2.26	2.11	1.77	2.38	2.17
COM 5	2.52	2.90	2.33	2.18	1.00	2.61	2.48	2.31	2.56	2.54
COM 6	2.28	2.64	2.18	1.76	1.00	2.41	2.21	1.92	2.25	2.37
COM 7	2.51	2.71	2.52	2.24	1.43	2.61	2.45	2.38	2.47	2.55
COM 8	1.85	2.07	1.76	1.59	1.14	1.98	1.79	1.38	1.84	1.94
COM 9	2.01	2.12	2.06	1.94	1.00	2.17	1.89	1.85	1.91	2.08
COM 10	1.85	2.08	1.88	1.35	1.00	2.07	1.73	1.62	1.84	1.90
COM 11	1.56	1.76	1.39	1.29	1.29	1.54	1.58	1.23	1.47	1.66
COM 12	2.96	3.36	2.85	2.35	1.57	3.46	2.61	3.23	2.94	2.92

Source: Authors' Elaboration

2.96, followed by dedicated section in the company website (2.59) and a separated social report or environmental report (2.52). The least used tools are the info-points and the multimedia terminals (1.56).

Crossing the level of utilization of communication tools with the description of respondents there are differences in their perception if we take into account the firm size variable. In fact, the average level of utilization within large firms corresponds to 2.50 (the average evaluation of the entire sample is equal to 2.25) (Table 6).

As for the industry variable, the firms operating in manufacturing industry give an average evaluation of 2.39, which is higher than the one of the sample (2.25).

On the contrary, with reference to the organizational function, the top management declares a lower rate than the average rate of the sample (respectively 2.06 and 2.25).

Correlations are mostly present with firm size (Table 7). In particular, the correlations are negative within SME, referring to a dedicated section in company website (-.208 **), separate social report/environmental report (-.242 ***), environmental report integrated in the annual report (-.248 ***), advertising (-.188 **), in-store advertising (-.204 **), info points and multimedia terminals (-.205 **) and certifications (-.255 ***).

As it is reasonable to expect manufacturing companies are positively correlated with the use of certifications (.265 ***), which are particularly pertinent to what they produce. No significant correlation has emerged regarding the corporate role held.

Table 7. Correlations between communications tools and descriptive variables of the sample

Construct	Code	SME	Manifacture	Board
Communication α = .944	COM 1	-.126	.049	.104
	COM 2	-.208**	.045	-.020
	COM 3	-.117	.027	.035
	COM 4	-.119	.057	.011
	COM 5	-.242***	.038	-.014
	COM 6	-.248***	.068	-.070
	COM 7	-.153	.057	-.038
	COM 8	-.188**	.080	-.098
	COM 9	-.083	.103	-.070
	COM 10	-.204**	.143	-.052
	COM 11	-.205**	-.016	-.127
	COM 12	-.255***	.265***	.033

Source: Authors' Elaboration

In short, the respondents do not yet see the communication as a strategic tool through which they can spread and enhance their adoption of the principles of circular economy and thus obtain a competitive advantage over their competitors. From the point of view of communication channels and tools, respondents do prefer traditional tools to the detriment of, for instance, social media.

The firm size turns out to be a determining variable for this type of activity that still sees smaller firms in an embryonic state.

SOLUTIONS AND RECOMMENDATIONS

The present exploratory work aims to provide an overview of how and how much Italian firms have adopted the principles of circular economy and the performances achieved. In particular, the research analysed the attitude, the motivations, the actions undertaken and the benefits achieved. The work thus enriches the topic debated in the literature of the circular economy at the micro level (Ghisellini et al., 2016).

The results of the research show that the level of knowledge on circular economy is medium to high among the respondents, the level of transposition in actions and perceived performances is medium and that the attitude (Xue et al., 2010; Singh et al., 2017) is more inclined towards some aspects of circular economy. Regarding the attitude, respondents lead the circular economy mainly to a strategy to reduce waste and emissions (EC, 1997; Gwehenberger et al., 2003; Frondel et al., 2004), as well as to increase energy efficiency (Brown and Stone, 2007; Li et al., 2010). The vision of respondents has not yet come to embrace the circular economy in all its potentialities, passing from a first stage in which circular economy is an integral part of the firm's environmental strategies to a stage in which the "new way of doing business" (Andersen, 2007; Bocken et al., 2016) integrates these strategies with the entire industrial system or the entire society (Ghisellini et al., 2016).

The results are in line with the plentiful studies that indicate that both the internal and external factors are responsible for the firm's circular economy behaviour (Zhang et al., 2013). Among the motivations that push towards circular economy (Clarkson, 1995; Yayan, 2007; Agan et al., 2013; Helmig et al., 2016) the internal motivations are the strongest ever. In particular, the strongest internal motivation is that given by the vision of the entrepreneur or of the managers who intercept in the circular economy an opportunity for development. This result confirms the previous literature which shows that the owner-manager can drive environmental initiatives (Corral, 2003, Singh et al., 2014; Sangle, 2010) and his/her commitment can affect the firm's actions devoted to circular economy significantly (Liu and Bai, 2014; Agnello et al., 2015; Xue et al., 2010). The motivational factor of the manager can be a driver of change for the entire organization: the manager can choose whether to involve the whole staff more, training it and making it more aware of the circular economy and its benefits, leading them to work more convincingly and effectively on these principles.

Among the external motivations, listening to the demands and expectations of the market is the first answer option chosen by respondents. Results are in line with previous studies, which recognise the role of social pressure in the transition of the firm towards circular economy (Mutz, 2015; Agnello et al., 2015; Bhupendra and Sangle, 2016). The market demands accessible, environmentally friendly products that minimize their impact on the environment. It is up to the enterprise to seize a business opportunity in these needs.

Looking at the actions put in place (Agan et al., 2013), respondents react to circular economy with a medium level intensity. This indicates that the implementation of its principles is not yet consolidated among respondents. In particular, the actions related to the implementation of energy efficiency and waste reduction gain a slightly higher evaluation than those devoted to eco-design, where respondents declare a particular effort towards environmentally friendly business processes.

The transition towards the circular economy implies the adoption of eco-design and cleaner production actions. From the point of view of the actions, it is important to note that eco-design (Winkler, 2011) and cleaner production (especially energy savings, the use of air and water filters) are the actions mostly taken by Italian firms to develop the circular economy principles. In particular, respondents pay attention to the environmental impact of a product since the earliest stages of design with the aim of promoting the improvement of material and resource use (Sherwin and Evans, 2000, Prendeville et al., 2014). Eco-design is related to more environmentally friendly products and processes focusing, which can drive to higher quality standards and higher product performance (Graedel and Allenby, 2010; Ramani et al., 2010).

This signals that the process of adoption of circular economy has started but that firms need to go beyond material and energy loops (Wells and Seitz, 2005; Stahel, 2010; Govindan et al., 2015) in order to get to new business models (Browne and Stone, 2007; Bocken et al., 2016).

From the point of view of marketing objectives (Agan et al 2013, Schramm-Klein et al., 2015) respondents are aware that investing in circular economy can also bring results in terms of brand image and brand reputation, and social acceptance of their work, as the community considers circularity an increasingly important issue. Investing in factors that the demand perceive as increasingly important - such as attention to the environment, waste reduction, price transparency, longer life cycle of the product - can differentiate the offer of the firm, strengthen its positioning and at the same time increase its competitiveness. Regarding communication

(Schramm-Klein et al. 2015), research evidence shows that respondents do not see it as a strategic tool. In fact, they produce contents on circular economy, especially in product communication - for example through certification - but they rarely use it to nurture the relationship with the client or to strengthen the company's brand image or brand reputation. Communicating what the company means by circular economy, which are the points of contact between its values and the principles of circularity and how it is translating these principles into decisions and actions is an aspect of positioning and credibility far from trivial. Therefore, seizing the opportunities offered by communication almost exclusively on the certification front seems to be at least reductive, although certifications can make the company's commitment easily recognizable by the market. From the point of view of communication channels, the traditional ones are the most used, while social media operate in a more marginal way. Instead, circularity could be the basis of new communication constructs and be conveyed through the entire marketing communication mix.

Regarding performance (Rao, 2002; Zhu et al., 2007; Zailani et al., 2012; Agan et al., 2013; Schramm-Klein, 2015), the introduction of circular economy approach should provide both environmental benefits and economic benefits to the firm, reducing costs and wastes (Ghisellini et al., 2016). At the same time it could also enable the firm increase its efficiency, while reducing environmental hazards and possible damage for humans (Van Berkel, 2000; Brown and Stone, 2007; Li et al., 2010). In the research, the benefits most frequently encountered by those who approach circular economy are referred to better relationships with their customers, followed by better environmental performance and finally by better economic performance. Circularity is an ongoing process, in which the respondents are seizing different opportunities and advantages. However, in overall terms, the circular economy paradigm has not yet been completely metabolized in the decision-making and organizational processes of respondents. The phenomenon is probably due to its novelty and the fact that, although the practices put in place are now numerous, there is neither a full awareness nor a clear strategic vision on its potential. Scholars can also support enterprises, further deepening in their studies the relationship between circular economy and business models.

Finally, by crossing the answers with the personal data of the respondents, there are discrepancies with respect to the average evaluations, if we consider firm size. In particular, large enterprises give a higher assessment of internal and external motivations that push them towards the circular economy, on eco-design actions and on the use of air filters, as well as on environmental performances. Medium-sized enterprises give a higher score than the sample average on economic and marketing performance. In short, while for large firms the most important impacts of being circular are on environmental performance - followed by better relations with customers and higher economic performance - for SMEs the order is relations with customers as the highest performance, followed by environmental performance and economic one.

The research also shows that larger firms perceive greater external pressures in terms of market, community and financial institutions. Finally, large firms communicate more the contents of circular economy within their own channels. Therefore, the dimensional variable seems to affect the way they implement the principles of circular economy. It also seems that large firms can play a leading role in their industry, providing a good example to smaller companies on how to approach the principles of circular economy.

The sector affects the types of actions undertaken, the perception of environmental performance and communication. The respondents that are active in the manufacturing industry give higher ratings on eco-design - conducting R&D on environmental issues, designing environmentally friendly products and production processes, and developing environmentally friendly packaging - and higher ratings on product management - using water filtering systems. On average, respondents in manufacturing perceive higher benefits than respondents that operate in service industry. In particular, positive and significant correlations emerge in environmental performance with significant improvement in the compliance to the environmental standards and with a significant reduction in consumption of hazardous materials. The respondents of manufacturing are also more active in certifications that are used as a tool to communicate and enhance their product. These evidences demonstrate how the adoption of circular economy is currently more product-oriented - including eco-design and the management of product life cycle - and to the efficiency of production and procurement systems. This is consistent with the fact that the most active and satisfied respondents belong to the manufacturing industry, which is traditionally more focused on the product. It should also be noted that in service sector the adoption of circularity is more difficult to monitor (Ghisellini et al., 2016) being the core business mainly base in intangibles. Within the responding sample, however, there are also positive results among those working in services, demonstrating the fact that all sectors can adopt - in a contextual manner – the principles of circular economy.

In sum, respondents have not yet metabolized the circular economy paradigm in their decisional and organizational processes of, although there are a few respondents who declare an advanced practice on it.

To complete the transition, companies should redesign their business model by seeing circular economy as a general management theme. The trend that seems, therefore, to arise is the need to move from a tactical and product-oriented approach, to a more strategic approach in which intangibles can become factors of competitiveness.

FUTURE RESEARCH DIRECTIONS

The research presented in this chapter is explorative and focused on Italian firms and provides interesting evidence on how and how much the principles of the circular economy are incorporated in today's Italian industrial and production context. In particular, the research investigates the motivations that drive respondents to this type of economy, as well as their level of knowledge and orientation to circular economy and what are the benefits they think they obtained in terms of performance - economic, environmental and relationship with the client – when approaching circular economy.

Since circular economy is a subject of great interest and relevance for the world economic development, it would be advisable to extend the research to enterprises that are active in other countries, so to check if there are any differences in orientation and level of implementation of the principles of circular economy in diverse geographical contexts.

The present research also investigates the relationship between circular economy and business models. The implementation of a qualitative phase aimed at deepening individual cases could help to focus on the evolutionary paths and identify best practices to be used as a model for those enterprises that are approaching the principles of circular economy.

Another line of research could be devoted to the analysis of the causal relationships between the various constructs and of the determinants of firm performance through a SEM - Structural Equation Model.

In addition, future research could get into detail of perceptive performance, introducing indicators to measure and quantify the impact of circular economy on the various types of the detected performances.

CONCLUSION

The work deals with a topic of great criticality and scientific interest, namely the circular economy, wondering if it could represent a business opportunity and how Italian companies are facing this transformation.

The results of the research show that the process of adopting the principles of circular economy is in progress among respondent, although it is not yet fully completed. The first area of activation, which is already underway, concerns the modification of production processes according to the principles of cost containment, reduction of energy consumption, production efficiency and eco-design. This area is the one that brings together the largest number of initiatives of responding companies, especially those of large size, in favour of circular economy. A second area is today just mentioned and concerns the communication activities of the adoption of the principles of circular economy towards the outside. Although respondents consider the intangible aspects - such as image and reputation - as the main benefits deriving from the adoption of circular economy, communication does not adequately value these strategic assets.

Within this evolutionary process, there seems to be the need for the respondents to assume circularity as a guiding principle for redesigning the whole business model and the strategies that lie behind it in the light of the challenges that circularity poses and that the same market requires. Although respondents sample have implemented actions with positive impacts on their business, the adherence to the principles of circularity can have an even greater impact on their competitiveness if it becomes a founding value, which guides the entire firm's strategy and action.

REFERENCES

Agan, Y., Acar, M. F., & Borodin, A. (2013). Drivers of environmental processes and their impact on performance: A study of Turkish SMEs. *Journal of Cleaner Production*, *51*, 23–33. doi:10.1016/j.jclepro.2012.12.043

Agnello, X., Naveen, J., Ravichandran, M., & Balamurugan, J. (2015). Clean technology and its efficacy: Strategies of environmental management. *J. Environ. Soc. Sci*, *2*(2), 1–10.

Andersen, M. S. (2007). An introductory note on the environmental economics of the circular economy. *Sustainability Science*, *2*(1), 133–140. doi:10.100711625-006-0013-6

Bakker, C., den Hollander, M., Van Hinte, E., & Zljlstra, Y. (2014). *Products that last: Product design for circular business models*. TU Delft Library.

Bhupendra, K. V., & Sangle, S. (2016). Pollution prevention strategy: A study of Indian firms. *Journal of Cleaner Production*, *133*, 795–802. doi:10.1016/j.jclepro.2016.05.169

Bocken, N. M., de Pauw, I., Bakker, C., & van der Grinten, B. (2016). Product design and business model strategies for a circular economy. *Journal of Industrial and Production Engineering*, *33*(5), 308–320. doi:10.1080/21681015.2016.1172124

Brown, G., & Stone, L. (2007). Cleaner production in New Zealand: Taking stock. *Journal of Cleaner Production*, *15*(8-9), 716–728. doi:10.1016/j.jclepro.2006.06.025

CEN - Circular Economy Network. (n.d.). Retrieved from http://www.circular-europe-network.eu/

Charonis, G. (2012). Degrowth, steady state economics and the circular economy: three distinct yet increasingly converging alternative discourses to economic growth for achieving environmental sustainability and social equity. *World Economic Association Sustainability Conference 2012*. Available: http://sustainabilityconference2012.worldeconomicsassociation.org/wp-content/uploads/WEASustainabilityConference2012_Charonis_Alternative-Discoursesto-Economic-Growth.pdf

Chiu, A. S., & Yong, G. (2004). On the industrial ecology potential in Asian developing countries. *Journal of Cleaner Production*, *12*(8-10), 1037–1045. doi:10.1016/j.jclepro.2004.02.013

Clarkson, M. E. (1995). A stakeholder framework for analyzing and evaluating corporate social performance. *Academy of Management Review*, *20*(1), 92–117. doi:10.5465/amr.1995.9503271994

Corral, C. M. (2003). Sustainable production and consumption systems—cooperation for change: Assessing and simulating the willingness of the firm to adopt/develop cleaner technologies. The case of the In-Bond industry in northern Mexico. *Journal of Cleaner Production*, *11*(4), 411–426. doi:10.1016/S0959-6526(02)00063-X

Darnall, N., Jolley, G. J., & Handfield, R. (2008). Environmental management systems and green supply chain management: Complements for sustainability? *Business Strategy and the Environment*, *17*(1), 30–45. doi:10.1002/bse.557

EC. (1997). *Review of Cleaner Production*. Available: http://ec.europa.eu/environment/enveco/eco_industry/pdf/annex2.pdf

Ehrenfeld, J., & Gertler, N. (1997). Industrial ecology in practice: The evolution of interdependence at Kalundborg. *Journal of Industrial Ecology*, *1*(1), 67–79. doi:10.1162/jiec.1997.1.1.67

Ellen MacArthur Foundation (EMAF). (2013). Towards the Circular Economy. Economic and Business Rationale for an Accelerated Transition. Ellen MacArthur Foundation.

Erkman, S. (1997). Industrial ecology: An historical view. *Journal of Cleaner Production*, *5*(1-2), 1–10. doi:10.1016/S0959-6526(97)00003-6

EUROSTAT. (2016). *Material flow accounts and resource productivity*. Retrieved from http://ec.europa.eu/eurostat/statistics-explained/index.php/Material_flow_accounts_and_resource_productivity

Frondel, M., Horbach, J., & Rennings, K. (2007). End-of-pipe or cleaner production? An empirical comparison of environmental innovation decisions across OECD countries. *Business Strategy and the Environment*, *16*(8), 571–584. doi:10.1002/bse.496

Frosch, R. A. (1992). Industrial ecology: A philosophical introduction. *Proceedings of the National Academy of Sciences of the United States of America*, *89*(3), 800–803. doi:10.1073/pnas.89.3.800 PMID:11607255

Geissdoerfer, M., Savaget, P., Bocken, N. M., & Hultink, E. J. (2017). The Circular Economy–A new sustainability paradigm? *Journal of Cleaner Production*, *143*, 757–768. doi:10.1016/j.jclepro.2016.12.048

Geng, Y., Zhang, P., Ulgiati, S., & Sarkis, J. (2010). Emergy analysis of an industrial park: The case of Dalian. China. *The Science of the Total Environment*, *408*(22), 5273–5283. doi:10.1016/j.scitotenv.2010.07.081 PMID:20805000

Ghisellini, P., Cialani, C., & Ulgiati, S. (2016). A review on circular economy: The expected transition to a balanced interplay of environmental and economic systems. *Journal of Cleaner Production*, *114*, 11–32. doi:10.1016/j.jclepro.2015.09.007

Govindan, K., Soleimani, H., & Kannan, D. (2015). Reverse logistics and closed-loop supply chain: A comprehensive review to explore the future. *European Journal of Operational Research*, *240*(3), 603–626. doi:10.1016/j.ejor.2014.07.012

Graedel, T. E., & Allenby, B. R. (2003). *Industrial Ecology* (2nd ed.). New York: Prentice Hall.

Graedel, T. E., & Allenby, B. R. (2010). *Industrial ecology and sustainable engineering*. Upper Saddle River, NJ: Prentice Hall.

Guide, V. D. R. Jr, & Van Wassenhove, L. N. (2009). OR FORUM—The evolution of closed-loop supply chain research. *Operations Research*, *57*(1), 10–18. doi:10.1287/opre.1080.0628

Gwehenberger, G., Erler, B., & Schnitzer, H. (2003). *A Multi e Strategy Approach to Zero Emissions*. Paper Presented at Technology Foresight Summit 2003, Budapest, Hungary. Retrieved from http://www.unido.org/.

Hall, J. (2001). Environmental supply-chain innovation. *Greener Management International*, 105-12.

Helmig, B., Spraul, K., & Ingenhoff, D. (2016). Under positive pressure: How stakeholder pressure affects corporate social responsibility implementation. *Business & Society*, *55*(2), 151–187. doi:10.1177/0007650313477841

Italian Ministry of the Environment. (2017). Towards a circular economy model for Italy. Ministry for the Environment and Protection of the Territory and the Sea in collaboration with the Ministry of Economic Development.

Judge, W. Q., & Elenkov, D. (2005). Organizational capacity for change and environmental performance: An empirical assessment of Bulgarian firms. *Journal of Business Research*, *58*(7), 893–901. doi:10.1016/j.jbusres.2004.01.009

King, A. A., & Lenox, M. J. (2001). Lean and green? An empirical examination of the relationship between lean production and environmental performance. *Production and Operations Management*, *10*(3), 244–256. doi:10.1111/j.1937-5956.2001.tb00373.x

Kleindorfer, P. R., Singhal, K., & Wassenhove, L. N. (2005). Sustainable operations management. *Production and Operations Management*, *14*(4), 482–492. doi:10.1111/j.1937-5956.2005.tb00235.x

Korhonen, J., Nuur, C., Feldmann, A., & Birkie, S. E. (2018). Circular economy as an essentially contested concept. *Journal of Cleaner Production*, *175*, 544–552. doi:10.1016/j.jclepro.2017.12.111

Lett. L. A. (2014). *Global threats. Waste recycling and the circular economy concept*. Academic Press.

Li, H., Bao, W., Xiu, C., Zhang, Y., & Xu, H. (2010). Energy conservation and circular economy in China's process industries. *Energy*, *35*(11), 4273–4281. doi:10.1016/j.energy.2009.04.021

Lieder, M., & Rashid, A. (2016). Towards circular economy implementation: A comprehensive review in context of manufacturing industry. *Journal of Cleaner Production*, *115*, 36–51. doi:10.1016/j.jclepro.2015.12.042

Liu, Y., & Bai, Y. (2014). An exploration of firms' awareness and behavior of developing circular economy: An empirical research in China. *Resources, Conservation and Recycling*, *87*, 145–152. doi:10.1016/j.resconrec.2014.04.002

Mirabella, N., Castellani, V., & Sala, S. (2014). Current options for the valorisation of food manufacturing waste: A review. *Journal of Cleaner Production*, *65*, 28–41. doi:10.1016/j.jclepro.2013.10.051

Molteni, L., & Troilo, G. (2007). *Ricerche di marketing*. McGraw-Hill.

Murphy, J., & Gouldson, A. (2000). Environmental policy and industrial innovation: Integrating environment and economy through ecological modernisation. *Geoforum*, *31*(1), 33–44. doi:10.1016/S0016-7185(99)00042-1

Mutz, D. (2015). *Circular Economy and Informal Waste Management in India – a Contradiction Institute of Development Studies*. Resource Politics 2015.

Naustdalslid, J. (2014). Circular economy in China e the environmental dimension of the harmonious society. *International Journal of Sustainable Development of World Ecology*. doi:10.1080/13504509.2014.914599

OECD. (2016). *Green growth indicators (Edition 2016)*. OECD Environment Statistics. doi:1.1787/5710f950-en

OECD. (2017). *Green growth indicators (Edition 2017)*. OECD Environment Statistics. doi:1.1787/9789264268586-en

Park, J., Sarkis, J., & Wu, Z. (2010). Creating integrated business and environmental value within the context of China's circular economy and ecological modernization. *Journal of Cleaner Production*, *18*(15), 1494–1501. doi:10.1016/j.jclepro.2010.06.001

Pearce, D. W., & Turner, R. K. (1990). *Economics of natural resources and the environment*. JHU Press.

Prendeville, S., Sanders, C., Sherry, J., & Costa, F. (2014). *Circular economy: is it enough*. EcoDesign Centre. Available from: http://www. edcw. org/en/resources/circulareconomy-it-enough

Preston, F. (2012). *A Global Redesign?: Shaping the Circular Economy*. London: Chatham House.

Ramani, K., Ramanujan, D., Bernstein, W. Z., Zhao, F., Sutherland, J., Handwerker, C., & Thurston, D. (2010). Integrated sustainable life cycle design: A review. *Journal of Mechanical Design*, *132*(9), 091004. doi:10.1115/1.4002308

Rao, P. (2002). Greening the supply chain: A new initiative in South East Asia. *International Journal of Operations & Production Management*, *22*(6), 632–655. doi:10.1108/01443570210427668

Sangle, S. (2010). Empirical analysis of determinants of adoption of proactive environmental strategies in India. *Business Strategy and the Environment*, *19*(1), 51–63.

Sarkis, J. (Ed.). (2006). Greening the supply chain. Springer Science & Business Media.

Schramm-Klein, H., Morschett, D., & Swoboda, B. (2015). Retailer corporate social responsibility: Shedding light on CSR's impact on profit of intermediaries in marketing channels. *International Journal of Retail & Distribution Management*, *43*(4/5), 403–431. doi:10.1108/IJRDM-04-2014-0041

Schroeder, R. G., Bates, K. A., & Junttila, M. A. (2002). A resource-based view of manufacturing strategy and the relationship to manufacturing performance. *Strategic Management Journal*, *23*(2), 105–117. doi:10.1002mj.213

Seuring, S., & Müller, M. (2008). From a literature review to a conceptual framework for sustainable supply chain management. *Journal of Cleaner Production*, *16*(15), 1699–171. doi:10.1016/j.jclepro.2008.04.020

Sherwin, C., & Evans, S. (2000, May). Ecodesign innovation: is. In *Proceedings of the 2000 IEEE International Symposium on Electronics and the Environment. ISEE-2000* (pp. 112-117). IEEE. 10.1109/ISEE.2000.857634

Singh, M. P., Chakraborty, A., & Roy, M. (2016). The link among innovation drivers, green innovation and business performance: Empirical evidence from a developing economy. *World Review of Science, Technology and Sustainable Development*, *12*(4), 316–334. doi:10.1504/WRSTSD.2016.082191

Singh, M. P., Chakraborty, A., & Roy, M. (2017). Developing an extended theory of planned behavior model to explore circular economy readiness in manufacturing MSMEs. India. *Resources. Conservation and Recycling*.

Singh, N., Jain, S., & Sharma, P. (2014). Determinants of proactive environmental management practices in Indian firms: An empirical study. *Journal of Cleaner Production*, *66*, 469–478. doi:10.1016/j.jclepro.2013.11.055

Stahel, W. (2010). *The performance economy*. Springer.

Stahel, W. R. (2013). The business angle of a circular economy–higher competitiveness. higher resource security and material efficiency. *A New Dynamic: Effective Business in a Circular Economy*, 45-53.

Stindt, D., & Sahamie, R. (2014). Review of research on closed loop supply chain management in the process industry. *Flexible Services and Manufacturing Journal*, *26*(1-2), 268–293. doi:10.100710696-012-9137-4

Su, B., Heshmati. A. Geng, Y., & Yu, X. (2013). A review of the circular economy in China: Moving from rhetoric to implementation. *Journal of Cleaner Production*, *42*, 215–227. doi:10.1016/j.jclepro.2012.11.020

Van Berkel, R. (1999). *Building a cleaner world: Cleaner Production, its role in Australia, lessons from overseas, and its future applications. Presentation for Futures Think Tank*. Perth, Australia: John Curtin International Institute, Curtin University of Technology.

Van Berkel, R. (2000). Sustainable development and cleaner production in minerals and energy production. In *Sixth International Symposium on Environmental Issues and Waste Management in Energy and Mineral Production* (pp. 1-17). Academic Press.

Van Berkel, R., Willems, E., & Lafleur, M. (1997). The relationship between cleaner production and industrial ecology. *Journal of Industrial Ecology*, *1*(1), 51–66. doi:10.1162/jiec.1997.1.1.51

Wells, P., & Seitz, M. (2005). Business models and closed-loop supply chains: A typology. *Supply Chain Management*, *10*(4), 249–251. doi:10.1108/13598540510612712

Wen, Z., & Meng, X. (2015). Quantitative assessment of industrial symbiosis for the promotion of circular economy: A case study of the printed circuit boards industry in China's Suzhou New District. *Journal of Cleaner Production*, *9*, 211–219. doi:10.1016/j.jclepro.2014.03.041

Winkler, H. (2011). Closed-loop production systems—A sustainable supply chain approach. *CIRP Journal of Manufacturing Science and Technology*, *4*(3), 243–246. doi:10.1016/j.cirpj.2011.05.001

Xue, B., Chen, X. P., Geng, Y., Guo, X. J., Lu, C. P., Zhang, Z. L., & Lu, C. Y. (2010). Survey of officials' awareness on circular economy development in China: Based on municipal and county level. *Resources, Conservation and Recycling*, *54*(12), 1296–1302. doi:10.1016/j.resconrec.2010.05.010

Yap, N. U. (2005). Towards a circular economy: Progress and challenges. *Green Management International*, *50*, 11–24.

Yayan, I. (2007). *The responsibilities of SME's within the scope of environmental management in adaptation process to EU and application in the Malatya organized industrial field* (PhD thesis). Inonu University.

Yu. F. Han, F., & Cui, Z. (2015). Evolution of industrial symbiosis in an eco-industrial park in China. *Journal of Cleaner Production*, *87*, 339–347. doi:10.1016/j.jclepro.2014.10.058

Zailani Hanim Mohamad, S., Eltayeb, T. K., Hsu, C. C., & Choon Tan, K. (2012). The impact of external institutional drivers and internal strategy on environmental performance. *International Journal of Operations & Production Management*, *32*(6), 721–745. doi:10.1108/01443571211230943

Zaman, A. U., & Lehmann, S. (2013). The zero waste index: A performance measurement tool for waste management systems in a 'zero waste city'. *Journal of Cleaner Production*, *50*, 123–132. doi:10.1016/j.jclepro.2012.11.041

Zhang, B., Yang, S., & Bi, J. (2013). Enterprises' willingness to adopt/develop cleaner production technologies: An empirical study in Changshu, China. *Journal of Cleaner Production*, *40*, 62–70. doi:10.1016/j.jclepro.2010.12.009

Zhu, Q., Geng, Y., & Lai, K. H. (2010). Circular economy practices among Chinese manufacturers varying in environmental-oriented supply chain cooperation and the performance implications. *Journal of Environmental Management*, *91*(6), 1324–1331. doi:10.1016/j.jenvman.2010.02.013 PMID:20223586

Zhu, Q., Sarkis, J., & Lai, K. H. (2007). Green supply chain management: Pressures. practices and performance within the Chinese automobile industry. *Journal of Cleaner Production*, *15*(11-12), 1041–1052. doi:10.1016/j.jclepro.2006.05.021

ADDITIONAL READING

Daddi, T., Iraldo, F., Frey, M., Gallo, P., & Gianfrate, V. (2016). Regional policies and eco-industrial development: The voluntary environmental certification scheme of the eco-industrial parks in Tuscany (Italy). *Journal of Cleaner Production*, *114*, 62–70. doi:10.1016/j.jclepro.2015.04.060

Frey, M. (2013). La green economy come nuovo modello di sviluppo. *Impresa Progetto-Electronic Journal of Management*, (3).

Chapter 7
An Approach to Solve Fuzzy Knapsack Problem in Investment and Business Model

Vishnu Pratap Singh
Visvesvaraya National Institute of Technology Nagpur, India

ABSTRACT

In this chapter, the author studies the knapsack problem with fuzzy weights for single and bi-objective function. The knapsack problem has been widely used in the investment and business model. In real-world decision-making situations, the existence of fuzziness of the weights and the profit is a common requirement. To overcome this difficulty, these weights and profit can be considered as a triangular fuzzy number. Thus, a fuzzy knapsack problem is introduced. The author introduces the possibility index which gives the possibility of choosing the items with fuzzy weights for knapsack with crisp capacity. The possibility index gives an idea to choose the solution according to the decision maker's choice. The dynamic programming approach using multi-stage decision making has been given for the different type of decision makers to find the solution. An investment problem in an imprecise environment has been defined as a fuzzy knapsack problem and the solution procedure is given to demonstrate the methodology.

DOI: 10.4018/978-1-5225-7850-5.ch007

INTRODUCTION

The knapsack problem is one of the most relevant mathematical programming problem with numerous applications in different areas. The knapsack problem (Martello et al, 199) is a problem where a tramper is searching for a combination of different items for filling the knapsack. The objective is to optimize the total utility value of all chosen items by the tramper subject to the total weight of chosen items is less than the capacity of a knapsack. The knapsack may correspond to a ship, truck or a resource. There are varieties of applications available for fuzzy knapsack problem such as various packing problem, cargo loading, cutting stock or economic planning. For example the problem of making investment decisions in which the size of an investment is based on the amount of money required, the knapsack capacity is the amount of available money to invest, the investment profit is the expected return. Knapsack problem has a simple structure which permits it to study in combinatorial optimization problems.

In the real world, the utility value used for knapsack problem is imprecise in nature because of the presence of inherent subjectivity. Some researcher used fuzzy theory to solve this type of problem. (Singh et al, 2017) proposed the fuzzy set theory, using this theory (Okada et al, 1994) described multiple-choice knapsack problem with fuzzy coefficients. (Kasperski eta 1, 2007) solved the 0-1 knapsack problem with fuzzy data. (Lin et al, 2001) described fuzzy knapsack problem (FKP) by taking each weight w_i, $i=1,2,\ldots,n$ as imprecise value. They consider $\tilde{w}_i = \left(w_i - \Delta_{i1}, w_i, w + \Delta_{i2}\right)$ as fuzzy number such that the decision maker should determine an acceptable range of values for each $\tilde{w}_i$, which is the interval $\left[w_i - \Delta_{i1}, w_i + \Delta_{i2}\right], 0 \le \Delta_{i1} < w_i$ and $0 \le \Delta_{i2}$. Then the decision maker chooses a value from the interval $\left[w_i - \Delta_{i1}, w_i + \Delta_{i2}\right]$ as an estimate of each weight. Estimate is exactly w_i if the acceptable grade is 1, otherwise, the acceptable grade will get smaller when the estimate approaches either $w_i - \Delta_{i2}$ or $w_i + \Delta_{i2}$. To calculate an estimate of the fuzzy weight defuzzification of the fuzzy number $\tilde{w}_i$ from the interval $\left[w_i - \Delta_{i1}, w_i + \Delta_{i2}\right]$ has been used.

The main idea of this chapter is to solve fuzzy knapsack problem in multi-stage decision making situation. Here, we choose the weight as a triangular fuzzy number and solved it without defuzzification. Defuzzification of fuzzy number gives a real value corresponding to that fuzzy number with some loss of information. Defuzzification of fuzzy number converts the fuzzy knapsack problem into crisp knapsack problem. Since the weights are fuzzy in nature we can fill the weights with some possibility, having any value between [0, 1]. (Sengupta et al, 2000) introduced acceptability index to order two intervals in terms of value. Similarly, we introduced a possibility index for calculating the possibility (Dubois et al, 1988) of putting fuzzy weight within a knapsack. Proposed possibility index provides the measure whether the knapsack can hold fuzzy weight or not. If the possibility index is 1 we can fill that weight completely in the knapsack and if it is zero we can not fill that weight. If the possibility index lies between [0, 1] we can fill the weight with this much possibility. Possibility index may be near 1 and also may be closer to zero. It depends on the decision maker how he chooses the weight. There are three types of decision makers (North et al, 1968) who want to get the solution namely Pessimistic decision maker, Optimistic decision maker and Moderator. An optimistic decision maker can take the worst case for optimizing the solution i.e. he tolerates the less possibility index for expected higher utility value and on the other hand pessimistic decision maker always chooses the highest possibility index even for total low utility value. A Moderator can choose the middle value of the possibility.

The bi-objective fuzzy knapsack problem is an extension of fuzzy knapsack problem. For solving bi-objective fuzzy knapsack problem, first, we optimize each objective function using proposed dynamic programming algorithm for single objective fuzzy knapsack problem. We select number of copies for both the objective functions separately and the pareto optimal frontier is generated by using these numbers of copies. Then the compromise ratio method (Guha et al, 2008) for decision maker under fuzzy environment has been used for selecting the best compromise solution.

The notable features of our approach are as follows:

- A new possibility index for calculating the possibility of putting fuzzy weight into a knapsack of crisp capacity has been developed. Possibility index gives an opportunity to the decision maker's to select the fuzzy weight according to their choice.
- A recursion based dynamic programming algorithm has been introduced to solve fuzzy knapsack problem which gives the optimal solution with some possibility index. The selection of possibility index may vary as the choice of decision maker's.
- For solving bi-objective fuzzy knapsack problem, the pareto optimal frontier is generated using the optimal values of each objective. Then the compromise ratio method for decision maker under fuzzy environment has been used for selecting the best compromise solution.

Due to possibility index, it is possible to solve fuzzy knapsack problem without doing defuzzification of its weight. Possibility index also gives an opportunities to decision makers for selecting the items according to their choice of possibility.

The chapter is organized as follows. The concept of possibility index has been introduced in Section 2. Fuzzy knapsack problem in multi-stage decision making for single objective, bi-objective and an algorithm is given in section 3. Numerical example is given in section 4. Section 5 concludes the work.

THE POSSIBILITY INDEX

Let us consider two fuzzy numbers $\tilde{A} = \left(a_1, a_2, a_3\right)$ and $\tilde{B} = \left(b_1, b_2, b_3\right)$ whose membership functions can be calculated by equation 1.

$$\mu_{\tilde{A}}\left(x\right) = \begin{cases} 0, & x < a_1 \\ \dfrac{x - a_1}{a_2 - a_1}, & a_1 \le x \le a_2 \\ \dfrac{a_3 - x}{a_3 - a_2}, & a_2 \le x \le a_3 \\ 0, & x > a_3 \end{cases} \tag{1}$$

Now if we take a knapsack of capacity $\tilde{B}$ and we want to fill the weight $\tilde{A}$ into the knapsack of capacity $\tilde{B}$ then we have three possibilities for filling the weight in the knapsack which is classified as follows.

1. $\tilde{A}$ can be completely filled into the knapsack of capacity $\tilde{B}$ i.e. possibility is one.
2. $\tilde{A}$ cannot be filled into the knapsack of capacity $\tilde{B}$ i.e. possibility is zero.
3. $\tilde{A}$ can be filled with some possibility into the knapsack of capacity $\tilde{B}$ i.e. possibility lies between zero and one.

If $\tilde{A} = \left(a_1, a_2, a_3\right)$ and $\tilde{B} = \left(b_1, b_2, b_3\right)$ are two fuzzy numbers then the possibility index for filling fuzzy weights in given capacity is denoted by $PI\left(\tilde{A} \blacktriangle \tilde{B}\right)$ i.e. the possibility of filling $\tilde{A}$ in $\tilde{B}$ and given by

$$PI\left(\tilde{A}\blacktriangle\tilde{B}\right)=\begin{cases}1-y_1\dfrac{\left(a_3-b_3\right)}{\left(a_3-a_1\right)}, & if\ \ b_3<a_3\ \ and\ \ a_2\le b_2\\ y_2\dfrac{\left(b_3-a_1\right)}{\left(a_3-a_1\right)}, & if\ \ b_3\left\langle a_3\ \ and\ \ a_2\right\rangle b_2\\ 1, & if\ \ b_3\ge a_3\\ 0, & if\ \ b_3\le a_1\end{cases} \tag{2}$$

where

$$y_1=\left\{\mu_{\tilde{D}}\left(x\right)\mid\mu_{\tilde{A}}\left(x\right)=\mu_{\tilde{B}}\left(x\right)for\,x\ge b_2\right\}$$

$$y_2=\{\max\ \mu_{\tilde{D}}\left(x\right)\mid\mu_{\tilde{D}}\left(x\right)=\min(\mu_{\tilde{A}}\left(x\right),\mu_{\tilde{B}}\left(x\right)\}$$

and $\mu_{\tilde{D}}\left(x\right)$ represents the membership value of fuzzy set $\tilde{D}=\tilde{A}\cap\tilde{B}$. Figure 1 shows some sets which defines above condition for calculating the possibility index.

When $b_3<a_3$ and $a_2<b_2$, the possibility index can be calculated as:

Figure 1. Sets of fuzzy numbers

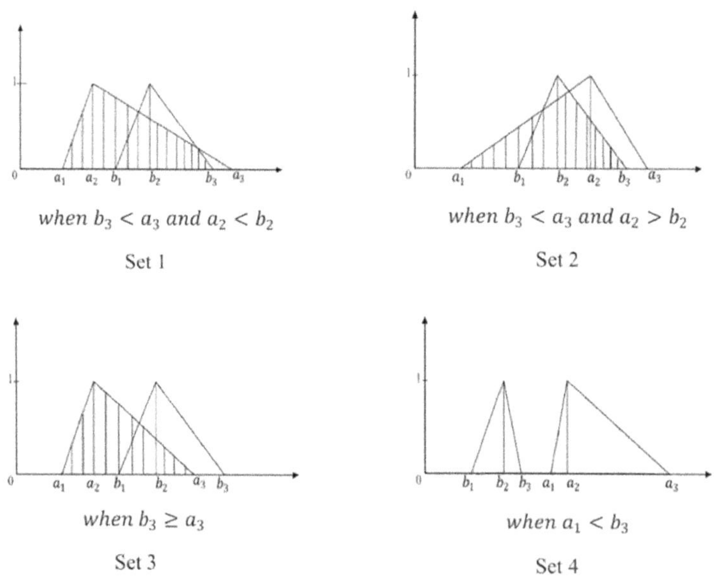

$$PI\left(\tilde{A}\blacktriangle\tilde{B}\right)=\frac{Area\ occupied\ by\ \tilde{A}\ in\ the\ knapsack\ of\ capacity\ \tilde{B}}{Total\ area\ of\ \tilde{A}}=1-y_1\frac{\left(a_3-b_3\right)}{\left(a_3-a_1\right)}$$

where

$$y_1=\{\mu_{\tilde{D}}\left(x\right)\mid\mu_{\tilde{A}}\left(x\right)=\mu_{\tilde{B}}\left(x\right) for x\geq b_2\}$$

and $\mu_{\tilde{D}}\left(x\right)$ represents the membership value of fuzzy set $\tilde{D}=\tilde{A}\cap\tilde{B}$.

When $b_3<a_3$ and $a_2>b_2$ the possibility index can be calculated as:

$$PI\left(\tilde{A}\blacktriangle\tilde{B}\right)=\frac{Area\ occupied\ by\ \tilde{A}\ in\ the\ knapsack\ of\ capacity\ \tilde{B}}{Total\ area\ of\ \tilde{A}}=y_2\frac{\left(b_3-a_1\right)}{\left(a_3-a_1\right)}$$

where

$$y_2=\{\max\mu_{\tilde{D}}\left(x\right)\mid\mu_{\tilde{D}}\left(x\right)=\min(\mu_{\tilde{A}}\left(x\right),\mu_{\tilde{B}}\left(x\right)\}$$

and $\mu_{\tilde{D}}\left(x\right)$ represents the membership value of fuzzy set $\tilde{D}=\tilde{A}\cap\tilde{B}$.

When $b_3\geq a_3$ the possibility index can be calculated as:

$$PI\left(\tilde{A}\blacktriangle\tilde{B}\right)=\frac{Area\ occupied\ by\ \tilde{A}\ in\ the\ knapsack\ of\ capacity\ \tilde{B}}{Total\ area\ of\ \tilde{A}}=1$$

When $a_1\geq b_3$ the possibility index can be calculated as:

$$PI\left(\tilde{A}\blacktriangle\tilde{B}\right)=\frac{Area\ occupied\ by\ \tilde{A}\ in\ the\ knapsack\ of\ capacity\ \tilde{B}}{Total\ area\ of\ \tilde{A}}=0$$

Since the knapsack capacity is crisp value. Let $\tilde{B}=\left(b,b,b\right)$ i.e. a crisp value b is knapsack capacity which is shown in figure 2. Now our possibility index can be given as:

Figure 2. PI of $\tilde{A} = (a_1, a_2, a_3)$ *for different value of b(crisp)*

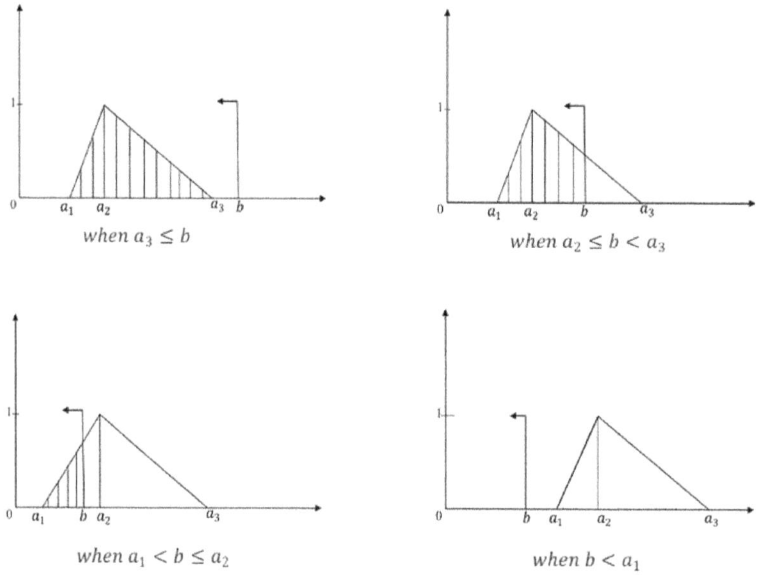

$$PI\left(\tilde{A} \blacktriangle b\right) = \begin{cases} 1, & if \;\; a_3 \leq b \\ 1 - \mu_{\tilde{A}}\left(b\right)\dfrac{\left(a_3 - b\right)}{\left(a_3 - a_1\right)}, & if \;\; a_2 \leq b < a_3 \\ \mu_{\tilde{A}}\left(b\right)\dfrac{\left(b - a_1\right)}{\left(a_3 - a_1\right)}, & if \;\; a_1 < b < a_2 \\ 0, & if \;\; b \leq a_1 \end{cases} \tag{3}$$

FUZZY KNAPSACK PROBLEM BY MULTI-STAGE DECISION PROCESS

In the classical Knapsack problem all the weights and utility value of items are assumed to be crisp in nature. Mathematically, it is defined as,

$$\max \sum_{i=1}^{n} u_i x_i$$

$$s.t\sum_{i=1}^{n} w_i x_i \leq W, i = 1,\ldots,n, \tag{4}$$

If the items are n in number and u_i represents the utility value of each item for i=1,2,…,n and w_i represents the crisp weight of each item with knapsack capacity W. Without loss of generality all weights and utility value of the items are assumed to be a positive numbers. In practice, we see many knapsack problems with items whose weights or price value are imprecise. Here we consider the problem in which weights of the items are triangular fuzzy number $\tilde{w} = \left(w_{1i}, w_{2i}, w_{3i}\right)$, knapsack capacity W and utility value are crisp or also may be considered as fuzzy. Now the fuzzy knapsack problem as a linear programming model is described by

$$\max \sum_{i=1}^{n} u_i x_i$$

$$s.t\sum_{i=1}^{n} \tilde{w}_i x_i \blacklozenge W, i = 1,\ldots,n, \tag{5}$$

After first stage when we have filled some weight in knapsack, the capacity of the knapsack will be fuzzy and the linear programming model is now described by

$$\max \sum_{i=1}^{n} u_i x_i$$

$$s.t\sum_{i=1}^{n} \tilde{w}_i x_i \blacklozenge \tilde{W}', i = 1,\ldots,n, \tag{6}$$

where $\widetilde{W'}$ is fuzzy weight.

A fuzzy knapsack problem may be viewed as n stage decision making process where the fuzzy stage transformation equation unite all the stages. In a dynamic programming structure of fuzzy knapsack problem, the stage transformation equation transforms input state variable and decision variable to an output state which works as an input state variable for its next stage and this process continues up to n^{th} stage. If S^0 is the input decision variable for 1st stage and d^1 is the state variable then stage 1 will consume some part of input state and decision variable and it will give an immediate return in the form of utility value (f_1) and possibility index(PI_1) at first stage. At first stage, state variable has a crisp value while from 2nd stage onwards it becomes fuzzy. If we have S^{j-1} as input decision fuzzy variable at j^{th} stage which is output from the (j-1) stage and $\tilde{d}^j$ for (j>1) is state variable then the immediate return at stage j is given by (f_j,PI_j). Similarly at n^{th} stage we get an optimal return f_n with possibility PI_n. This optimal value will be our solution and by moving backward direction with respect to the corresponding decision variable we calculate the non-dominated set of items. Here possibility index plays an important role at each stage. Since the decision makers have values of possibility index at each stage so that they can select the optimal value according to their tolerance limits. The selection of possibility index will change the solution according to DM's choices.

Similarly, a bi-objective fuzzy knapsack problem in multi-stage decision making can be defined with two objective function. Here, we represent a bi-objective fuzzy knapsack problem in multi-stage decision making approach by the figure 3 given below.

Methodology for Single Objective Fuzzy Knapsack Problem

A dynamic programming technique of decision making in fuzzy environment is given to solve FKP using the possibility index introduced in the previous section. The solution obtained by this method depends upon the DM who chooses the profit with respect to possibility index at each state of every stage. In the dynamic programming approach we divide an n items (variable) problem into n single stage problem and each stage provide the selection of copies of one item with the optimal selection of the item from its previous stages and then it used backward recursive approach to get the solution of the overall problem. Following steps are given to solve fuzzy knapsack problem.

Figure 3. Multistage decision making process for a bi-objective FKP

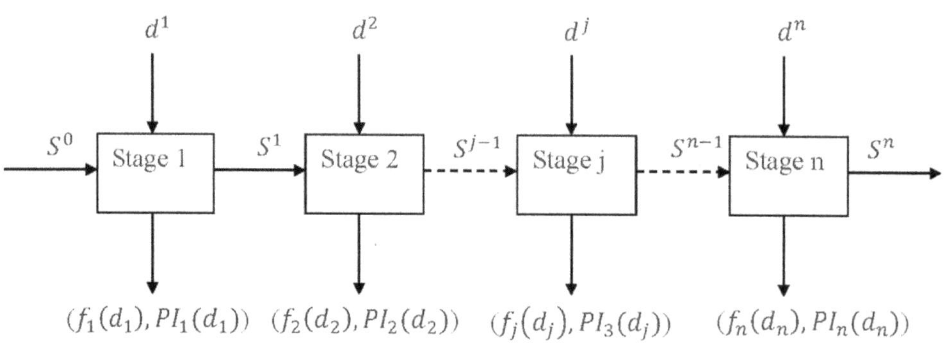

1. First we formulate the problem by defining the symbol given below-
   x_i: Number of copies of an item *i* selected for knapsack.
   d_i: State variable (Available weight at each stage *i*).
   u_i: Utility value of an item *i* selected for knapsack.
   $F_i(x_i)$: Return value in stage i given x_i number of copies.
   $f_i^{N_t}\left(d_i\right)$: Maximum possible value chooses for stage *i* to *n* according to the decision makers tolerance limit N_t for *t*=1,2,3.
   $PI_i(x_i)$: Possibility index at stage *i* for weights selected in the knapsack.
2. 2. We start from n^{th} item and calculate the optimal value and possibility index of weight for this item. In the next stage we take n^{th} and $(n-1)^{th}$ item and again calculate the optimal value and possibility index of weights. Continuing in this manner at i^{th} stage we have *i* number of item, for calculating the optimal value and possibility index which is selected by the DM in each stage we require optimal value and possibility index from previous stage. So we defined stage transformation equations for utility value and the possibility index –

$$F_i\left(x_i, d_i\right) = x_i * u_i + f_{i+1}^{N_t}\left(d_i^{'}\right) \tag{7}$$

$$PI_i\left(x_i, d_i\right) = \frac{1}{2}\left(PI\left(\left(x_i * \tilde{w}_i\right) \blacktriangle d_i\right) + PI\left(\widetilde{ow_i} \blacktriangle \widetilde{rw_i}\right)\right) \tag{8}$$

$$f_i^{N_t}\left(d_i\right) = \max\{F_i\left(x_i, d_i\right) \mid \max\left\{PI_i\left(x_i, d_i\right)\right\} \in N_t\} \tag{9}$$

Here $d_i^{'} =$�rw_{i3}� , $\widetilde{rw_i} = d_i - \left(x_i * \tilde{w}_i\right)$ is the remaining fuzzy weight at stage i and $\widetilde{ow_i} = \sum_{j=i+1}^{n} x_j^{*} \tilde{w}_j$ is the optimal weight at stage *i* due to its all previous stages where x_i^{*} is the optimal value at stage i. $PI_i\left(\widetilde{ow_i} \blacktriangle \widetilde{rw_i}\right)$ represent the possibility index of two fuzzy number which is calculated by equation 2. Initial values are given by the equations.

$$f_{n+1}^{N_t}\left(d_i\right) = 0 \tag{10}$$

$$PI_{n+1}\left(\widetilde{ow_n}\blacktriangle\widetilde{rw_n}\right) = PI\left(\left(x_i * \tilde{w}_i\right)\blacktriangle d_i\right) \tag{11}$$

3. Once we calculate the value of $f_i^{N_t}\left(d_i\right)$, $PI_i(x_i)$ at first stage it depends upon the decision maker to choose the optimal value in next stage. Here N_1, N_2, N_3 are the tolerance limit for the optimistic, moderator and pessimistic decision makers respectively. Then the selection of $PI_i(x_i)$ for next stage has been showed in the figure 4 depending on the selected decision maker and the corresponding $f_i^{N_t}\left(d_i\right)$ value will be optimal value for profit.
4. Now we have utility values and possibility index for all stages. Moving backward by considering the optimal value (chooses by DM) corresponding to remaining weight from first stage to n^{th} stage will give the solution for that decision maker. Similarly for other decision makers they can select there tolerance limit.

Methodology for Bi-Objective Fuzzy Knapsack Problem

In the classical bi-objective Knapsack problem all the weights and item profits are assumed to be crisp in nature. Mathematically, it is defined as,

$$\max f_k\left(x\right) = \sum_{i=1}^{n} u_i^k x_i \quad for \quad k = 1,2$$

Figure 4. Selection of Possibility index by DM

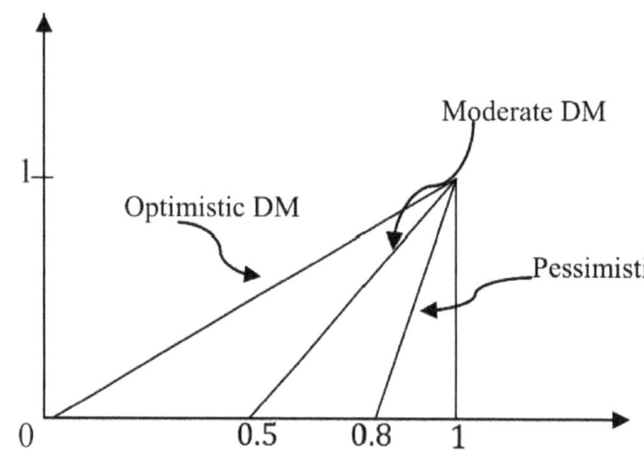

$$s.t\sum_{i=1}^{n} w_i x_i < W, i = 1,\ldots,n.$$

If the item are n in number and u_i^1 and u_i^2 (i=1,2,…,n) represents the utility values of item i for first and second objective respectively and w_i represents the crisp weight of each item with knapsack capacity W. In the formulation of bi-objective fuzzy knapsack problem, the used weights are fuzzy in nature. In practice, we see many knapsack problems involves items whose weights or price value are imprecise. Here we consider the problem in which weights of the items are triangular fuzzy number $\widetilde{w_i} = \left(w_{1i}, w_{2i}, w_{3i}\right)$, knapsack capacity W and utility values are crisp. After fuzzifying the crisp value W we obtain $\tilde{W} = \left(W_1, W_2, W_3\right)$. Now the bi-objective fuzzy knapsack problem as a linear programming model is described by

$$\max f_k\left(x\right) = \sum_{i=1}^{n} u_i^k x_i \quad for \quad k = 1,2$$

$$s.t\sum_{i=1}^{n} w_i x_i < W, i = 1,\ldots,n.$$

Following steps are given to solve bi-objective fuzzy knapsack problem.

1. First we formulate the problem by defining the symbol given below-
   x_i: Number of copies of an item i selected for knapsack.
   y_k^i : Upper bound of an item i for k^{th} objective.
   d_i: State variable (Available weight in each stage i).
   u_i^k : Utility value of an item i for k^{th} objective (k=1,2) selected for knapsack.
   $F_k^i\left(x_i\right)$: Return value in stage i given x_i number of copies for k^{th} objective (k=1,2).
   $f_k^{i,N_t}\left(d_i\right)$: Maximum possible utility value selected at stage i to n for k^{th} objective (k=1,2) according to the decision makers tolerance limit N_t for t=1,2,3.
   $PI_i(x_i)$: Possibility index in stage i for weights selected in the knapsack.
2. 2. We start from n^{th} item and calculate the optimal value for each objective functions and possibility index of weight for this item. In the next stage we take n^{th} and $(n-1)^{th}$ item and again calculate the optimal value and possibility index of weights. Continuing in this manner at i^{th} stage we have i number of

item, for calculating the optimal value and possibility index which is selected by the DM in each stage we require optimal value and possibility index from previous stage. So we defined stage transformation equations for profit and the possibility index -

$$F_k^i\left(x_i, d_i\right) = x_i * u_i + f_k^{i+1,N_t}\left(d_i\right) \quad for\ k = 1,2 \tag{12}$$

$$PI_i\left(x_i, d_i\right) = \frac{1}{2}\left(PI\left(\left(x_i * \tilde{w}_i\right) \blacktriangle d_i\right) + PI\left(\widetilde{ow_i} \blacktriangle \widetilde{rw_i}\right)\right) \tag{13}$$

$$f_k^{i,N_t}\left(d_i\right) = \max\{F_k^i\left(x_i, d_i\right) \mid \max\left\{PI_i\left(x_i, d_i\right)\right\} \in N_t\ for\, t = 1,2,3\} \tag{14}$$

Here $d' =$�$\widetilde{rw_{i3}}$�, $\widetilde{rw_i} = d_i - \left(x_i * \tilde{w}_i\right)$ is the remaining fuzzy weight at stage i and $\widetilde{ow_i} = \sum_{j=i+1}^{n} x_j^* \tilde{w}_j$ is the optimal weight at stage *i* due to its all previous stages where x_i^* is the optimal value at stage i. $PI_i\left(\widetilde{ow_i} \blacktriangle \widetilde{rw_i}\right)$ represent the possibility index of two fuzzy number which is calculated by equation 2. Initial values are given by the equations.

$$f_k^{n+1,N_t}\left(d_i\right) = 0 \tag{15}$$

$$PI_{n+1}\left(\widetilde{ow_n} \blacktriangle \widetilde{rw_n}\right) = PI\left(\left(x_i * \tilde{w}_i\right) \blacktriangle d_i\right) \tag{16}$$

3. Once calculate the value of $f_k^{i,N_t}\left(d_i\right)$, $PI_i(x_i)$ at first stage it depends upon the decision maker to choose the optimal value in next stage. Let N_1, N_2, N_3 are the tolerance limit for the optimistic, moderator and pessimistic decision makers respectively. Then the selection of $PI_i(x_i)$ for next stage has been shown in the figure 4 depending on the selected decision maker and the corresponding $f_k^{i,N_t}\left(d_i\right)$ value will be optimal value for profit.

4. Now we have utility values and possibility index for all stages. Moving backward by considering the optimal value (chooses by DM) corresponding to remaining weight from first stage to n^{th} stage will give the solution and the selected number of copies of item for that decision maker and the selected number of copies . Similarly for other decision makers they can select there tolerance limit.
5. 5. According to the decision maker's tolerance limit select the upper bound of each item for each objective. Here we select only those values of x_i for which the possibility index $PI_i \in N^t$ at $d_i = W$. Now stage transformation equations for uniting all the stages in case of mixed approach

$$F_k^i\left(x_i, d_i\right) = x_i * u_i^k + f_k^{i+1,N_t}\left(d'\right)$$

$$f_k^{i,N_t}\left(d_i\right) = \max\{F_k^i\left(x_i, d_i\right) \mid \max\left\{PI_i\left(x_i, d_i\right)\right\} \in N_t\}$$

6. Now, we select number of copies for both the objective by moving in backward direction with maximum objectives values provided the possibility index for $d_i = W$ at last stage ($i = 10$) should not be less than from possibility index at $d_{i-1} = W$.

NUMERICAL EXAMPLE

Example 1: Consider the fuzzy knapsack model given in table 1. Our objective is to optimize the utility value subject to knapsack capacity (10 unit) and find number of copies per item.

Mathematical model as defined in section 3 can be written as

$$\max 20x_1 + 50x_2 + 60x_3$$

Table 1. Data for knapsack problem

Weight	$\tilde{1} = \left(0.5, 1, 2\right)$	$\tilde{2} = \left(1.5, 2, 3\right)$	$\tilde{2} = \left(1.5, 2, 3\right)$
Profit	20	50	60
Type	A	B	C

$s.t\tilde{1}x_1 + \tilde{2}x_2 + \tilde{2}x_3 ◆ \widetilde{10}, i = 1,2,3.$

These tables represent the solution of fuzzy knapsack problem given above. We can solve this problem for three decision makers' i.e. pessimistic DM, moderator and optimistic decision maker. The given tables show the solution for moderator who chooses the maximum profit with the maximum possibility which lies in the interval [0.5, 1].

In table 3 calculating the profit value when d=7, x_2=1, we have available weight 7 unit in which we can fill 1 copy of item B with possibility index 1. Now we have remaining weight $\widetilde{rw_i} = (4, 5, 5.5)$ this implies $d' = 6$. From the previous stage at d=6 we have optimal profit is 120 with $x_3^* = 2$. So the optimal profit becomes 170 with possibility index 0.97.

From tables 2, 3 and 4, it is clear that a moderator can choose three copies of type C, one copy of type B and five copies of type A so that the optimal solution is 330 with possibility 0.5, another solution with the same possibility is given by two copies of type C, three copies of type B and three copies of type A.

Example 2: Let us consider that there is a truck with 10 tons loading capacity. The decision makers' have two types of items A and B with fuzzy weights. Here f_1 represents the profits on the items of type A and B respectively f_2 represent the remaining amount of material used in manufacturing the items of the type A and B respectively. Our objective is to optimize both the objective functions

Table 2. Solution for stage 3 problem for FKP

d	$x_3 = 0$	$x_3 = 1$	$x_3 = 2$	$x_3 = 3$	$x_3 = 4$	$x_3 = 5$	max	x_3
1	-	-	-	-	-	-	-	-
2	-	(60, 0.34)	-	-	-	-	(60, 0.34)	1
3	-	(60, 1)	-	-	-	-	(60, 1)	1
4	-	(60, 1)	(120, 0.34)	-	-	-	(60, 1)	1
5	-	(60, 1)	(120, 0.83)	(180, 0.03)	-	-	(120, 0.83)	2
6	-	(60, 1)	(120, 1)	(180, 0.34)	-	-	(120, 1)	2
7	-	(60, 1)	(120, 1)	(180, 0.7)	(240, 0.08)	-	(180, 0.7)	3
8	-	(60, 1)	(120, 1)	(180, 0.92)	(240, 0.34)	(300, 0.01)	(180, 0.92)	3
9	-	(60, 1)	(120, 1)	(180, 1)	(240, 0.62)	(300, 0.12)	(240, 0.62)	4
10	-	(60, 1)	(120, 1)	(180, 1)	(240, 0.83)	(300, 0.34)	(240, 0.83)	4

Table 3. Solution for stage 2 problem for FKP

d	$x_2 = 0$	$x_2 = 1$	$x_2 = 2$	$x_2 = 3$	$x_2 = 4$	$x_2 = 5$	max	x_2	x_3
1	-	-	-	-	-	-	-	0	1
2	(60, 0.34)	(50, 0.34)	-	-	-	-	(60, 0.34)		
3	(60, 1)	(50, 1)	-	-	-	-	(60, 1)	0	1
4	(60, 1)	(110, 0.84)	(100, 0.34)	-	-	-	(110, 0.84)	1	1
5	(120, 0.83)	(110, 1)	(160, 0.55)	(150, 0.03)	-	-	(160, 0.55)	2	1
6	(120, 1)	(170, 0.75)	(160, 1)	(150, 0.34)	-	-	(170, 0.75)	1	2
7	(180, 0.7)	(170, 0.97)	(160, 1)	(210, 0.66)	(200, 0.08)	-	(210, 0.66)	3	1
8	(180, 0.92)	(230, 0.72)	(220, 0.83)	(210, 0.96)	(260, 0.2)	(250, 0.01)	(230, 0.72)	1	3
9	(240, 0.62)	(230, 0.9)	(220, 1)	(270, 0.65)	(260, 0.81)	(250, 0.12)	(270, 0.65)	3	2
10	(240, 0.83)	(290, 0.78)	(280, 0.77)	(270, 0.96)	(260, 0.91)	(310, 0.11)	(290, 0.78)	1	4

Table 4. Solution for stage 1 problem for FKP

d	$x_1 = 0$	$x_1 = 1$	$x_1 = 2$	$x_1 = 3$	$x_1 = 4$	$x_1 = 5$	$x_1 = 6$	$x_1 = 7$	$x_1 = 8$	$x_1 = 9$	$x_1 = 10$	max
10	(290,0.78)	(310,0.58)	(310,0.54)	(330,0.50)	(310,0.58)	(330,0.50)	(330,0.47)	(350,0.43)	(330,0.48)	(350,0.26)	(360,0.17)	(330,0.50)

subject to knapsack capacity (W=10) and find number of copies per item which gives the compromise solution for both the objectives.

If a moderator is trying to find the solution then the selected possibility index should be greater than 0.5. Here the solution is given for moderator. First we solve it by taking each objective separately using our proposed dynamic programming algorithm.

From table 6, 6, 8 and 9 it is clear that we select x_2=0,1,2,3,4 and x_1=0,1,2,3,4 since the possibility index at x_1=x_2=5 is less than 0.5.

The following pareto frontier can be generated for the above problem

Table 5. Data for knapsack problem

Weight	$\tilde{2} = (1.5, 2, 3)$	$\tilde{2} = (1.5, 2, 3)$
f_1	6	10
f_2	20	3
Type	A	B

Table 6. Solution for first objective at stage 1

d_2	$x_2 = 0$	$x_2 = 1$	$x_2 = 2$	$x_2 = 3$	$x_2 = 4$	$x_2 = 5$	$\max f_1$	x_2
1	-	-	-	-	-	-	-	-
2	-	(10, 0.34)	-	-	-	-	(10, 0.34)	1
3	-	(10, 1)	-	-	-	-	(10, 1)	1
4	-	(10, 1)	(20, 0.34)	-	-	-	(10, 1)	1
5	-	(10, 1)	(20, 0.83)	(30, 0.03)	-	-	(20, 0.83)	2
6	-	(10, 1)	(20, 1)	(30, 0.34)	-	-	(20, 1)	2
7	-	(10, 1)	(20, 1)	(30, 0.7)	(40, 0.08)	-	(30, 0.7)	3
8	-	(10, 1)	(20, 1)	(30, 0.92)	(40, 0.34)	(50, 0.01)	(30, 0.92)	3
9	-	(10, 1)	(20, 1)	(30, 1)	(40, 0.62)	(50, 0.12)	(40, 0.62)	4
10	-	(10, 1)	(20, 1)	(30, 1)	(40, 0.83)	(50, 0.34)	(40, 0.83)	4

Table 7. Solution for first objective at stage 2

d_1	$x_1 = 0$	$x_1 = 1$	$x_1 = 2$	$x_1 = 3$	$x_1 = 4$	$x_1 = 5$	$\max f_1$	x_1	x_2
1	-	-	-	-	-	-	-	0	1
2	(10, 0.34)	(6, 0.34)	-	-	-	-	(10, 0.34)		
3	(10, 1)	(6, 1)	-	-	-	-	(10, 1)	0	1
4	(10, 1)	(16, 0.84)	(12, 0.34)	-	-	-	(16, 0.84)	1	1
5	(20, 0.83)	(16, 1)	(22, 0.55)	(18, 0.03)	-	-	(22, 0.55)	2	1
6	(20, 1)	(26, 0.75)	(22, 1)	(18, 0.34)	-	-	(26, 0.75)	1	2
7	(30, 0.7)	(26, 0.97)	(22, 1)	(28, 0.66)	(24, 0.08)	-	(30, 0.7)	0	3
8	(30, 0.92)	(36, 0.72)	(32, 0.83)	(28, 0.96)	(34, 0.2)	(30, 0.01)	(36, 0.72)	1	3
9	(40, 0.62)	(36, 0.9)	(32, 1)	(38, 0.65)	(34, 0.81)	(30, 0.12)	(40, 0.62)	0	4
10	(40, 0.83)	(46, 0.78)	(42, 0.77)	(38, 0.96)	(34, 0.91)	(40, 0.11)	(46, 0.78)	1	4

Table 8. Solution for Second objective at stage 1

d_2	$x_2 = 0$	$x_2 = 1$	$x_2 = 2$	$x_2 = 3$	$x_2 = 4$	$x_2 = 5$	$\max f_2$	x_2
1	-	-	-	-	-	-	-	-
2	-	(3, 0.34)	-	-	-	-	(3, 0.34)	1
3	-	(3, 1)	-	-	-	-	(3, 1)	1
4	-	(3, 1)	(6, 0.34)	-	-	-	(3, 1)	1
5	-	(3, 1)	(6, 0.83)	(9, 0.03)	-	-	(6, 0.83)	2
6	-	(3, 1)	(6, 1)	(9, 0.34)	-	-	(6, 1)	2
7	-	(3, 1)	(6, 1)	(9, 0.7)	(12, 0.08)	-	(9, 0.7)	3
8	-	(3, 1)	(6, 1)	(9, 0.92)	(12, 0.34)	(15, 0.01)	(9, 0.92)	3
9	-	(3, 1)	(6, 1)	(9, 1)	(12, 0.62)	(15, 0.12)	(12, 0.62)	4
10	-	(3, 1)	(6, 1)	(9, 1)	(12, 0.83)	(15, 0.34)	(12, 0.83)	4

Table 9. Solution for second objective at stage 2

d_1	$x_1 = 0$	$x_1 = 1$	$x_1 = 2$	$x_1 = 3$	$x_1 = 4$	$x_1 = 5$	$\max f_2$	x_1	x_2
1	-	-	-	-	-	-	-	1	0
2	(3, 0.34)	(20, 0.34)	-	-	-	-	(20, 0.34)		
3	(3, 1)	(20, 1)	-	-	-	-	(20, 1)	1	0
4	(3, 1)	(23, 0.84)	(40, 0.34)	-	-	-	(23, 0.84)	1	1
5	(6, 0.83)	(23, 1)	(43, 0.55)	(60, 0.03)	-	-	(43, 0.55)	2	1
6	(6, 1)	(29, 0.75)	(43, 1)	(60, 0.34)	-	-	(43, 1)	2	1
7	(9, 0.7)	(29, 0.97)	(43, 1)	(63, 0.66)	(80, 0.08)	-	(63, 0.66)	3	1
8	(9, 0.92)	(38, 0.72)	(46, 0.83)	(63, 0.96)	(83, 0.2)	(100, 0.01)	(63, 0.96)	3	1
9	(12, 0.62)	(38, 0.9)	(46, 1)	(66, 0.65)	(83, 0.81)	(100, 0.12)	(83, 0.81)	4	1
10	(12, 0.83)	(50, 0.78)	(49, 0.77)	(66, 0.96)	(83, 0.91)	(103, 0.11)	(83, 0.91)	4	1

- (40,12) ◆ (0,4)
- (38,66) ◆ (3,2)
- (34,83) ◆ (4,1)

Now fuzzy decision matrix is given by

Table 10. Solution for both objectives at stage 1

d_2	$x_2 = 0$	$x_2 = 1$	$x_2 = 2$	$x_2 = 3$	$x_2 = 4$	$\max f_1, f_2$
1	-	-	-	-	-	-
2	-	(10,3,0.34)	-	-	-	(10,3,0.34)
3	-	(10,3,1)	-	-	-	(10,3,1)
4	-	(10,3,1)	(20,6,0.34)	-	-	(10,3,1)
5	-	(10,3,1)	(20,6,0.83)	(30,9,0.03)	-	(20,6,0.83)
6	-	(10,3,1)	(20,6,1)	(30,9,0.34)	-	(20,6,1)
7	-	(10,3,1)	(20,6,1)	(30,9,0.7)	(40,12,0.08)	(30,9,0.7)
8	-	(10,3,1)	(20,6,1)	(30,9,0.92)	(40,12,0.34)	(30,9,0.92)
9	-	(10,3,1)	(20,6,1)	(30,9,1)	(40,12,0.62)	(40,12,0.62)
10	-	(10,3,1)	(20,6,1)	(30,9,1)	(40,12,0.83)	(40,12,0.83)

Table 11. Solution for both objectives at stage 2

d_1	$x_1 = 0$	$x_1 = 3$	$x_1 = 4$	$Max f_1$	$Max f_2$
10	(40,12,0.83)	(38,66,0.96)	(34,83,0.91)	(40,12,0.83)	(34,83,0.91)

$$\tilde{Y} = (\tilde{f}_{ij})_{2\times 3} = \begin{pmatrix} (0;0;0) & (6;1.5;3) & (8;2;4) \\ (8;2;4) & (4;1;2) & (2;0.5;1) \\ \end{pmatrix}$$

After calculating normalized fuzzy decision matrix fuzzy Positive ideal solution and fuzzy negative ideal solution is given by $\tilde{a}^+ = \{(0.67;0.16;0.34), (0.67;0.16;0.34)\}$ and $\tilde{a}^- = \{(0;0;0), (0.16;0.04;0.08)\}$ respectively.

So Using compromise ratio method we get the solution which is 3 copies of type A and 2 copies of type B with the possibility index 0.96. Where decision at each stage for selecting the possibility depends upon the tolerance limit of moderator.

CONCLUSION

For modeling an investment problem in a real-world phenomenon, the crisp knapsack problem is extended into fuzzy knapsack problem and solve it without defuzzification. The resulting value of optimal return changes with the selection of possibility index by DM. The possibility index of selecting fuzzy amount in available fuzzy amount gives the opportunity to DM to select the optimal return according to their choice of decision. The proposed dynamic programming technique provides us with a useful way to deal with the knapsack problem in the fuzzy environment for an investment problem.

REFERENCES

Dubois, D., & Prade, H. (1988). *Possibility theory*. Springer. doi:10.1007/978-1-4684-5287-7

Guha, D., & Chakraborty, D. (2008). *Compromise ratio method for decision making under fuzzy environment using fuzzy distance measure*. Academic Press.

Kasperski, A., & Kulej, M. (2007). The 0-1 knapsack problem with fuzzy data. *Fuzzy Optimization and Decision Making*, *6*(2), 163–172. doi:10.100710700-007-9000-3

Lin, F. T., & Yao, J. S. (2001). Using fuzzy numbers in knapsack problems. *European Journal of Operational Research*, *135*(1), 158–176. doi:10.1016/S0377-2217(00)00310-6

Martello, S., & Toth, P. (1990). *Knapsack Problems*. Wiley.

North, D. W. (1968). A tutorial introduction to decision theory. Systems Science and Cybernetics. *IEEE Transactions on*, *4*(3), 200–210.

Okada, S., & Gen, M. (1994). Fuzzy multiple choice knapsack problem. *Fuzzy Sets and Systems*, *67*(1), 71–80. doi:10.1016/0165-0114(94)90209-7

Sengupta, A., & Pal, T. K. (2000). On comparing interval numbers. *European Journal of Operational Research*, *127*(1), 28–43. doi:10.1016/S0377-2217(99)00319-7

Singh, V. P., & Chakraborty, D. (2017). Solving bi-level programming problem with fuzzy random variable coefficients. *Journal of Intelligent & Fuzzy Systems*, *32*(1), 521–528. doi:10.3233/JIFS-152354

Zadeh, L. A. (1965). Fuzzy sets. *Information and Control*, *8*(3), 338–353. doi:10.1016/S0019-9958(65)90241-X

Chapter 8
Spiral Management:
New Concept of the Social Systems Management

Justína Mikulášková
Slovak University of Technology in Bratislava, Slovakia

Miloš Čambál
Slovak University of Technology in Bratislava, Slovakia

Ľuboš Polakovič
Lotes Centrum s.r.o., Slovakia

Petra Urbanovičová
Slovak University of Technology in Bratislava, Slovakia

ABSTRACT

Spiral management and its principles are based on the long-term successful existence of living systems. The principles can be applied to the enterprise and organization management. Living systems manage long-term success by acquiring energy from their surroundings (through nutrition), while enterprises acquire customers and employees' energy in order to eliminate entropy (in enterprises manifested as economic losses). Spiral management is based on the synergy of living systems. It describes behavior patterns in the cyclical development of enterprises as well as the ability of the latter to diagnose their own strategic decisions, including the instructions of how to drive an enterprise towards a long-term success. The chapter describes theoretical basis of spiral management while providing a novel insight into this unique managerial approach and emphasizing its importance for the human resources management. Also introduced are the elements of spiral management applied in the enterprises that want to be competitive and survive turbulent periods.

DOI: 10.4018/978-1-5225-7850-5.ch008

INTRODUCTION

The world of the 21st century is characterized by dynamism, turbulence and uncertainty. There is a need for change of the complex paradigm of thinking in society and humanity, as well as in organizations and enterprises at every market level. The current crisis differs from the previous ones; it is a crisis of consciousness, a crisis of paradigm, when the commonly accepted rules and procedures stop working. Companies are struggling with fluctuation, disproportionate cost of production quality, increasing pressure on growth and expansion versus social responsibility, or traditionalism versus multiculturalism etc.

In order to survive, companies need to address the issue of changing their own management paradigm. Otherwise, they are likely to fail. Over the past two hundred years, industrial system had built the basis of economy and society throughout the periods of birth, boom and gradual exhaust of their development potential up to the phase of decline. As early as in the first half of the 20th century, the first symptoms of the industrial system depletion appeared, invoking the need to find an alternative to the existing system, i.e. possibilities of its rectification. Gravity center of technology growth between the years 1792 and 1989 ended up with the excess of the technology growth potential. (Polakovič & Krempaský, 2012)

Modern society faces numerous questions: Is today's society in crisis? Is the contemporary society, with consumption dominating, sustainable? What is the impact of globalisation on the stability of society? Is there another, a real alternative for the current society? Regarding the current state, can another type of society be considered? Facing the abysmal difference between the rich and the poor, is the current society sustainable? Are there consistent political elites able to navigate the current society in solving topical problems? What are the societal limits and prospects? Is it possible to reform society, or is the humanity condemned to extinction?

The above-mentioned problems have been investigated by the authors considering the collapse of the society (Tainter, 2009) and seeking new scientific paradigms for theoretical reflection of the changing world. (Bachelard, 1981) In the first half of the 20th century, Oswald Spengler in *The Decline of the West*, Pitrim Sorokin in *The Crisis of our* Age, Julien Benda in *The Betrayal of the Intellectuals* and Arnold Toynbee in *A Study of History* pointed out the emergence of the elements of crisis related to the industrial system. In the mid-sixties, the industrial system began to change gradually; its development triggered certain internal impulses acting towards transformation of the system (Staněk, 2010). The emerging system was initially called a post-industrial society or a service society. Later, as information started playing the decisive role in the economy and society, the first concepts of the information society or the Third Wave or, as Alvin Toffler the American futurologist called it, a civilisation transformation. Daniel Bell described the emerging transformation in his books *The Coming of Post-Industrial Society* and *Cultural Controversies of Capitalism*. Zbigniew Brzezinski in his book *Between Two Ages: America's Role in the Technetronic Era*, Yoneji Masuda in his book *The Information Society as Post-Industrial Society*, Alvin Toffler in his trilogy *Future Shock, The Third Wave and Powershift*, John Naisbitt in *Megatrends, Reinventing the Corporation,* and *Global Paradox*, Peter Drucker in *The Age of Discontinuity* and *Post-Capitalist Society*, or Francis Fukuyama in his trilogy (*The End of History, Trust and The Great Disruption), they all* describe the continual decay of the industrial society/the industrial system, trying to identify the potential trends in the future development of society and civilisation. (Klinec, 2005)

A new direction within the economy and society will require a change. The change of society and economy will inevitably necessitate the change at all the levels of enterprise, family and an individual.

The change will always concern the whole enterprise, never just a part of it. Unlike in the situation where it is enough just to survive stormy times, the future will be typical for a degree of adaptation to the new performance requirements that will always follow the change (the cyclicality of turbulent changes). Enterprises should be thus perceived as living organisms or systems. Humanity is approaching the moment of transition from the mechanistic paradigm to the holistic one. It is therefore necessary to address the issue of complexity in perceiving an enterprise as a living organism. Comprehensive systems require changes in time affecting the current state of enterprise. The key role of management is to influence, steer and manage an enterprise towards success. A comprehensive system must be influenced. However, managers never know the system absolutely, they just know certain principles; other features may be completely hidden from them. Representing the most important segment of complex systems, people are the major driving force behind the enterprise. Spiral Management is here to offer the tools for the modern management of people, enterprises and organisations.

BACKGROUND

Humans are living the time when individual areas of knowledge are connected by numerous links (unimaginable in the past), and traditionally established boundaries between disciplines are being erased. Reality does not appear as fragmented and isolated segments; on the contrary, it is perceived as an interconnected whole. When focusing on the whole, humans are able to go beyond our current needs, personal interests and momentary obsessions. Such interdisciplinarity and consistency of insight naturally raises the sense of responsibility, shifting the European way of thinking from the classical concept of science, education and progress to the post-classical or post-modernistic one. (Erban, 2003)

Table 1 indicates the shift expressed as a change of the mechanical, inanimate image of the world modelled according to a perfect and intelligible machine towards the vitalistic concept perceiving the world as a living organism spontaneously manifesting itself, subject to constant change and connected by complex links on various levels. There the role of a scientist is that of an involved observer rather than an independent expert. Such concept is a diversion from the classical division into spiritual and material, and appears to be a natural tendency to adopt the religious and ethical attitudes also in the field of the exact natural sciences. (Erban, 2003)

Several major futurologists and visionaries talk about the transition from the entropic stage towards the syntrophic stage of human civilization. Currently, human civilization is in the entropic stage, since it is primarily profit-oriented; transformation is connected with the human mind, and the mind is primarily connected with syntropy, creation of the new paradigms, and overcoming the entropy. (Erban, 2003)

Satish Kumar sees the roots of the current global ecological crisis in the wrong system of values. In fact, the key idea of the modern industrial society is that people are superior to nature which is here for them, and they are here to manage and control it (human centrism, human supremacy). (Kumar, 2014)

Satish Kumar sees the roots of the current global ecological crisis in the wrong system of values. In fact, the key idea of the modern industrial society is that people are superior to nature which is here for them, and they are here to manage and control it (human centrism, human supremacy). (Kumar, 2014)

Such perception of ourselves needs to be changed for a few reasons; the most important being the fact that it could lead to our own annihilation. Sara Parkin argues that "what really is the driving force of the economic system is our value system." (Erban, 2003), (Parkin, 1991)

Holistic interpretation of the current new economic reality served as the basis of the holistic economic theory and its key concepts (Klinec, 2011):

- Perception of economy as an open subsystem or an integral part of higher systems such as society, nature or universe;
- Perception of the global world economy as an indivisible whole, an implicated order; economic development is perceived as a holomovement;
- Perception of individual economic theories and theoretical schools and directions as fragmentary views developing the implications of a particular-undivided reality; i.e. economics, as a science composed of individual partial economic theories complementing each other and creating a map of economic theories, where each has its own location, purpose, time and limits of performance, and no economic theory can be considered absolute;

Table 1. Major differences between the classical and post-classical paradigms

Classical paradigm	Post-classical (postmodern) paradigm
Facts	Connections
Truth	Significance
Features	Symbol, metaphor
Analysis	Synthesis
Rationality	Intuition, inspiration (role of unconsciousness)
Reduction (simplification)	Ambiguity, incomprehensibility
Basic building units	Unifying principle
Elements	Relationships
Static model, mechanism	Vitalism, organicism
Sustainability, state of being	Transformation
Development, progress, unilinearity	Plurality of developmental lines, regression, "blind street"
Adaptation, competition ("fight for life")	Creativity, collaboration (symbiosis)
Purpose	Spontaneity, playfulness, coincidence, chaos
Cultivation vs. spontaneity	Permeation of nature and education culture
Isolation of the item under investigation (laboratory conditions)	Inserting into context (natural conditions)
Individuality/Particularity, segment of reality	Holistic perception (grasping reality globally)
Unidirectional relationships (dependencies), hierarchies	Feedback, cohesion
Subject and object (recognising vs. recognised)	Relativisation of the subject and object's duality
Retraction, ab extra view	Engagement
Description, explanation	Interpretation, understanding
Mathematization, abstraction, theory	Literature, practice, experience
Science vs. experience	Experience as a source of scientific inspiration
Differentiation of scientific disciplines	Interdisciplinarity
Unity, universality, majority, standardisation	Diversity, plurality, minorities, exceptions
Eurocentrism	Multiculturalism
Scientific vs. unscientific	Inspiration by myths, imagination, game
Separation of science form public	Popularisation, application, public involvement
Independence of science	Ethical, societal and cultural aspects

Source: Erban, 2003

- Change in perception of the economic processes reversibility in favor of their irreversibility, with an emphasis on economic dynamics rather than economic statics;

- Introduction of the concept of entropy, i.e. uncertainty or disorganization, into economic theory; perception of its relation to the economic structure as a whole rather than using the notion of uncertainty only in relation to the decision-making and management of economic processes;
- Change of viewing the relation between information and economy and economic theory; understanding information as a structural factor generating the profile and the structure of the economics instead of viewing it exclusively in terms of the decision-making and management of economic processes;
- Understanding the economy as a structure dissipating energy, raw materials, materials and information, while creating a structure around the attractors in the form of the factors determining the structure and profile of economy, society and civilization; the value reorientation of a human and civilization based on the holistic perception of the changed economic reality and respect for the world and natural laws;
- Understanding the emergence of the global economy as a chance to restore the original importance of economics as a science of management, while overcoming the alienation from its original meaning in the industrial age. In the global world economy, a person must behave first as an economist and only then as a trader or financier.

Fritjof Capra (1982) argues that in terms of a systemic view, economy is a living system composed of living beings and social organizations in constant interaction with each other, while interacting simultaneously with the surrounding ecosystems on which they depend. Similar to individual organisms, ecosystems are self-organizing systems in which the animals, plants, microorganisms and inorganic components are interconnected by a complex network of interdependencies, including the mass and energy exchange in continuous cycles.

The holistic interpretation of the current changed economic reality and gradual development and articulation of the holistic economic theory can significantly contribute to changing the human activity on Earth and harmonizing people‘s relationship to nature. (Henderson, 1991) The expanding global crisis of mankind gives rise to numerous economic theories aimed at harmonizing economy with the new economic and civilization reality, and thus sustaining the Earth's environment. (Gore, 1992)

SPIRAL MANAGEMENT AS PART OF SYSTEM DYNAMICS

Spiral Management is based on the general theory of systems devised by Ilya Prigogine, a Belgian scientist. Inspired by his work and publications, and summarising the issue, Andrej Kopčaj wrote a comprehensive publication "Spiral Management". (Kopčaj, 2007)

Ilya Prigogine who won the Nobel Prize for his contribution to non-equilibrium thermodynamics and his theory of dissipative structures in particular, in 1984 together with Isabelle Stengers published a book by the title "Order out of Chaos" and the subtitle "Man's new dialogue with nature", in which they presented their idea of the world development based on dissipative structures, second law of thermodynamics, and irreversible processes as sources of order generation. The futurist Alvin Toffler, in the preface to the Ilya Prigogin and Isabelle Stengers' book, introduces the Prigoginian paradigm. What Toffler thinks has made the Prigoginian paradigm particularly interesting is the shift of attention to those aspects of reality that characterise today's accelerated social change, such as disorder, instability, diversity, imbalance, non-linear relationships, and temporality (increased sensitivity to the time flow etc.). (Kopčaj, 2007)

The essence of Spiral Management, as the name implies, is the so-called spiral growth, which can be understood as asymmetry of idea and symmetry of source; in other words: wise and unusual ideas and high integration of motivated promoters. The above-mentioned characteristics define the spiral growth of success as a result of the growing potential of success. The principle of spiral growth is ubiquitous in nature - the growth of galaxies in the universe, the growth of embryo in mother's womb, shape of hurricanes, the Milky Way or the DNA helical (spiral) structure. (Kopčaj, 2007)

The effectiveness of spiral growth can be also observed e.g. in the evolution of trees. Instead of the energy-consuming pumping of water from the earth in the anti-gravity direction used by people, trees have developed a capillary rise, osmosis and evaporation. Similar examples of such evolutionary process can be found in many plant and animal species: every rule blocking the dynamics of spiral growth is compensated by many patterns strengthening its dynamics. (Kopčaj, 2007)

An important contribution to the spiral growth theory was that of Leonardo of Pisa (original name Leonardo Fibonacci) and his Fibonacci sequence, which was developed after observing rabbit reproduction. It is a sequence of numbers where the following number is the sum of the two preceding ones, and it looks like this: 0, 1, 1, 2, 3, 5, 8, 13, 21, 34, 55, 89, 144, 233, 377, 610, 987, 1597 ....

When determining the ratio of neighbouring numbers, the result is 1.61803 which is typical for infinite decimal development and is called the number Φ of the Golden Ratio or the Divine Proportion. (Kopčaj, 2007)

Figure 1 shows the geometric expression of the golden ratio. The golden ratio refers to dividing a segment into two parts so that the ratio of the smaller part to the larger one will be the same as the ratio of the larger part to the whole segment.

Figure 1. Geometrical illustration of golden ratio
Source: Janoštiak, 2015

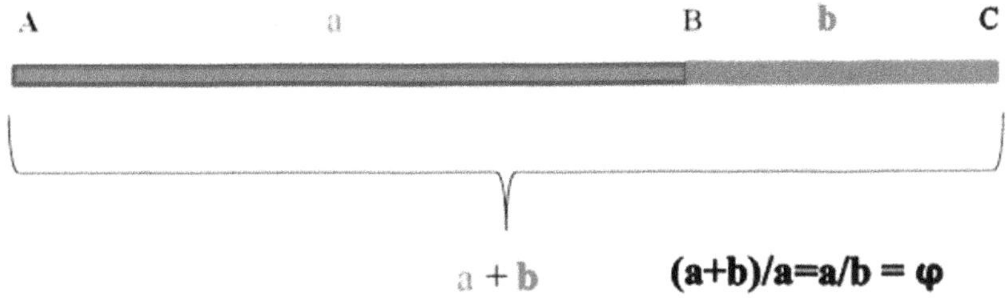

In the course of evolution, all living organisms have tried to optimise their growth and use resources efficiently. The Fibonacci sequence and the number of the golden ratio have proven to be the optimum possibility. Many plants place the leaves on the stalk in a spiral (helix), so that each further leaf grows shifted at a certain angle regarding the previous one. Then, if to calculate which leave in the order will be exactly above the first one, and give the result in proportion to the number of the spiral rotations created by the leaves, we would get the so-called phyllotaxia number, e.g. 1/3, 2/5, 3/8 - all numbers of the Fibonacci sequence. Mathematical modelling has proven that by setting leaves in such a way, the plant optimises the amount of sunlight and the amount of water supplied to each leaf (Figure 2). (Kopčaj, 1997)

Ratio of finger segments of human hand is also an example of the Fibonacci sequence. Not only the lengths of individual segments are in the golden ratio; besides, when bending our fingers and making a fist, the space is optimally filled (Figure 3).

Spiral Management is based on the continuous struggle of living systems for their own existence. Generally, it concerns the natural patterns of spontaneous development of the living and non-living systems. Spiral Management says that the goal of each system is its successful existence; to achieve a unique spiral (helical) growth, it is necessary to break the resistance of the average active balance culture and continue up to the critical (initial) point of the spiral growth. Neither failure to achieve the limit nor significant excess of the critical point will start the spiral growth. Being successful in terms of Spiral Management means to extricate from average and simultaneously not to go beyond the time and its needs. (Kopčaj, 2007)

Spiral Management will not allow companies to "be abreast of the time" in the sense of building an ideal company respecting the moral, ethical, or socially sustainable principles. Using Spiral Management principles in business can, however, help avoid the mistakes that may consequently slow down the company development; i.e. to solve the issues before it becomes necessary. At the same time, it will help utilise natural laws and resources without disturbing or only minimally upsetting

Figure 2. Optimisation of plants´ growth
Source: Janoštiak, 2015

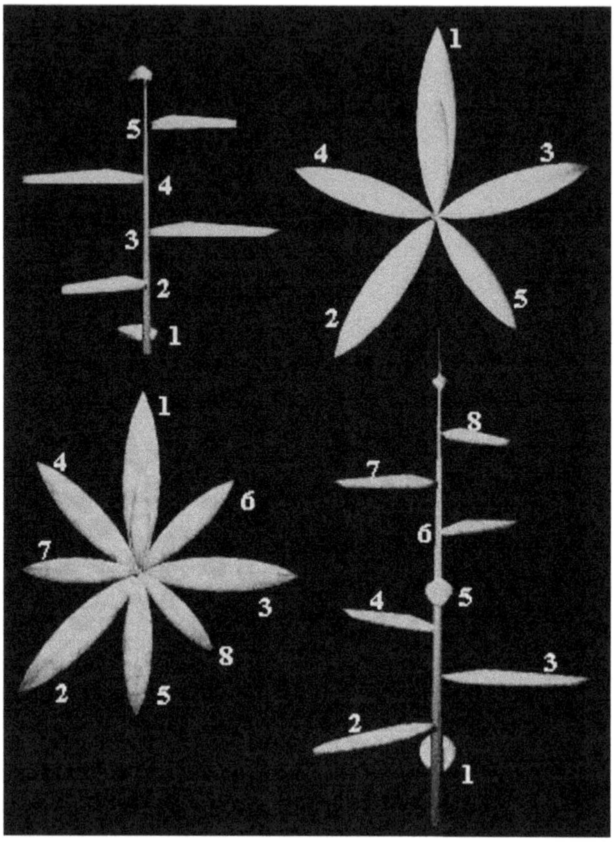

Figure 3. Golden ratio illustrated by a human hand example
Source: Janoštiak, 2015

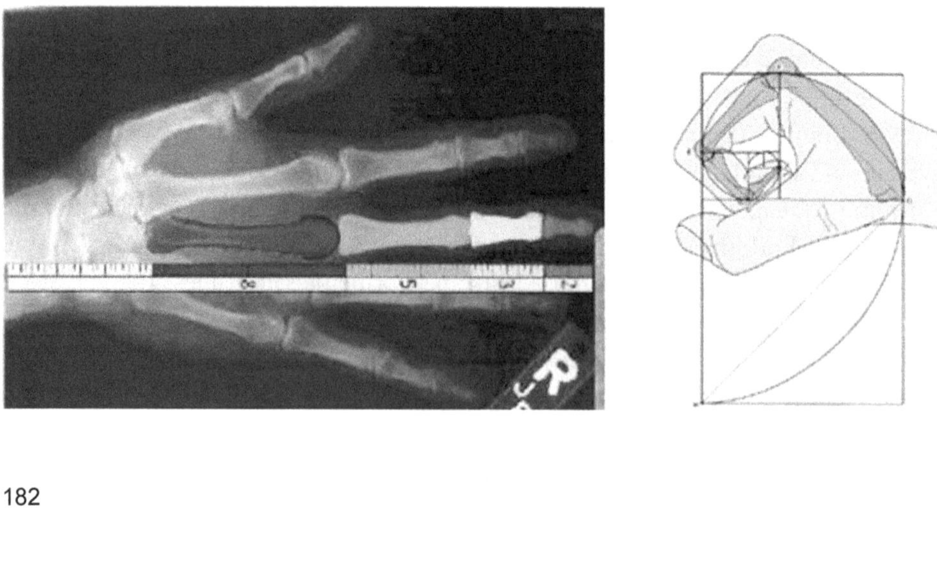

the fragile balance in nature, so that to eliminate the entropy emerging in the system and its environment. Just like in the nature. (Mikulášková, 2017)

Entropy in Spiral Management

Entropy is a status function of the second thermodynamic law, which expresses the tendency of all natural processes towards unidirectionality. In terms of the related law, for example, it is impossible to transfer heat from a cooler body to a warmer one, but always vice versa. Entropy comes from a Greek word for *transformation* or *direction* of conversion; it is actually a measure of the tendency to the spontaneous heat convection, and, in combination with the first thermodynamic law, it forms the multiform world of equations that can describe the spontaneous direction of chemical reactions. (Kopčaj, 1997)

Entropy can be viewed as a molecular disorder. When two bodies, a hot and a cold, come into contact, they exchange heat. The originally warm body will record a loss of entropy, while the originally cold one will record an increase of entropy. The total entropy will, however, increase in both cases, since the energy degradation will result in a temperature drop. That means that everything in the universe is directed towards an increase of entropy, which grows along with chaos and disorder. (Skácel, 2002) The law of the entropy growth says that spontaneous development of self-governed systems (left to themselves) exhibits tendency towards an increasing disorder. (Šimon, 2015).

Entropy and its growth in nature, in a closed system of our environment, label our path to extinction and self-destruction. In terms of energy, the use of non-renewable energy sources, nuclear energy and the means exceeding the natural balance represent a burden to the environment. The burden keeps rising together with entropy and chaos in the form of hurricanes, excessive heat, drought or rain. Nature itself does not know chaos, it has its firm order; it is us who introduce chaos along with the increase of entropy by utilising physical laws to extremes that are not inevitable. (Skácel, 2002) The notion of entropy is used in physical chemistry or mathematics, as well as in biology, sociology and, most recently, in management. According to the second Prigogin Law, the prerequisite for existence of living systems is their ability to eliminate entropy by expelling it to the outer environment. (Plchová, 2013)

For management, entropy thus represents an unwanted phenomenon challenging the search for creative solutions to its minimisation. According to Kopčaj (2007), entropy in management is characterised by:

- Rate of degradation,
- Rate of disorder of states and malfunction of processes,
- Rate of lack or inversion of information,

- Rate of the extinction probability.

The Role of Corporate Culture in Spiral Management

Common management approaches utilise various economic theories and their applications in order to achieve the required economic indicators such as profit, cost optimisation, economic stability or competitiveness and performance. Spiral Management introduces a new concept into management, viewing a company as a system comprising two different sub-systems:

- Technical subsystem – nonalive,
- Social subsystem – alive.

According to Kopčaj, corporate culture assures a "struggle for the existence" and the stability of any community, including that of enterprise. (Kopčaj, 1999)

Spiral Management views corporate culture as an artificial product of the human community (enterprise) with its key mission to cultivate the orientation of the ego-evaluation energy (EEE) of the individuals within the enterprise in favour of the growth of both components of the community (enterprise)'s wealth, i.e. its product and potential. Product is an objective component of wealth (product, service), while potential is a subjective one (probability of its effective transformation into product). (Kopčaj, 2007) The technical subsystem comprises both, material (tangible) and intangible knowledge and processes, as well as the revitalisation of potential and its exploitation into the product.

Fundamental enterprise processes or macro-processes comprise (Kopčaj, 1999):

- Marketing/Sales,
- Research/Development,
- Economy/Finance,
- Purchase/Storage,
- Production/Maintenance,
- Logistics/Informatics,
- Administration/Personnel Policy.

The social subsystem of an enterprise involves the ego-evaluation energy of employees. Its size is not directly proportional to the number of employees in the enterprise, but to the amount of integrated vital energy. Development and management of human resources means working with the energy units obtained to embellish wealth, rather than reckoning on the number of employees. Various people have various goals which generally fall into two simple categories:

- To survive (assurance of existence),
- To enjoy (improvement of life quality).

If goals of an individual are contrary to the goals of enterprise, then energy of an individual will be egocentric and the individual will tend to behave according to the slogan: "Who does not steal, robs his own family." The opposite extreme is the complete harmonisation of both wealth components of an individual and enterprise; then the energy flow will be ethnocentric. Existence of an organization depends on whether it is energy or entropy what it acquires from its members. (Kopčaj, 1999)

Spiral Management in Managerial Practice

For management, it is essential to manage the organization unit that is deficient. Historically, the management of technical resources was the first to appear. In the distant past, there was a lack of material, such as stone (flint) in the Stone Age, bronze in the Bronze Age, iron in the Iron Age, production means in the Middle Ages, up to the lack of machinery in the Industrial Age. There was a lack of inanimate systems; people were just forced to work, usually based on fear. That worked for over 2,000 years. Then a management based on economic laws emerged. However, it only works in a static and stable environment, which, however, is no longer sufficient as a concept of the world or market.

In a dynamic turbulent environment, possibilities of economy and its laws are very limited. People have become a costly item. The current situation requires the management able to manage people in a turbulent and dynamic environment. Principally, all HR approaches agree that people need to be motivated to work; they need to develop their feeling of ownership and identify themselves with the goals of the enterprise. In such a way, an ordinary employee becomes an invaluable human asset that brings about the unique component of work that cannot be replaced even by robotics, i.e. creativity. In future, creativity and the ability to think ahead will be the key principles of the most successful businesses worldwide. (Lockwood, 2005)

The problem of majority of the HR approaches, however, is measurability and manageability. Most managers act intuitively. A company may have a well-functioning remuneration system, implemented the optimal corporate culture and regular teambuilding, yet those cannot be directly measured and thus managed effectively. The managers can only state that the activity/event/measure was successful in the past and is likely to be improved in future. They cannot say, however, what, when, how much etc.

Spiral Management primarily addresses the management of a company's social system, as the only supplier of creative energy within the enterprise. This is logical, since it is people's energy that is utilised by businesses to meet their own goals.

Spiral Management applies the laws of the living systems manageability, along with the theory of system stability, which serve as the fundamentals for the spiral management development as a unified and coherent theory.

From the Spiral Management's point of view, a manager has to achieve results in three areas of enterprise:

1. **Utilisation of potential** and its transformation to product. This brings money.
2. **Development of potential**. This assures future.
3. **Protection of potential**. This reduces a risk of collapse/failure (e.g. maintenance of technical equipment, insurance).

For a manager, the ratio in which to address individual fields depends on the external environment and the state of enterprise.

At present, it is possible to manage a product, process and technical potential of an enterprise at the maximum efficiency. Now, it is the time to master the management of social (human) potential (Figure 4). To manage anything, it is necessary to divide it into parts that behave homogeneously, i.e. unambiguously respond to the steering impulse.

The level of energy and stability is dominant in terms of management, since it determines the degree of utilising other components and the result. Table 2 shows the classification of employees according to the degree of cooperation, their relationship to knowledge, the utilisation of their working time, the environment they work in and the work results they generate.

The key issues being dealt within Spiral Management are as follows:

Figure 4. Managerial Line
Source: Mikulášková, 2017

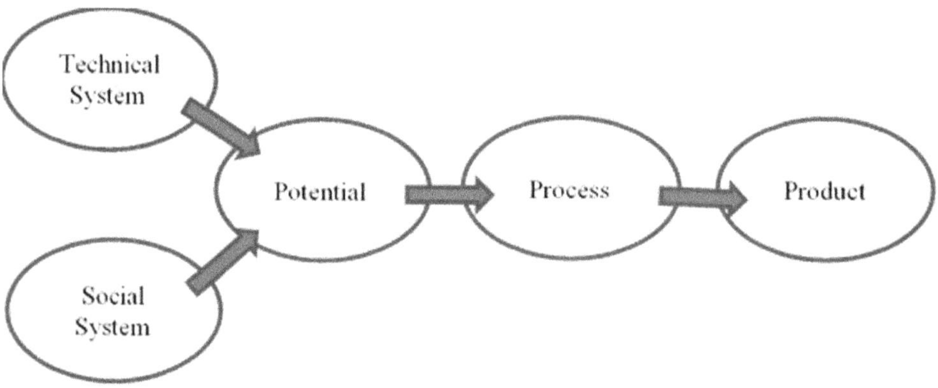

Table 2. Employees levels from the Spiral Management point of view

Level	Knowledge	Processes (time)	Environment	Result
I.	produce	acquire spare time of others	abrupt changes	new fields
II.	apply	invest their spare time	continuous changes	improvement of position
III.	utilise	utilise work time	stable	maintaining position
IV.	misuse	do not utilise work time	destabilise	worsening position
V.	destroy	destroy within work time	destroy	drop out of competition

Source: Polakovič & Krempaský, 2012

1. The current situation in the world is characterised by high turbulence and instability.
2. It is necessary to gain profit (i.e. to control product) while developing and protecting one's own potential, the one represented by social system in particular.
3. Creativity of employees should be controlled.
4. Both teams and individuals should be controlled.
5. The most effective methods and tools should be selected.
6. There's no time for the "attempt - error" method. Instead, act immediately and effectively.

That means it is high time for companies to master the social system management based on their own actual energy and stability level. It is a role of line managers. The line managers are not any more the smartest ones in terms of technology. It is the executive officers who are more competent in their fields since they have competencies, authorisations and certificates. Line managers have to adopt a role of preparing the environment and energy of social system. They have to learn how to motivate individuals and teams, and shape their qualities and personalities.

Employees Typology within Spiral Management

As follows from the first Prigogin law, living systems, including the social ones, should be explored in the interaction with their surroundings: "Open systems must acquire energy from the outside environment". All the processes in the universe are based on energy flows (energy exchange). Spiral Management examines the energy flows between the social element and the environment.

For example, let us take a social system: Employee declares he will perform something. However, whether it will be done, depends on the amount of energy put into action. If there is a lack of energy, the result will not occur, despite the employee's declaration and persuasion. Such systems can be described by partial differential equations that, however, cannot be solved so far. (Krempaský, 2001) Yet, their investigation proves that the solutions exhibit several levels of stability. From a managerial point of view, there are five levels:

1. System acquires much energy from the environment up to losing its structural stability, and thus giving rise to a developmental leap.
2. System acquires enough energy from the environment to develop, yet only within the existing structure.
3. System acquires just enough energy from the environment to survive.
4. System loses energy, it is still structurally stable, yet its performance decreases.
5. System loses much energy, thus letting the structure fail.

In terms of management, the above-mentioned typology exhibits the following characteristics:

1. Within the *level,* system behaves homogeneously, responding predictably to the external interventions.
2. Interfaces between *levels* are sharp and measurable. It is where the change in number of degrees of freedom occurs.
3. It covers all the possible states.

Applying the above-mentioned to the "employee/company" system, Spiral Management get five levels of stability.

1. "Creator" – exhibits a strong link to the company and exerts a lot of energy to change the existing structures and processes for better.
2. "Innovator" – exhibits a strong link to the company and uses the exerted energy to increase effectiveness within the existing structures and rules, thus increasing also productivity.
3. "Professional" – exhibits a link rather to his/her own expertise than to the company, while focusing energy on product.
4. "Slacker" – focuses interest to his/her benefit, utilising his/her energy to get the energy from the company (pay) without bringing the anticipated value to the company.
5. "Destructor" – focuses interest exclusively to his/her benefit, while stealing and destroying.

From the managerial point of view, it is important that:

1. Everyone (employee) may be on each of the above-mentioned levels, while passing from one to another as necessary. What only makes difference is how long an employee stays on individual levels.
2. Profile (time ratio on individual levels) of multiple systems (company) is stable.
3. The shift from unwanted levels to the desirable is manageable.

4. Energy flows are difficult to measure.
5. Time profile of a company in individual states is measurable.
6. Time profile can be used to calculate a complementary quantity of energy, i.e. entropy of system.
7. Each social system is therefore typical for particular entropy level.
8. An entropy level can help assume energy level and thus also the system behaviour and its anticipated results.

SOLUTIONS AND RECOMMENDATIONS

Application of the Spiral Management Principles in HR Management

Having determined the typology of employees and the way of identifying various types of human-beings in the organization, managers should use an appropriate strategy to manage individual types of employees. It would not be efficient to apply a uniform strategy to all employees; and therefore, four basic strategies were identified within the Spiral Management (Kopčaj, 2007):

- **ES1**: Removal, displacement of the critical aspects (materialization of entropy), while cleaning the system from entropy;
- **ES2 Product**: Incentive remuneration for fulfilling and adhering to orders and bans making a successful product;
- **ES2 Potential**: Incentive remuneration for creating and implementing new ideas;
- **ES3**: Incentive remuneration for success rate growth.

The lines below will explore the possibilities of applying individual strategies to certain employees' energy levels:

Destructor (Egocentric): The state can be cultivated by the ES1 strategy; in a critical situation it means "trimming" dry branches and, in less critical situations, it means displacing critical (entropic) elements of behaviour. In progressive types of enterprises and organizations, ES1 becomes a sort of an immune system (searching for entropic tendencies); employees are aware of the consequences of their behaviour.

Slacker: Cultivation of this state governed by the slogan "Do not work but make money" begins with the ES2 product energy strategy, i.e. by introducing an accountable remuneration system conditioning the remuneration of the work results by meeting the criteria defined by quality and other attributes of a product Or service.

Professional: Their cultivation consists in transformation into an open system, i.e. the state where the source is the enterprise. Employees have stifled their creativity, using it more in the private sphere rather than at work. They are guided by the slogan: "Nothing is for free in this world". They are not interested in work, considering it "a necessary evil". There is a transition from egocentrism to ethnocentrism. In such a case, it is reasonable to apply the ES3 strategy and stimulatory ES2 potential strategy, which activate willingness and desire to contribute creatively to the common goals. The resulting transformation accrues from ethics and morality on the one hand, and "egoistic virtue" on the other hand, where the personal effect via cooperation grows faster than the personal effect without co-operation.

Innovator: Is guided by the slogan: "Everything can be done better." Unlike professionals, innovators are more aware of both, their role (mission) within the company and their responsibility for the work they perform. They are not only concerned with the standards that, for a professional, represent the limits that do not need to be exceeded. A key strategy here is ES2 potential, since incentive remuneration for work improvement contributes to the growth of corporate success potential. To become an innovator, it is necessary to deepen the ES3 energy strategy, which activates the innovator's internal responsibility for the growth of the success potential through the transformation of both, enterprise and innovator.

Creator: Is guided by the idea that everything is possible if you have knowledge/skill and will. Decisive here is the ES3 strategy that deepens the internal responsibility for the long-term success of the organization as the best way of achieving personal goals. (Kopčaj, 2007)

Role of HR Manager within Spiral Management

An HR manager currently makes use of large databases on employees (information on their age, knowledge, training, practice, etc.). However, the information on the employees' willingness to invest *their energy* for the benefit of the company is missing there, maybe except of some verbal description that cannot be used for the managerial purposes. The HR managers frequently work with the concepts such as employee's performance, personal goals, their fulfilment, and so on. However, these are just partial management tools, almost inapplicable when managers do not know what to manage (energy) and how much of it (quantification). If teams of managers do not know what to manage and what amount to manage, the tools are just useless.

Beginning in the 1980s, HR Management began to experience a transformation from being an administrative maintenance function to being viewed as a core business function that could contribute to organizational effectiveness. The role of the HR manager keeps changing significantly. From an officer often underestimated in the corporate hierarchy (starting his sentences by saying: "It would be reasonable

...”), he is being upgraded to the level of other top managers who can quantify their demands and guarantee results. Imagine the situation when the budget for the next year is set in the company. The CEO says: “Our company needs 15 machines and raw materials to ensure the required volume.” The Economist states: “To ensure marketing activities, machines and raw materials, our company needs 2 million euros “. In compliance with the Spiral Management principles, the HR manager should add: “In order to ensure the required development, it could be useful to reduce entropy of the social system by 2 tenths, which means: To increase the share of level I by 5%, the share of level II by 7%, to maintain the share of level III, to reduce the share of level IV by 10% and to reduce the share of level V by 0.2%. This altogether can provide a sufficient creative social and implementation potential to achieve the scheduled goals.”

Such an approach is inevitable to manage future results. Only the social system is able to be creative and bring the energy of change into organization. Those who prefer a past technocratic track will restrain the social system. Automation and robotization will win. But who will design the robotic factory? The key to success is a flexible and highly creative company with proper management of social system.

The HR managers have to abandon general “best practices” and proceed to “individual best practice” focused on specific goals of the company and, predominantly, on level of its potential. That is why most of the working techniques do not work in a different environment. Based on the level of the social system, Spiral Management can guess which techniques will work and which will fail: it is only the transmission between the equal levels of energy and stability that works.

Scientific Prospects of Spiral Management

From the scientific point of view, it is essential whether we only want to explore and describe the past, or to make reasonable forecasts for the future. Social research is mostly oriented on the past. Forecasts for the years to come are limited to extrapolation in the same conditions.

The area of the social systems management is extremely promising for practical application. Management is supposed to take appropriate measures today in order to achieve the desirable results in the future. This, however, requires sufficiently precise and quantified development patterns and managerial techniques. Until now, the social systems used mainly the knowledge of sociology and psychology, quantifiability of which is quite limited, and thus the accuracy of managerial decisions is inadequate. It is the area very desirable to develop. Spiral Management has the potential to be successful even in research, ideally combining several disciplines, particularly management, sociology, psychology, biology, anthropology and pedagogy. In terms of successful management of social systems, strict separation of individual sciences should be replaced by the holistic approach combining several scientific disciplines.

FUTURE RESEARCH DIRECTIONS

In the future, Spiral Management principles can be applied in managing individual employees (as mentioned above) as well as managing performance of various generations of employees. Companies started considering generations in the mid-20th century, when the first sociologists noticed certain personal differences between the people born before and after the World War II. Later, several sociological and anthropological theories dividing the human population into generations according to their most distinctive features were developed. From the managerial point of view, the basic question is: "How can be various generations of employees in various organisations managed effectively?"

The current labour market is to face a unique situation: five different generations of employees will be working side by side within an organization: Traditionalists, Baby Boomers, Generation X, Generation Y and Generation Z. The labour market conditions (along with the lack of specific labour workforce in developed countries) call for the need to manage individual generations of employees in the work process. Conventional approaches describe a wide scale of the skills, knowledge and experience required; sometimes including psychological traits. When combining these features, managers may be confronted with a precarious unmanageable situation.

Spiral Management is able to provide solutions by using so-called theory of developmental cycles (Kopčaj, 2007). Within the cyclical exploration of the human society, Kopčaj defined individual stages and certain rules of development (about 105,000 years ago up to the present), plotting a timeline (time axis). Built on the natural mathematical constants (Golden ratio, Feigenbaum constant), the axis expresses the time shortening of each subsequent development stage, generally just like in the case of other living systems in nature. If applying the phenomenon to the development of human generations, it was found that the curve (i.e. the time limits of generations) of generations keeps decreasing (Figure 5).

A developmental cycle consists of the thermodynamic and energy parts. The former describes the development of thermodynamic parameters of the system. In enterprises, it includes machines, equipment, as well as knowledge and experience of employees. The latter describes the development of the human energy invested. Both parts consist of five accelerating stages, each describing typical behaviour of the system. Acceleration of the thermodynamic part is $\boldsymbol{\varphi = 1.62}$ (golden ratio), while that of the energy part is $\boldsymbol{\tau = 4.66}$ (Feingenbaum constant). A cycle closes when both the thermodynamic and energy parts end up.

Figure 5. Cycle of euro-atlantic civilization
Source: Polakovič & Krempaský, 2012

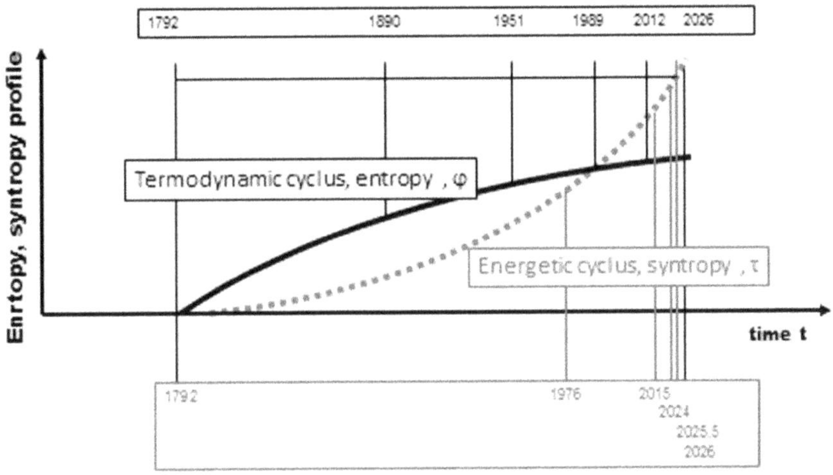

Kopčaj 's theory of developmental cycles was later developed by Polakovič (Figures 6 and 7), whose conclusions could be further elaborated and applied to manage the performance of individual generations of employees (Polakovič & Krempaský, 2012).

It is also possible to measure the potential, both social and technical, of individual generations of employees. Consequently, it would make possible to determine the level of the company in the areas of:

- Potential utilisation,
- Potential development,
- Potential protection.

If entropy of the generation is similar or lower, it can be assumed that the members of a given generation will be of benefit to the particular company segment, and they can be successfully incorporated in it.

CONCLUSION

The manager's job is to ensure that people know how to work and want to work at the highest level of energy. This subsystem, however, cannot be effectively managed purely by making intuitive decisions. In order to be able to manage, managers need to know the system to be managed and the way of how to influence it.

Figure 6. Developmental cycles of X, Y employee generations
Source: Polakovič & Krempaský, 2012

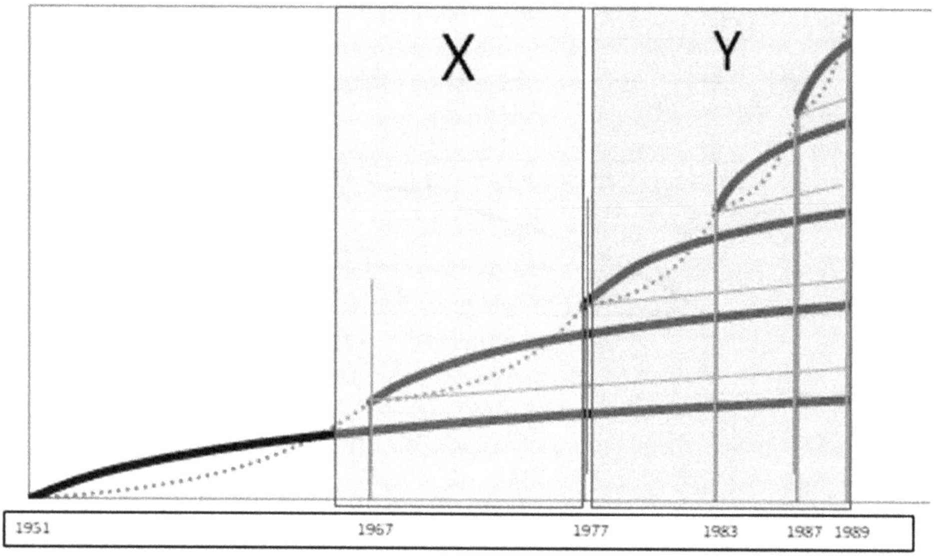

Figure 7. Developmental cycles of millennials employee generations
Source: Polakovič & Krempaský, 2012

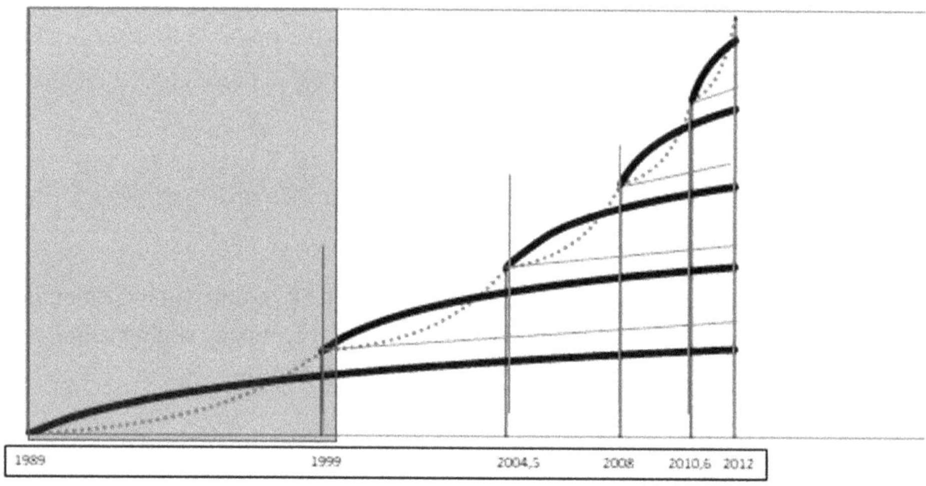

Spiral Management combines the knowledge from a variety of disciplines (psychology, anthropology, biology, mathematics, physics, management, etc.), providing a "manual" for managing a social subsystem in an enterprise. Such approach is unique since it can be mathematically quantified, and the dependencies of individual factors with respect to sustainability or increase of the company's success potential can be measured.

If the object of management is a human being or a social group, the management theories should provide an effective methodology to ensure effective management. The role of scientific research should be to design a system that will be universally valid, generally applicable and effective, while taking into account the time factor in the sense of the constant need for change and in the sense of the time relativity.

ACKNOWLEDGMENT

This research was supported by the Slovak Scientific Grant Agency - VEGA [grant number VEGA 1/0348/17] and by the Young Researcher of Slovak University of Technology Grant [grant number 1324].

REFERENCES

Bachelard, G. (1981). *The Poetics of Space*. Beacon Press.

Bell, D. (1976a). *The Coming of Post-industrial Society: A Venture in Social Forecasting*. New York: Basic Books. doi:10.1080/00131727609336501

Bell, D. (1976b). *The Cultural Contradictions of Capitalism*. New York: Basic Books.

Benda, J. (1955). *The Betrayal of the Intellectuals*. Boston: Beacon Press.

Brzezinski, Z. (1967). *America in the Technetronic Age*. School of International Affairs, Columbia University.

Capra, F. (1982). *The Turning Point: Science, Society and the Rising Culture*. Flamingo Press.

Drucker, F. P. (1992). *The Age of Discontinuity: Guidelines to our Changing Society*. New York: Harper & Row.

Drucker, F. P. (1993). *Post-capitalist Society*. New York: Harper Business.

Erban, V. (2003). New paradigm? From mechanistics to holistics, from part to whole. In *UNImagazín. XIII. roč. University of South Bohemia in České Budějovice, 2003* (pp. 31-34). ABOPRESS. Retrieved from http://www2.tf.jcu.cz/~erban/paradigma.pdf

Fukuyama, F. (1996). *Trust: The Social Virtues and the Creation of Prosperity*. New York: Free Press Paperbacs.

Fukuyama, F. (2007). *The end of history and the last human*. Prague: Rybka Publishers.

Fukuyama, F. (2015). *Political Order and Political Decay: From the Industrial Revolution to the Globalization of Democracy*. New York: Farrar, Straus and Giroux.

Gore, A. (1992). *Earth in the Balance. Ecology and the Human Spirit*. Boston: Houghton Mifflin Company.

Henderson, H. (1991). *Life Beyond Economics. Knowledge Systems*. Berrett-Koehler Publishers.

Janoštiak, R. (2015). When Matematics Uncover the Secrets of the Nature - Fibonnaci Sequence and Golden Ratio. *InVivo magazín*. Retrieved from https://invivomagazin.sk/ked-matematika-prezradza -tajomstva-prirody-fibonacciho-postupnost-a-zlaty-rez_399.html

Klinec, I. (2005). Alternative economic theories in terms of sustainable development. In J. Hejda (Ed.), Sustainability and quality of life in managerial and civic decision-making process. Chapter: Alternative economic theories in the context of sustainable development (pp. 46–87). Prague: Academic Press.

Klinec, I. (2011). *The Outline of the Holistic Economics Theory*. Economic Institute of the Slovak Academy of Sciences, Ekonomic theory, Prognostics (futurology).

Kopčaj, A. (1997). Multiplying the Wealth. Kopčaj - Silma ´90.

Kopčaj, A. (1999). *Management of Change - The common way how to achieve extraordinary development*. Prague: Grada Publishing.

Kopčaj, A. (2007). *Spiral management*. Bratislava: Alfa.

Krempaský, J. (2001). Quantitative theory of evolution. Metodické centrum.

Kumar, S. (2014). *No Destination: Autobiography of a Pilgrim* (4th ed.). Cambridge, UK: Green Books.

Lockwood, N. R. (2005). *Crisis Management in Today's Business Environment*. Society for Human Resource Management.

Masuda, Y. (1980). *The Information Society as Post-industrial Society*. Chicago: World Future Society.

Mikulášková, J. (2017). *Usage of Living Systems Management Principles by increasing of the Influence of Corporate Culture related to Sustain Long-term Potential of Success* (Unpublished doctoral dissertation). Slovak University of Technology, Faculty of Materials Science and Technology in Trnava.

Naisbitt, J. (1984). *Megatrends: Ten New Directions Transforming Our Lives.* New York: Warner Books.

Parkin, S. (1991). *Green Future. Agenda for 21st Century.* Fount.

Plchová, J. (2013). New Approaches to Human Resources Management in the Company. Journal of Knowledge Society, 1(1), 1-8.

Plchová, J., & Polakovič, Ľ. (2015). Quantification in Human Resources Management - Spiral Management. *International May Conference on Strategic Management – IMKSM 2015,* 662-672.

Polakovič, Ľ., & Krempaský, J. (2012). Quantitative management theory of enterprises as unimodal systems. ATP Journal, 19, 44-46.

Prigogin, I. (2003). *Is Future Given?* London: World Scientific Publishing Co. doi:10.1142/5352

Šimon, P. (2015). *Entropia – málo chápaná fyzikálna veličina s veľkým dosahom.* EnergeticaWeb. Retrieved from https://www.energiaweb.sk/2015/12/09/entropia-malo-chapana-fyzikalna-velicina-s-velkym-dosahom/

Skácel, D. (2002). What is it the entropy? *Alternativní energie 1/2002. CEMC - České ekologické manažerské centrum.* Retrieved from http://www.tzb-info.cz / casopisy/alternativni-energie

Sorokin, P. (1992). *The Crisis of Our Age.* London: Oneworld Publications.

Spengler, O. (1991). *The Decline of the West.* Oxford, UK: Oxford University Press.

Staněk, P. (2010). *Global crisis - a threat or a challenge?* Bratislava: Sprint.

Tainter, A. J. (2009). *Collapse of sophisticated societies.* Praha: Dokořán.

Toffler, A. (1971). *Future Shock.* New York: Bantam Books.

Toffler, A. (1981). *The Third Wave.* Hampshire, UK: Pan Macmillan Limited.

Toynbee, J. A. (1972). *A Study of History.* Oxford, UK: Oxford University Press.

ADDITIONAL READING

Ashkenas, R. (2009). *Simply effective. How to cut trough complexity in your organization and get things done*. Boston: Harvard Business Press.

Hazy, J. K., Goldstein, J. A., & Lichtenstein, B. B. (2015). *Complex Systems Leadership Theory: New Perspectives from Complexity Science on Social and Organizational Effectiveness (Exploring Organizational Complexity)*. Mansfield: ISCE Publishing.

Janáček, K., & Janáčková, S. (2017). *Ekonomický úpadek Evropy. (Economic Decline of the Europe)*. Praha: Institut Václava Klause.

Kohl, Ch. T. (2013). *Buddhismus und Quantenphysik. (The Buddhism and Quantum Physics)*. WindPferd Verlag. Oberstdorf.

Kopčaj, A. (1997). Košatění bohatství. (Enhancing of the Wealth). SILMA 90. Ostrava.

Piketty, T. (2015). Kapitál v 21. storočí. (The Capital in the 21. Century). IKAR, Bratislava.

Sedláček, T. (2011). *Ekonómia dobra a zla – Po stopách ľudských otázok od Gilgameša po finančnú krízu. (Economics of Good and Evil - The Quest for Economic Meaning from Gilgamesh to Wall Street)*. England: Oxford University Press.

Stroh, D. P. (2015). *Systems Thinking for Social Change: A Practical Guide to Solving Complex Problems, Avoiding Unintended Consequences, and Achieving Lasting Results*. New York: Chelsea Green Publishing.

KEY TERMS AND DEFINITIONS

Complex Systems Theory: Is a new and rapidly developing field. The ideas and principles that have already been proposed must be studied in a multitude of actual examples. And new principles must be sought. Complex systems theory cuts across the boundaries between conventional scientific disciplines. It makes use of ideas, methods and examples from many disparate fields. And its results should be widely applicable to a great variety of scientific and engineering problems.

Corporate Culture: Is the set of assumptions, beliefs, values, and norms shared by an organization's members.

EEE (Ego-Evaluation Energy): Of the individual. It is the rate of the energy (characterized by engagement, motivation, passion, etc.) that is the employee willing to invest into general good of the enterprise.

Entropy: In the physics – rate of system´s messiness or disorder in a physical system. In the social systems theory – social entropy is a sociological theory that evaluates social behaviors using a method based on the second law of thermodynamics.

Holistic Approach: Is the idea that systems (physical, biological, chemical, social, economic, mental, linguistic) and their properties should be viewed as wholes, not just as a collection of the parts.

Human Resource Management: Includes conducting job analyses, planning personnel needs, recruiting the right people for the job, orienting and training, providing benefits and incentives, evaluating performance, resolving disputes, and communicating with all employees at all levels. Examples of core qualities of HR management are extensive knowledge of the industry, leadership, and effective negotiation skills.

Social System: Is a complex set of human relationships interacting in many ways. Two points stand out in the complex interactions among people in a social system. 1) The behavior of any one member can have an impact, directly or indirectly, on the behavior of any other. 2) Any social system engages in exchanges with its environment, receiving input from it and providing output to it.

Spiral Management: The theory of social systems management based by Czech scientist and manager Andrej Kopčaj. Spiral management follows the complex systems theory and Prigogine laws.

Chapter 9
Legal and Ethical Aspects of CSR:
Potential in New Business Models Development

Ewa Barbara Wójcik
University of Economics, Poland

Katarzyna Olejko
University of Economics, Poland

ABSTRACT

The increasingly important role of sustainability issues and CSR in business activity has been widely recognized. In order to promote socially responsible decisions, changes in the macro- and micro-environment should be examined. The study offers insight into different aspects of CSR and defines those whose importance is growing, discusses trends, reasons for the state of affairs, and formulates conclusions of possible effects. The focus is on ethical values, in particular trust, and their changing perception which may lead to new business models strengthening and further development.

INTRODUCTION

Contemporary world has faced challenges of development and in order to ensure they are met profound understanding of the real nature of main problems and obstacles is necessary. There is big potential in sustainable business decisions which are often in line with their CSR practices. In order to promote such decisions motivations

DOI: 10.4018/978-1-5225-7850-5.ch009

and driving forces of both firms' decision makers, as well as individuals providing labour and ultimately using the offerings, should be examined.

The study offers insight into different aspects of CSR and defines those whose importance is growing, discusses trends, reasons for the state of affairs and formulates conclusions of possible effects.

The focus is on ethical values, in particular trust and their changing perception which may lead to new business models strengthening and further development.

Aspects of CSR

While economic responsibility at the base of the Caroll's Corporate Social Responsibility pyramid remains to be considered as the foundation as well as the final verifier of the sense or relevance of any economic activity, the importance of the other levels has been altered. It can be stated that from the tip of the Caroll's CSR pyramid where philanthropic activities are placed, the focus shifted towards the central levels comprising legal and ethical responsibility. (Caroll, 1991) Legal responsibility should be understood as an observance of legal regulations, but also contractual obligations and consumer rights protection. Ethical responsibility involves avoidance of undesired behaviour and acting according to law, which shows the interdependence of the two levels. At present, due to vital changes in perceiving some core ethical values, it seems likely the shift is more towards values rooted deeply in the human nature rather than derivative of legal rules or regulations.

Ethical issues, intangible, complex and difficult to trace or standardize need to be given particular attention in the era of global business operating in different parts of the globe. Such businesses should understand the diversity of the environment they operate in from the perspective of human nature. While legal rules even in remote countries are complied with, very often by using the expertise of outsourced specialised local companies, there is no equivalent way to enable understanding of the specific features or requirements of the human component in local business. The trend of glocalization does not seem to be specifically considered in the capacity of human values. They are understood rather as universal values, which implies they should be applied all over the world in the same way.

Such an attitude is not responsive to the logic of the network economy profoundly and to the highest degree ever based on individual ties. In the future, it should be assumed, it is individuals, their personal connections and independent decisions that will shape contacts and relations also within the framework of business which is less dependent on physical place, but more dependent on moral features of the staff working from different parts of the globe. Therefore, regional differences in approach to ethical values may gain importance in the years to come. Cross-cultural analyses of values may contribute to understanding the different attitudes of individualist and collectivist cultures, or such societies as the Polish one which, according to researchers, is on the borderline between the two.

The turn of the 20th and 21st centuries has brought significant change in the perception of ethical issues on corporate grounds. Such "utilitarian ethics" principles were to ensure that company activities are not contradictory to shareholders' expectations or interests. The focus was more on businesses' relations with the environment, in particular, the society as one of the core stakeholders. Attempts were made to organize and structure efforts that incorporate ethical issues into company strategy and operational activity. Over the first decade of the 21st century, the debate of the importance of Corporate Social Responsibility amplified bringing to the public attention the need of combining financial performance and market valuation with non-financial, environmental and social issues such as the satisfaction of employees, contractors, investors, cooperating institutions and customers. (Wolska, 2013)

The global economy, which brings about new challenges, demands that the ethics of business activity are considered on a multinational level. According to the suggestions of ISO regarding principles of ethical behavior to be integrated into companies' core organizational decisions ethical behaviour is defined as "behaviour that is in accordance with accepted principles of right or good conduct in the context of a particular situation and is consistent with international norm of behaviour"(ISO 26000, 2.7)

An international norm of behaviour should be understood as "expectations of socially responsible organizational behaviour derived from the customary international law, generally accepted principles of international law, or intergovernmental agreement that are universally or nearly universally recognized" ISO 26000, 2.11)

Organizational governance is a core subject and should imply that leaders practice and promote ethical behaviour, accountability and transparency. ISO 26000 suggests tools for integrating Social Responsibility into core organizational decisions, but international guidelines are in a natural way not very specific as business solutions and ethical dilemmas are country or region specific and need to be tackled in different ways.

As a moral subject business entity should act ethically for the inner imperative, while it is often argued that CSR activity is only aimed at improving company image or enticing consumers in order to improve profitability. Moreover, employees are treated as assets and as such they are only means to generate profit rather than human beings whose ethical behaviour can add value but the fact they deserve the same courtesy from employers is often ignored.

Responsible Business Forum (Forum Odpowiedzialnego Biznesu) carried out two studies "Managers 500 and responsible business. Knowledge-attitudes-practice." in Poland in 2003 in cooperation with the World Bank and the Academy of Philanthropy Development and in 2010 with GoodBrand & Company Polska, an international firm specializing in sustainable development implementation into company strategy. The project was based on the opinions of managers selected according to their knowledge and engagement in business social responsibility (Leader CSR research) from 500 biggest firms in Poland listed in "Polityka" magazine ranking. The results of both studies show it was rather the need to build the brand and create an image that made firms engage in CSR, the motivation behind decisions of 72% and 76% of the respondents in 2003 and 2010 respectively. It was noted, however, that equally important motivator in the later research was the desire to build relations with local communities, which increased by over one third from 42% to 74%. Also, the perspective of CSR long-run influence on financial results was claimed to be an important motivator of engagement in such activities (up from 30% to 56%) by the companies surveyed.

Legal Regulations

In the environment where ethical issues are gaining more and more importance, leading global organizations and regional blocks, have been recognizing the need to encourage practices that society approves and expects businesses to comply with in order to protect the moral rights of stakeholders such as consumers, shareholders and employees.

Thus, ethical responsibility has been discussed on different forums involved in Corporate Social Responsibility as well as sustainability agendas, eg the United Nations (the Goals in the 2030 Agenda for Sustainable Development of the United Nations General Assembly), the European Union (inter alia the Final Report, 2018 of EU High-Level Group on Sustainable Finance). The aspects of sustainable development frequently overlapping with companies' CSR activities, such as the environment protection, inclusion of all social groups, or education, are also central for organizations operating in the structures of the EU responsible for regulations shaping business activity within the member countries. The Directive 2014/95/EU of the European Parliament and of the Council of 22 October 2014 on the disclosure of non-financial and diversity information by certain large undertakings and groups pointed to the need of increasing the transparency of social and environmental information submitted by entities of all sectors in all Member States. The objective is to increase EU companies' transparency and performance on environmental and social matters and, therefore, to contribute effectively to long-term economic growth and employment, to improve relations with consumers and stakeholders. The regulatory step is expected to bring consistency and comparability to companies' activity in non-financial areas, commitment to socially and environmentally important issues aimed at improving social wellbeing.

It is stipulated organisations operating within the EU and seeking formal approach to CSR should take into consideration the internationally recognized principles and guidelines, in particular the updated OECD guidelines for multinational enterprises, Three-party Declaration of Principles for Multinational Enterprises and Social Policy of the International Labor Organization (ILO) and the UN Guiding Principles on Business and Human Rights. The set of guidelines should be acknowledged as a general framework for corporate social responsibility. The nature of the documents implies the multidimensional nature of the CSR principles and guidelines, which cover human rights, work and employment practices (such as training, diversity, gender equality and health and well-being of employees), environmental issues, supply chain, life cycle assessment, as well as combating bribery and corruption. Issues of the disabled integration and protection of consumers interests, including privacy, volunteering of employees and good governance in the area of tax also fall within the scope of the CSR. (European Commission, 2011)

The United Nations Global Compact initiative formulated the Ten Principles based on the Universal Declaration of Human Rights, the International Labour Organization's Declaration on Fundamental Principles and Rights at Work, the Rio Declaration on Environment and Development, and the United Nations Convention Against Corruption in order to facilitate implementation of universal principles in business practice.

"This…[principles-based approach to doing business]… means operating in ways that, at a minimum, meet fundamental responsibilities in the areas of human rights, labour, environment and anti-corruption". "By incorporating the Ten Principles of the UN Global Compact into strategies, policies and procedures, and establishing a culture of integrity, companies are not only upholding their basic responsibilities to people and planet but also setting the stage for long-term success." (the United Nations Global Compact)

What is particularly interesting in the light of this study is the section "Labour" which stipulates all forms of forced or compulsory labour and discrimination in respect of employment and occupation should be eliminated.

Employer-employee relationship building and developing as well as creating ties between employees should be understood as an essential element of a wide spectrum of methods used to establish a socially responsible enterprise. The foundation of this complex structure of relations is laid by both domestic as well as international external regulators.

The legal acts adopted by the Polish regulator, in particular, the Labour Code, constitute a source of law which defines the rights and obligations of the parties to the employment relationship, and also rules of conduct in case of infringement of the accepted rights.

In order to adjust the general solutions to the specific corporate activity and work conditions and harmonize them with characteristics of the employees, more specific solutions are required in the form of internal regulations, though. In the Labour Code (article 104), the regulator assuming the criterion of the number of employees imposes an obligation to create detailed solutions to the organization and order in the work process as well as to define related rights and obligations of the employer as well as employees. According to the regulation, in principle, in organisations employing over 50 employees a bylaw, document called "Work Rules and Regulations" shall be adopted. The introduction of the regulations is not obligatory provided it is replaced by the binding provisions of the collective agreement.

It should be emphasized that the statutory regulations, including the Labor Code, relate in large part to the so-called "Hard relationships" which manifest themselves in concrete actions, or failure to act. However, there are also references to ethical standards. Particular attention should be paid to section four of the Code, which specifies the obligations of employers and employees. The regulations, including objectivity and justice in the evaluation and remuneration of employees, constitute the basis for shaping the ethical behaviour of both employers and employees.

Creating specific norms of behaviour expressed in bylaws and other internal regulations, which indirectly or directly influence interpersonal relations, requires special care. Therefore, it is not advisable to blindly copy the solutions adopted by other organizations. Unfortunately, many Polish enterprises build their system of internal regulations through the reproduction of already existing solutions. Involvement in the process of preparing a company bylaw of an external consultant who completes the task without thoroughly examining the individual needs of the business unit does not provide for a tailored solution. Often, specialized consultancy companies offer unified solutions that can be implemented in many business units. However, they do not take into account the very specific features characteristic of an organization.

The internal regulatory solutions implemented by an employer are characterized by far-reaching freedom regarding both the scope of the regulated area as well as the depth and specificity of the solutions adopted. Depending on the importance of factors influencing a good working climate, which may stimulate employee involvement, it is possible to limit or extend the scope of the regulations. One of the criteria determining the shape of a bylaw should be generational differentiation, which may be expressed inter alia in contradictory approaches to work organization or doing certain jobs, as well as in diversified expectations towards other employees and an employer.

In connection with the intensifying conflicts observed in enterprises resulting, for example, from big generational differences referred to later on in this study, the construction of a well thought-out system of mutually complementary internal regulations is of particular importance. It should be understood not as an obligation but rather an opportunity to create systemic solutions that might protect the employer against violation of the codified regulations in ethical aspects, but simultaneously maximize employees' satisfaction, increase their commitment and, consequently, the efficiency of human resources.

Intergenerational Relations

Parallel to "local" ethical dimension, there is global demographic dimension reflected in the changing makeup of age groups and generations in the society. Such changes are likely to result, not only, in the need for the development of systemic solutions in social systems and policies in spheres ranging from finance, through healthcare to education, but they will need a common corporate level approach to intergenerational issues. For decision makers in order to face the challenges and address the issues that may occur in business practice, understanding of intergenerational relations is necessary.

The median age of workers in 2015 was 42.3, the highest in history as the oldest Baby Boomers retired or approached retirement. In order to guarantee intergenerational transfer and synergy and ensure replacement, commitment to age diversity will be required of employers. For companies, it is important to create conditions and ensure the atmosphere will prompt employee satisfaction and stimulate engagement because companies with "highly engaged" employees prove they are able to outperform organizations with less engaged employees. In 2013 the cost of disengagement was estimated by Gallop poll at $450-550 billion in lost productivity per year. It was reported that only one-third of the American employees were engaged.

An important problem at work likely to contribute to employee's dissatisfaction is a potential conflict between the workforce. As reported by the authors of Lee Hecht Harrison survey, 60% of employees are experiencing intergenerational conflicts, which implies there is not enough effort made to ensure different generations find common grounds to make the best use of their combined abilities.

The four generations that make their presence on the labour market are Traditionalists, Baby Boomers, Gen. Xers, and Gen Ys also called Millennials. (Table 1)

According to statistics (projections from the U.S. Census Bureau, as of July 1, 2016), the number of Generation Y representatives is likely to surpass the number of previous generations in the labour market in 2019. As they outnumber the other generations, Millennials with their distinguishing features and demands will need to be principally taken into account by business decision makers, such as employers and marketers.

In Europe, in particular, the Millennial generation is specific as the first one to have shaped its identity in Europe without military or ideological conflicts, borders or regional divisions, in Europe of hyper-intense integration processes. It is also the first generation to ignore all political divisions between countries or blocks and to have full, unrestricted access to common territory and space within the EU.

However, it is also the first generation expected to operate in a multicultural work environment in companies with strong international connections multiplied by technology, in the aura of cross-cultural differences which call for understanding and tolerance for the number of immigrants not be neglected.

Moreover, in certain countries, such as Poland, Gen Y is outstanding in the capacity of the first generation with "global" characteristics, the one in which irrespective of the place of birth all individuals show similar features.

It should be stressed, Millennials are likely to be the first generation to much longer coexist with the older ones in the place of work for the challenge of the ageing societies.

Such societies will not only demand shifts in social policies or new service offering but may also call for development in sectors that help avoid brain drain and make longer working lives possible. Lifelong learning or activities within the scope of edutainment are the areas which must catch up with the increasing demands of the silver economy. Additional efforts will also be needed in the financial industry, including services and solutions providing support for pension systems.

What causes intergenerational differences, first of all, is their living and getting mature at varying times in history, sharing common experience within the generation, the experience not understood by other generations. Each generation has its specific timelines, spectacular events and influencers. For instance, Baby Boomers were raised by parents who lived through the depression and WW II, the two experiences reflected in their thrift to be prepared for the unexpected, and hard work. Millennials, on the other hand, were raised in the period of the uniting Europe, they saw their parents building up capital (in the well-developed countries) or purchasing things to catch up with the rest of the well-developed world. They do not have memories of military conflicts but share the experience of fear of terrorist attacks. Some of them may have recollections of the last crises when assets were lost as a result of collapse on the stock markets, and parents lost their jobs and were unable to pay back their mortgage.

The matter of particular interest in the context of labour relations is the fact that Baby Boomers and Traditionalists generations came of age professionally before ethics and compliance offices were well established and are therefore not prepared to deal with dilemmas in the office or utilize resources the way Millennials are. According to the Report of National Business Ethics Survey in the USA, Boomers, on the other hand, are more likely to ask leaders or follow management on ethical matters. They are more responsive to ethics/compliance programs included in formal systems, are more aware of corporate standards/ systems of accountability and more responsive to signals from people in formal positions or in power. It seems they pose less risk based on their characteristics but may make employers vulnerable to unethical conduct. (Table 1)

The behaviour of the four generations differs in aspects relevant to work, such as communication or reaction to misconduct. Representatives of the same generation are found to share characteristics and interests all over the world in the era of globalization. However, across Europe, there will be differences resulting from the political systems they grew up in. For example, in Poland, there are still remains of socialist rules at work connected, for example, with the use of equipment for private

Table 1. Generations at workplace

Generations	Traditionalists	Baby Boomers	Gen. Xers	Gen. Ys
Age/ number	73+ 2015- 30 mln	53-72 2015- 74.9 mln	38-52 2015- 66 mln	17-37 2015- 75.4 mln
Communication	Letter/memo	Phone calls, personal interaction	Voicemail, email	Text messages, blogs, emails
Workplace	Positive attitude and impression	Want to use company standards of conduct, formal systems of ethical conduct, need to feel prepared to deal with problems which may occur	Less likely to report without formal advice, want guidelines publicized, e.g. where to report	Want to feel prepared to handle the situation, need to know resources for seeking advice. Without training less likely to report
Relations with management	Confident can speak honestly	In search of ethical leadership by management	Learned teamwork, used to mentoring	Low loyalty, no authority
Misconduct	22% would turn blind eye to misconduct to avoid layoffs or reduced benefits 36% viewed and 39% reported misconduct at work	44% observed misconduct, 64% reported misconduct	45% observed, 69% reported misconduct	49% observed misconduct, 67% reported misconduct
Employment	"Joiners", cradle to grave employment, a strong sense of loyalty, respect authority	Lifelong employment common	No longer cradle to grave employment	No lifelong employment Lifelong access to digital technology

Source: Based on Tammy Ericson: *Generations Around the Globe*. "Harvard Business Review"; Paul Fiorelli: *Generational Ethics: A Battle of the Ages*

purposes commonly found ethical. On the other hand, Poland faced revolutionary changes where certain stages of the development did not occur, certain systems and elements of business culture were brought by foreign investors from developed countries.

Gen X representatives can be perceived as the "bridge" between the previous and the following generation. They resemble Baby Boomer generation in their loyalty of life-long employees. Generation X is less likely to turn to formal systems for help with ethical questions but do so more often than the two earlier generations. They act more like Millennials in terms of reporting and more readily respond to the elements of ethics and compliance programs, but in a way that involves social interaction or formalized mechanisms for seeking advice, helplines or training. (Table 1)

Millennials, on the other hand, observe fewer boundaries than previous generations and are more flexible about ignoring them and more likely to engage in or tolerate behaviour considered to be unacceptable. Discussing work activity even in public is likely for this open and transparent generation. As a result, they may be the most at risk of the four generations for the potential to observe misconduct, shine a light on it and experience retaliation after reporting it. (Ericson, 2011)

The observation of generational values leads to the following conclusion: they evolved and were incorporated in different ethical frameworks, from an "old-fashioned" work ethic, through materialistic ethic, up to the present day "participative" model ethic. On the corporate grounds, the changes are evident in work ethos replaced by "efficiency" ethos, supplemented more recently with environmental awareness often constituting a part of the business ethos.

Business Moral Standards

A business entity comprehended as a moral subject should be responsible to the environment (understood as stakeholders) and for the environment (in a broader meaning, comprising the whole society, the nature) in all aspects of its activity.

Professor Aniela Dylus in her paper included in the work of PAN (Polish Academy of Science) Sociology Committee on the moral condition of the Polish society stated that business entity treated as a moral subject should be scrutinized as such, the approach resulting in areas of deficiency identified as follows:

1. Relations with competitors, unfair competition,
2. Clients and consumers being misled or cheated by producers/service providers,

Employee relations discrimination, expected availability as a form of slavery. (Dylus, 2002)

Apparently, the problems communicated at the beginning of the century, at the end of its second decade are still relevant. The most vulnerable groups of business stakeholders are the ones listed as the second and the third one in the list and improvement of their position may demand that regulators take protective measures.

A vulnerable group is defined by ISO as "a group of individuals who share one or several characteristics that are the basis of discrimination or adverse social, economic, cultural, political or health circumstances, and that cause them to lack the means to achieve their rights or otherwise enjoy equal opportunities" (ISO 26000, 2.26)

According to the definition, employees can be treated as such a group, in particular recently when relaxed employer-employee relations connected with fewer life-long jobs, professions disappearing and more temporary jobs available have been commonplace. The unavoidable changes involve on the one hand lower loyalty, on the other hand, less job security.

In Poland, the attempts to improve the situation of employees take a form of implied protection by changes in the Labour Code concerning employment contracts. The fundamental clause shall provide for work to be performed under two types of employment: on the basis of a contract of employment (which corresponds to the current employment contracts, ie. full-time employment) and self-employment.

The so-called non-business contracts, based on the provisions of the Civil Code (civil law contracts of mandate and contracts of work, commonly referred to as "junk" contracts) are to be liquidated and only exceptionally permitted. In order to replace civil law agreements and provide for a more liberal form of non-permanent employment an equivalent of the solution used in Great Britain- zero-hour contract should appear. The provisions of the new Labour Code may limit flexibility and restrict freelancing or extra hours worked for certain professions, though. This is an example of legislation providing for the protection of employees against employers whose decisions to offer "junk contracts" reflected lack of interest in their security and focus on business efficiency by means of employment cost reductions. Thus employment relations were often poor, employment treated temporarily and loyalty questionable. In such an environment, standards of work ethics were not valued high and morally wrong decisions or unethical behaviour were not rare.

Ethical Values and Perception of Trust

Individuals' attitude towards ethical values, such as trust, in today's economy, should not be underappreciated. Numerous economists point out to the fact that lack of trust can be detrimental to the society and its economic performance. Professor Douglass North, the economic historian and Nobel Prize winner in 1993, argued that a low level of trust can cause stagnation and economic collapse.

According to Young, markets could not survive without trust and this way free markets promote ethical behaviour of buyers and sellers. Negative experience with a partner who cannot be trusted will result in refusal to deal with them on their conditions. The law declares contracts void and null if they are based on untrue data, fraudulent practices or unfair rules and penalizes breach or violation of commitments. Such legal rules are similar in all cultures and they are represented in communities in such a way as to promote trust. Where fraud, distrust and breach of promises predominate, markets shrink and are limited to barter and economic minimalism. Only sellers of well-established reputation can develop business and increase customer base. Immoral partners will be excluded from markets as fewer people will decide to be exposed to threats of risky transactions. (Young, 2003)

The importance of social trust has been stressed by professor Janusz Czapiński who leads the team of researchers of Social Diagnosis, a comprehensive study prepared every other year in Poland. He claims that trust, being the foundation of social capital, which determines healthy social relations, caring for the common good and cooperation, is not only about coexistence with others, but should be treated as the basis of social well-being.

From this perspective, the results of research carried out by Edelman Trust Barometer in 28 countries seem worrying. They show that many countries have recorded a decline in social trust towards different public institutions, with the record low values in the United States and Italy. In Poland, where historically the lowest levels of trust have been recorded, the results have improved slightly over the last year.

The results of research by CBOS (the office for public opinion testing in Poland) into trust show that over two-thirds of the respondents (68%) demonstrate lack of trust and careful attitude to people, with a quarter of definitely negative stance of extreme lack of trust. In all aspects of the research, the surveyed identified with an option of care in human relations and limited trust to people. The other extreme is people – a quarter of the surveyed- who can be defined as amiable and approaching others with trust.

High level of trust was an attribute of only every eleventh respondent (9%). The average value of the trust index in 2018 was -0,89, the negative number proving that lack of trust and care in relations predominate over trustful and open stance. Such lack of confidence in others prevailed in all groups irrespective of the social and demographic features, but its highest level was typical of low educated people and those with the lowest per capita income.

According to the research carried out for the Quarterly „IUSTITIA" the most trusted in Poland are Fire Fighters with 65% of the respondents in 2016 claiming the institution was trustworthy. 14% of the people interviewed said universities were trustworthy, while 12% decided it was the NBP (National Bank of Poland) which can be trusted. Extremely low numbers of the respondents (3%) pointed to courts and the Sejm, and ZUS – the Social Security Office (2%) as trustworthy institutions. Such a negative attitude can derive from publicity given to affairs reflecting the unethical conduct of some companies.

Recently the world has heard of many financial and moral scandals on a huge scale, in which managers and executives' behaviour -far from moral- lead to extremely high losses. In fact, it is only the enormous amount of loss resulting from the scam that gives the affairs publicity, while minor misdemeanour may remain unnoticed.

One of the widely discussed, as associated with the last crises, was Lehman Brothers Scandal of 2008, the result of over $50 billion hidden in loans disguised as sales by this global financial services firm's executives and company's auditors Ernst & Young.

Another affair which was given huge publicity was Bernie Madoff Investment Securities LLC, a wall street investment firm's scandal of 2008, in which the owner cheated investors out of 64.8 billion through the largest Ponzi scheme.

Saytam scandal took place in 2009 when this Indian IT services and back-office services firm falsely boosted revenue by $1.5 bln. The founder and Chairman was charged with breach of trust, conspiracy, cheating and falsification of records, but released after the Central Bureau of Investigation failed to file charges on time.

According to the Fortune magazine, more recently, in 2017 there was a lot morally wrong conduct on a smaller scale, such as:

- Samsung, the family-run conglomerate, and the heir Lee Jae-Yong who was charged with offering bribes to Park, former South Korean President, embezzlement and hiding assets overseas
- Kobe Steel falsified information on items sold to Boeing, Ford and Toyota
- Mitsubishi Materials providing fake data on auto and aeroplane parts
- Nissan and Subaru allowing unqualified inspectors to perform a final examination of their cars
- Wells Fargo's consumer banking division having created 1.4 million fake accounts on top of 2.1 million previously disclosed as opened without permission of the clients
- Wells Fargo's insurance division having persuaded 570,000 consumers to buy unnecessary auto insurance
- Apple having purposely slowed down older iPhones to compensate for decaying batteries
- Equifax, credit rating firm selling personal, often sensitive information to financial institutions and lenders to boost its profits, the data breach which affected 145 mln people after hackers could take advantage of the system flow which was disclosed two months following the discovery. The top executives

are being investigated by the Justice Department for insider dealing after they sold $1.8 billion in shares before the breach was disclosed. (Fortune, 2017)

Banking Industry: Institutions of Public Trust?

The industry where high moral standards are central is the financial sector with banks traditionally referred to as public trust institutions. Contemporary research shows that customers' confidence in different aspects of financial institutions activity is very low. After the financial crises of the first decade of the 21st century, it seemed the lost trust will prompt financial institutions to apply more transparent and clear procedures in the industry where the gap between clients and employees knowledge is extremely wide.

In order to ensure the information gap is narrowed down, legislation was needed to protect clients applying for a credit which in Poland took a form of Consumer Credit Act resulting, inter alia, in the imposed obligation of referring to RRSO (real annual interest rate) when advertising a credit or loan.

However, numerous examples of unethical practices in banking can still be quoted. One of the high street banks in Poland included in their Cash Loan Agreement, which was 7 pages long, such a clause:The scope and direction of the tariff change and the amount in fees and commissions:

The fee or commission may not increase by more than 200% in relation to its previous amount.

This restriction does not apply to change in the tariff in case of:

1. Introducing a new fee or commission,
2. Increasing the fee or commission, whose value was PLN 0 or 0%
3. Changing the tariff resulting from a change in:
    a. The reference rate, the deposit rate, the Lombard rate, the change in the opposite direction to the rate change,
    b. The mandatory reserve rate of WIBOR for one-month or three-month deposits on the interbank market, any of the consumer price growth rates, average monthly wages and salaries in the enterprise sector, excluding payments from profit – the change in line (the same direction) with the change in these ratios".

Such wordy, complex "legalese" language in credit agreements is typical in Poland, resulting in many clients signing them without reading (or understanding). The level of financial education in Poland is very low with the information gap very wide and the gap of understanding even wider. It is, therefore, thanks to the implicit protection that clients may decide to sign agreements with financial institutions.

There is a register of abusive clauses in banking agreements available on the website of UOKiK (Office of Competition and Consumers Protection) which proves cases of unethical behaviour in these institutions are not rare.

In the period 2011-2017 UOKiK analysed the offering of credits, in particular mortgage and the general information policy on credit and risk. The main concern, it was concluded, should be the way of informing consumers about the interest rate risk referring to credit with a variable rate of interest. There was lack of mortgage with the fixed interest rate for the whole period of the credit agreement or its bigger part, as an alternative for variable interest rate credit and consumers were not always aware of the risk involved in such credit agreement. UOKiK expressed its concerns and hopes that banks work out such procedures to provide complex and clear information about risks involved in a mortgage, in particular, interest rate risk. Such information should be provided at the initial stage, ie, when signing the agreement, but also in the course of the credit agreement. Financial institutions should consider the client's situation at every stage of the agreement, and respond to their needs as there is a huge gap in legal and financial knowledge. It was recommended that banks work out procedures and systems of early warning, informing clients about detrimental changes in the markets that can result in increased interest rates. On client's request, such alert could initiate preparation of stabilization mechanism to mitigate negative effects directly affecting clients.

Another form of unethical practice in banking is "hidden" payment for banking services claimed to be free-of-charge when small amounts are charged for certain services specified in agreements which lay dormant for a limited time and become active when clients are likely to forget about them. Information may be sent by SMS referring to the website where the changed conditions of certain service are described. Clients are most likely to ignore such information or forget about it until they find themselves being charged for too few payments by their credit card or too little amount of monthly payments by a card or an overdraft which was free at the beginning. As a rule, clients decide not to lodge a complaint because the amount is minuscule, but a scale of such practices is big and banks being able to earn significant amounts of money without negative feedback do not withdraw such clauses.

Another ethical problem in banking is a lack of independent advisors, impartial in offering financial services of different institutions rather than employees of certain institutions selling the same product to all clients irrespective of their needs. Added to this is the bonus system in banking based on sales and motivational programs rewarding employees for high volume of sales.

The issue of employee relations in the context of ethics in banking has been analysed recently by Robert Rogowski who applied the quantitative and qualitative method in research based on a specialist Internet forum devoted to the banking industry employees. The study includes analyses of 817 comments posted on the forum in the period 2011-2016. The biggest number of comments were from Credit Agricole, Alior Bank, Bank PKO, Getin Bank, and ING.

21% of all comments pointed to a bad atmosphere at work. The biggest number of negative comments were made by employees of BPH (27%), Alior Bank (24%), Bank Zachodni WBK, and Credit Agricole.

Relations between employees were claimed to be objectified and depersonalized in particular when referring to the attitude of managers to employees which illustrates strong pressure to constantly increase sales. Sales were identified as the focal point of all activities. In 24% of all posts, it was stated that the management expectation was: "at any cost increase sales of financial products", with Getin Bank at the highest of 29%.

Comments also referred to high staff turnover and employment of staff who guarantee a high increase in sales irrespective of their level of knowledge or education in banking and finance. The main criterion of recruitment was an ability to sell and win new customers even at costs of ethics. Pressure on sales was identified as the main element of corporate culture. Comments even included lies that employees had to rely on to sell in order to reach the sales targets set by managers.

The third problem referred to was the negative evaluation of managerial staff in 19% of posts. The highest percentage of negative comments were about the managers with Credit Agricole accounting for 30% of all negative comments. Most frequently comments included: lack of competence and managerial skills, main focus being placed on sales and results, constant controls of effects and the requirement to justify targets not met, stressful atmosphere and "instrumental treatment" of workers, lack of fairness in bonus schemes, atmosphere of destructive competition, mobbing, bullying and threats of losing a job or being transferred to another branch.

Other issues addressed at the forum included lack of training courses or their low quality and the requirement to self-train in banking procedures or IT system operating. All training courses, it was claimed, focused on repeating sales scenes/ dramas and conference calls associated with sales. It was also noticed that the key to promotion was either good result in sales or (family) connections resulting in managers being recruited without any skills or competencies. Employees also realise the fact that managers role is purely to increase sales and therefore they are controlled constantly by directors, regional directors and headquarters so everyone is focused on gaining the best results in selling banking products, in particular, those most profitable.

Mobbing was reported in lots of banks, eg in PKO BP and BZ WBK 21% and 16% of comments respectively referred to it.

A trend towards decreasing remuneration and commission on sales was noted, as well as no increases in staff salary, lack of extra hour pay and unclear or unfair bonus schemes.

What is particularly noticeable is the fact that negative comments dominated. Only about 9% of comments included positive elements. Relatively most positive estimates were those of Raiffeisen POLBANK and positive comments about the atmosphere at work referred to this bank. In other banks, satisfaction was only attributed to salaries and sometimes to the nature of work based on personal contacts with clients.

Even overall positive comments sometimes included unethical elements, eg salary is high but at a high cost, or at a cost of persuading clients they should buy the product. (Rogowski, 2016)

While there is a reference to employer-employee relations in the mission statement or strategy of the majority of the big banks operating in Poland, the trend of immoral treatment of employees seems strong. In June 2018 there was the first in the history of Polish banking so wide-reaching protest of Pekao SA employees (it was estimated at least 70% of staff participated wearing black) demanding "real increase in salaries in reference to the bank's results, unreal sales targets liquidation as well as change of the arrogant and objectified treatment of employees".

This kind of "specific" morality was addressed by Aniela Dylus who described it as "marginal" ("borderline") morality, a kind of ethos "the other way round" incorporated in activities taken in order to prove smarter than others in the pursuit of success at any cost. Applying the economic principles of efficiency, it should be understood as the lowest possible "input of morality" that should maximize the economic result. This way this specific, distorted business "culture" or pseudo-culture is formed, which is then transformed into the pressure imposed on the members of the organization. Aniela Dylus calls it the "borderline" pressure and identifies it as a factor making people take measures that are often morally questionable but promise success and enable adaptation to common practice and avoidance of failure. (Dylus, 2002).

Financial institutions when given negative publicity may, to some extent, affect the image of the industry as a whole and raise the interest of journalists and regulators which was the case of Amber Gold affair, Swiss Franc credits in Poland, or the recent Get Back affair. Such increased interest often finally results in certain adjustment, supplementary regulation or educational activities to ensure there will be no irregularities of the same nature again. Unfortunately, this kind of a posteriori actions proves there is always a risk, finally taken by the public and the protection of the government and its bodies is not guaranteed.

The results of the research carried out in Poland by the Conference of Financial Enterprises prove that clients notice some crucial aspects of financial institutions activity they doubt are fair and trustworthy.

84% of the surveyed think the information from banks, insurance and leasing companies is not clear or transparent. According to the authors of the survey, the most critical aspect of financial market institutional regulation is the confidence the offering is not fair or reliable for the lack of complex, full and clear information. Clients opinions are based on both personal experiences as well as mass information about such practices. The negative experience resulted from being persuaded to purchase products which were not tailored to the needs or risky, "hidden" detrimental conditions in agreements, ignoring or neglecting risk, and fraudulent or misleading advertising. Only every sixth person believed the offering was fair and had "no strings attached".

The research into a financial situation of the Poles ("Sytuacja materialna Polaków") showed that respondents were most afraid of indebtedness and considered high amount of credit the riskiest, hence mortgage was considered as the sort of credit posing most threats to their financial stability.

Clients of financial institutions also find high commissions not justified, the opinion true for 78% of the surveyed.

It is possible such opinion results from financial markets crises and heavily criticised extremely high bonuses of managers held irresponsible for their bad decisions. On the other hand, there seems to be awareness of certain commissions being unreasonably high, e.g. money transfers abroad that reach 20% of the amount transferred.

Insurance companies are also frequently subjected to criticism, in particular in reference to compensation which, in the opinion of 77% of the respondents, is not fairly calculated, the amount usually too low. 18% of the surveyed doubt the valuation is fair and think it is therefore justified to reciprocate dishonest behaviour when consciously increasing the value of the loss suffered. The respondents openly confirmed this and treated it as a compensation for the insurer likely to increase the premium anyway. Only one in four surveyed thought the calculation of the compensation was honest.

The percentage of people whose perception of financial institutions in Poland is negative is exceptionally high. In the opinion of nearly every four in five respondents, the financial market communicates in an unclear way, underestimates due amounts of compensation in insurance while overestimating own commission. Such a high percentage of critical or dissatisfied clients who claim the offering is unclear, difficult to understand and exposing them to unjustified cost seems unprecedented.

Consumers' Role in New Business Models Emergence

Consumers who were addressed in the previous part of this study, sub-headed "Business moral standards", as one of the most vulnerable groups for their lack of knowledge and experience, seem to be in a changing position over the last years.

One of the reasons, paradoxically, can be a new perception of trust. The notion rightly seems to be central today and is gaining even more attention with the advent of the era of sharing/ access business models. An explanation can also be provided by the altered understanding of the concept of value creation.

The new perception of value, as defined by Vargo & Lusch, the authors of service-dominant logic, is likely to keep consumers involved and engaged to such an extent that they cooperate with service providers, influence and even shape their final offering. Consumer empowerment seems to predominate the economic reality today. The impressive performance of companies which grew on consumers' active participation (such as Allrecipes- sharing recipes site, now with 85 million users globally and 1.5 billion users annually or peer to peer lending which increased sevenfold between 2014 and 2015, from $9 bln to $64 bln) proves it is an opportunity which may result in business success.

Similarly, impressive results achieved by companies which emerged on the basis of peer-to-peer communication with roots in social media (such as Uber, AirB&B) thus creating business models "from the bottom up" prove that the unprecedented role of individuals is not to be neglected. Surprisingly, the main principles on which success of such firms is based are peer-to-peer trust and lack of regulation or protection by law. This, in turn, signifies that the regulatory environment may cease to have a dominant role in contemporary consumers' perceptions and evaluations, while the decision-making process is likely to be reliant more on individual ethical values. New consumers' focus on self-driven solutions and more participative models is an evident reflection of their intensified confidence in peer-to-peer transactions and may lead to further development of the sharing economy primarily and profoundly based on trust.

Customer shifted expectations of a variety of choice and their preferences towards efficient use of resources are materialized in the sharing economy which is presumed to have an immense growth potential, especially in the five main industries: financial services, transportation, accommodation and tourism, as well as labour. It takes different forms of lending/ borrowing, barter, making resources, such as time, money and skills available for other users. According to PricewaterhouseCoopers, peer to peer lending may expand further to at least $150 bln while aggregate income from sharing economy in the aforementioned five core areas is estimated to account for $335bln by 2025.

The financial industry has been ranked very high among sectors which are likely to be influenced most by market "disruptors", institutions emerging from societal forces operating on a peer-to-peer basis in the sharing or access economy. According to PricewaterhouseCoopers, the sharing economy will be one of the most disruptive forces the banking sector has experienced by 2020. The principles of access economy in financial services sector already manifest themselves in decentralized asset ownership and innovations that match financial counterparts, such as peer-to-peer lending, insurance, crowdfunding and social payments. The potential of sharing economy, to a high extent, derives from altered consumer perception of value materialized in company offerings.

Moreover, consumers evaluate owning as opposed to using in a different way. A new consumer is more focused on experience rather than attached to possession. Recent research carried out by PricewaterhouseCoopers on sharing economy shows that consumers' way of thinking about value added by ownership is evolving: 81% of respondents agree that it is more efficient to use other people's possessions than actually own them, 43% of the surveyed think that ownership of resources is an unnecessary burden for the budget and 57% claim that access to resources and goods is an attractive alternative to owning them. The approach appears to be the response to the last crisis and urbanization, the need to avoid indebtedness as well as inconvenience related, for example, to parking space limitations. Additional benefits, such as reduced negative effects of pollution resulting from optimization and efficient use of resources (cuts in car manufacturing, economizing on fuel, etc.) should not remain unnoticed.

The evolving attitude of individuals is derivative of many factors, with technology/ innovation in the centre. The emergence of new generations, more and more dependent and reliant on technology necessitates changes in business models adequate for different stakeholders.

According to Manuel Castells, the world's third most-cited social science scholar, network society is characterized by the breakdown of "rhythms" incorporated in the concept of the life cycle. Organisational and technological solutions, as well as cultural events typical of the new, emerging society, undermine this ordered lifecycle without any alternative suggested. (2007)

He claims that contemporary societies are organised around the two opposing poles: the "Net" and the Self". The former reflecting the network organisations which predominantly replace previous vertically integrated hierarchies. The latter term implies reaffirming social identity and meaning by individuals in a constantly changing cultural environment. (Castells, 1996)

This perspective confirms the view that the trends are likely to result in strengthening the sharing of participative models as main forms of business organisations with an increasingly critical role of individuals with their values. Such values will be founded on knowledge as well as strong inner confidence in the reliability of institutions.

As stipulated by last year's Nobel Prize winner in economic sciences, Richard Thaler, the author of the nudge concept, people are not responsive to regulations, orders or bans, but can be much more effectively influenced by stimuli which correspond to their specific needs.

Such positive motivation based not necessarily on financial stimulation and strengthened by educating and communicating different benefits can increase the level of trust and result in better understanding and acceptance of solutions and expected decisions.

It seems there is an urgent need for more activities aimed at improving consumers' knowledge, awareness and responsiveness to responsible and ethical behaviour.

Sharing economy is evidence of profound social changes where consumers decide of forms of their participation in the economy. Bitcoin and its development are based on consumers drive to streamline transactions. Trust consumers have in each other illustrates their altered need to have confidence in peers.

Challenges the global economy is facing demand that ethical dilemmas are viewed from a different angle. Primarily, it is the notion of trust that needs to be better understood and examined. According to research trust depends, to a high degree, on education as well as income and therefore it should be assumed that the reasons for its varied level will be different across countries. However, the trend towards sharing economy models seems to result from the widespread access to technology and should, therefore, be understood as a global phenomenon.

CONCLUSION

It can be concluded that a clear message about the organization's moral norms plays a significant role in the process of creating a socially responsible organization. It facilitates the enforcement of socially acceptable behaviour of employees. Respecting the adopted standards should be an obligation of all participants of the organization, both employees and employers. At the same time, the utility of the ethical system created in the enterprise depends on its coherence with generally binding moral standards. Therefore, especially in large business organizations, employers are developing and adopting so-called ethical codes in which desirable behaviour patterns are described as well as unacceptable behaviours and consequences related to non-compliance with specific rules of conduct. Such a document reflects the ethical values that the organization respects and observes.

The important question in the context of ethical values, however, is if trust without understanding can be real and long-standing and, if so, what can be its sources. As exemplified in the study the gap of understanding in certain industries is really wide and therefore without improving education in the society there can be no trust based on values from within the organisation. It seems that trust, if be based on assumptions which are not derivative of inner qualities of the institutions, but on the government guarantees of exercising control over them is not valuable.

The quality of so defined trust seems to be inferior to confidence naturally laid on the institution because of its strengths and values from inside of the organisation.

Analyses of the new consumers' expectations and position may lead to the conclusion that businesses suffering from moral problems between main stakeholders will find it difficult to survive in the era of innovation, information and consumer empowerment.

Individuals' drive towards new business models may be a natural result of disappointment in the old solutions and given the new opportunities, they feel encouraged to try something new, even though also risky or unknown.

The answer to the question if business models should be adjusted to the needs of the public and follow the trend from the bottom up seems obvious. In the light of the changes, the contemporary world is facing there is no other alternative. Consumers' power is the fact of life and developing technology can only strengthen the trend.

REFERENCES

Carroll, A. B. (1991). The Pyramid of Corporate Social Responsibility: Toward the Moral Management of Organizational Stakeholders. *Business Horizons*, *34*(4), 39–48. doi:10.1016/0007-6813(91)90005-G

Castells, M. (1996). *The Rise of the Network Society: The Information Age: Economy, Society, Culture* (Vol. 1). Oxford, UK: Blackwell Publishers.

Castells, M. (2007). *Społeczeństwo sieci*. Warszawa: PWN.

Castells, M. (2009). The Rise of the Network Society: The Information Age: Economy, *Society, and Culture.* Wiley-Blackwell.

CBOS (Centrum Badania Opinii Społecznej). (2018). *O nieufności i zaufaniu*. Komunikat z Badań.

Dylus, A. (2002). Erozja standardów etycznych w biznesie. In J. Mariański (Ed.), *Kondycja moralna społeczeństwa polskiego* (pp. 273–303). Kraków: WAM.

Ericson T. (n.d.). Generations Around the Globe. *Harvard Business Review*.

Ethics Resource Centre, Generational Differences in Workplace. (2011). *Ethics: A Supplemental Report of the 2011 National Business Ethics Survey*. Retrieved from http://www.ethics.org/ecihome/research/nbes/nbes-reports/nbes-2013

Fiorelli, P. (n.d.). *Generational Ethics: A Battle of the Ages.* Retrieved from https://www.corporatecompliance.org/Portals/1/PDF/Resources/past_handouts/Higher_Ed/2017/V1__ses_401_2slides.pdf

Lewicka-Strzałecka, A. (n.d.). *Moralność Finansowa Polaków.* Instytut Filozofii i Socjologii PAN, Konferencja Przedsiębiorstw Finansowych

Relative Ranking of a Selected Pool of Leading Scholars in the Social Sciences by Number of Citations in the Social Science Citation Index. (2000-2014). Retrieved from https://web.archive.org/web/20160307132846/http://www.manuelcastells.info/sites/default/files/sscisocialranking_eng.pdf

Rogowski, R. (2016). Ethical Problems at Work in the Opinion of Employees of Selected Banks. *Annales. Ethics in Economic Life, 19*(3).

United Nations Global Compact. (n.d.). Retrieved from https://www.unglobalcompact.org/what-is-gc/mission/principles

Ustawa o kredycie konsumenckim (Consumer Credit Act). (n.d.). Retrieved from http://prawo.sejm.gov.pl/isap.nsf/DocDetails.xsp?id=WDU20111260715

Wolska, G. (2013). Corporate social responsibility in Poland – theory and practice. *Journal of International Studies, 6*(2), 45–53. doi:10.14254/2071-8330.2013/6-2/4

Young, S. (2003). *Moral Capitalism: Reconciling Private Interest with the Public Good.* Berrett-Koehler Publishers, Inc.

KEY TERMS AND DEFINITIONS

Business Ethics: The belief that companies should behave, as individuals, in a way universally considered to be good and moral.

Consumer Empowerment: The trend in consumer behavior visible in their independence and determination to actively participate in co-creating value with companies and service providers.

Corporate Social Responsibility: The belief that apart from generating profits companies should contribute to the society by performing socially important activities to benefit the society as a whole and its certain groups.

Generations: Groups coexisting in the society, born at different times and showing specific features.

Sharing Economy: The economy based on sharing goods rather than owning them, also called access economy to emphasize that consumers need to use products, which is possible without possessing them.

Trust: The confidence in a person or organisation based on a belief that they act in compliance with moral standards and will behave in an expected way, according to certain, established rules.

Values: The set of believes and attitudes that each individual has.

Chapter 10
Circularity in Portugal:
Features of New Business Challenges

Ana Cristina Pego
Nova University, Portugal

ABSTRACT

The use of renewable energy and recycling products is one of the main achievements of organizations. The circular economy (CE) is a new concept which evolves out of a new management assumption in organizations based on recycling, reuse, and repurposing of products. The circular economy provides a framework for facing challenges and a guide for rethinking and redesigning the future. This chapter analyzes the Portuguese market for circular economy organizations based on discussion of the CE conceptual model. The circular economy is expected to contribute positively by introducing new methodologies for the production of raw materials, with new production processes and giving value to eco products. The challenge for Portuguese organizations is to create management "vectors" which promote networking innovation, labor, capital, and eco products. Overall, the conceptual model presented gives importance to Portuguese business decision making for sustainable consumption, which provides advancements in business for the green supply chain.

INTRODUCTION

The concept of the circular economy (CE) has gained momentum both among scholars and practitioners (Kirchherr et al., 2017:221). Business models and market dynamics in the circular economy are based on economic empirical or modelling approaches to understanding why and how companies or organizations are pursuing circular economy opportunities. The CE and the business models face a singularity

DOI: 10.4018/978-1-5225-7850-5.ch010

of a new assumption on how to be efficient in "green" markets. The importance of this assumption is to give an opportunity to new products which will be related to the environment and sustainable production. However, it needs to draw on an efficient model which deals with the relationship between the social and economic impact, consumers and producers towards a new concept of "eco". In this research article, the conceptual model for Portuguese organization is presented. In order to answer the research question: "Which are the most important vectors in circularity in Portugal?", the methodology was based on the conceptual market framework where it was compared to the following vectors: positive and negative impact from changing to a CE model; stakeholders which are important for implementing the business model; uses of natural resources in the value chain; and market strategy. The goal is to identify the most important features in the Portuguese CE and build a conceptual model based on that statement. The article is divided into six main points: the CE concept, the circular conceptual model, the Portuguese organization and the circularity, results from the research, further development discussion about CE and a conclusion.

BACKGROUND

The objective of this study is to analyse the vectors which influence circularity in Portugal. This section will characterize the organisations and the conceptual model. This means that not only are the positive and negative impacts from using circularity analysed but also the stakeholders, the use of natural resources and market strategies which comprise the circular Portuguese conceptual model. The goal is to create an analogy between the organisations which use circular products and describe the conceptual model homogeneously from different sectors.

The Circular Economy

The term circular economy has both a linguistic and a descriptive meaning. Linguistically it is an antonym of a linear economy. Murray et al. (2017:371).

Definition of the Circular Economy

According to Boulding, K. (1966: 2), the circular economy is "a closed system, the outputs of all parts of the system is linked to the inputs of other parts. There are no inputs from outside and no outputs to the outside; indeed, there is no outside at all". The closed system inside the organization allows re-use of resources to promote new products. The challenge is to create new products which can be re-used. In view of these goals, organizations need to be innovative in their product design, revenue model associated with it, and engage in social and institutional innovation to be competitive. There is no single accepted definition of the circular economy.

The precise meaning of a "transition to a circular economy" varies across the current literature but tends to involve a reduced demand for certain natural resources and the materials that are derived from them (McCarthy et al., 2018:8). One of the main achievements for the organization was to rethink a new business model where materials can be re-used to be competitive in the market. As such, organizations needed to address new forms of managing attitudes towards a new concept of production. However, these changes need to be based on decisions where the model could construct a reverse cycle in the market, i.e., re-using, recycling and producing products which could be accepted by consumers or organizations in order to be in the economic value chain again.

According to the Action Plan for Circular Economy (APCE)(2017:10), materials are preserved, restored and reintroduced cyclically into the system with economic benefits for suppliers and users, and environmental benefits due to lower extraction and imports of raw materials, reduced waste production and lower associated emissions. The circular economy is a closed system. From the EU (European Union) perspective, the circular economy has had an increased participation in the economy.

EU policy on the CE has discussed resource efficiency and sustainable use of natural resources. The policy focuses on topics related to eco-innovation, chemicals and plastic, waste, water management, marine pollution and urban environmental best practices. These issues are also related to innovative business for welfare and environment solutions.

According to the EU,[1] Circular Economy Missions are conceived with three clear objectives: *to increase* cooperation between the EU and third countries in the field of environmental policy. This can be achieved by signing political agreements directed at fostering the circular economy, green public procurement and innovative, sustainable and inclusive growth; *to achieve* a better understanding of the environmental challenges faced by third countries; *to promote* green solutions through business partnerships abroad. In this regard, the missions will organize matchmaking events between European and local entrepreneurs and will engage in an exchange of views with targeted audiences. In order to address the circular economy in Europe and the relationship between the stakeholders, the European Commission has developed a platform with strategies for the transition to a circular economy adopted at national, regional or local level by public authorities (https://circulareconomy.europa.eu/platform/en/strategies?, consulted 31/07/2018). The intention is to exhibit strategies from European countries about the transition to a circular economy.

Impacts of Circularity on the Economy

The impacts of circularity are evaluated with when the benefits, strategies, and barriers to circular transition are analysed. These vectors influence organizations and their relation to the market. However, any organization should study them overall. The goal is maximized goods utility for consumers and the production value chain.

Pego (2018a) points out some benefits to the economy of using a CE, namely fostering competitiveness by creating savings and reducing raw materials and energy dependency; security of supply and control of rising costs; contributing to EU climate change policy by reducing greenhouse gas emissions; employment opportunities; reducing environmental impact of resource extraction and waste disposal; opportunities for new businesses by selling goods or offering services. The importance of the CE in the economic system is consistent with the relationship between economic agents. This means that there are direct inputs and outputs where the impacts on the economic system can be explored.

In other words, the CE is a concept which involves a set of useful competencies for welfare. This means a network with the ability to foster system thinking, goals, strategy and their adoption, with external and internal effects, and which promotes positive externalities in the economy. CE components are the positive vectors which allow linear economy for saving resources.

It is important to study the impacts of a circular economy transition at the macroeconomic level (McCarthy et al., 2018:13) because even while creating positive impacts (Figure 1), organizations need to adapt to circularity. At the macroeconomic level, organizations are confronted with supply and demand and circular material flows. The goal is to achieve a methodology where organizations can contribute positively to better re-use, re-building and re-thinking about materials and economic flux. The question is to "design" the market and the methodology to

Figure 1. The simplified circular economy (r Recycling, W waste, P production, C consumption, K capital goods, U utility, R natural resources)
Source: Pego (2018a:316)

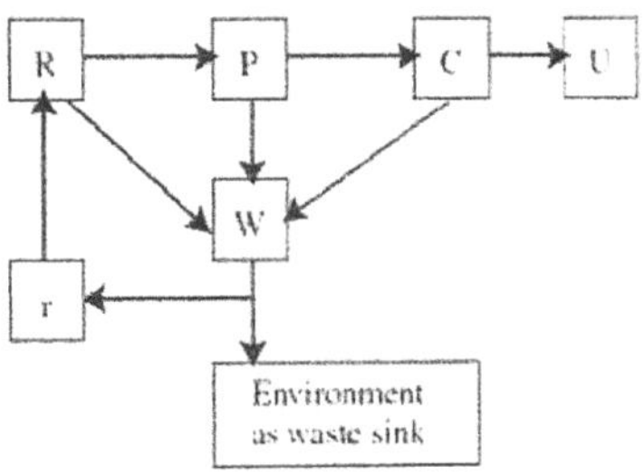

achieve equilibrium between macroeconomic agents. There is a perfect combination of these macroeconomic vectors (supply, demand and circular economy).

There are perfect symbioses between the supply and circular economy if there is a possibility to change from secondary materials by recycling primary materials when there is improved material productivity via technological change, substitute renewable inputs for non-renewable, substitute labour or capital for material and design longer-lived products (DFE). From the demand side, the linkages between circular economies are made by substituting repaired and remanufactured goods for their new equivalent (repaired and remanufactured), when goods are replaced with services, improving assets utilization (sharing economy).

In order to achieve marginal utility in the market for consumers and production, organizations need to change strategies from a linear economy to a circular economy. The strategies are based on a few aspects, such as design, technologies, new business models, reverse cycles, and promoters. The goal is not to lose externalities in the value chain and to gain with new products.

However, there are market imperfections which are called "barriers" to development. These constitute obstacles to the circular economy transition. The business model followed by organizations should take it into account to implement their decision to "change".

Another perspective from Kirchherr et al. (2018) points out the circular economy transition according to value chain and key factors. Cultural, regulatory, market, and techniques may be the key factor for CE transition, where effectively hesitant company culture, lacking consumer awareness and interest, as well as operation in a

Figure 2. Circular economy strategies
Source: APCE (2017:11)

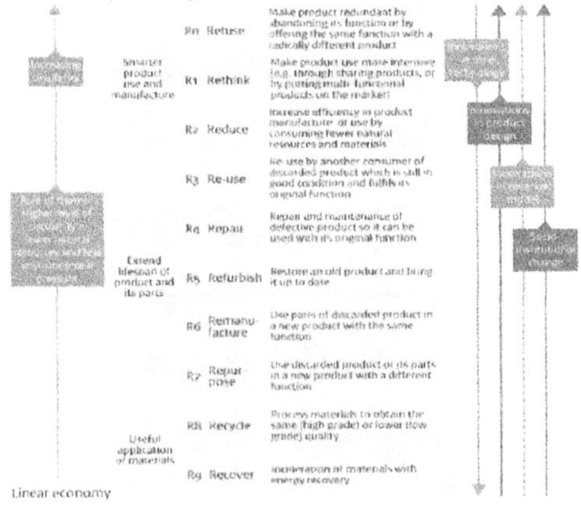

Table 1. Barriers to the circular economy transition

Economic	*Profitability:* Further innovation and learning by doing are required to reduce costs or realize benefits; Realistic projections of the profitability of the technology in the long run are difficult to make; *Barriers to financing the new technologies; Uncertainty about future costs and revenues; Technology is not available at scale;*
Market failures	*Externalities* (societal costs and benefits that are not reflected in market prices); *Insufficient public goods, including infrastructure ; - Insufficient competition on markets; competition on the wrong criteria - Imperfect information, e.g. asymmetric information; Split incentives (agency problems) when parties have different goals; Transaction costs, such as the costs of bargaining;*
Regulatory failures	*Inadequately defined legal frameworks; Poorly defined targets and objectives; Implementation and enforcement failures; Unintended consequences of existing regulation that hamper circular practices;*
Social factors	*Capabilities and skills; Customs and habits; Social resistance; Political resistance;*

Source: Woltjer, G. (2018: 9)

linear system, are the most pressing barriers, because of the organizational culture. Another pressing barrier is the market, where prices and investments are the most important factor to achieve the CE.

According to the APCE (2017), some European countries have shown positive CE performance. The impact on jobs and the economy has contributed to a positive development in some sectors, and to a competitive advantage from a market process, structural industry analysis, resource skills or capabilities and dynamics sector (Pego, 2018b). From Woltjer's (2018:19) perspective, circular opportunities in an economy may generate GDP increases by various means: through the environmental effect; reducing demand for primary resources may reduce their relative scarcity; increase in additional productivity ; reduction in externalities via the tax and regulatory systems; and effect of increased demand.

Figure 3. Key CE barriers and their interaction
Source: Kirchherr et al. (2018: 270)

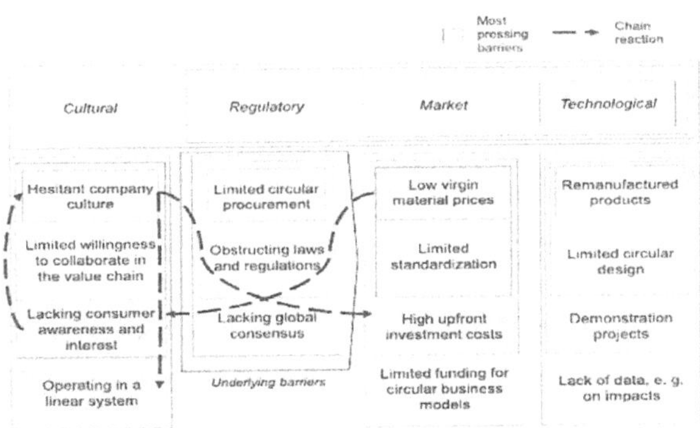

To address the impact of the CE on the economy, it is important to study relevant indicators for macroeconomic evaluation: changes in factor productivity, i.e. input requirements per unit of output, where one has to be aware that the quality of the output may also change; changes in trade flows, especially imports of raw materials; amount of investment needed; changes in quantity of employment, wherein it is important to prove that the jobs generated are additional to baseline employment; composition of labour demand compared with scarcities on the labour market; externalities in production that may be reduced by the circular opportunity; welfare effects of the externalities that may be reduced; whether the circular opportunity create skills and/or knowledge that provide a competitive advantage or that can be exported to other regions of the world (Woltjer, 2018:27).

Circular Economy and Clusters

The following figure identifies the CE position in the economy, as well as its participation. Clusters become one of the main figures in the CE if the relationship between the products, the sectors, waste materials, raw materials, knowledge, and investments is identified. The purpose is to create links between these variables for the CE to perform economic and social impacts.

Clusters reflect a phenomenon where the organizations and market perspective can be seen. The clusters establish development strategies in a particular activity sector, associated with increasingly specialized services. Clusters are related to smart specialization, knowledge, and innovation (Pego, 2018b). The collaboration between activities will end in innovative clusters, where new activities are explored, building up existing capacities and promoting strengths in new products and activities, capitalizing upon regional competences to diversify into new activity areas and to develop emerging industries; capturing cross-sectoral linkages; adopting an inclusive and participatory cluster approach.

Therefore, clusters should have an international perspective on value chains and build partnerships at the European level (Pego, 2018b).

THE CONCEPTUAL MODEL

The first question is *how to study a CE business model.* The concept of the business model is based on industrial innovation of future productivity and competitiveness between organizations. CE business model solutions can be improved if companies transfer knowledge from their previous experience based on the relationship between customers and stakeholders (Pego, 2018a:316). The circular economy is based on a different business model which aims to be competitive with linear products. As such,

Figure 4. Conceptual activities in the CE
Source: APCE (2017:19)

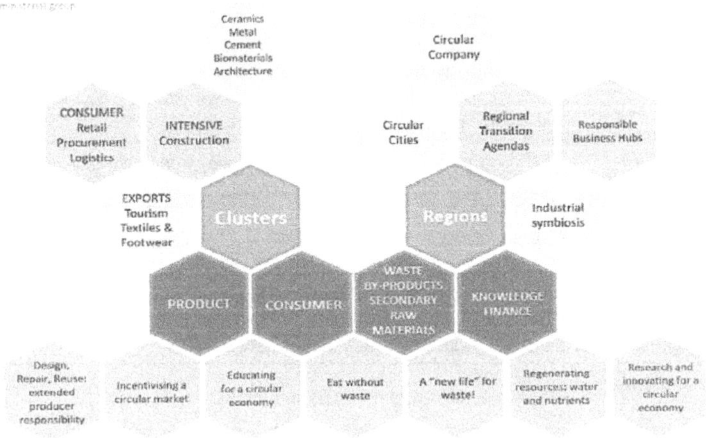

organizations, besides new strategies, must develop a new conception of business related to the perception of re-using, re-building and re-producing new products.

The business models developed in the circular economy create value in the products and build necessities in consumers. This means that by developing new ways to be in the market, producers and consumers can rely on new forms of goods utility. From the producer's side, the savings which come from the use of raw materials, equipment and value added in the new products are important. From the perspective of Planing, P. (2015:4), the business model from the producer's view has more consistent gains with products with long life, innovation, and collaborative consumption.

From the consumer's side, the re-use of goods will affect the environment and welfare. The business models which comprise consumers are based on re-use of the products for new utility in the long term (Planing, P., 2015:4). The business model which comprises the CE is complex because it needs to be adjusted to a few variables, such as, environment, materials and re-use of products towards new methods of production, innovation, investments and consumers.

The conception of a circular business model put forward by Lewandowski (2016:43) identified the main characteristics of the business and how those characteristics will influence the economy. The importance of this conceptualization is the identification of circularity components for a new methodology of production based on green business models and innovation (Pego, 2018b).

Another point of view put forward by Bocken et al. (2016) describes the circular business model with a comparison between products and strategies in the market. The

Table 2. Circular business model strategy

New business models and dematerialization	Use of virtual services and pay-per-use platforms where it is created rental services to maximize the productivity and equipment by resources savings.
Design, eco-conception	Design/ redesign of circular products and production process where it used renewable materials and raw material recovered. The products can be used in other products, lifelong product design with labels where it can be seen how to re-use the product;
Clean production/ eco-efficient	Efficient production with low use of energy and materials; efficient net systems in productivity and resources;
Cycle life extension: re-use, re-manufacture and reconditioning	*Downcycling*, re-use of residuals to create new products with low value; *upcycling*, re-use of residuals to create new products with a high value added;
Industrial symbioses (urban, local, regional)	Business strategies between entities which works together on an efficient system towards a positive natural externalities;
Sub products and waste valuation	New products from residuals sub-products or products
Social awareness and engagement	Social awareness about the citizens participation in circular economy

Source: http://eco.nomia.pt/pt/economia-circular/diagrama-de-sistemas, consulted in 31th july 2018.

Figure 5. The concept of developing a framework of business model for the circular economy
Source: Lewandowski, M. (2016:43)

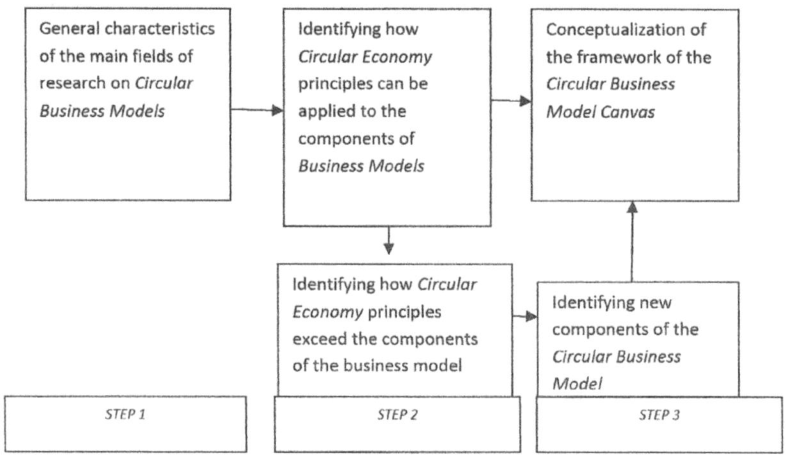

circular business model is made with the comparison between the slowing and closing strategies. According to this point of view, interest is based on long-life products, with long-life value, as well as industrial symbioses and a long-life technological cycle. The value of products is adjusted to long-life cycles in the economy.

Figure 6. Circular economy product and business model strategy framework.
Source: Bocken et al. (2016: 316)

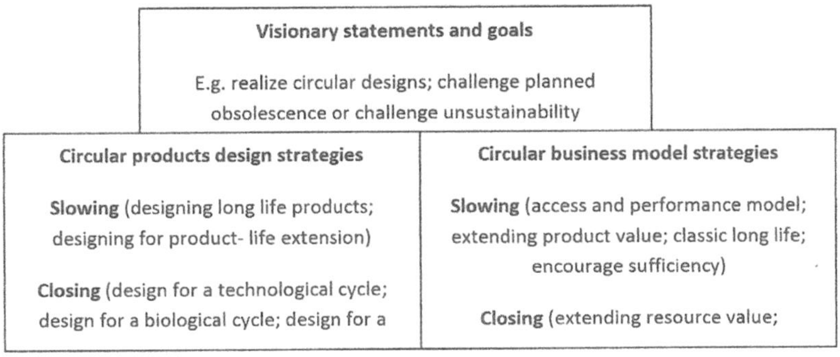

A business strategy based on the CE needs to optimize materials and energy flows inside the regions or industrial ecosystems. This creates a new challenge for resource recovery and tax exemption in reverse supply chain activities. Additionally, the stakeholder's expectations regarding the CE business model on production, value chain, and competitiveness constitute an important vector for social, environmental and resources effectively in the economy (Pego, 2018a).

Planing, P. (2015:7) describes why consumers should not accept the circular economy. The change will be to optimize the value proposition of circular economy business models by not only regarding rational but also non-rational motives of consumer behaviour. This includes the habits and routines of individuals (Planing, P., 2015:9). From his point of view, consumers are the important part of the circular system and face a few problems in accepting circularity:

Customer Irrationality: Customers only evaluate the transaction cost at the point of sale (purchase price) even if the net present value of upgrading to a more expensive but more durable product would be more economical. Consumers prefer ownership of a product, even if temporary usage is more economical;

Conflict of Interest Within Companies: Higher capital or cash required to change an existing product design or to move from a sales-based to a usage-based revenue model;

Misaligned Profit-Share Along the Supply Chain: Imperfect design at the beginning of the supply chain if the profits from a better design would only occur at the end-of-use phase;

Geographic Dispersion: Since the value chain of today's product is spreading over multiple countries, national initiatives often lose their potential impact.

THE PORTUGUESE ORGANIZATIONS AND THE CIRCULAR ECONOMY

Action plans and strategic directions are the vectors for the future of the CE in Europe (Pego, 2018a: 317). The roadmap for CE in Portugal was created with the (APCE).[2] The vectors which support this plan are:

1. A carbon-neutral economy that is efficient and productive in its use of resources: neutral GHG emissions and effective use of materials (a significant fall in the extraction and importing of materials, a significant fall in final waste generated, better management and value extraction from the resources in circulation);
2. Knowledge as imputes: focusing on research and innovation creates solutions – in products, services, business models, consumption/use, behaviour – with lower emissions and intensity of resources, integrated into business models that spur creation of jobs, efficient and effective use of mobilized resources, and their lasting economic value;
3. Inclusive and resilient economic prosperity: economic development that impacts all sectors of society is resilient against price and risk volatility and gradually decoupled from negative environmental and social impacts;
4. A flourishing, responsible, dynamic and inclusive society: an informed, participative and more collaborative society – a society guided by being and caring, rather than wanting and possessing and which conserves and cares for its natural capital.

It is important to build circularity in three main vectors: macro, meso (sectorial) or micro (regional/local). In these vectors, the links within the value chain and the productivity are presented, as well as the positive effects on the economy through intentions between all players. The *macro* level is defined as actions which are structural in scope and that produce transversal and systematic effects which enable society to appropriate the principles of the circular economy; the *meso* (sectorial) is defined as actions or intentions defined and accepted by all players in the value chain of the sectors relevant to raising productivity and the efficient use of the country's resources, seizing economic, social, and environmental benefits; the *micro* (regional/local) is defined as action and intentions defined and accepted by all regions and/ or local government, economic and social actors which incorporate a local economic aspect and which emphasise this in the approach to social challenges (APCE, 2017:17).

In order to develop circularity in Portugal, there are a few financing opportunities available, divided by European initiatives, programmes, or instruments for which Portuguese organizations can apply (2014-2020) (APCE, 2017:23). The goal is to support activities where environmental impacts can be reduced; reduce disposable packaging and plastics in the transportation, storage, exhibition and marketing of products through the reuse of sustainable products; promote the adoption of a rationale of sustainability, circular economy and sharing economy; promote a sustainable culture through education and implementation of environmental values.

Portuguese circularity is based on two macro guidelines: products and consumers. Both aim to be in the market to promote positive externalities based on innovation and R&D products. The equilibrium point between those is the self-regulatory framework where consumers benefit from long-life products and the product benefits from the supply services which benefit the consumer's needs in the long run.

The latest data for Portuguese organizations which use the CE shows that the growth in many economic sectors has contributed positively to new business models related to new products, R&D, and investment. Although it appears that there is an emergent cluster related to circularity, this means an emergent market with circular products, investments, expertise labour and R&D, where links can be made between the organization, government and research activities.

From Table 4, it is possible to conclude that the sectors with the greatest CE impact on the Portuguese economy are those where citizens have a direct participation as consumers, and also where the value chain is shorter, namely agro-food and waste management.

Table 3. Portuguese macro action guidelines for circularity

Products	Develop partnerships involving national R&D, e.g. in design, to analyse products with a view to boosting manufacturing innovation; Interact with manufacturers to develop strategies to extend product working life: e.g. servitization, "designing to last", component and service repair/remanufacturing; Assess the introduction of differentiated financial allocations (eco-value, in short), awarding the introduction of circular requirements into products (e.g. eco-labeling, consumer information on the period of availability of spare parts and repair services, information on repairs by independent bodies or repair manuals for the final consumer, software or product update options, product return incentives, easy repair design);Cut the maximum size of family packs across the board (to be agreed with sugary drink producers and distributors), from a self-regulatory stand point;
Consumer	Encourage repair & reuse: support development of a network of repair facilities, e.g. by backing initiatives promoted by councils, such as repair cafés, local swap shops and repairer banks, encouraging local and/or traditional repair activities (linked to the Environment Fund, regional agendas–circular cities); Establish partnerships with municipalities to train and disseminate repair and reuse networks –resale, social support; Develop tools to communicate to consumers the benefits of extending the useful life of goods/equipment, e.g. information on warranties, repair instructions, replacement parts, eco- labeling; Develop banks of reused school books in the public network of educational establishments.

Source: APCE (2017: 29)

CIRCULARITY IN PORTUGAL: A NEW BUSINESS CHALLENGE

This chapter will focus on the conception of a model from Portuguese organisations which use circular products. The research presented in this chapter will provide valuable knowledge on positive and negative aspects of the circular economy faced by Portuguese organisations when undertaking circularity as well as a conceptual model for business performance.

Methodology

The research objective of this paper is to study the conceptual model and its applicability to the Portuguese circular sector. The research question is: *Which are the most important vectors in circularity in Portugal?* In order to achieve the goal three organizations from different economic sectors were studied (Soja Portugal, NAE Fashion with Comparison, and Fruta Fea), which have a high impact in the national and international market, and how the organizations are dealing with circularity.

Table 4. Portuguese organisations using CE

Sectors Typology	Nº	Percentage
Agro- Food and food (included urban waste)	32	*14.8*
Ceramic	4	1.8
Communication, marketing and design	1	0.5
Building construction	11	5
Packaging	5	2.3
Energy	10	4.6
Electronic and electric equipment	9	4.1
Mining, metallurgy and metalworking	4	1.8
Financial	6	2.8
Waste management	23	*10.6*
Cosmetics and hygiene	1	0.5
R&D and teaching activities	20	*9.2*
Distribution and logistics	6	2.8
Wood and other similar products	1	0.5
Furniture	5	2.3
Transports and other mobility services	6	2.8
Chemical industry	4	1.8
Other manufacturing industries	1	0.5
Other services not specified	37	*17.1*
Paper paste	2	0.9
Plastics	6	2.8
Telecommunications	2	0.9
Textiles and Footwear	19	*8.8*
Tourism	2	0.9
Total	217	100

Source: www.eco.nomia.pt (consulted in 29th July 2018)

Table 5. Portuguese circular economy conceptual model

Positive Impacts	Environmental sustainability; eco-value (product value from ecological production); consumers responsibility; resources valuation; eco-design products; re-use of natural materials; innovation; research and development of eco-design; waste of agriculture products for local markets;
Negative Impacts	Financial costs in short run; high research &innovation expenses;
Stakeholders	Supply Portuguese organisation; European organisation; research centers; universities; domestic consumers (agro-industry);supermarket, local market (agro-industry sector);
Uses of natural Resources	Use of natural resources; use of renewable energy (e.g. biomass, onshore wind energy, water) except in agro-industry sector;
Market Strategies	Product differentiation; use of website to promote the organisation; help producers to sell their production (agro –industry sector); network logistic system; long life products (except on agro industry sector); ecological quality; Partnership with international organisations in the value chain; scale economy; eco –market share;

Results

From the organizational study, a table was produced which shows the capacity to be in the market and the positive and negative impacts on the environment, organizational partners, social responsibility, the use of natural resources, and the value chain.

Despite the new era of a conceptual model for Portuguese CE organization, a new challenge is being faced in the European economy. First, the concept of circularity is new in business Portuguese networks and consumers need more time to evaluate and understand the concept of circularity. Second, the sectors which are beginning to grow under this concept are those with a short value chain, like the agro-industry. Sectors with ahigh economic specialization and expert knowledge constitute a low share in the CE overall; third, there is a market strategy for growth at European level or other markets; fourth, production factors constitute a negative impact on circularity; positive externalities in the market (national or international) are one of the goals of the CE in Portugal.

It is expected that other sectors (Table 5) will have an important contribution in the CE Portugal and promote a value in eco-products and the ecosystem itself. It is important to build awareness in Portuguese consumers and producers about the importance and benefits of circularity in Portuguese's business network. The business model which Portuguese organizations should follow is to build self-assurance about the potentialities about the CE in Portugal. Moreover, vectors such as the positive and negative impact on the economy (local/regional/national), stakeholders, use of natural resources and market strategies constitute the conceptual model for circularity in Portugal.

FUTURE RESEARCH DIRECTIONS

The importance of studying a Portuguese conceptual model when the organization uses circularity is to show how the organization is changing towards a circular business model.

From the Portuguese business network perspective, the CE is constituted by emergent sectors in this field; sectors such as agriculture, waste management and technology and research activities are the most important sectors in CE. It is expected that others sectors with low impact will increase their participation in the direct and indirect impact on the economy. Questions such as: "Who we are?", "How can we avoid the problem?" and "What should the environmental, social and technical changes be?" form the basis for a new business methodology to achieve circularity in the economy. The question is to demonstrate how it is important to change attitudes and decision in organizations towards circularity, and therefore the APCE (2017) will have an important contribution to this achievement.

CONCLUSION

Circularity in Europe has become an important issue due to the fact of new methodologies for understanding challenges for the circular economy. The critical changes of the conceptual model that most organizations face are production costs and acceptance of new products by the consumers. However, creating needs for the consumers and some organizations is the most important marketing factor. Working through this strategy and "eco" definitions (e.g. eco-design, eco-production, raw material) is a powerful methodology to set up a useful business model. The new challenges about Portuguese circularity have arisen because organization performance in the market has gained a powerful meaning in business strategies.

Therefore, it is important to set up concrete guidelines to design a conceptual model based on innovation, technologies and products. Portuguese circularity faces multiple factors which influence its business model. It is necessary to understand the positive and negative impacts, stakeholders, use of natural resources and market strategy to build a conceptual model in the long run. Furthermore, the value added from the production as well as the use of raw materials and design are the most important figures to understand in the Portuguese market. These vectors need to be consistent with the consumers' needs and desires.

To conclude, it is known that the circularity is a concept which has gained space in Portuguese organizations. This concept is associated with the value-added product, eco-design, eco-materials, re-use of products, and long-life living standards. It is important to build a conceptual model where organizations and consumers can deal with ecosystem values.

REFERENCES

APCE. (2017). *Leading the Transition: Action Plan for Circular Economy in Portugal 2017-2020*. Ministério do Ambiente, República Portuguesa.

Bocken, N. M., de Pauw, I., Bakker, C., & van der Grinten, B. (2016). Product design and business model strategies for a circular economy. *Journal of Industrial and Production Engineering*, *33*(5), 308–320. doi:10.1080/21681015.2016.1172124

Boulding, K. (1966). *The economics of the coming spaceship earth*. Academic Press.

Kirchherr, J., Piscicelli, L., Bour, R., Kostense-Smit, E., Muller, J., Huibrechtse-Truijens, A., & Hekkert, M. (2018). Barriers to the Circular Economy: Evidence From the European Union (EU). *Ecological Economics*, *150*, 264–272. doi:10.1016/j.ecolecon.2018.04.028

Kirchherr, J., Reike, D., & Hekkert, M. (2017). Conceptualizing the circular economy: An analysis of 114 definitions. *Resources, Conservation and Recycling*, *127*, 221–232. doi:10.1016/j.resconrec.2017.09.005

Lewandowski, M. (2016). Designing the business models for circular economy—Towards the conceptual framework. *Sustainability*, *8*(1), 43. doi:10.3390u8010043

McCarthy, A., Dellink, R., & Bibas, R. (2018). *The Macroeconomics of the Circular Economy Transition: A Critical Review of Modelling Approaches (No. 130)*. OECD Publishing.

Murray, A., Skene, K., & Haynes, K. (2017). The circular economy: An interdisciplinary exploration of the concept and application in a global context. *Journal of Business Ethics*, *140*(3), 369–380. doi:10.100710551-015-2693-2

Pego, A. (2018a). In S. Cubico, G. Favretto, J. Leitão, & U. Cantner (Eds.), *The pentagonal problem and the offshore energy sector in Portugal. Why does it matter? In Entrepreneurship along the Industry Life Cycle: The changing role of Entrepreneurial Activities and Knowledge Competencies* (pp. 313–327). Sringer Book.

Pego, A. (2018b). *The offshore energy cluster. A geographic and an economic overview* (PhD Thesis). Lisbon: Universidade Nova de Lisboa.

Planing, P. (2015). Business model innovation in a circular economy reasons for non-acceptance of circular business models. *Open Journal of Business Model Innovation, 1*(11).

Woltjer, G. (2018). *Methodologies for measuring the macroeconomic and societal impacts of the circular economy.* European Union.

KEY TERMS AND DEFINITIONS

Circular Economy: a new concept of re-use, re-cycling and re-defining where a new product is created which is needed by consumers. It is a non-linear concept of a relationship between consumers and producers. The circular economy defines new capacity for production, using raw materials and others in order to create a new value in products and a new value chain. There is a maximization of product utility by consumers. Nothing is lost, but transformed in order to create a necessity in consumers/organizations.

Conceptual Model: Model used by a certain number of organizations, which shows some similarity in some vectors (e.g., markets, strategies).

Management Decision: Organizational objective decisions practiced by mangers.

Strategy: Reaching management goals in short, medium or long runs. Organizations position themselves in their market to achieve goals and objectives.

ENDNOTES

1 http://ec.europa.eu/environment/international_issues/missions_en.htm, consulted 30/07/2018.

2 Diário da República n.º 236/2017, 2º Suplemento, Série I de 2017-12-11.

Chapter 11
Influence of Practice Management Software on Dental Services:
A Case Study Approach

Alba Demneri Kruja
Epoka University, Albania

Kei Hysi
Epoka University, Albania

ABSTRACT

In the 21st century, the main focus of technological advances is on data. Practice management software (PMS) is having its highest demand in the international market as a tool helping dental services operate in a better way. The main focus of this research is on analyzing the role of the implementation of PMS in dental clinics in Tirana, capital city of Albania. Qualitative and quantitative data through semi-structured interviews and surveys was collected to analyze the case. Low purchasing power, lack of knowledge, and informality in Albania are some of the limitations that restrain dentists implement new technologies. The results show that PMS implementation adds value to dental clinics through more effective and efficient services and improved customer relationship management.

DOI: 10.4018/978-1-5225-7850-5.ch011

INTRODUCTION

Nowadays it is difficult to imagine a world without technology. The digital revolution that is transforming every aspect of the life is also impacting dentistry and medicine in many ways. Healthcare industry is one of the earliest to implement and integrate healthcare technologies. Yet, the paper system has stymied the ability of care givers to access the information vital to the delivery of care (Omachonu & Einspruch, 2010). During the past several decades healthcare has experienced an explosion of innovations designed to improve life expectancy and quality of life of patients. From electronic record-keeping and data analysis to the latest innovative diagnostic tools, technology has proved to be revolutionizing the healthcare industry. As Govindarajan (2007) emphasize, new digital information, nanotechnology, semiconductor products, and genetic engineering are revolutionizing health care, making old assumptions invalid and creating unanticipated prospects for innovation and improvement of existing processes

The adoption of technologies such as practice management software by the dentistry has enabled dentists to focus on the patients and improvement of customer relationship by allowing dentists to perform multiple tasks such as generating and compiling clinical, administrative and financial data efficiently. The state-of-the-art software solutions also enable dentists to manage their workflow and maximize the chair time utilization by attending more patients which leads to profit increase. Thus, the innovation that comes along with dental practice management software has completely transformed the dentistry sector worldwide.

Dentem is more than just a customer relationship management platform or electronic health record. It is a practice management software which allows dental practices to be more reliable and flexible. It offers a very neat and user-friendly page where dental practice can have a presence online and show the most important information. It also comes in the form of an application which provides some extremely helpful services to the dentists. Agenda management, patients and staff management, image uploading is only some of the services offered by this platform.

Dental health service in Albania is provided by both public and private sector. Private sector is considered the main provider since all dental clinics in Albania are privately owned and many patients with average incomes prefer private dental care clinics for the quality they provide. The good conditions and latest technology used to have a competitive advantage in the market make the private sector way more efficient and responsive to the needs of the patients; while public dental services exist at low efficiency.

Even though it has been decades now that technology and innovation has improved the way dental clinics operate in the market, this doesn't seem to be the case of Albania. Schwab (2017), in the Global Competitiveness Report for 2017-

2018, classifies Albania as an efficiency-driven economy, which needs to invest in business sophistication and innovation to become an innovation-driven one. Berwick (2003), emphasize that "diffusion of innovations is a major challenge in all industries including health care". According to Kruja (2013b) the main weaknesses of enterprises in Albania "are generally related to a higher or lower degree of accessibility to the main resources: finance, technology, knowledge". Only lately some of the largest and best dental clinics in Albania have started to implement innovative technologies and use equipment which are helpful to their business and to the patients as well. However, the majority still is not applying any type of technology while stubbornly continues doing its job in the old-fashioned way not understanding that this not only cause problems to their business but might also harm the relationship with the patients. The large amount of space that images, agenda and X-rays take, the time wasted while waiting for the patients, the difficulty of managing the staff or keeping records of the treatment plans and invoices, are problems in the dentistry move the focus of the dental clinics away from the patients and does not help in creating long lasting relationships with them.

The purpose of this study is to examine whether the dental clinics of Tirana implement any practice management software and the impact that the software usage has on their daily operations and customer relationship management. What is important about this study is not only the fact that it researches the dentistry market and analyzes the benefits of using practice management software, but it also gives some insights about the contribution of technology and innovation in dentistry and analyzes whether the Albanian dental clinics are conscious about their benefits and if they do implement such technologies.

THEORETICAL BACKGROUND

Innovation and Healthcare Industry

Schumpeter (1911/34) see innovation to lead to a new production function, such as: (1) introduction of a new good; (2) introduction of new method of production; (3) opening of a new market; (4) conquest of a new source of supply of a raw material; or (5) carrying out of a new organization of an industry. On the other side according to Drucker (1985), innovation is the specific tool to exploit changes as an opportunity for a different business or service. Montensen & Bloch (2005), defined innovation as "the implementation of a new or significantly improved product (good or service), or process, a new marketing method, or a new organizational method in business practices, workplace organization or external relations. In the third edition of the Oslo Manual they classified it into four groups, as:

- *Product innovation, which contains significant changes in the use of goods and services;*
- *Process innovation, which involves significant changes in production and transport methods;*
- *Marketing innovation, which includes the application of new marketing methods;*
- *Organizational innovation, which involves the using of new organizational methods.* (Montensen & Bloch, 2005)

So, everything that is new to the market or comes in an improved form is considered an innovation. Lewrick et al. (2010), point out that innovation is "the production, diffusion, and use of new and economically useful knowledge, a key factor for competitiveness and growth. Knowledge is the key element of the innovation systems and the institutions which have an important role in its development can be stated as: universities and academic institutions (develop and transfer knowledge); government organizations; innovative enterprises (Kruja, 2013a). Innovation is the distinct implement of entrepreneurs, knowledge is the crucial element of the innovation system, and the synergy between the participants of these innovation systems is vital to becoming a "laboratory for knowledge based economic development" (Kruja A. D., Synergic Individual Entrepreneurial Orientation of University Students: A New Measurement Model, 2019).

Innovation is changing the way of life, and it has drastically improved the economy of different countries that have implemented it. It is considered to be the engine for long term economic development and a key driver of competitiveness. In order for companies to compete and to give dynamism to the national economy, innovation together with technical development have become of the main sources (Kruja, 2012). Smith & Estibals (2011) emphasize that an effective innovation policy requires recognition that innovation is not the exclusive realm of the private sector, but the public sector is also a major player in the innovation system and at the origins of many radical technological innovations.

Healthcare innovation can be defined as the introduction of a new concept, idea, service, process, or product aimed at improving treatment, diagnosis, education, outreach, prevention and research, and with the long-term goals of improving quality, safety, outcomes, efficiency and costs (Omachonu & Einspruch, 2010).

The healthcare industry is experiencing maybe its most rapid pace of innovation ever. Technology has held a great role in this process by presenting value to the market. Nowadays the main focus is not providers and doctors; rather it is patients and their data. Varkey, Horne, & Bennet (2008), see innovations in health care to be "related to product, process, or structure". In order to guarantee uninterrupted operations, healthcare industry and organizations must implement innovative technologies and modernized IT systems.

Medical technology can be considered the biggest innovation in healthcare industry. The application of modern technology into medical field has advanced medicine, improved human life, transformed the way information flows, has made patient care easier and has reduced the business costs. Nowadays doctors can make diagnosis for patients across the globe, can transfer the patient's history and health records with the click of a mouse in another country and can even get information from a patient without having to make a physical appointment. Nowadays technology can also protect the patient's data. Proper cyber security can protect sensitive health records from being stolen by third parties. Beside this, technology can also provide to the patients the ability to access their own information from everywhere, anytime and in any device.

Even though medical science has advanced a lot during the past decades there still is the issue that paper system is vital for doctors and patients in order to access information, which makes the process very inefficient and costly. But paper work can be erroneous, and the sharing of information and data delivery can be very challenging or even impossible at times. Not to mention the time that is needed to go through the patient's data history. That is why the electronic record keeping would benefit not only the doctors but also the patients. It would reduce costs and time and would allow patients to have immediate access to their own records and be able to transmit or carry it from one healthcare provider to another.

However, during the past two decades electronic health records have started to become quite popular. This has made possible to capture and analyze huge amounts of information about patients. This trend has laid the foundation for the data-driven healthcare, which is becoming a revolution.

Innovation in Dentistry and Dental Practice Management Software

Innovation has had a great effect also in dental care. New technologies applied, and innovative solutions have improved the way dentists operate and the relationship with their patients. But it has not always been like this. During the twentieth century dentist could only do the process of tooth extraction. But since that time many changes have occurred, dentists expanded their knowledge and with the help of new equipment and technologies they are now able to solve almost all of their patients' problems.

Nowadays the term digital dentistry is often used. Digital dentistry refers to the usage of digital methods instead of traditional techniques in dental services. Thus, dentist can perform their work more effectively and can provide better diagnosis and treatments for their patients while removing wasted costs and money. But still studies about the implementation of innovation in the field of dentistry are rarely done.

Dental Practice Management Software is an innovation that is transforming dentistry. It is both an administrative and clinical tool designed to help dental professionals to manage their workflow efficiently and effectively. Some of the features provided are appointment scheduling, patient communication features, e-billing and e-insurance claiming facilities, cashless payment facilities which represent the administrative tools and the treatment planning, dental imaging integration, clinical charting which represent the clinical tools. Of course, these are only some of the features provided. Dental practice management software increases overall work efficiency of dental practices and helps dentist manage huge number of patients' data.

Dentistry and Innovation in Albania

Dental health service is provided by public and private dental health care (Demishaj & Radonshiqi, 2016). The main provider of dental care in Albania is private sector which means private dental clinics. These clinics offer a better service and have all the necessary equipment and technologies, something that is often missing in the public sector.

Albania is transforming into a major tourist destination. Tourism is one of the most crucial sectors contributing to country development (Ferizi & Kruja, 2018). The majority of tourists to Albania come for holidays, as opposed to business purposes (Kruja, 2012b). However, they come also for dental tourism. Medical tourism captured worldwide attention only in 2006, when medical journals started to publish papers on the topic, as awareness of the phenomenon in both developing and industrial countries was increasing (Horowitz, Rosensweig, & Jones, 2007). According to Connell (2006), a medical tourist is someone who in order to minimize his costs of health care decides to travel abroad and becomes a tourist. According to the Medical Dental Association, dental tourism is the act of a person traveling from one country to another for dental care (Nexhipi, 2018). During the last 10-years there has been a great increase in dental tourism in Albania because of the low prices. This kind of tourism is very beneficial to Albania and especially to dental clinics that have a huge amount of work during summer months when the highest number of tourists visit Albania.

According to the "The Ordre des Dentists of Albania", whose mission is to maintain high standards in the organization and practice of the dentist profession and to protect the patients and the public from misuse of this profession, the number of the current licensed dentists in Albania is 1647 (see USSH, 2018).

METHODS

Case Study Research Practice Management Software Implementation in Tirana

The main objective of the study is to examine through a questionnaire whether the dental clinics of Tirana, capital of Albania, have had a better performance from the implementation of PMS. Also, since there are no previous studies done in the application of technology and innovation in the field of dentistry in Albania, this study aims to provide some insights about it.

The methodology used in this research is a mixed one since it is composed of an integration of quantitative and qualitative data analysis. Quantitative data were collected through a questionnaire which was prepared in two languages, English and Albanian, and was distributed online but also physically to the dentists of Tirana. At the same time qualitative data collection and analysis were conducted from interviews with the CEO (Chief Executive Officer) of Dentem Mr. Alen Saqe, COO (Chief Operations Officer) Mr. Fatjon Saqe and CTO (Chief Technology Officer) Mr.Rexhin Vorpsi, Mr. Grej Malo from "The Ordre des Dentists of Albania" and many dentists interviewed through the process of questionnaires distribution.

Dentem is the first Albanian mobile practice management software (see Dentem, 2018). It can be used as web-based software but as well as an application. This provides a competitive advantage for Dentem but also for the dental clinics that implement it. Dentem is a B2B (Business to Business) company, which means it is a business that provides a solution to the other businesses, in this case to the dental clinics. This platform allows dental practices to be more reliable and flexible. They provide software services to help dentists grow their business and make sense of big amounts of data.

Dentem provides many helpful features to the dental clinics which include storing health records, X-rays and data on the cloud, scheduling appointments and sending automated messages to the patients, planning patients' treatment, managing the staff and the patients. And the cost of implementing this software is €150 per year for the Albanian market. Its competitors in Albania are separated in two groups. The first group includes the traditional way of doing business in dentistry, by still using pen and paper to manage the agenda, plan the treatment of the patients and schedule appointments. In the second group are the other software used in dental clinics, which provide similar functionalities as Dentem. But still Dentem has a competitive advantage by being one of the first mobile and cloud-based practice management in Albania.

Dentem started three years ago when one dentist in Tirana, capital of Albania, lost all his patients' data the moment his computer was attacked by a virus. This intrigued the two brothers, Alen and Fatjon Saqe, to create cloud-based software where data could not be lost. In 2015 Dentem started as a project in Tirana by a small team. Later on, after the first tests they decided to represent Albania in Pirate Summit in Koln, Germany, a startup competition where they had to pitch their project. At the finals the team got an invitation to participate in ABC- accelerator in Ljubljana Slovenia. After the acceleration, Dentem became a registered business in the beginning of 2016 in Tirana, Albania. As the company's vision was always to became global and because of the difficulties and limitations that the local market provided, Dentem decided to register in Delaware USA to have an international branch. After two years of developing the software and growing as a company, Dentem now has its headquarters in Toronto, Canada after getting a seed investment.

The sole purpose of Dentem is to make life easier at the dental practice. As its slogan says, "Empower your dental practice!" Dentem started from feedback of just one dentist and now they have feedbacks from hundreds of customers and testers. The platform is always growing through an ongoing process. Dentem tackles the main pain-points in the dental practices, creating a paperless environment and making work easy in the practice. Dentem provides many features, from scheduling, to electronic dental records, to online bookings and AI powered X-rays analytics. Reports are easier done and dental practices increase ROI (Return on Investment) by implementing Dentem. Research and Innovation are a core part of the product. DX-Vision & D Assistant are two R&D projects that Dentem is working right now with a team of professional developers, dentists and at the same time it is bringing universities and researchers together in these projects. Dentem is a next generation dental platform being mobile first and focusing on being easy and helpful. They focus on user experience and user interface and kill unwanted features while working on the new things that customers want.

Dentem is really working for some interesting projects which include artificial intelligence and innovation. The first one is D Assistant, a virtual assistant with a human interface. Its main purpose is to allow dentists to communicate with Dentem hands-free, only by voice commands, in this way it will serve a lot of busy dental practitioner. D Assistant features Natural Language Processing, Hot Word Detection, Speech Recognition and Speech Synthesis and it will be integrated with third party assistant like Google Assistant. This project is still at its first steps and many improvements must be made. But it will surely change the way dentists use their software and the way they work.

DX Vision is the second project that Dentem is working on. DX Vision is a computer vision algorithm that detects problems within dental X-rays. By using it, the computer will be the one that will detect different problems of patients' dental health from the X-rays like implants, fillings and many more. This algorithm is being trained and data are added each day to make it better. This is a three-stage project.

The first stage is to leverage artificial intelligence and build an algorithm to detect different objects. After some tests it is concluded that the accuracy of detection was over 99%. The second stage, which is also the current stage of the project, is to build a model and to train the model to label multiple objects within the same X-ray. The algorithm is being trained by many data. After finishing the second stage the algorithm will be enabled to a few early access users and it will be further trained to get ready for the third stage. During the last stage the feedbacks from all the dental practitioners will be taken into consideration to better train the algorithm. Dentem team believes that the implementation of the modern techniques of machine learning will forever change the way dental practices use and analyze X-rays.

Sample and Data Collection

More than half of the dental clinics are located in the capital of Albania, Tirana. Also, since Tirana is the economic center of Albania, the probability of new technologies and innovations implemented in dental clinics there is higher than in other cities. Dentem too has most of his clients in Tirana. The person that had to answer the questionnaire had to be a dentist working in the dental clinic, but not necessary the owner. Four approaches were used in order for the questionnaire to reach the dentists: personal delivery, social media, cold emailing and through Dentem. The questionnaire was distributed to 15 dental clinics in Tirana in three days, from which only 6 of them were filled. The online version of the questionnaire was posted in a Facebook group called "Dentistët Shqipëtar", whose members are dentists from all over Albania. Also, the online questionnaire was delivered to 11 dentists through LinkedIn platform. The next approach was to send the online questionnaire to 245 dental clinics in Tirana through cold email. Mr. Fatjon Saqe was very helpful since he sent the online questionnaire to the clients of Dentem that were located in Tirana. The data was collected throughout May 2018. In total were collected 101 answers from the online questionnaire, from which 4 were excluded because they were not seen as reliable. Together with the 6 questionnaires that were gathered through personal delivery, the sample size of this study is 103. From which, 55 dentists claim not to implement any software. 33 used Dentem and 15 use other software.

The questionnaire was prepared in two languages, English and Albanian because some of the dentists operating in Albania are foreigners. It was delivered physically but also in an online version.

The questionnaire was divided in 4 sections. In the first one there are 5 questions of general information about the dentist surveyed. The second section includes 14 questions that are related to the implementation of Dentem while the third section includes 18 questions related to the dentists that implement other software rather than Dentem. In the last section of this questionnaire there are 7 questions related to the dentists that do not implement any software in their dental clinics. So, the questionnaire has in total 44 questions. Also, in the beginning of the questionnaire was included an introduction of the survey and what was it about and the definitions of some words that were mentioned in English and could cause confusions such as mobile or cloud.

RESULTS

Descriptive Analysis

The investigation conducted by this research was based on the answers of the 103 dentists operating in the Tirana. Sample detailed characteristics are provided in Table 1.

37% of respondents have been working as dentists from 1 to 5 years, 30% from 6 to 10 years, 17% from 11 to 15 years, 1% from 16 to 20 and the remaining 15% for more than 20 years. 39% of the surveyed dentists have had also an abroad experience.

In 41% of the surveyed dental clinics there work only one dentist, two - three dentists work in 47% of them, and more than four in the remaining 12%. It is apparent that most of the dental clinics in this sample are small.

18% of respondents have less than 50 patients per month, 32% have 51 to 100 patients, 25% of respondents have 101 to 150 patients, 8% of respondents have 151 to 200, while 17% of them have more than 200 patients per month.

32% of the respondents have implemented Dentem practice management software, 15% have implemented other software, while 53% have not implemented any software.

Dentem vs. Other Software Usage

From 103 surveyed dental clinics, 48 of them adopted software of which 33 Dentem and 15 other ones. The majority of Dentem as well as other software users, use them very frequently (Table 2). Most of the Dentem users use the software for managing agenda, scheduling appointments, managing patients and uploading photos of the patients, while the other software users, use these functions at a lower rate. Since most of clinics had one or a low number of dentists employed, staff management function is not very used, while online booking function is not currently offered by Dentem.

The software implementation seems not to have affected the number of staff in the clinics and the number of patients has slightly increased. About half of Dentem users (48%) need to use pen and paper method too in their operations, but in the other clinics the ratio is higher (73%).

Table 1. Sample characteristics (n=103)

Variable	Item	Frequency	Percentage
Work Experience	1-5	38	36.89%
	6-10	31	30.10%
	11-15	18	14.48%
	16-20	1	0.79%
	More than 20	15	14.56%
Dentist No.	1	42	40.78%
	2	33	32.04%
	3	15	14.56%
	4	5	4.85%
	5	3	2.91%
	6	3	2.91%
	8	1	0.97%
	10	1	0.97%
Abroad Experience	Yes	40	39%
	No	63	61%
Clients per Month	Less than 50	19	18.45%
	50-100	33	32.04%
	101-150	26	25.24%
	151-200	8	7.77%
	More than 200	17	16.50%
Dentem Implementation	Yes	33	32.04%
	Other Software	15	14.56%
	No Software	55	53.40%

To measure the impact of software on the clinic operations, dentists were asked in session II and III to evaluate questions 6 to 9 12 using a 5- point Likert scale (1 – "strongly disagree"; 2 – "disagree"; 3 – "neutral"; 4 – "agree"; 5 – "strongly agree"). The average evaluation of dentists is reported in Table 2. It is clear that both users are very satisfied from the software, since it has improved their customer relationship management and improved client data store - access easiness and efficiency. Related to cost and patient delay reduction as well as being helpful to the business, Dentem users are more satisfied than the other ones.

Impact of General Information on Software Implementation

From the total sample of the study, 48 dental clinics have implemented Dentem or other software, and 55 dental clinics have not implemented any software to support their operations. Univariate Analysis of Variance (ANOVA) is used to analyze whether software implementation is affected from the general information of the sample (Table 3). Since the sample is not that big a 10% significant level was taken to analyze impact significance.

Table 2. Dentem vs other software usage

Question	Variable	Dentem N=33	Other software N=15
1	Usage frequency Always Very often Often Not that often	64% 30% 6%	67% 13% 13% 7%
2	Functions Agenda Management Online Booking Patients Management Staff Management Gallery Appointment Scheduling	88% 0% 73% 30% 70% 82%	53% 33% 53% 27% 33% 53%
3	No. of staff Increased Decreased Not effected	18% 0% 82%	27% 0% 73%
4	No. of patients Increased Decreased Not effected	24% 0% 76%	33% 0% 67%
5	Pen & paper usage Yes No	48% 52%	73% 27%
6	Satisfaction	4,82	4,67
7	CRM Improvement	4,73	4,13
8	Cost reduction	4,36	3,13
9	Patient delay reduction	4,79	3,27
10	Data store & access easiness	4,76	4,47
11	Data store & access efficiency	4.61	4,27
12	Being helpful	4,56	3,47

Table 3. Impact of general information on software implementation

Dependent Variable:	Software Implementation				
Source	**Type III Sum of Squares**	**df**	**Mean Square**	**F**	**Sig.**
Corrected Model	16.333[a]	58	.282	1.333	.161
Intercept	8.904	1	8.904	42.139	.000
Years	1.184	4	.296	1.400	.250
Dentist No.	3.158	7	.451	2.135	.059
Abroad	.630	1	.630	2.982	.091
Patients No.	1.965	4	.491	2.325	.071

- The impact of number of dentists working in the dental clinic on software implementation is significant with a p-value 0.059.
- Whether the dentists have had an experience abroad is also significant with a p-value 0.091.
- Number of patients per month has a significant impact on software implementation too, with a p-value 0.071.
- But the years spent working in the profession of dentist have no impact in software implementation since p-value is not significant at any significance level.

As a conclusion from the data analysis, the number of dentists working in a dental clinic, the number of patients per month and the experience abroad has an impact on the implementation of the software by the dental clinics.

Impact of General Information on Number of Patients

ANOVA is again used to test whether the monthly number of patients is affected from the general information of the sample at a 10% significance level (Table 4). The test results show that the number of dentists working in a dental clinic (p-value = 0.000) as well as the implementation of a software (p-value = 0.001) has a significant impact on the number of patients per month. The situation is not the same for experience abroad and years of working since they do not have a significant impact on the number of patients per month.

Table 4. Software impact on number of patients per month

Dependent Variable:	Patients Number				
Source	**Type III Sum of Squares**	**df**	**Mean Square**	**F**	**Sig.**
Corrected Model	129.804[a]	44	2.950	3.638	.000
Intercept	419.716	1	419.716	517.607	.000
Years	2.096	4	.524	.646	.632
Dentist No.	41.428	7	5.918	7.299	.000
Abroad	1.611	1	1.611	1.987	.164
Software Impl.	9.932	1	9.932	12.248	.001

Software Implementation Impact on General Information

Software implementation has a great impact on the number of patients per month (p-value = 0.001) significant at 5% and 10% level of significance (Table 5). This means that the implementation of software positively effects the number of patients per month.

General Information Impact on Dentem Implementation

From 48 clinics that have adopted software, 33 of them have implemented. ANOVA analysis is used to test whether there is an impact of general information in Dentem implementation (Table 6).

The impact of number of dentists (p-value = 0.086) working in the dental clinic and the experience abroad (p-value = 0.084) are significant on software implementation at 10% significance level.

Number of patients per month and number of years working as a dentist do not have any impact in the Dentem implementation at any significance level.

Table 5. Impact of software implementation on general information

Source		Type III Sum of Squares	df	Mean Square	F	Sig.
Software	Nr.P	19.777	1	19.777	12.718	.001
	Abroad	.217	1	.217	.904	.344
	Nr.D	5.260	1	5.260	2.181	.143
	Years	.078	1	.078	.042	.838

Table 6. General information impact on Dentem implementation

Dependent Variable:	Dentem				
Source	Type III Sum of Squares	df	Mean Square	F	Sig.
Corrected Model	11.792[a]	47	.251	1.136	.342
Intercept	4.862	1	4.862	22.018	.000
Years	.943	4	.236	1.068	.385
Dentist No.	2.667	6	.445	2.013	.086
Patients No.	1.396	4	.349	1.581	.198
Abroad	.692	1	.692	3.135	.084

As a conclusion dentist with an abroad experience and with many other dentists working in their clinic, will be more willing to implement Dentem.

Impact of Dentem Implementation on General Information

Dentem implementation has a very significant impact on the number of patients per month at 5% and 10% significance level, with a p-value of 0.014 (Table 7) and it can be concluded that implementation of Dentem increases the number of patients per month.

DISCUSSION

Mr. Alen Saqe provided some necessary information about Dentem and its growth as a company. When asked about the Albanian market he stated that things were a little messy. For example, the law that exists for submitting the dental records to the state causes a double work for the dentists, since besides keeping the dental records in the software they also have to fill them in paper. Such a law does not

Table 7. Impact of Dentem implementation on general information

Source		Type III Sum of Squares	df	Mean Square	F	Sig.
Dentem	Nr.P	9.001	1	9.001	6.308	.014
	Abroad	.007	1	.007	.029	.865
	Nr.D	.001	1	.001	.000	.984
	Years	.876	1	.876	.527	.470

exist in Canada. Another disadvantage here in Albania is the fact that Albanians are afraid of taxes and these leads the market toward informality. This is why Dentem has deleted the feature of invoices in its application, but now that they are working in Canadian market where things are more stable, the feature of invoices will be added again. He also said that Albanian market has some problems with insurances.

Mr. Fatjon Saqe provided the information about Dentem journey and its future which are presented in the literature review of this paper. Also, when asked about the decision to move away from Albania, Mr. Fatjon said that Albanian market is a small one and the purchasing power is low. They have had offers from England, France, Germany and Canada (where they are right now). The reason for choosing Canadian market was because it is a really big market. There are 20000 dental clinics there and 100000 dental employees, who are of different profiles like dentists, assistant etc. “In Germany for example the state is separated in lands and each land has its own laws which make it difficult, beside this Europe has many languages”, said Mr. Fatjon Saqe when asked why choosing Canada and not Europe.

Mr. Rexhin Vorpsi has provided some technical information and also created a Dentem account for me to better see how the software works. According to him, the software nowadays is having some updates, improving the current features and adding other ones like invoices and online booking. Soon the Dentem application will also be provided to the patients in the future.

There are three packets offered by Dentem. For Albanian market, Dentem Premium costs €150/year. Dentem Pro costs €120/year, while Dentem Scheduler costs €100/year. These packets differentiate from the features that they provide to the dentists. Dentem Scheduler offers agenda management but no dental records of the patients, Dentem Pro offers agenda management and dental records of the patients while Dentem Premium beside these also offers financial operations and image uploads. The prices offered in Albanian market by Dentem are much lower than in Canada, because of the purchasing power in Albania is lower too.

Mr. Grej Malo is part of Dentists Order (created by Ministry of Health) whose mission is to maintain high standards in the organization and practice of the dentist profession and to protect the patients and the public from misuse of this profession. During an interview with him I got useful information about dentistry in Albania. In Albania dental care is provided by both public and the private sector. Public dental care is provided for free amongst 0-18 years old people. However, the private sector is the main provider in our market.

According to him there about 1200 licensed dental clinics in Albania, from which 680 are located in the capital Tirana. It is clear that more than half of the dental clinics of Albania are located in its capital. Mr. Grej said that dental clinics in Albania have a 15% to 20% tendency for technology implementation.

When asked about the implementation of different software, he claimed that there are many laws who make it difficult for the software to be implemented in Albania. There are some laws about privacy and transparency of the patients' data which may cause problems to the dentists if broken. In order to control the patients' data, government requires dental records from every dentist.

Most of the dentists used X-ray software to also keep the patient's data. So, when one dental clinic buys an X-ray machine, it is also supplied with software that keeps the X-rays of the patients, the name, surname and age. This was helpful to the dentists for keeping patients' data.

Another interesting fact is that dentists used Google Drive to keep the patients' data and to also send automated messages to their patients. Other programs implemented were personalized programs, which mean that the dentists had paid for having a personal program in their computer.

CONCLUSION AND RECOMMENDATIONS

Innovation and technology are making great changes in the way we live. They are no longer a future we hope for, but instead have become part of our daily life. Innovation and technology have great impact also on healthcare sector by making it easier for the doctors to perform their job and as well as for the patients to get their treatment. In 21th century, the main focus of technological advances is on data. Innovative solutions that help doctors have a better and quicker access to patients' information and data history and that help patients have control on their health data are being applied in dentistry as well. Practice management software is having its highest demand in the international market nowadays as a tool that helps dental services operate in a better way.

In Albania the situation is a little bit different. From the results of the questionnaire, the majority of dental clinics in Tirana do not implement any software. From 103 respondents, 55 of them did not use any software in their dental clinics. The lack of innovative technologies implemented in dentistry is also emphasized by one of the interviewees, dentist Mr. Grej Malo, who said that there is only 15-20% tendency for technology implementation.

The respondents of the questionnaire that did implement software in their clinics are separated in Dentem users and other software user. There is a difference between these two groups as well as there are similarities. Both groups are very satisfied or adequately satisfied with their software and both groups believe that software implementation has improved customer relationship management, even though the percentage of Dentem users that strongly agree with this statement is higher. The majority of Dentem users agree that Dentem implementation has reduced the costs of the business, while only a minority agrees on this statement in the second group of other software users. Also, Dentem users agree that Dentem implementation has increased the number of patients, while only a minority agrees on this statement in the other software users. The majority of Dentem users agree that the software has helped them reduce the delays of the patients, while only 47% of other software users agree on this statement. Both groups agree that with the implementation of the software it is easier to store and access data, even though there is a higher percentage in Dentem users that agrees on this statement. Both of the groups also agree that time needed to store, and access data is reduced after implementing software. Advantages of implementing Dentem are that it is cloud based software and a mobile application, while this is not the case in the other group where only a minority used cloud-based software and mobile applications. Both groups of respondents believe that software implementation has helped them have competitive advantage in the market, even though the percentage of the Dentem users that agrees on this statement is higher, exactly 97%. When asked whether the respondents still felt the need for using pen and paper, both groups said yes. This is because of the law that exists in Albania for the dental clinics that have to keep physical dental records of their patients.

But the paper system is not efficient at all. It can be erroneous; it takes lots of space and is difficult to be managed. When asked in the questionnaire, the respondents that do not implement any software in their dental clinic, they agree that using physical dental records takes a huge amount of space, while 47% of them agree that it takes lots of time. When asked whether dentists wanted to implement software that can store data of patients, can schedule appointments and send automated messages to the patients, the majority of them said yes. The majority of respondents of this group also believe that the software can improve customer relationship management. It is clear that there is a willingness amongst dentist to implement practice management software in their dental clinics. However, the main reasons why the dentists are not implementing software are because of price that is considered to be high, lack of knowledge or small number of patients.

From the statistical analyses it was clear that the implementation of any software does have an impact on the number of patients per month. And even when test is done specifically for Dentem again there is an impact of Dentem implementation on the number of patients per month. Also, it was seen that having an experience abroad, number of staff and number of patients per month have an impact on software implementation. When it comes to Dentem, only having an experience abroad and number of staff was seen to have an impact on Dentem implementation.

As a conclusion the Albanian market is willing to implement software that improve the dental services but is still not ready to do so. There are many limitations like the low purchasing power, laws, lack of knowledge and informality which also forced Dentem founders leave Albania for a market that could offer more. It should be mentioned the fact that Dentem provides way more benefits for the dental services than other software. But in general, the implementation of software in dental clinics improves the way they operate.

This research recommends government to highlight the impact of innovation and technology on the healthcare sector and it should not put constrains such as the law for keeping physical records. It is needed to take the example of other developed countries where dentists are no obliged to keep physical dental records. In fact, government should be more supportive to the new technological advances and the benefits that they offer.

Also, there must be done more in the information of dentists about these innovative solutions since a large number of respondents claimed that they lacked the information about software. Maybe workshops, seminars and training must be organized in order to inform the dentists. I also believe that this kind of information should be given from the beginning, when they are still studying dentistry. The universities should provide specific subjects about professionalism in patient care and practice management where students can get informed about the new technologies that improve their dental practice.

As a last but not least recommendation, this research strongly recommends the dentists to use Dentem practice management software because as seen from this study, it does provide more benefits than other software in the market and beside this, it is a cloud-based software and a mobile application. It can be used in an iPad or Smartphone as well as in a computer. The price is not that high compared to other software and a free trial is provided so the dentists can see by themselves whether they would like to implement it or not. Also taking into consideration the fact that it is created by an Albanian staff, it means that it fits the needs of our market.

REFERENCES

Berwick, D. M. (2003). Disseminating innovations in health care. *Journal of the American Medical Association*, *289*, 1969–1975. PMID:12697800

Connell, J. (2006). Medical tourism: Sea, sun, sand and surgery. *Tourism Management*, 1093–1100.

Demishaj, A., & Radonshiqi, R. (2016). Public and private sector services (Case study of dental services). *Science Arena Publications Specialty Journal of Accounting and Economics*, 15-18.

Dentem. (2018). *Dentem*. Retrieved from Dentem: Dental Practice Management Software: https://www.dentem.co/

Drucker, P. F. (1985). *Innovation and entrepreneurship*. New York: Harper & Row.

Ferizi, V., & Kruja, A. D. (2018). Coastline hospitality industry performance, challenges, and opportunities: evidence from Durres coastline. In D. Batabyal (Ed.), Managing Sustainable Tourism Resources (pp. 14-38). IGI Global.

Govindarajan, V. (2007). *The Importance of Strategic Innovation*. Retrieved from http:/www.vijaygovindarajan.com/2006/03/the_importance_of_strategic_in.htm

Horowitz, M. D., Rosensweig, J. A., & Jones, C. A. (2007). *Medical Tourism: Globalization of the Healthcare Marketplace*. Medscape General Medicine Journal.

Kruja, A. (2012a). Entrepreneurship, knowledge, innovation and sustainable development. *Mediterranean Journal of Social Sciences*, 21–25.

Kruja, A. (2012b). The impact of tourism sector development in the Albanian economy. *Economia. Seria Management, 15*(1), 205-218.

Kruja, A. (2013a). Entrepreneurship and knowledge-based economies. *Revista Românească pentru Educaţie Multidimensională, 5*(1), 7-17.

Kruja, A. D. (2013b). The contribution of SMEs to the economic growth (Case of Albania). *EuroEconomica, 32*(1), 55–67.

Kruja, A. D. (2019). Synergic Individual Entrepreneurial Orientation of University Students: A New Measurement Model. In *Handbook of Research on Ethics, Entrepreneurship, and Governance in Higher Education*. IGI Global.

Lewrick, M., Omar, M., Raeside, R., & Saier, K. (2010). Education for entrepreneurship and innovation: `Management capabilities for sustainable growth and success. *World Journal of Entrepreneurship, Management and Sustainable Development*, *6*(1/2), 1–18.

Montensen, P. S., & Bloch, C. W. (2005). *Oslo manual-guidelines for collecting and interpreting innovation data: Proposed guidelines for collecting and interpreting innovation*. OECD.

Nexhipi, O. (2018). Medical Tourism Management Challenges - The Case of Dental Tourism in Albania. *European Journal of Interdisciplinary Studies*.

Omachonu, V. K., & Einspruch, N. G. (2010). Innovation in healthcare delivery systems: A conceptual framework. *The Innovation Journal*, *15*(1), 1–20.

Schumpeter, J. (1911/34). *The theory of economic development*. Cambridge, MA: Harvard University Press.

Schwab, K. (2017). *The global competitieness report 2017-2018.* Geneva: World Economic Forum.

Smith, K., & Estibals, A. (2011). Innovation and Research Strategy for Growth. London: BIS Department for Business Innovation and Skills.

USSH. (2018). *Urdhëri i Stomatollogut Shqiptar*. Retrieved from http://ussh.org.al/

Varkey, P. A., Horne, A., & Bennet, K. E. (2008). Innovation in health care: A primer. *Journal of Medical Quality*, *23*, 382–388. PMID:18820143

KEY TERMS AND DEFINITIONS

Business Performance: Encompasses areas of business outcomes such as financial performance, product market performance, and shareholder return.

Dental Practice Management Software: Improving customer relationship management by allowing dentists to perform multiple tasks such as generating and compiling clinical, administrative and financial data efficiently.

Dentem Practice Management Software: A practice management software which allows dental practices to be more reliable and flexible by offering a neat and user-friendly page where dental practice can have a presence online and show the most important information. It also comes in the form of an application which provides some extremely helpful services to the dentists such as agenda management, patient and staff management, image uploading, etc.

Digital Dentistry: Usage of digital methods instead of traditional techniques in dental services.

Technological Innovation: Providing new products and processes or technological advancements of already existing products and services.

APPENDIX: SURVEY QUESTIONNAIRE

This questionnaire aims to gather data to examine whether the dental clinics of Tirana implement any software and specifically Dentem practice management software and the impact that the software usage has on their daily operations and customer relationship management.
Participation in this survey is volunteer. The reported information is confidential and will be used only for generalization purposes.
Your contribution is very important and will provide an essential support in the realization of this research.

General Information

1. For how many years have you been working as a dentist?
    a. 1 - 5
    b. 6 - 10
    c. 11 - 15
    d. 16 – 20
    e. More than 20
2. How many dentists are employed in your clinic?
    ....
3. Do you have any abroad experiences in dental service?
    a. Yes
    b. No
4. What is the number of clients that you have per month?
    a. Less than 50
    b. 51-100
    c. 101-150
    d. 151 – 200
    e. More than 200
5. Do you implement Dentem software in your dental services?
    a. Yes, I have implemented Dentem
    b. No, I use another software
    c. No, I do not use any software

Dentem Users

1. How often do you use Dentem in daily basis?
    a. Always

b. Very often
c. Often
d. Not that often

2. Which of its functions do you use?
 a. Agenda Management
 b. Online booking
 c. Patients Management
 d. Staff Management
 e. Gallery
 f. Appointments Scheduling
3. Has it affected the number of staff?
 a. Yes, it has increased it
 b. Yes, it has decreased it
 c. No, it hasn't affected it
4. Has it affected the number of patients?
 a. Yes, it has increased it
 b. Yes, it has decreased it
 c. No, it hasn't affected it
5. Do you still feel the need to use pen and paper even after the implementation of Dentem?
 a. Yes
 b. No
6. Are you satisfied with Dentem platform?
 a. Strongly Agree
 b. Agree
 c. Neutral
 d. Disagree
 e. Strongly Disagree
7. Dentem has improved my customer relationship management.
 a. Strongly Agree
 b. Agree
 c. Neutral
 d. Disagree
 e. Strongly Disagree
8. Dentem has reduced the costs of the business.
 a. Strongly Agree
 b. Agree
 c. Neutral
 d. Disagree
 e. Strongly Disagree

9. Dentem has reduced the delays of customers.
    a. Strongly Agree
    b. Agree
    c. Neutral
    d. Disagree
    e. Strongly Disagree
10. With Dentem it is easier to store and access clients' data.
    a. Strongly Agree
    b. Agree
    c. Neutral
    d. Disagree
    e. Strongly Disagree
11. Dentem has reduced the amount of time needed to store and access clients' data.
    a. Strongly Agree
    b. Agree
    c. Neutral
    d. Disagree
    e. Strongly Disagree
12. Being a mobile application, it has helped my business a lot.
    a. Strongly Agree
    b. Agree
    c. Neutral
    d. Disagree
    e. Strongly Disagree

Other Software Users

1. How often do you use this software?
    a. Always
    b. Very often
    c. Often
    d. Not that often
2. Which functions does it offer to your clinic?
    a. Agenda Management
    b. Online booking
    c. Patients Management
    d. Staff Management
    e. Gallery

   f. Appointments Scheduling
3. Has it affected the number of staff?
   a. Yes, it has increased it
   b. Yes, it has decreased it
   c. No, it hasn't affected it
4. Has it affected the number of patients?
   a. Yes, it has increased it
   b. Yes, it has decreased it
   c. No, it hasn't affected it
5. Do you still feel the need to use pen and paper after the implementation of software?
   a. Yes
   b. No
6. Are you satisfied with this software?
   a. Strongly Agree
   b. Agree
   c. Neutral
   d. Disagree
   e. Strongly Disagree
7. The software has improved my customer relationship management.
   a. Strongly Agree
   b. Agree
   c. Neutral
   d. Disagree
   e. Strongly Disagree
8. The software has reduced the costs of the business.
   a. Strongly Agree
   b. Agree
   c. Neutral
   d. Disagree
   e. Strongly Disagree
9. Has it reduced delays of patients?
   a. Strongly Agree
   b. Agree
   c. Neutral
   d. Disagree
   e. Strongly Disagree
10. With the software it is easier to access clients' data.
   a. Strongly Agree
   b. Agree

c. Neutral
d. Disagree
e. Strongly Disagree

11. This software has reduced the amount of time needed to store and access clients' data.
    a. Strongly Agree
    b. Agree
    c. Neutral
    d. Disagree
    e. Strongly Disagree
12. This software has helped me have a competitive advantage.
    a. Strongly Agree
    b. Agree
    c. Neutral
    d. Disagree
    e. Strongly Disagree

No Software Used

1. Do you still use pen and paper to schedule appointments with the patients?
    a. Yes
    b. No
2. Do your clients' health records, X-rays and data use a huge amount of physical space?
    a. Yes
    b. No
3. Does is take a lot of time to store and access clients' data?
    a. Yes
    b. No
4. Would you like to implement software that can store health records, X-rays and data on the cloud?
    a. Yes
    b. No
5. Would you like to implement software that can schedule appointments and send automated messages to the patients?
    a. Yes
    b. No
6. Do you think software implementation can improve your customer relationship management?

   a. Yes
   b. No

7. What reasons prevent you from implementing software?
   a. Price
   b. Lack of knowledge
   c. Small number of clients
   d. You do not need one
   e. Other (Please specify) ....

Compilation of References

Abdelkafi. N. (2012). Open Business Models for the Greater Good – A Case Study from the Higher Education Context. *Die Unternehmung, 60*(3).

Accenture Strategy. (n.d.). *Circular Advantage Innovative Business Models and Technologies to Create Value in a World without Limits to Growth.* Retrieved from https://www.accenture.com/t20150523T053139Z__w__/usen/_acnmedia/Accenture/ConversionAssets/DotCom/Documents/Global/PDF/Strategy_6/Accenture-Circular-Advantage-Innovative-Business-Models-Technologies-Value-Growth.pdf

Acquiera, A., Daudigeosb, T., & Pinksec, J. (2017). Promises and paradoxes of the sharing economy: An organizing framework. *Technological Forecasting & Social Change*, 125.

Acquier, A., Daudigeos, T., & Pinkse, J. (2017). Promises and paradoxes of the sharing economy: An organizing framework. *Technological Forecasting and Social Change, 125*, 1–10. doi:10.1016/j.techfore.2017.07.006

ADEME. (2014). *Economie Circulaire: Notions*. Author.

Agan, Y., Acar, M. F., & Borodin, A. (2013). Drivers of environmental processes and their impact on performance: A study of Turkish SMEs. *Journal of Cleaner Production, 51*, 23–33. doi:10.1016/j.jclepro.2012.12.043

Agnello, X., Naveen, J., Ravichandran, M., & Balamurugan, J. (2015). Clean technology and its efficacy: Strategies of environmental management. *J. Environ. Soc. Sci, 2*(2), 1–10.

Airbnb. (2016). *About Us*. Retrieved 12 July 2018, from https://press.atairbnb.com/about-us/

Akbar, Y. H., & Tracogna, A. (2018). The sharing economy and the future of the hotel industry: Transaction cost theory and platform economics. *International Journal of Hospitality Management, 71*, 91–101. doi:10.1016/j.ijhm.2017.12.004

Amaro, S., Andreu, L., & Huang, S. (2018). Millenials' intentions to book on Airbnb. *Current Issues in Tourism, 0*(0), 1–15. doi:10.1080/13683500.2018.1448368

Amit, R., & Zott, C. (2010). *Value Drivers of E-commerce Business Models.* Working Paper No. 2000-2006. INSEAD.

Andersen, M. S. (2007). An introductory note on the environmental economics of the circular economy. *Sustainability Science*, *2*(1), 133–140. doi:10.100711625-006-0013-6

Anticainen, M., Uusitalo, T., & Kivikyto-Reponen, P. (2018). Digitalisation as an Enabler of Circular Economy. *Procedia CIRP*, 73.

APCE. (2017). *Leading the Transition: Action Plan for Circular Economy in Portugal 2017-2020*. Ministério do Ambiente, República Portuguesa.

Bachelard, G. (1981). *The Poetics of Space*. Beacon Press.

Baden-Fuller, C., MacMillan, I., Demil, B., & Lecocq, X. (2010). Long Range Planning call for papers for the Special Issue on "Business Models" by Volume 43. Issues 2–3. Pages 143-462 (April–June 2010). Academic Press.

Bakker, C., den Hollander, M., Van Hinte, E., & Zljlstra, Y. (2014). *Products that last: Product design for circular business models*. TU Delft Library.

Barnett-Page, E., & Thomas, J. (2009). Methods for the Synthesis of Qualitative Research: A Critical Review. *BMC Medical Research Methodology*, *9*(1), 59. doi:10.1186/1471-2288-9-59 PMID:19671152

Baron, R. A., & Markman, G. D. (2003). Beyond social capital: The role of entrepreneurs' social competence in their financial success. *Journal of Business Venturing*, *18*(1), 41–60. doi:10.1016/S0883-9026(00)00069-0

Bastien, T., Roelofs, E., Rietveld, E., & Hoogendoorn, A. (2013). *Opportunities for a Circular Economy in the Netherlands*. TNO, Report commissioned by the Netherlands Ministry of Infrastructure and Environment.

Beauchamp, M., Krysztofiak-Szopa, J., & Skala, A. (2017). *Polskie startupy. Raport 2017*. Warszawa, Poland: Fundacja Startup Poland.

Beauchamp, M., Krysztofiak-Szopa, J., & Skala, A. (2018). *Polskie startupy. Raport 2018*. Warszawa, Poland: Fundacja Startup Poland.

Belk, R. (2014). You are what you can access: Sharing and collaborative consumption online. *Journal of Business Research*, *67*(8), 1595–1600. doi:10.1016/j.jbusres.2013.10.001

Belk, R. W. (1988). Possessions and the Extended Self. *The Journal of Consumer Research*, *15*(2), 139–168. doi:10.1086/209154

Bell, D. (1976a). *The Coming of Post-industrial Society: A Venture in Social Forecasting*. New York: Basic Books. doi:10.1080/00131727609336501

Bell, D. (1976b). *The Cultural Contradictions of Capitalism*. New York: Basic Books.

Benda, J. (1955). *The Betrayal of the Intellectuals*. Boston: Beacon Press.

Bergman, M. M., Bergman, Z., & Berger, L. (2017). An Empirical Exploration, Typology, and Definition of Corporate Sustainability. *Sustainability*, 9.

Berwick, D. M. (2003). Disseminating innovations in health care. *Journal of the American Medical Association*, *289*, 1969–1975. PMID:12697800

Beulque, R., & Aggeri, F. (2016). Circular Business Model Innovation: Key Patterns and Challenges to unleash recycling value creation potential. EGOS.

Bhupendra, K. V., & Sangle, S. (2016). Pollution prevention strategy: A study of Indian firms. *Journal of Cleaner Production*, *133*, 795–802. doi:10.1016/j.jclepro.2016.05.169

Bin, F., Qiang, Y., & Law, R. (2016). Effect of sharing economy on tourism industry employment. *Annals of Tourism Research*, *57*, 264–267. doi:10.1016/j.annals.2015.11.018

Blank, S., & Dorf, B. (2012). *The Startup Owner's Manual. The Step-By-Step Guide for Building a Great Company*. Pescadero, CA: K&S Ranch Press.

Bocken, N. M. P., Short, S. W., Rana, P., & Evans, S. (2014). A literature and practice review to develop sustainable business model archetypes. *Journal of Cleaner Production*, 65.

Bocken, N. M., de Pauw, I., Bakker, C., & van der Grinten, B. (2016). Product design and business model strategies for a circular economy. *Journal of Industrial and Production Engineering*, *33*(5), 308–320. doi:10.1080/21681015.2016.1172124

Böcker, L., & Meelen, T. (2017). Sharing for people, planet or profit? Analysing motivations for intended sharing economy participation. *Environmental Innovation and Societal Transitions*, *23*, 28–39. doi:10.1016/j.eist.2016.09.004

Boons, F., Montalvo, C., Quist, J., & Wagner, M. (2013). Sustainable innovation, business models and economic performance: An overview. *Journal of Cleaner Production*, 45.

Botsman, R. (2013). *The Sharing Economy Lacks A Shared Definition*. Retrieved 12 July 2018, from https://www.fastcompany.com/3022028/the-sharing-economy-lacks-a-shared-definition

Botsman, R., & Rogers, R. (2010). *What's Mine Is Yours: The Rise of Collaborative Consumption*. New York: Harper Business.

Boulding, K. (1966). *The economics of the coming spaceship earth*. Academic Press.

Boulding, K. (1966). The Economics of the Coming Spaceship Earth. In H. Jarrett (Ed.), *Environmental Quality in a Growing Economy*. Baltimore, MD: Johns Hopkins University.

Boyoung, K., Hyojin, K., & Youngok, J. (2018). Critical Success Factors of a Design Startup Business. *Sustainability*, *10*(9), 1–15. doi:10.3390u10092981 PMID:30607262

Bressanelli, G., Adrodegari, F., Perona, M., & Saccani, N. (2018). The role of digital technologies to overcome Circular Economy challenges in PSS Business Models – and exploratory case study. *Proccedia CIRP*, 73.

Brown, G., & Stone, L. (2007). Cleaner production in New Zealand: Taking stock. *Journal of Cleaner Production, 15*(8-9), 716–728. doi:10.1016/j.jclepro.2006.06.025

Brzezinski, Z. (1967). *America in the Technetronic Age*. School of International Affairs, Columbia University.

Calvo, N., & Villarreal, O. (2018). Analysis of the growth of the e-learning industry through sustainable business model archetypes: A case study. *Journal of Cleaner Production, 191*, 26–39. doi:10.1016/j.jclepro.2018.04.211

Cambridge Econometrics and BIO Intelligence Service. (2014). *Study on modelling of the economic and environmental impacts of raw material consumption*. Final Report prepared for the European Commission.

Capra, F. (1982). *The Turning Point: Science, Society and the Rising Culture*. Flamingo Press.

Carroll, A. B. (1991). The Pyramid of Corporate Social Responsibility: Toward the Moral Management of Organizational Stakeholders. *Business Horizons, 34*(4), 39–48. doi:10.1016/0007-6813(91)90005-G

Castells, M. (1996). *The Rise of the Network Society: The Information Age: Economy, Society, Culture* (Vol. 1). Oxford, UK: Blackwell Publishers.

Castells, M. (2007). *Społeczeństwo sieci*. Warszawa: PWN.

Castells, M. (2009). The Rise of the Network Society: The Information Age: Economy, *Society, and Culture*. Wiley-Blackwell.

CBOS (Centrum Badania Opinii Społecznej). (2018). *O nieufności i zaufaniu*. Komunikat z Badań.

CEN - Circular Economy Network. (n.d.). Retrieved from http://www.circular-europe-network.eu/

Chang, W.-L., & Wang, J.-Y. (2018). Mine is yours? Using sentiment analysis to explore the degree of risk in the sharing economy. *Electronic Commerce Research and Applications, 28*, 141–158. doi:10.1016/j.elerap.2018.01.014

Charonis, G. (2012). Degrowth, steady state economics and the circular economy: three distinct yet increasingly converging alternative discourses to economic growth for achieving environmental sustainability and social equity. *World Economic Association Sustainability Conference 2012*. Available: http://sustainabilityconference2012.worldeconomicsassociation.org/wp-content/uploads/WEASustainabilityConference2012_Charonis_Alternative-Discoursesto-Economic-Growth.pdf

Cheng, M. (2016). Sharing economy: A review and agenda for future research. *International Journal of Hospitality Management, 57*, 60–70. doi:10.1016/j.ijhm.2016.06.003

Cheng, X., Fu, S., & de Vreede, G.-J. (2018). A mixed method investigation of sharing economy driven car-hailing services: Online and offline perspectives. *International Journal of Information Management, 41*, 57–64. doi:10.1016/j.ijinfomgt.2018.03.005

Chesbrough, H. (2010). Business Model Innovation: Opportunities and Barriers. *Long Range Planning*, 43.

Chiu, A. S., & Yong, G. (2004). On the industrial ecology potential in Asian developing countries. *Journal of Cleaner Production, 12*(8-10), 1037–1045. doi:10.1016/j.jclepro.2004.02.013

Choi, H. R., Cho, M. J., Lee, K. B., Hong, S. G., & Woo, C. R. (2014). *The Business Model for the Sharing Economy between SMEs* (Vol. 11). WSEAS Transactions on Business and Economics.

Cho, S., & Gumeta, H. (2015). Factors affecting university students' start-up intention: Comparative study on Korean and Chinese universities. *Journal of Korean Entrepreneurship, 10*(3), 150–152.

Clarkson, M. E. (1995). A stakeholder framework for analyzing and evaluating corporate social performance. *Academy of Management Review, 20*(1), 92–117. doi:10.5465/amr.1995.9503271994

Club of Rome. (2015). *The Circular Economy and Benefits for Society Jobs and Climate Clear Winners in an Economy Based on Renewable Energy and Resource Efficiency*. Retrieved from www.clubofrome.org

Club of Rome. (2016). *The Circular Economy and Benefits for Society Jobs and Climate Clear Winners in an Economy Based on Renewable Energy and Resource Efficiency*. Retrieved from www.clubofrome.org

Cohen, B., & Munoz, P. (2017). *Sharing Business Model Compass*. Retrieved from https://ladiaria.com.uy/articulo/2017/4/un-modelo-para-entender-la-economia colaborativa/#

Communication from the Commission to the European Parliament, the Council, the European Economic and Social Committee, & the Committee of the Regions. (2005). *Closing the loop - An EU action plan for the Circular Economy*. COM/2015/0614 final.

Compass. (2015). *The Global Startup Ecosystem Ranking 2015*. Retrieved https://ec.europa.eu/futurium/en/system/files/ged/the_global_startup_ecosystem_report_2015_v1.2.pdf

Connell, J. (2006). Medical tourism: Sea, sun, sand and surgery. *Tourism Management*, 1093–1100.

Corral, C. M. (2003). Sustainable production and consumption systems—cooperation for change: Assessing and simulating the willingness of the firm to adopt/develop cleaner technologies. The case of the In-Bond industry in northern Mexico. *Journal of Cleaner Production, 11*(4), 411–426. doi:10.1016/S0959-6526(02)00063-X

Czakon. W. (2011). Metodyka systematycznego przeglądu literatury. *Przegląd Organizacji*, 3.

Darnall, N., Jolley, G. J., & Handfield, R. (2008). Environmental management systems and green supply chain management: Complements for sustainability? *Business Strategy and the Environment, 17*(1), 30–45. doi:10.1002/bse.557

Daunoriene, A., Draksaite, A., Snieska, V., & Valodkiene, G. (2015). Evaluating Sustainability of Sharing Economy Business Models. *Procedia: Social and Behavioral Sciences*, 213.

de Pádua Pieronia, M., Pigossoa, D. C. A., & McAloonea, T. C.,(2018). Sustainable qualifying criteria for designing circular business models. *Procedia CIRP*, 69.

Deloitte. (2016). *Diagnoza ekosystemu startupów w Polsce*. Retrieved https://www2.deloitte.com/content/dam/Deloitte/pl/Documents/Reports/pl_Deloitte_raport_startupy.pdf

Demil, B., & Lecocq, X. (2010). Business Model Evolution: In Search of Dynamic Consistency. *Long Range Planning*, *43*(2-3), 227–246. doi:10.1016/j.lrp.2010.02.004

Demishaj, A., & Radonshiqi, R. (2016). Public and private sector services (Case study of dental services). *Science Arena Publications Specialty Journal of Accounting and Economics*, 15-18.

Den Hollander, M., & Bakker, C. (2016). Mind the Gap Exploiter: Circular Business Models for Product Lifetime Extension. *Proceedings of the Electronics Goes Green.*

Dentem. (2018). *Dentem*. Retrieved from Dentem: Dental Practice Management Software: https://www.dentem.co/

Directive 2009/125/EC of the European Parliament and of the Council of 21 October 2009 establishing a framework for the setting of ecodesign requirements for energy-related products (Text with EEA relevance), Official Journal of the European Union L 285/10

Directive 2010/30/EU of the European Parliament and of the Council of 19 May 2010 on the indication by labelling and standard product information of the consumption of energy and other resources by energy-related products (Text with EEA relevance), Official Journal of the European Union L 153/1

Directive 2010/75/EU of the European Parliament and of the Council of 24 November 2010 on industrial emissions (integrated pollution prevention and control) Text with EEA relevance, Official Journal of the European Union L 334/17

Dixon-Woods, M., Debbie Cavers, S., Agarwal, A. E., Arthur, A., Harvey, J., Hsu, R., … Sutton, A.J. (2006). Conducting a Critical Interpretive Synthesis of the Literature on Access to Healthcare by Vulnerable Groups. *MC Medical Research Methodology*, 6. doi:10.1186/1471-2288-6-35

Drucker, F. P. (1992). *The Age of Discontinuity: Guidelines to our Changing Society*. New York: Harper & Row.

Drucker, F. P. (1993). *Post-capitalist Society*. New York: Harper Business.

Drucker, P. F. (1985). *Innovation and entrepreneurship*. New York: Harper & Row.

Dubin, R. (1983). Theory Building in Applied Areas. In Handbook of Industrial and Organizational Psychology. Wiley.

Dubois, D., & Prade, H. (1988). *Possibility theory*. Springer. doi:10.1007/978-1-4684-5287-7

Dylus, A. (2002). Erozja standardów etycznych w biznesie. In J. Mariański (Ed.), *Kondycja moralna społeczeństwa polskiego* (pp. 273–303). Kraków: WAM.

EC. (1997). *Review of Cleaner Production*. Available: http://ec.europa.eu/environment/enveco/eco_industry/pdf/annex2.pdf

EEA (European Environment Agency). (2014). *Resource-efficient Green Economy and EU policies*. Luxembourg: Publications Office of the European Union.

EEB (European Environmental Bureau). (2014). Advancing Resource Efficiency in Europe: Indicators and waste policy scenarios to deliver a resource efficient and sustainable. *Europe*.

Ehrenfeld, J., & Gertler, N. (1997). Industrial ecology in practice: The evolution of interdependence at Kalundborg. *Journal of Industrial Ecology*, *1*(1), 67–79. doi:10.1162/jiec.1997.1.1.67

Elen MacArthur Foundation. (2012). *Towards the Circular Economy: Vol. 1. An economic and business rationale for an accelerated transition*. Retrieved from https://www.ellenmacarthurfoundation.org/publications

Elkington, J. (1999). *Cannibals with forks: the triple bottom line of 21. century business*. Oxford, UK: Capstone.

Ellen MacArthur Foundation (EMAF). (2013). Towards the Circular Economy. Economic and Business Rationale for an Accelerated Transition. Ellen MacArthur Foundation.

Ellen MacArthur Foundation and McKinsey Center for Business and Environment. (2015). *Growth Within: A Circular Economy Vision for a Competitive Europe*. Retrieved from https://www.ellenmacarthurfoundation.org/publications

Ellen MacArthur Foundation and SYSTEMIQ. (2017). *Achieving 'Growth Within': A €320-Billion Circular Economy Investment Opportunity Available to Europe up to 2025*. Retrieved from https://www.ellenmacarthurfoundation.org/publications

Ellen MacArthur Foundation. (2013). *Towards the Circular Economy: Vol. 2. Opportunities for the consumer goods sector*. Retrieved from https://www.ellenmacarthurfoundation.org/publications

Ellen MacArthur Foundation. (2015). *Towards a Circular Economy: Business rationale for an accelerated transition*. Retrieved from https://www.ellenmacarthurfoundation.org/publications

EMF. (2015a). *Towards a Circular Economy - Business Rationale for an Accelerated Transition*. EMF.

Erban, V. (2003). New paradigm? From mechanistics to holistics, from part to whole. In *UNImagazín. XIII. roč. University of South Bohemia in České Budějovice, 2003* (pp. 31-34). ABOPRESS. Retrieved from http://www2.tf.jcu.cz/~erban/paradigma.pdf

Ericson T. (n.d.). Generations Around the Globe. *Harvard Business Review*.

Erkman, S. (1997). Industrial ecology: An historical view. *Journal of Cleaner Production*, *5*(1-2), 1–10. doi:10.1016/S0959-6526(97)00003-6

Ert, E., Fleischer, A., & Magen, N. (2016). Trust and reputation in the sharing economy: The role of personal photos in Airbnb. *Tourism Management*, *55*, 62–73. doi:10.1016/j.tourman.2016.01.013

Ethics Resource Centre, Generational Differences in Workplace. (2011). *Ethics: A Supplemental Report of the 2011 National Business Ethics Survey*. Retrieved from http://www.ethics.org/ecihome/research/nbes/nbes-reports/nbes-2013

European Commission. (2013). *Flash Eurobarometer 367: Attitudes of Europeans towards building the single market for green products*. Author.

European Commission. (2014). *Flash Eurobarometer 388: Attitudes of Europeans towards waste management and resource efficiency*. Author.

European Commission. (2015). *Commission Staff Working Document: Additional analysis to complement the impact assessment SWD (2014) 208 supporting the review of EU waste management targets*. Author.

European Commission. (n.d.). *Press releases database*. Retrieved from http://eu-ropa.eu/rapid/press-release_MEMO-15-6204_pl.htm

European Economic and Social Committee 2014/C 67/05: Opinion of the European Economic and Social Committee on 'Towards more sustainable consumption: industrial product lifetimes and restoring trust through consumer information' (own-initiative opinion). *Official Journal of the European Union, C*, *67*(23).

EUROSTAT. (2016). *Material flow accounts and resource productivity*. Retrieved from http://ec.europa.eu/eurostat/statistics-explained/index.php/Material_flow_accounts_and_resource_productivity

Fagerstrøm, A., Pawar, S., Sigurdsson, V., Foxall, G. R., & Yani-de-Soriano, M. (2017). That personal profile image might jeopardize your rental opportunity! On the relative impact of the seller's facial expressions upon buying behavior on Airbnb™. *Computers in Human Behavior*, *72*, 123–131. doi:10.1016/j.chb.2017.02.029

Fahimnia, B., Sarkis, J., & Davarzani, H., (2015). Green supply chain management: A review and bibliometric analysis. *International Journal Profuction Economics*, 162.

Feeny, D., Berkes, F., McCay, B. J., & Acheson, J. M. (1990). The Tragedy of the Commons: Twenty-two years later. *Human Ecology*, *18*(1), 1–19. doi:10.1007/BF00889070 PMID:12316894

Ferizi, V., & Kruja, A. D. (2018). Coastline hospitality industry performance, challenges, and opportunities: evidence from Durres coastline. In D. Batabyal (Ed.), Managing Sustainable Tourism Resources (pp. 14-38). IGI Global.

Ferrell, O. C., Ferrell, L., & Huggins, K. (2017). Seismic Shifts in the Sharing Economy: Shaking Up Marketing Channels and Supply Chains. *Journal of Marketing Channels*, *24*(1-2), 3–12. do i:10.1080/1046669X.2017.1346973

Fiedor, B. (Ed.). (2002). Podstawy ekonomii środowiska i zasobów naturalnych. Wydawnictwo C.H.Beck.

Fiorelli, P. (n.d.). *Generational Ethics: A Battle of the Ages*. Retrieved from https://www.corporatecompliance.org/Portals/1/PDF/Resources/past_handouts/Higher_Ed/2017/V1__ses_401_2slides.pdf

Foss, N.J., & Saebi, T. (2017). Business Models and Business Model Innovation: Between Wicked and Paradigmatic Problems. *Long Range Planning*. doi:10.1016/j.lrp.2017.07.006

Friends of the Earth. (2010). *More Jobs Less Waste - Potential for Job Creation through higher rates of recycling in the UK and the EU*. Author.

Frondel, M., Horbach, J., & Rennings, K. (2007). End-of-pipe or cleaner production? An empirical comparison of environmental innovation decisions across OECD countries. *Business Strategy and the Environment*, *16*(8), 571–584. doi:10.1002/bse.496

Frosch, R. A. (1992). Industrial ecology: A philosophical introduction. *Proceedings of the National Academy of Sciences of the United States of America*, *89*(3), 800–803. doi:10.1073/pnas.89.3.800 PMID:11607255

Fukuyama, F. (1996). *Trust: The Social Virtues and the Creation of Prosperity*. New York: Free Press Paperbacs.

Fukuyama, F. (2007). *The end of history and the last human*. Prague: Rybka Publishers.

Fukuyama, F. (2015). *Political Order and Political Decay: From the Industrial Revolution to the Globalization of Democracy*. New York: Farrar, Straus and Giroux.

Geissdoerfer, M., Morioka, S., Monteiro de Carvalho, M., & Evans, S. (2018). Business models and supply chains for the circular Economy. *Journal of Cleaner Production*, 190.

Geissdoerfer, M., Savaget, P., Bocken, N. M., & Hultink, E. J. (2017). The Circular Economy–A new sustainability paradigm? *Journal of Cleaner Production*, *143*, 757–768. doi:10.1016/j.jclepro.2016.12.048

Geng, Y., & Doberstein, B. (2008). Developing the Circular Economy in China: Challenges and Opportunities for Achieving 'Leapfrog Development'. *International Journal of Sustainable Development & World Ecology*, 15.

Geng, Y., & Doberstein, B. (2008). Developing the circular economy in China: Challenges and opportunities for achieving 'leapfrog development'. *International Journal of Sustainable Development and World Ecology*, *15*(3), 231–239. doi:10.3843/SusDev.15.3:6

Geng, Y., Zhang, P., Ulgiati, S., & Sarkis, J. (2010). Emergy analysis of an industrial park: The case of Dalian. China. *The Science of the Total Environment*, *408*(22), 5273–5283. doi:10.1016/j.scitotenv.2010.07.081 PMID:20805000

Ghisellini, P., Cialani, C., & Ulgiati, S. (2016). A review on circular economy: The expected transition to a balanced interplay of environmental and economic systems. *Journal of Cleaner Production*, *114*, 11–32. doi:10.1016/j.jclepro.2015.09.007

Gibbs, C., Guttentag, D., Gretzel, U., Morton, J., & Goodwill, A. (2018). Pricing in the sharing economy: A hedonic pricing model applied to Airbnb listings. *Journal of Travel & Tourism Marketing*, *35*(1), 46–56. doi:10.1080/10548408.2017.1308292

Gonzalez-Padron, T. L. (2017). Ethics in the Sharing Economy: Creating a Legitimate Marketing Channel. *Journal of Marketing Channels*, *24*(1-2), 84–96. doi:10.1080/1046669X.2017.1347005

Gore, A. (1992). *Earth in the Balance. Ecology and the Human Spirit*. Boston: Houghton Mifflin Company.

Govindan, K., Soleimani, H., & Kannan, D. (2015). Reverse logistics and closed-loop supply chain: A comprehensive review to explore the future. *European Journal of Operational Research*, *240*(3), 603–626. doi:10.1016/j.ejor.2014.07.012

Govindarajan, V. (2007). *The Importance of Strategic Innovation*. Retrieved from http:/www.vijaygovindarajan.com/2006/03/the_importance_of_strategic_in.htm

Graebner, M. E., Martin, J. A., & Roundy, P. T. (2012). Qualitative data: Cooking without a recipe. *Strategic Organization*, *10*(3), 276–284. doi:10.1177/1476127012452821

Graedel, T. E., & Allenby, B. R. (2003). *Industrial Ecology* (2nd ed.). New York: Prentice Hall.

Graedel, T. E., & Allenby, B. R. (2010). *Industrial ecology and sustainable engineering*. Upper Saddle River, NJ: Prentice Hall.

Grow Advisors. (2017). *The Startup Ecosystem. White Paper*. Retrieved http://www.startupcommons.org

Grudzewski, W. M., Hejduk, I. K., Sankowska, A., & Wańtuchowicz, M. (2010). *Sustainably w biznesie czyli przedsiębiorstwo przyszłości. Zmiany paradygmatów i koncepcji zarzadzania*. Warszawa: Wyd. Poltext.

Guha, D., & Chakraborty, D. (2008). *Compromise ratio method for decision making under fuzzy environment using fuzzy distance measure*. Academic Press.

Guide, V. D. R. Jr, & Van Wassenhove, L. N. (2009). OR FORUM—The evolution of closed-loop supply chain research. *Operations Research*, *57*(1), 10–18. doi:10.1287/opre.1080.0628

Guinée, J. B. (2002). Handbook on Life Cycle Assessment: Operational Guide to the ISO Standards. Springer Science+Business Media B.V. doi:10.1007/BF02978897

Guttentag, D. (2015). Airbnb: Disruptive innovation and the rise of an informal tourism accommodation sector. *Current Issues in Tourism*, *18*(12), 1192–1217. doi:10.1080/13683500.2013.827159

Guttentag, D. A., & Smith, S. L. J. (2017). Assessing Airbnb as a disruptive innovation relative to hotels: Substitution and comparative performance expectations. *International Journal of Hospitality Management*, *64*, 1–10. doi:10.1016/j.ijhm.2017.02.003

Guttentag, D., Smith, S., Potwarka, L., & Havitz, M. (2018). Why Tourists Choose Airbnb: A Motivation-Based Segmentation Study, Why Tourists Choose Airbnb: A Motivation-Based Segmentation Study. *Journal of Travel Research*, *57*(3), 342–359. doi:10.1177/0047287517696980

Gwehenberger, G., Erler, B., & Schnitzer, H. (2003). *A Multi e Strategy Approach to Zero Emissions*. Paper Presented at Technology Foresight Summit 2003, Budapest, Hungary. Retrieved from http://www.unido.org/.

Haaker, T., Bouwman, H., Janssen, W., & De Reuver, M. (2017). Business model stress testing: A practical approach to test the robustness of a business model. *Futures*, *89*, 14–25. doi:10.1016/j.futures.2017.04.003

Habibi, M. R., Davidson, A., & Laroche, M. (2017). What managers should know about the sharing economy. *Business Horizons*, *60*(1), 113–121. doi:10.1016/j.bushor.2016.09.007

Hall, J. (2001). Environmental supply-chain innovation. *Greener Management International*, 105-12.

Hamari, J., Sjöklint, M., & Ukkonen, A. (2016). The sharing economy: Why people participate in collaborative consumption. *Journal of the Association for Information Science and Technology*, *67*(9), 2047–2059. doi:10.1002/asi.23552

Hardin, G. (1968). The tragedy of the commons. *Science*, (162): 1243–1248. doi:10.1126cience.162.3859.1243 PMID:5699198

Heck, P. (2006). *Circular Economy related international practices and policy trends: Current situation and practices on sustainable production and consumption and international Circular Economy development policy summary and analysis. Institut für angewandtes Stoffstrommanagement*. IfaS.

Helmig, B., Spraul, K., & Ingenhoff, D. (2016). Under positive pressure: How stakeholder pressure affects corporate social responsibility implementation. *Business & Society*, *55*(2), 151–187. doi:10.1177/0007650313477841

Henderson, H. (1991). *Life Beyond Economics. Knowledge Systems*. Berrett-Koehler Publishers.

Horowitz, M. D., Rosensweig, J. A., & Jones, C. A. (2007). *Medical Tourism: Globalization of the Healthcare Marketplace*. Medscape General Medicine Journal.

http://odpowiedzialni.gpw.pl/

Italian Ministry of the Environment. (2017). Towards a circular economy model for Italy. Ministry for the Environment and Protection of the Territory and the Sea in collaboration with the Ministry of Economic Development.

Jabłoński, A. (2016). Longitudinalne badania modeli biznesu przedsiębiorstw. *Zeszyty Naukowe Uniwersytetu Ekonomicznego w Krakowie*, *6*(954), 95–110. Doi:10.15678/ZNUEK.2016.0954.0606

Jabłoński, A., & Jabłoński, M. (2016). Research on Business Models in their Life Cycle. *Sustainability*, 8.

Janoštiak, R. (2015). When Matematics Uncover the Secrets of the Nature - Fibonnaci Sequence and Golden Ratio. *InVivo magazín*. Retrieved from https://invivomagazin.sk/ked-matematika-prezradza -tajomstva-prirody-fibonacciho-postupnost-a-zlaty-rez_399.html

Jeon, Y. (2018). Analysis of the impact of start-up mentoring on strengthening business capabilities of one-man design entrepreneur-focusing on 'Creative Maestro Job Creation Project'. *Journal of Digital Convergence*, *16*, 343–349.

Jin, S. T., Kong, H., Wu, R., & Sui, D. Z. (2018). Ridesourcing, the sharing economy, and the future of cities. *Cities (London, England)*, *76*, 96–104. doi:10.1016/j.cities.2018.01.012

Judge, W. Q., & Elenkov, D. (2005). Organizational capacity for change and environmental performance: An empirical assessment of Bulgarian firms. *Journal of Business Research*, *58*(7), 893–901. doi:10.1016/j.jbusres.2004.01.009

Kaczmarek, M., Olejnik, I., & Springer, A. (2016). Badania jakościowe. metody i zastosowania. CeDeWu.

Kagermann, H., Helbig, J., Hellinger, A., & Wahlster, W. (2013). *Recommendations for Implementing the Strategic Initiative INDUSTRIE 4.0: Securing the Future of German Manufacturing Industry. Final Report of the Industrie 4.0 Working Group*. Forschungsunion.

Karlsson, L., Kemperman, A., & Dolnicar, S. (2017). May I sleep in your bed? Getting permission to book. *Annals of Tourism Research*, *62*, 1–12. doi:10.1016/j.annals.2016.10.002

Kasperski, A., & Kulej, M. (2007). The 0-1 knapsack problem with fuzzy data. *Fuzzy Optimization and Decision Making*, *6*(2), 163–172. doi:10.100710700-007-9000-3

Key, T. M. (2017). Domains of Digital Marketing Channels in the Sharing Economy. *Journal of Marketing Channels*, *24*(1-2), 27–38. doi:10.1080/1046669X.2017.1346977

Kim, B., & Cho, S. (2014). Factors affecting university students' start-up intentions: Focus on knowledge and technology based start-up. *Journal of Korean Entrepreneurship*, *9*(4), 86–106.

Kimberly, J. R. (1976). Issues in the Design of Longitudinal Organizational Research. *Sociological Methods & Research*, *4*(3), 321–348. doi:10.1177/004912417600400303

Kim, K., Baek, C., & Lee, J.-D. (2018). Creative destruction of the sharing economy in action: The case of Uber. *Transportation Research Part A, Policy and Practice*, *110*, 118–127. doi:10.1016/j.tra.2018.01.014

Kim, Y. G., Woo, E., & Nam, J. (2018). Sharing economy perspective on an integrative framework of the NAM and TPB. *International Journal of Hospitality Management*, *72*, 109–117. doi:10.1016/j.ijhm.2018.01.008

King, A. A., & Lenox, M. J. (2001). Lean and green? An empirical examination of the relationship between lean production and environmental performance. *Production and Operations Management, 10*(3), 244–256. doi:10.1111/j.1937-5956.2001.tb00373.x

Kirchherr, J., Piscicelli, L., Bour, R., Kostense-Smit, E., Muller, J., Huibrechtse-Truijens, A., & Hekkert, M. (2018). Barriers to the Circular Economy: Evidence From the European Union (EU). *Ecological Economics, 150*, 264–272. doi:10.1016/j.ecolecon.2018.04.028

Kirchherr, J., Reike, D., & Hekkert, M. (2017). Conceptualizing the circular economy: An analysis of 114 definitions. *Resources, Conservation and Recycling, 127*, 221–232. doi:10.1016/j.resconrec.2017.09.005

Kleindorfer, P. R., Singhal, K., & Wassenhove, L. N. (2005). Sustainable operations management. *Production and Operations Management, 14*(4), 482–492. doi:10.1111/j.1937-5956.2005.tb00235.x

Klinec, I. (2005). Alternative economic theories in terms of sustainable development. In J. Hejda (Ed.), Sustainability and quality of life in managerial and civic decision-making process. Chapter: Alternative economic theories in the context of sustainable development (pp. 46–87). Prague: Academic Press.

Klinec, I. (2011). *The Outline of the Holistic Economics Theory*. Economic Institute of the Slovak Academy of Sciences, Ekonomic theory, Prognostics (futurology).

Kopčaj, A. (1997). Multiplying the Wealth. Kopčaj - Silma ´90.

Kopčaj, A. (1999). *Management of Change - The common way how to achieve extraordinary development*. Prague: Grada Publishing.

Kopčaj, A. (2007). *Spiral management*. Bratislava: Alfa.

Korhonen, J., Nuur, C., Feldmann, A., & Birkie, S. E. (2018). Circular economy as an essentially contested concept. *Journal of Cleaner Production, 175*, 544–552. doi:10.1016/j.jclepro.2017.12.111

Krempaský, J. (2001). Quantitative theory of evolution. Metodické centrum.

Kruja, A. (2012b). The impact of tourism sector development in the Albanian economy. *Economia. Seria Management, 15*(1), 205-218.

Kruja, A. (2013a). Entrepreneurship and knowledge-based economies. *Revista Românească pentru Educaţie Multidimensională, 5*(1), 7-17.

Kruja, A. (2012a). Entrepreneurship, knowledge, innovation and sustainable development. *Mediterranean Journal of Social Sciences*, 21–25.

Kruja, A. D. (2013b). The contribution of SMEs to the economic growth (Case of Albania). *EuroEconomica, 32*(1), 55–67.

Kruja, A. D. (2019). Synergic Individual Entrepreneurial Orientation of University Students: A New Measurement Model. In *Handbook of Research on Ethics, Entrepreneurship, and Governance in Higher Education*. IGI Global.

Kumar, V., Lahiri, A., & Bahadir Dogan, O. (2018). A strategic framework for a profitable business model in the sharing Economy. *Industrial Marketing Management*, 69.

Kumar, S. (2014). *No Destination: Autobiography of a Pilgrim* (4th ed.). Cambridge, UK: Green Books.

Lacy, P., & Rutqvist, J. (2015). *Waste to Wealth. The Circular Economy Advantage*. Palgrave Macmillan.

Laubscher, M., & Marinelli, T. (2014). Integration of Circular Economy in Business. *Proceedings of the Conference: Going Green—CARE INNOVATION*.

Laurell, C., & Sandström, C. (2018). Comparing coverage of disruptive change in social and traditional media: Evidence from the sharing economy. *Technological Forecasting and Social Change*, *129*, 339–344. doi:10.1016/j.techfore.2017.09.038

Lawton, Carter, Lee, Tan, de Prado Trigo, Luscombe, & Briscoe. (2013). *The opportunities to business of improving resource efficiency*. Study prepared by AMEC Environment & Infrastructure and Bio Intelligence Service.

Lee, S. H., & Noh, S. H. (2014). A study on the success factors of ICT Convergence type-specific start-up enterprise - Mainly the case study. *Journal of Digital Convergence*, *12*(12), 203–215. doi:10.14400/JDC.2014.12.12.203

Lee, S., & Kim, D.-Y. (2018). Brand personality of Airbnb: Application of user involvement and gender differences. *Journal of Travel & Tourism Marketing*, *35*(1), 32–45. doi:10.1080/10548408.2017.1284030

Lett. L. A. (2014). *Global threats. Waste recycling and the circular economy concept*. Academic Press.

Lewandowski, M. (2016). Designing the business models for circular economy—Towards the conceptual framework. *Sustainability*, *8*(1), 43. doi:10.3390u8010043

Lewicka-Strzałecka, A. (n.d.). *Moralność Finansowa Polaków*. Instytut Filozofii i Socjologii PAN, Konferencja Przedsiębiorstw Finansowych

Lewrick, M., Omar, M., Raeside, R., & Saier, K. (2010). Education for entrepreneurship and innovation: `Management capabilities for sustainable growth and success. *World Journal of Entrepreneurship, Management and Sustainable Development*, *6*(1/2), 1–18.

Liang, S., Schuckert, M., Law, R., & Chen, C.-C. (2017). Be a "Superhost": The importance of badge systems for peer-to-peer rental accommodations. *Tourism Management*, *60*, 454–465. doi:10.1016/j.tourman.2017.01.007

Lieder, M., & Rashid, A. (2016). Towards circular economy implementation: A comprehensive review in context of manufacturing industry. *Journal of Cleaner Production, 115*, 36–51. doi:10.1016/j.jclepro.2015.12.042

Li, H., Bao, W., Xiu, C., Zhang, Y., & Xu, H. (2010). Energy conservation and circular economy in China's process industries. *Energy, 35*(11), 4273–4281. doi:10.1016/j.energy.2009.04.021

Linder, M., & Williander, M. (2015). Circular Business Model Innovation: Inherent Uncertainties. *Bus. Strateg. Environ.*

Lin, F. T., & Yao, J. S. (2001). Using fuzzy numbers in knapsack problems. *European Journal of Operational Research, 135*(1), 158–176. doi:10.1016/S0377-2217(00)00310-6

Liu, S. Q., & Mattila, A. S. (2017). Airbnb: Online targeted advertising, sense of power, and consumer decisions. *International Journal of Hospitality Management, 60*, 33–41. doi:10.1016/j.ijhm.2016.09.012

Liu, Y., & Bai, Y. (2014). An exploration of firms' awareness and behavior of developing circular economy: An empirical research in China. *Resources, Conservation and Recycling, 87*, 145–152. doi:10.1016/j.resconrec.2014.04.002

Lockwood, N. R. (2005). *Crisis Management in Today's Business Environment.* Society for Human Resource Management.

Lombardi, P., & Schwabe, F. (2017). Sharing economy as a new business model for energy storage systems. *Applied Energy, 188*, 485–496. doi:10.1016/j.apenergy.2016.12.016

Łopusiewicz, A. (2013). *Start-up Od Pomysłu Do Sukcesu.* Warszawa, Poland: Edgard.

Lorek, E. (2007). *Polska polityka energetyczna w warunkach integracji z Unią Europejską.* Wyd. AE Katowice.

Lorek, E., & Lorek, A. (2011). *Efektywne zarządzanie dobrami środowiskowymi w ujęciu modelowym.* Uniwersytet Ekonomiczny w Krakowie.

Lüdeke-Freund, F. (2010). *Towards a Conceptual Framework of 'Business Models for Sustainability.* Paper presented at Knowledge Collaboration & Learning for Sustainable Innovation, Delft, The Netherlands.

Lutz, C., & Newlands, G. (2018). Consumer segmentation within the sharing economy: The case of Airbnb. *Journal of Business Research, 88*, 187–196. doi:10.1016/j.jbusres.2018.03.019

Magretta, J. (2003). *What Management Is. How it Works and Why It Is Everyone's Business.* London: Profile Books.

Mair, J., & Reischauer, G. (2017). Capturing the dynamics of the sharing economy: Institutional research on the plural forms and practices of sharing economy organizations. *Technological Forecasting and Social Change, 125*, 11–20. doi:10.1016/j.techfore.2017.05.023

Manninen, K., Koskela, S., Antikainen, R., Bocken, N., Dahlbo, H., & Aminoff, A. (2018). Do circular economy business models capture intended environmental value propositions? *Journal of Cleaner Production*, 171.

Martello, S., & Toth, P. (1990). *Knapsack Problems*. Wiley.

Masuda, Y. (1980). *The Information Society as Post-industrial Society*. Chicago: World Future Society.

Mauri, A. G., Minazzi, R., Nieto-García, M., & Viglia, G. (2018). Humanize your business. The role of personal reputation in the sharing economy. *International Journal of Hospitality Management*, *73*, 36–43. doi:10.1016/j.ijhm.2018.01.017

McCarthy, A., Dellink, R., & Bibas, R. (2018). *The Macroeconomics of the Circular Economy Transition: A Critical Review of Modelling Approaches (No. 130)*. OECD Publishing.

McDowall, W., Geng, Y., Huang, B., Bartekov'a, E., Bleischwitz, R., Türkeli, S., . . . Doménech, T. (2017). Circular Economy Policies in China and Europe. *Journal of Industrial Ecology*. Retrieved from https://www.researchgate.net/publication/316722262

Mikulášková, J. (2017). *Usage of Living Systems Management Principles by increasing of the Influence of Corporate Culture related to Sustain Long-term Potential of Success* (Unpublished doctoral dissertation). Slovak University of Technology, Faculty of Materials Science and Technology in Trnava.

Mirabella, N., Castellani, V., & Sala, S. (2014). Current options for the valorisation of food manufacturing waste: A review. *Journal of Cleaner Production*, *65*, 28–41. doi:10.1016/j.jclepro.2013.10.051

Mitchell, P. (2015). Employment and the circular economy - Job Creation through resource efficiency in London. Report produced by WRAP for the London Sustainable Development Commission, the London Waste and Recycling Board and the Greater London Authority.

Möhlmann, M. (2015). Collaborative consumption: Determinants of satisfaction and the likelihood of using a sharing economy option again. *Journal of Consumer Behaviour*, *14*(3), 193–207. doi:10.1002/cb.1512

Molteni, L., & Troilo, G. (2007). *Ricerche di marketing*. McGraw-Hill.

Montensen, P. S., & Bloch, C. W. (2005). *Oslo manual-guidelines for collecting and interpreting innovation data: Proposed guidelines for collecting and interpreting innovation*. OECD.

Morgan, J., & Mitchell, P. (2015). Employment and the circular economy Job creation in a more resource efficient Britain. *Green Alliance*. Retrieved from https://tinyurl.com/gmrnosb

Mourougan, S. (2015). Corporate Social Responsibility for sustainable business. *IOSR Journal of Business and Management, 17*(5).

Murphy, J., & Gouldson, A. (2000). Environmental policy and industrial innovation: Integrating environment and economy through ecological modernisation. *Geoforum*, *31*(1), 33–44. doi:10.1016/S0016-7185(99)00042-1

Murray, A., Skene, K., & Haynes, K. (2017). The circular economy: An interdisciplinary exploration of the concept and application in a global context. *Journal of Business Ethics*, *140*(3), 369–380. doi:10.100710551-015-2693-2

Mutz, D. (2015). *Circular Economy and Informal Waste Management in India – a Contradiction Institute of Development Studies*. Resource Politics 2015.

Nadler, S. (2014). *The sharing economy: what is it and where is it going?* (Thesis). Massachusetts Institute of Technology. Retrieved from http://dspace.mit.edu/handle/1721.1/90223

Naisbitt, J. (1984). *Megatrends: Ten New Directions Transforming Our Lives*. New York: Warner Books.

Naustdalslid, J. (2014). Circular economy in China e the environmental dimension of the harmonious society. *International Journal of Sustainable Development of World Ecology*. doi: 10.1080/13504509.2014.914599

Neumeyer, X., & Santos, S. C. (2018). Sustainable business models, venture typologies, and entrepreneurial ecosystems: A social network perspective. *Journal of Cleaner Production*, 172.

Nexhipi, O. (2018). Medical Tourism Management Challenges - The Case of Dental Tourism in Albania. *European Journal of Interdisciplinary Studies*.

Nielsen, C., & Bukh, N. (2008). *What Constitutes a Business Model.: The Perception of Financial Analysts. Working Paper.* Series Department of Business Studies No.4. Aalborg University.

North, D. W. (1968). A tutorial introduction to decision theory. Systems Science and Cybernetics. *IEEE Transactions on*, *4*(3), 200–210.

OECD. (2016). *Green growth indicators (Edition 2016)*. OECD Environment Statistics. doi:1.1787/5710f950-en

OECD. (2017). *Green growth indicators (Edition 2017)*. OECD Environment Statistics. doi:1.1787/9789264268586-en

Okada, S., & Gen, M. (1994). Fuzzy multiple choice knapsack problem. *Fuzzy Sets and Systems*, *67*(1), 71–80. doi:10.1016/0165-0114(94)90209-7

Omachonu, V. K., & Einspruch, N. G. (2010). Innovation in healthcare delivery systems: A conceptual framework. *The Innovation Journal*, *15*(1), 1–20.

Orlowska. A.. Mazur. Z.. Raguna. M. (2017). Systematyczny przegląd literatury: Na czym polega i czym różni się od innych przeglądów. *Ogrody Nauk i Sztuk*, 7. doi:10.15503/onis2017.350.363

Osterwalder, A., & Pigneur, Y. (2012). *Tworzenie modeli biznesowych. Podręcznik wizjonera.* Gliwice: Helion.

Parente, R. C., Geleilate, J.-M. G., & Rong, K. (2018). The Sharing Economy Globalization Phenomenon: A Research Agenda. *Journal of International Management, 24*(1), 52–64. doi:10.1016/j.intman.2017.10.001

Parkin, S. (1991). *Green Future. Agenda for 21st Century.* Fount.

Park, J., Sarkis, J., & Wu, Z. (2010). Creating integrated business and environmental value within the context of China's circular economy and ecological modernization. *Journal of Cleaner Production, 18*(15), 1494–1501. doi:10.1016/j.jclepro.2010.06.001

Pearce, D. W., & Turner, R. K. (1990). *Economics of Natural Resources and the Environment.* Baltimore, MD: Johns Hopkins University Press.

Pearce, D. W., & Turner, R. K. (1990). *Economics of natural resources and the environment.* JHU Press.

Pearce, D., Barbier, E., & Markandya, A. (1990). *Sustainable Development, Economics and the Enviroment in the Third World.* Edward Elgar Pub.

Pego, A. (2018b). *The offshore energy cluster. A geographic and an economic overview* (PhD Thesis). Lisbon: Universidade Nova de Lisboa.

Pego, A. (2018a). In S. Cubico, G. Favretto, J. Leitão, & U. Cantner (Eds.), *The pentagonal problem and the offshore energy sector in Portugal. Why does it matter? In Entrepreneurship along the Industry Life Cycle: The changing role of Entrepreneurial Activities and Knowledge Competencies* (pp. 313–327). Sringer Book.

Phua, V. C. (2018). Perceiving Airbnb as sharing economy: The issue of trust in using Airbnb. *Current Issues in Tourism, 0*(0), 1–5. doi:10.1080/13683500.2018.1440539

Piscione, D. P. (2013). *Secrets of Silicon Valley: What Everyone Else Can Learn from the Innovation Capital of the World.* New York, NY: Palgrave Macmillan.

Planing, P. (2015). Business model innovation in a circular economy reasons for non-acceptance of circular business models. *Open Journal of Business Model Innovation, 1*(11).

Plchová, J. (2013). New Approaches to Human Resources Management in the Company. Journal of Knowledge Society, 1(1), 1-8.

Plchová, J., & Polakovič, Ľ. (2015). Quantification in Human Resources Management - Spiral Management. *International May Conference on Strategic Management – IMKSM 2015,* 662-672.

Polakovič, Ľ., & Krempaský, J. (2012). Quantitative management theory of enterprises as unimodal systems. ATP Journal, 19, 44-46.

Polski Ruch Czystszej Produkcji. (2015). *Gospodarka o obiegu zamkniętym – nowe wytyczne Komisji Europejskie.* Retrieved from www.cp.org.pl/2015/12/forum-cp-j-baran-circular-economy.htm

Porter, M. E., & Heppelmann, J. E. (2014). How Smart, Connected Products Are Transforming Competition. *Harvard Business Review*.

Porter, M. E., & Heppelmann, J. E. (2015). How Smart, Connected Products Are Transforming Companies. *Harvard Business Review*.

Prayag, G., & Ozanne, L. K. (2018). A systematic review of peer-to-peer (P2P) accommodation sharing research from 2010 to 2016: Progress and prospects from the multi-level perspective. *Journal of Hospitality Marketing & Management*, *27*(6), 649–678. doi:10.1080/19368623.2018.1429977

Prendeville, S., Sanders, C., Sherry, J., & Costa, F. (2014). *Circular economy: is it enough.* EcoDesign Centre. Available from: http://www. edcw. org/en/resources/circulareconomy-it-enough

Preston, F. (2012). A Global Redesign? Shaping the Circular Economy. *Briefing Paper*. London: Chatham House.

Preston, F. (2012). *A Global Redesign?: Shaping the Circular Economy*. London: Chatham House.

Prigogin, I. (2003). *Is Future Given?* London: World Scientific Publishing Co. doi:10.1142/5352

Priporas, C.-V., Stylos, N., Rahimi, R., & Vedanthachari, L. N. (2017). Unraveling the diverse nature of service quality in a sharing economy: A social exchange theory perspective of Airbnb accommodation. *International Journal of Contemporary Hospitality Management*, *29*(9), 2279–2301. doi:10.1108/IJCHM-08-2016-0420

PwC. (2015). *The Sharing Economy - Consumer Intelligence Series*. Retrieved from https://www.pwc.com/us/en/industry/entertainment-media/publications/consumer-intelligence-series/assets/pwc-cis-sharing-economy.pdf

Qiao, F., & Qiao, N. (2013). Circular Economy: An Ethical and Sustainable Economic Development Model. *Prakseologia, 154*, 253-272.

Ramani, K., Ramanujan, D., Bernstein, W. Z., Zhao, F., Sutherland, J., Handwerker, C., & Thurston, D. (2010). Integrated sustainable life cycle design: A review. *Journal of Mechanical Design*, *132*(9), 091004. doi:10.1115/1.4002308

Rao, P. (2002). Greening the supply chain: A new initiative in South East Asia. *International Journal of Operations & Production Management*, *22*(6), 632–655. doi:10.1108/01443570210427668

Regulation (EC) No 1221/2009 of the European Parliament and of the Council of 25 November 2009 on the voluntary participation by organisations in a Community eco-management and audit scheme (EMAS), repealing Regulation (EC) No 761/2001 and Commission Decisions 2001/681/EC and 2006/193/EC, Official Journal of the European Union L 342/1

Regulation (EC) No 66/2010 of the European Parliament and of the Council of 25 November 2009 on the EU Ecolabel (Text with EEA relevance), Official Journal of the European Union L 27/1

Regulation (EU) 2017/1369 of the European Parliament and of the Council of 4 July 2017 setting a framework for energy labelling and repealing Directive 2010/30/EU (Text with EEA relevance.)

Regulation (EU) 2017/1369 of the European Parliament and of the Council of 4 July 2017 setting a framework for energy labelling and repealing Directive 2010/30/EU (Text with EEA relevance.), Official Journal of the European Union L 198/1

Relative Ranking of a Selected Pool of Leading Scholars in the Social Sciences by Number of Citations in the Social Science Citation Index. (2000-2014). Retrieved from https://web.archive.org/web/20160307132846/http://www.manuelcastells.info/sites/default/files/sscisocialranking_eng.pdf

Richard, B., & Cleveland, S. (2016). The future of hotel chains, The future of hotel chains: Branded marketplaces driven by the sharing economy, Branded marketplaces driven by the sharing economy. *Journal of Vacation Marketing*, *22*(3), 239–248. doi:10.1177/1356766715623827

Ries, E. (2011). *The Lean Startup. How Constant Innovation Creates Radically Successful Businesses*. London, England: VIKING.

Ries, E. (2011). *The Lean Startup: How Today's Entrepreneurs Use Continuous Innovation to Create Radically Successful Businesses*. New York, NY: Crown Publishing Group.

Rizos, V., Tuokko, K., & Behrens, A. (2017). *The Circular Economy. A review of definitions, processes and impacts.* CEPS Research Reports No 2017/8.

Rogowski, R. (2016). Ethical Problems at Work in the Opinion of Employees of Selected Banks. *Annales. Ethics in Economic Life, 19*(3).

Roh, T. H. (2016). The Sharing Economy: Business Cases of Social Enterprises Using Collaborative Networks. *Procedia Computer Science*, *91*, 502–511. doi:10.1016/j.procs.2016.07.129

Roos, G. (2014). Business model innovation to create and capture resource value in future circular material chains. *Resources*, 3.

Sangle, S. (2010). Empirical analysis of determinants of adoption of proactive environmental strategies in India. *Business Strategy and the Environment*, *19*(1), 51–63.

Sarkis, J. (Ed.). (2006). Greening the supply chain. Springer Science & Business Media.

Sauvé, S., Bernard, S., & Sloan, P. (2016). Environmental sciences, sustainable development and circular economy: Alternative concepts for trans-disciplinary research. *Environmental Development*, *17*, 48–56. doi:10.1016/j.envdev.2015.09.002

Sauvé, S., Bernard, S., & Sloan, P. (2016). Environmental sciences. sustainable development and circular economy: Alternative concepts for trans-disciplinary research. *Environmental Development*, 17.

Schaltegger, S., Hansen, E. & Lüdeke-Freund, F., (2015). Business Models for Sustainability: Origins, Present Research, and Future Avenues. *Organization & Environment.* . doi:10.1177/1086026615599806

Schaltegger, S., Lüdeke-Freund, F., & Hansen, E.G. (2016). Business Models for Sustainability - A Co-Evolutionary Analysis of Sustainable Entrepreneurship, Innovation, and Transformation. *Organization & Environment, 29.*

Schor, J. (2016). Debating the sharing economy. *Journal of Self-Governance and Management Economics*, *4*(3), 7–22. doi:10.22381/JSME4320161

Schramm-Klein, H., Morschett, D., & Swoboda, B. (2015). Retailer corporate social responsibility: Shedding light on CSR's impact on profit of intermediaries in marketing channels. *International Journal of Retail & Distribution Management*, *43*(4/5), 403–431. doi:10.1108/IJRDM-04-2014-0041

Schroeder, R. G., Bates, K. A., & Junttila, M. A. (2002). A resource-based view of manufacturing strategy and the relationship to manufacturing performance. *Strategic Management Journal*, *23*(2), 105–117. doi:10.1002mj.213

Schumpeter, J. (1911/34). *The theory of economic development.* Cambridge, MA: Harvard University Press.

Schwab, K. (2017). *The global competitieness report 2017-2018.* Geneva: World Economic Forum.

Sengupta, A., & Pal, T. K. (2000). On comparing interval numbers. *European Journal of Operational Research*, *127*(1), 28–43. doi:10.1016/S0377-2217(99)00319-7

Seuring, S., & Müller, M. (2008). From a literature review to a conceptual framework for sustainable supply chain management. *Journal of Cleaner Production*, *16*(15), 1699–171. doi:10.1016/j.jclepro.2008.04.020

Sherwin, C., & Evans, S. (2000, May). Ecodesign innovation: is. In *Proceedings of the 2000 IEEE International Symposium on Electronics and the Environment. ISEE-2000* (pp. 112-117). IEEE. 10.1109/ISEE.2000.857634

Silverman, D., & Marvasti, A. B. (2008). Doing Qualitative Research: A Comprehensive Guide. *Sage (Atlanta, Ga.).*

Šimon, P. (2015). *Entropia – málo chápaná fyzikálna veličina s veľkým dosahom.* EnergeticaWeb. Retrieved from https://www.energiaweb.sk/2015/12/09/entropia-malo-chapana-fyzikalna-velicina-s-velkym-dosahom/

Singh, M. P., Chakraborty, A., & Roy, M. (2017). Developing an extended theory of planned behavior model to explore circular economy readiness in manufacturing MSMEs. India. *Resources. Conservation and Recycling.*

Singh, M. P., Chakraborty, A., & Roy, M. (2016). The link among innovation drivers, green innovation and business performance: Empirical evidence from a developing economy. *World Review of Science, Technology and Sustainable Development, 12*(4), 316–334. doi:10.1504/WRSTSD.2016.082191

Singh, N., Jain, S., & Sharma, P. (2014). Determinants of proactive environmental management practices in Indian firms: An empirical study. *Journal of Cleaner Production, 66*, 469–478. doi:10.1016/j.jclepro.2013.11.055

Singh, V. P., & Chakraborty, D. (2017). Solving bi-level programming problem with fuzzy random variable coefficients. *Journal of Intelligent & Fuzzy Systems, 32*(1), 521–528. doi:10.3233/JIFS-152354

Skácel, D. (2002). What is it the entropy? *Alternativní energie 1/2002. CEMC - České ekologické manažerské centrum.* Retrieved from http://www.tzb-info.cz /casopisy/alternativni-energie

Smith, K., & Estibals, A. (2011). Innovation and Research Strategy for Growth. London: BIS Department for Business Innovation and Skills.

Snihur, Y., & Zott, C. (2013). *Legitimacy without Imitation: How to Achieve Robust Business Model Innovation.* Paper to be presented at the 35th DRUID Celebration Conference, Barcelona, Spain.

Sorokin, P. (1992). *The Crisis of Our Age*. London: Oneworld Publications.

Spengler, O. (1991). *The Decline of the West.* Oxford, UK: Oxford University Press.

Stahel, W. R. (2013). The business angle of a circular economy–higher competitiveness. higher resource security and material efficiency. *A New Dynamic: Effective Business in a Circular Economy*, 45-53.

Stahel, W. (2010). *The performance economy*. Springer.

Stahel, W., & Reday, G. (1976). *Report The Potential for Substituting Manpower for Energy*. New York: Vantage Press.

Stahel, W., & Reday, G. (1981). *Jobs for Tomorrow, the Potential for Substituting Manpower for Energy*. New York: Vantage Press.

Stańczyk-Hugiet, E. (2014). Badania longitudinalne w zarządzaniu. czyli jak dostrzec prawidłowości w dynamice. *Organizacja i Kierowanie*, 2.

Standing, C., Standing, S., & Biermann, S. (2018). The implications of the sharing economy for transport. *Transport Reviews, 0*(0), 1–17. doi:10.1080/01441647.2018.1450307

Staněk, P. (2010). *Global crisis - a threat or a challenge?* Bratislava: Sprint.

Startup Genome. (2017). *The Global Startup Ecosystem Report 2017.* Retrieved https://startupgenome.com

Stegeman, H. (2015). *The potential of the circular economy*. Retrieved from https:/economics.rabobank.com/publications/2015/july/the-potential-of-the-circular-economy

Stephany, A. (2015). *The Business of Sharing: Making it in the New Sharing Economy*. Palgrave Macmillan. doi:10.1057/9781137376183

Stindt, D., & Sahamie, R. (2014). Review of research on closed loop supply chain management in the process industry. *Flexible Services and Manufacturing Journal*, *26*(1-2), 268–293. doi:10.100710696-012-9137-4

Su, B., Heshmati, A., Geng, Y., & Yu, X. (2013). A review of the circular economy in China: Moving from rhetoric to implementation. *Journal of Cleaner Production*, *42*, 215–227. doi:10.1016/j.jclepro.2012.11.020

Szarucki, M. (2016). *Koncepcja doboru metod w rozwiązywaniu problemów zarządzania*. Kraków: Wydawnictwo Uniwersytetu Ekonomicznego w Krakowie.

Tainter, A. J. (2009). *Collapse of sophisticated societies*. Praha: Dokořán.

Täuscher, K., & Abdelkafi, N. (2015). Business Model Robustness: A System Dynamics Approach. *Proceedings of the 15th EURAM Conference*.

Tauscher, K., & Abdelkafi, N. (2018). Scalability and robustness of business models for sustainability: A simulation experiment. *Journal of Cleaner Production*, 170.

Teece, D.J. (2010). Business Models. business strategy and innovation. *Long Range Planning*, *43*(2).

Teece, D. J. (2010). Business models, business strategy and innovation. *Long Range Planning*, *43*(2), 172–194. doi:10.1016/j.lrp.2009.07.003

Teubner, T., Saade, N., Kawlitschek, F., & Weinhardt, C. (2016). It's only pixels, badges, and stars: On the economic value of reputation on Airbnb. *27th Australasian Conference on Information Systems*. Retrieved from http://ro.uow.edu.au/acis2016/papers/1/56

Timmers, P. (1998). Business Models for electronic markets. *Electronic Markets*, *8*(2), 3–8. doi:10.1080/10196789800000016

Toffler, A. (1971). *Future Shock*. New York: Bantam Books.

Toffler, A. (1981). *The Third Wave*. Hampshire, UK: Pan Macmillan Limited.

Toynbee, J. A. (1972). *A Study of History*. Oxford, UK: Oxford University Press.

Tussyadiah, I. P., & Park, S. (2018). When guests trust hosts for their words: Host description and trust in sharing economy. *Tourism Management*, *67*, 261–272. doi:10.1016/j.tourman.2018.02.002

Tussyadiah, I. P., & Pesonen, J. (2016). Impacts of Peer-to-Peer Accommodation Use on Travel Patterns, Impacts of Peer-to-Peer Accommodation Use on Travel Patterns. *Journal of Travel Research*, *55*(8), 1022–1040. doi:10.1177/0047287515608505

United Nations Global Compact. (n.d.). Retrieved from https://www.unglobalcompact.org/what-is-gc/mission/principles

USSH. (2018). *Urdhëri i Stomatollogut Shqiptar*. Retrieved from http://ussh.org.al/

Ustawa o kredycie konsumenckim (Consumer Credit Act). (n.d.). Retrieved from http://prawo.sejm.gov.pl/isap.nsf/DocDetails.xsp?id=WDU20111260715

Van Berkel, R. (2000). Sustainable development and cleaner production in minerals and energy production. In *Sixth International Symposium on Environmental Issues and Waste Management in Energy and Mineral Production* (pp. 1-17). Academic Press.

Van Berkel, R. (1999). *Building a cleaner world: Cleaner Production, its role in Australia, lessons from overseas, and its future applications. Presentation for Futures Think Tank*. Perth, Australia: John Curtin International Institute, Curtin University of Technology.

Van Berkel, R., Willems, E., & Lafleur, M. (1997). The relationship between cleaner production and industrial ecology. *Journal of Industrial Ecology*, *1*(1), 51–66. doi:10.1162/jiec.1997.1.1.51

Varkey, P. A., Horne, A., & Bennet, K. E. (2008). Innovation in health care: A primer. *Journal of Medical Quality*, *23*, 382–388. PMID:18820143

Varma, A., Jukic, N., Pestek, A., Shultz, C. J., & Nestorov, S. (2016). Airbnb: Exciting innovation or passing fad? *Tourism Management Perspectives*, *20*, 228–237. doi:10.1016/j.tmp.2016.09.002

Vision 2050: The New agenda for business. (n.d.). World Business Council for Sustainable Development (WBCS). Retrieved from http://www.wbcsd.org/vision2050.aspx

Wang, D., & Nicolau, J. L. (2017). Price determinants of sharing economy based accommodation rental: A study of listings from 33 cities on Airbnb.com. *International Journal of Hospitality Management*, *62*, 120–131. doi:10.1016/j.ijhm.2016.12.007

Wang, Z., & Sarkis, J. (2017). Corporate social responsibility governance, outcomes, and financial performance. *Journal of Cleaner Production*, 162.

WBCSD. (2017). *CEO Guide to the Circular Economy*. Retrieved from www.wbcsd.org/Clusters/Circular-Economy/Resources/CEO-Guide-to-the-Circular-Economy

Wells, P., & Seitz, M. (2005). Business models and closed-loop supply chains: A typology. *Supply Chain Management*, *10*(4), 249–251. doi:10.1108/13598540510612712

Wen, Z., & Meng, X. (2015). Quantitative assessment of industrial symbiosis for the promotion of circular economy: A case study of the printed circuit boards industry in China's Suzhou New District. *Journal of Cleaner Production*, *9*, 211–219. doi:10.1016/j.jclepro.2014.03.041

Winkler, H. (2011). Closed-loop production systems—A sustainable supply chain approach. *CIRP Journal of Manufacturing Science and Technology*, *4*(3), 243–246. doi:10.1016/j.cirpj.2011.05.001

Wolska, G. (2013). Corporate social responsibility in Poland – theory and practice. *Journal of International Studies*, *6*(2), 45–53. doi:10.14254/2071-8330.2013/6-2/4

Woltjer, G. (2018). *Methodologies for measuring the macroeconomic and societal impacts of the circular economy*. European Union.

World Economic Forum. (2018) *Collaboration between Start-ups and Corporates. A Practical Guide for Mutual Understanding*. White Paper. Author.

Xue, B., Chen, X. P., Geng, Y., Guo, X. J., Lu, C. P., Zhang, Z. L., & Lu, C. Y. (2010). Survey of officials' awareness on circular economy development in China: Based on municipal and county level. *Resources, Conservation and Recycling*, *54*(12), 1296–1302. doi:10.1016/j.resconrec.2010.05.010

Yang, S.-B., Lee, H., Lee, K., & Koo, C. (2018). The application of Aristotle's rhetorical theory to the sharing economy: An empirical study of Airbnb. *Journal of Travel & Tourism Marketing*, *0*(0), 1–20. doi:10.1080/10548408.2018.1455622

Yannopoulou, N., Moufahim, M., & Bian, X. (2013). User-Generated Brands and Social Media: Couchsurfing and AirBnb. *Contemporary Management Research*, *9*(1), 85–90. doi:10.7903/cmr.11116

Yap, N. U. (2005). Towards a circular economy: Progress and challenges. *Green Management International*, *50*, 11–24.

Yayan, I. (2007). *The responsibilities of SME's within the scope of environmental management in adaptation process to EU and application in the Malatya organized industrial field* (PhD thesis). Inonu University.

Yip, A. W. H., & Bocken, N. M. P. (2018). Sustainable business model archetypes for the banking industry. *Journal of Cleaner Production*, 174.

Young, S. (2003). *Moral Capitalism: Reconciling Private Interest with the Public Good*. Berrett-Koehler Publishers, Inc.

Yu. F. Han, F., & Cui, Z. (2015). Evolution of industrial symbiosis in an eco-industrial park in China. *Journal of Cleaner Production*, *87*, 339–347. doi:10.1016/j.jclepro.2014.10.058

Zacharakis, A., & Meyer, D. (2000). The potential of actuarial decision models: Can they improve the venture capital investment decision? *Journal of Business Venturing*, *15*(4), 323–346. doi:10.1016/S0883-9026(98)00016-0

Zadeh, L. A. (1965). Fuzzy sets. *Information and Control*, *8*(3), 338–353. doi:10.1016/S0019-9958(65)90241-X

Zailani Hanim Mohamad, S., Eltayeb, T. K., Hsu, C. C., & Choon Tan, K. (2012). The impact of external institutional drivers and internal strategy on environmental performance. *International Journal of Operations & Production Management*, *32*(6), 721–745. doi:10.1108/01443571211230943

Zaman, A. U., & Lehmann, S. (2013). The zero waste index: A performance measurement tool for waste management systems in a 'zero waste city'. *Journal of Cleaner Production*, *50*, 123–132. doi:10.1016/j.jclepro.2012.11.041

Zervas, G., Proserpio, D., & Byers, J. W. (2017). The Rise of the Sharing Economy: Estimating the Impact of Airbnb on the Hotel Industry. *JMR, Journal of Marketing Research*, *54*(5), 687–705. doi:10.1509/jmr.15.0204

Zhang, B., Yang, S., & Bi, J. (2013). Enterprises' willingness to adopt/develop cleaner production technologies: An empirical study in Changshu, China. *Journal of Cleaner Production*, *40*, 62–70. doi:10.1016/j.jclepro.2010.12.009

Zhang, T. C., Jahromi, M. F., & Kizildag, M. (2018). Value co-creation in a sharing economy: The end of price wars? *International Journal of Hospitality Management*, *71*, 51–58. doi:10.1016/j.ijhm.2017.11.010

Zhu, G., So, K. K. F., & Hudson, S. (2017). Inside the sharing economy: Understanding consumer motivations behind the adoption of mobile applications. *International Journal of Contemporary Hospitality Management*, *29*(9), 2218–2239. doi:10.1108/IJCHM-09-2016-0496

Zhu, Q., Geng, Y., & Lai, K. H. (2010). Circular economy practices among Chinese manufacturers varying in environmental-oriented supply chain cooperation and the performance implications. *Journal of Environmental Management*, *91*(6), 1324–1331. doi:10.1016/j.jenvman.2010.02.013 PMID:20223586

Zhu, Q., Sarkis, J., & Lai, K. H. (2007). Green supply chain management: Pressures. practices and performance within the Chinese automobile industry. *Journal of Cleaner Production*, *15*(11-12), 1041–1052. doi:10.1016/j.jclepro.2006.05.021

About the Contributors

Bogdan Nogalski's range of research interests incude the issues of Strategic Management [including valuation of goodwill, restructuring, ownership transformation, strategic change management, strategy design, multidisciplinary organization management, corporate governance issues, organizational culture and knowledge management, and strategic human resource management. Generally, the research interests of prof. B. Nogalski is concerned with the management of economic organizations and the improvement of management systems. Professor B. Nogalski is the author / co-author of more than 950 scientific, popular, scientific, theoretical, methodical and methodological and empirical publications, published in Polish, English and Russian in periodicals and scientific journals and publications of recognized scientific reputation in Poland and in the world. [Croatia, Greece, Spain, Germany, Kazakhstan, Russia, Ukraine, South Africa, USA, Moldova, Georgia]. Professor B. Nogalski is the author / co-author of 39 books related to the above-mentioned scientific interests. Professor B. Nogalski is the author / co-author of more than 250 scientific / implementation studies, as well as implemented privatization or restructuring projects and programs prepared for the commission of Polish and foreign companies and institutions of economic life.

Agnieszka Anna Szpitter is a specialist in range of: project management, business process management, innovation and business strategies. She concentrated on project and process management (including traditional and agile project management tools, project maturity, business processes, process maturity, knowledge flows, workflows, BPR, BPM, BMPN 2.0 business process modeling, business process architecture, etc.). Management innovation (including organizational innovation, product innovation, NPD, etc.). Strategic management (including competitiveness, business models, business strategies, competitive advantage, etc.). She is a laureate of many awards for individual and team work. She is the author of more than 80 scientific publications in Polish, English and French including the author or co-author of 4 scientific monographs. She has implemented projects funded by the Scientific Research Committee and the National Science Center.

Adam Jabłoński is an Associate Professor at WSB University in Poznań, Faculty in Chorzów. He is also Vice-President of the Board of "OTTIMA Plus" Ltd. of Katowice, a reputable management consulting company, and President of the "Southern Railway Cluster" Association of Katowice, which supports development in railway transport and the transfer of innovation, as well as cooperation with European railway clusters (as a member of the European Railway Clusters Initiative). He holds a postdoctoral degree in Economic Sciences, specializing in Management Science. Having worked as a management consultant since 1997, he has broadened his experience and expertise through co-operation with a number of leading companies in Poland and abroad. He is the author of a variety of studies and business analyses on business models, value management, risk management, the balanced scorecard and corporate social responsibility. He has also written and co-written several monographs and over 100 scientific articles in the field of management. Adam's academic interests focus on the issues of modern and efficient business model design, including Sustainable Business Models and the principles of strategy for building company value that includes the rules of Corporate Social Responsibility.

Marek Jabłoński is an Associate Professor at WSB University in Poznań, Faculty in Chorzów, Poland. He is the Head of Scientific Institute of Entrepreneurship and Innovation. He is also President of the Board of "OTTIMA Plus" Ltd. management consulting company, and Vice President of the "Southern Railway Cluster", as well as cooperation with European railway clusters (as a member of the European Railway Cluster Initiative). He holds a postdoctoral degree in Economic Science, specializing in Management Science in the following range of topics: Value Based Management, Performance Management, and Business Models. Having worked as a management consultant since 1997, he is the author of a variety of studies and business analysis on business models, creating shareholder value, the Balanced Scorecard, and implementing the High Performance Organization concept. He has also written and co-written several monographs and over 100 scientific articles in the field of strategic management, performance management and business models. Marek's academic interests focus on the issues of strategic value, innovative business models, measurement systems of results including companies listed on the stock exchange and the principles of creating shareholder value and new trends in this area.

* * *

Francesca Ceruti is a Researcher at ENEA, Department for Sustainability, Resource efficiency Division, Laboratory Resources Valorization (Italy). She received her PhD in Business Administration, Management, and Territorial Economics at

University of Milan – Bicocca and served on several advisory committees to the Italian Ministry of Economic Development. She teaches "Web Marketing" and "Management" at University of Milan – Bicocca. Her area of expertise is the application of management in raw materials, circular economy, as well as digital communication.

Angelo Di Gregorio is full professor of Management at the University of Milan-Bicocca (Italy), where he holds the position of Director of CRIET, Inter-University Research Center in Territorial Economics. He teaches Marketing Management, at the Faculty of Economics, Milan Bicocca University. He serves on several advisory committees to the Italian Ministry of Economic Development and he is a member of the steering committee of the various scientific disciplines and has published numerous contributions on business strategies, marketing and communication and has carried out consultancy activities in the areas of strategy, marketing, communication and business start-ups.

Marco Frey is Full Professor of Economics and Business Management and leader of the Sustainability Management Research Group at Sant'Anna School of Advanced Studies, Professor at IUSS (University School for Advanced Studies of Pavia), Fellow at IEFE (Centre for Research on Energy and Environmental Economics and Policy – Bocconi University, Milan). He has published several articles on major international journals on sustainability topics. Marco Frey is also chairman of Global Compact Italian Foundation – which is a body of the United Nations committed to sustainability, National President of Cittadinanzattiva, a non-profit organization which promotes civic participation and the protection of citizens' rights in Italy and Europe, President and Board Member of Symbola, Foundation for the Italian Qualities.

Laura Gavinelli is a Research Fellow in Management at the University of Milan-Bicocca (Italy). After a post degree couse in Marketing and Digital Economy and a PhD in Management, she collaborated with several public and private institutions for tourism, culture and competitiveness of SMEs for research projects and consultancy. She is the delegate of the Ministry of Economic Development for international technical boards on raw materials. She teaches "Marketing Management" and "Corporate Communication" at University of Milan-Bicocca. Her area of expertise is the application of management in raw materials, circular economy, digital reputation, as well as corporate communication.

Kei Hysi was born in February 19, 1997 in Berat, Albania. She has recently graduated with a bachelor degree in Business Informatics at Epoka University. During her time in university Kei was selected as the President of Student Council. She has also organized many different activities related to entrepreneurship, innovation and charity with student clubs. During her study period she managed to finish three internships, two of which were related to marketing and content creation in two Albanian companies Softmogul and EasyPay, both tech companies, and one of the internships was done in Albanian Investment Council. Kei has also been involved in voluntarism. She has been part of AIESEC, Albanian Skills and Leadership Development Association NGOs in Albania. She has been part of many competitions, conferences and workshops in Albania and abroad.

Waldemar Jędrzejczyk, DSc, PhD, Eng., Professor at Czestochowa University of Technology, Head of the Division of Information and Knowledge Manage¬ment in the Institute of Information Management Systems at the Faculty of Management of Czestochowa Univer¬sity of Technology. His research focuses on strategic management, information and knowledge management, human resource management, psychology, sociology and computing.

Alba Kruja is lecturer at Epoka University in Albania, Department of Business Administration. She holds an MBA degree from Nebraska University, Lincoln, USA and a PhD degree on Entrepreneurship from Agribusiness University of Tirana, Albania. At Epoka she teaches courses of Entrepreneurship and Management Science Research on Bachelor, Master and PhD level. At the same time, she holds the administrative duty of the Academic Coordinator of Business Informatics Program. Dr. Kruja has been a visiting professor at the Mainz University of Applied Sciences, Germany. She is author of many research articles and book chapters. Her main research focus is on Entrepreneurship, Innovation and Small Business Management.

Agnieszka Lorek, Ph.D., Assistant Professor in the Department of Social and Economic Policy at the University of Economics in Katowice, Poland. Member of the Polish Association of Environmental and Natural Resources Economists and the European Association of Environmental and Resource Economists (EAERE). Main scientific interests: environmental economics, theory and practice of sustainable development, ecological policy, ecosystem services and management of natural resources, problems of development of urban areas, "green" economy, renewable energy sources. In this respect author and co-author of approximately 76 publications.

Elżbieta Lorek, Ph.D., Professor at the Faculty of Business, Finance and Administration of the University of Economics in Katowice, Poland. A member of many scientific associations, including the Board of the Polish Association of Environmental and Natural Resources Economists, the Board of the Silesian Water Cluster, the Commission for the Protection of Mining Areas of the Polish Academy of Sciences, Polish Society for Environmental Engineering and co-founder of the

Polish-German Scientific Network for Sustainable Development. Author and co-author of approximately 210 scientific and research works, studies for economic practice and public institutions regarding the issues of economics and environmental management as well as issues related to sustainable development.

Katarzyna Olejko received the title of doctor in economic sciences at the University of Economics in Katowice (2011). She is the author of a number of publications on management accounting and controlling. In 2012 she was employed as a lecturer on Faculty of Finance and Insurance University of Economics in Katowice. Currently, she lectures at the Faculty of Business, Finance and Administration. At the same time, as a practitioner, she implements numerous business projects, covering the area of management accounting, internal audit and controlling. Her main area of interest is company accounting, corporate governance as well as non-financial reporting. Currently, she focuses her attention on issues related to new reporting obligations, including CSR reporting.

Fatih Pinarbasi is research assistant at Istanbul Medipol University, PhD student at Yildiz Technical University. Specialized in Marketing area.

Vishnu Pratap Singh has obtained his Ph.D. degree from Indian Institute of Technology Kharagpur (India) under the supervision of Dr. Debjani Chakraborty on the topic "Multi-stage Decision Making in Imprecise and Uncertain Environment." From July 2017 to March 2018, he has worked at National Institute of Technology Jamshedpur, India. In March 2018, he joined as an Assistant Professor in the Department of Mathematics at National Institute of Technology Nagpur, India. His interests of research are in the area of Optimization under uncertainty, Multi-stage Decision Making, Operation research. He has published many papers in national and international journals.

Ewa Wójcik, PhD, Senior Lecturer at the University of Economics in Katowice, Faculty of Business, Finance and Administration, and English for Specific Purposes (business, finance, and law) teacher with research interests in the field of banking, marketing, microeconomics, CSR and business ethics. As a lecturer and author of postgraduate programs and International Business studies supported by EFS and the Norway Grants, she was awarded many times for achievements of students by the London Chamber of Commerce and Industry. Writing widely on savings market, competition in financial services market, value co-creation, consumer behavior, CSR, ethics and sustainability issues she authors numerous scientific publications and co-authors textbooks for learning English for students of business, economics, banking and finance. As a reviewer, she has cooperated with Pearson as well as other international publishers.

Index

A

B

C

M

N

O

P

R

S

T

V

www.ingramcontent.com/pod-product-compliance
Lightning Source LLC
LaVergne TN
LVHW081334300926
849161LV00008B/1972